Forty Centuries of History

Here is a vivid and perceptive evaluation of forty centuries of history—a fascinating record of adventure, invention and territorial expansion.

L. J. Cheney surveys the entire field of Western civilization: politics, art, government, science, philosophy, religion. He traces the causes and effects of war, and he analyzes the character and motivation of the men and nations that shaped Western civilization and carried it abroad to other continents and the islands of the seas.

Colorful, yet factual, this sweeping narrative gives intimate details of the sights and sounds of times past, viewed through the lens of modern scholarship and research.

Other MENTOR Books You Will Enjoy

The Painter's Eye *by Maurice Grosser*
Brilliant analysis of conventions, principles, and techniques of painting, with reproductions of 32 masterpieces. (#MD159—50¢)

Enjoying Modern Art *by Sarah Newmeyer*
The unconventional lives and works of great modern painters, from early French rebels to today's masters of abstraction. 80 masterpieces reproduced. (#MD211—50¢)

The Renaissance *by Walter Pater.* New introduction *by Louis Kronenberger*
A great critic reveals the spirit of this artistic era by examining the work of da Vinci, Michelangelo, Boccaccio and others. (#MD265—50¢)

Good Reading (revised, up-to-date) edited by the Committee on College Reading.
Classified lists of over 1500 books to help you select your own reading program. (#MD178—50¢)

A HISTORY OF THE
WESTERN WORLD

L. J. CHENEY

A MENTOR BOOK

Published by THE NEW AMERICAN LIBRARY

FIRST PUBLISHED IN 1959

This book is copyright under the Berne Convention. Apart from any fair dealing for the purpose of private study, research, criticism or review, as permitted under the Copyright Act, 1956, no portion may be reproduced by any process without written permission. Inquiry should be made to the publisher, George Allen & Unwin Ltd., 40 Museum Street, London, W.C. 1.

© George Allen & Unwin Ltd., 1959

Published as a MENTOR BOOK
By Arrangement with George Allen & Unwin Ltd.

FIRST PRINTING, NOVEMBER, 1959

A handsome cloth-bound edition of this work is obtainable from George Allen & Unwin Ltd., *London*, 40 Museum Street, W.C. 1; *Auckland*, 24 Wyndham Street; *Bombay*, 15 Graham Road, Ballard Estate, Bombay 1; *Calcutta*, 17 Chittaranjan Avenue, Calcutta 13; *Cape Town*, 109 Long Street; *Karachi*, Metherson's Estate, Wood Street, Karachi 2; *New Delhi*, 13-14 Ajmeri Gate Extension, New Delhi 1; *São Paulo*, Avenida 9 de Julho, 1138-Ap. 51; *Singapore, South East Asia and Far East*, 36c Princep Street; *Sydney*, N.S.W., Bradbury House, 55 York Street; *Toronto*, 91 Wellington Street West.

MENTOR BOOKS are published by
The New American Library of World Literature, Inc.
501 Madison Avenue, New York 22, New York

PRINTED IN THE UNITED STATES OF AMERICA

CONTENTS

Introduction   *page ix*

1. AROUND THE GREAT SEA OR THE PEOPLES OF ANTIQUITY

B.C. and A.D. page 11. Before the Smiths 12. The Bronze Age 14. Archaeology 16. Where Civilization Began 18. Egypt of the Pharaohs 21. Lost Empires of the Ancient East 23. The Sea Power of Crete and the Land Power of Assyria 27. The Persians 30. The Greeks 32. The Glory and Decline of the Greek Cities 35. Alexander 38. Seafarers and Cities in the Western Mediterranean 40. How the Romans Spread upon the World 43. Caesar 48. Citizens of No Mean City 50. Ancient Religions and the Jews 55. Christianity 57. The Fall of Jerusalem 59. The Church in the Roman Empire. 60.

2. THE END OF THE ROMAN EMPIRE AND THE LOSS OF ANCIENT LEARNING

The Overrunning of the West page 65. Barbarians and Bishops 70. The Emperor Justinian 72.

3. THE BANNERS OF THE CROSS, OR KINGDOM, CASTLE AND CHURCH

Christendom: Pope Gregory the Great page 75. Men from the Desert 77. The First Repulse of the Crescent 79. Charlemagne 80. Men from the North 81. Alfred of Wessex 84. An Arabic Civilization 87. The Normans and the Great Crusades 89. Warfare and Worship: Castle and Church 94. Pilgrims to Canterbury 103. Knights and Chivalry 105. City Craftsmen 105. Lawyers and Clerks 107. Farmers 109. The Church 112. Seamen and Travelers 114. The Wars of the Cross 116. The End of Constantinople 117. The Fall of Granada in Spain 120. Southward Ho 120. Beyond Good Hope 122. Sunset Islands and Strange Empires 124. The World Enlarged 128. The Seaways 129.

4. THE REDISCOVERY OF ANCIENT KNOWLEDGE

Three Civilizations page 131. The Search Begins 134. The Renaissance 136. Printing 137. Earth and Heaven 139.

5. THE GREAT KINGDOMS OF THE WEST AND THE NEW WORLD OF AMERICA

Principalities and Powers page 141. Many Churches in Place of One 143. "Bluff King Hal" 146. Bibles for Plowmen 149. The Century of Spain 150. Mary Queen of Scots 151. The Dutch 153. The English Seamen and Drake 154. The Spanish Armada 156. Elizabethan England 158. A New Century 160. The Contrast: Britain 162. The Contrast: France 166. Westward Ho 168. Sultan and Tsar 172. Britain Against Louis XIV and Louis XV: 1689–1748 174. The Seven Years' War 178. Man and the Universe 183. The American Revolution 187. The Wealth of Nations 191.

6. THE FRENCH REVOLUTION

The Revolution page 199. Napoleon and the British Navy 203. Napoleon: Spain and Russia 208.

7. MANY INVENTIONS AND NEW KNOWLEDGE: THE WORLD OF TODAY

Three Adventures page 211. The Adventure of Politics: Kingdoms and Republicans 212. Politics: Freedom 214. Politics: The Mother of Parliaments 217. Invention: The Engineers 219. Invention: Roads and Canals 220. Invention: Coal, Iron, and Steam Power 222. Invention: Gains and Losses 227. Politics: The Year of 1848 in Europe 234. Politics: Italy and Germany 237. Politics: Russia and Revolution 241. Expansion 245. Expansion: The Tale of Empire and the Pax Britannica 246. Expansion: The British Dominions 249. Expansion: The United States of America 251. Expansion: India 256. Expansion: The Far East 258. Expansion: Africa 261. The Nations in Their Harness, 1914–1918 265. Fallen Empires 271. Twenty-one Years Between Wars, 1918–1939 276. The Nations in Their Harness, 1939–1945 280. Inventions Without End and People as the Sands of the Sea 284. The Present Passing into the Future 287.

8. EPILOGUE

News of This World page 291. News from Nowhere 292. The Living Past 294.

Index   296

MAPS

1.	The Ancient East	19
2.	Alexander's Greek Empire	39
3.	The Roman Empire	47
4.	The Barbarian Invasions of the West	69
5.	The Troubles of Western Europe: Ninth Century	85
6.	The Latin Crusading States	92
7.	Southern Ways out of the Atlantic	127
8.	The Spanish Attempt on England, 1588	157
9.	New England and New France, 1755–1763	180
10.	Napoleon's Military Empire, 1810	206
11.	The Unification of Italy	238
12.	The Westward Expansion of the U.S.A.	254
13.	The European Occupation of Africa	262
14.	The Hapsburg Empire, 1914	266
15.	The Fragmentation of Eastern Europe	273

INTRODUCTION

There is an old eastern tale of a young king who, suddenly and very properly, became full of curiosity about the Past. He sent for his learned men and commanded them to write the history of all that had gone before. Many years later he remembered his order, sent for the learned men, and asked how far they had progressed with the work. They were happy to tell him that they had but recently completed it—in sixty volumes. He praised them for their industry, pointed to his graying locks, and requested them to compress the work into three volumes. It took them ten more years to do this. The king had neither time nor strength to read these, and commanded them to reduce the whole narrative into one volume. With incredible labor they toiled at this task, and duly brought the book to the royal presence. But by this time the king was very old, very feeble, and partially blind. "Tell me," he said to the chief of the scholars, "you who have spent your whole life at the task, tell me in one sentence, what knowledge you have gained of the Past." "O king, live for ever," replied the aged scholar to the aged king, "I crave your mercy, but I cannot do this thing." But the king insisted, and the scholar, bowed down with years, said: "I have learned that many generations of men have been born, have toiled and loved, have suffered and died." Upon this, the king, justly annoyed because he could easily have said this himself, handed the scholar over to the public executioner, and lamented the shortness of human life and the length of History.

We are all, when young, in the position of that king. Luckily for us, hundreds of learned men have toiled through the ages for our instruction and delight, and while we are still young we can now satisfy our curiosity: and it is while we are young that we most desire to know how all the Past "fits together," to know it as one long story leading up to our own lives.

This book is a story of men and times and places, a story of what men did, and when, and where. It might of course (with incredible labor) be lengthened to sixty volumes—for it is only a fraction of the complete story. But even if all were told that could be told, there would still remain the greater part that we do not know and never shall know.

If you happen to be a prince (which is unlikely) you can find some record of your ancestors for a long way back. If you happen to be an ordinary person, you will not. Nevertheless, your own ancestors lived through all the times of the past. And if you reckon twenty-five years to each generation, a full busload of your ancestors would carry you back into the Roman Empire. Somehow, these ancestors of yours have transformed their language from Anglo-Saxon, or Romano-Celtic, or Danish, to present-day English. And they have changed their habits, their religion, and their ways of living as well as their speech. Your family has had its share in making the Present out of the Past, just as you are now helping to shape the Future by what you do in the Present.

So now to our story: which has no one hero but is full of heroes; which has no beginning because the records are lost; which has no ending because we are still, ourselves, part of it; which belongs to all men and women, all boys and girls; but which is here written for those who speak English and have been brought up in the Anglo-Saxon tradition.

1

AROUND THE GREAT SEA, OR THE PEOPLES OF ANTIQUITY

B.C. and A.D.

The tale of our civilization begins in the lands around the "Great Sea." We call it the *Mediterranean*, which means the Sea in the Middle of the World. At one time it did seem to be in the middle of the world to the men and women who lived around it: and they were all ruled by the same ruler—the Roman Caesar or emperor whose legions of soldiers had conquered their lands, and to whom they paid their taxes.

This was that mighty and famous Roman Empire in which Our Lord and His Apostles lived, and of which St. Paul was a citizen. In the east it reached to the river Euphrates; in the west to the Atlantic Ocean; in the north to the Rhine and the Danube; in the south to the Sahara Desert.

In those days a merchant could journey all the way from Babylon to York and be under the same government as he rode from tavern to tavern and from city to city along the paved highways, the long straight roads built by the Roman engineers. The sentinel who looked out from his post over the sands of the Sahara Desert might have been born in a Danube village: the man who stood guard in a camp on the Euphrates might have grown up in Spain. Jews from Palestine could be found trading in the Rhineland, and Greek merchants kept their shops by the River Tyne.

No wonder that the Romans sometimes called the Mediterranean *Mare Nostrum*—Our Own Sea; for across its tideless waters moved their cargo ships with the goods that enriched the life of their hundreds of cities: copper from Spain; olive oil and grain from North Africa; ivory, papyrus, and grain from Egypt; wines and pottery from Greece; hides and timber from France; and slaves from everywhere.

In the Gospel of St. Luke you will find these words: "It came to pass in those days that there went out a decree from Caesar Augustus that all the world should be taxed. And this taxing was first made when Cyrenius was governor of Syria. And all went to be taxed, every one to his own city."

St. Luke goes on to tell us how Joseph and Mary came to Bethlehem of Judea because of this decree, and how at Bethlehem Jesus Christ was born in the stable of an inn.

In that stable of that inn on that day our dates begin. They begin then, and run both ways, backwards and forwards: backwards, or B.C. (Before Christ) into the dim and mysterious past for ever and ever; and forwards, or A.D. *(Anno Domini*—In the Year of Our Lord) right down to our own day.

Augustus Caesar, who was the first of the Roman emperors, ruled from 27 B.C. to 14 A.D. He did not know this; for he reckoned his years from the foundation of Rome in 753 B.C. A little arithmetic will show that Augustus called the first year of his reign 726, and the last year 767. A little more arithmetic will show that, by his reckoning, our own year of A.D. 1958 would be called 2711 A.U.C., or, in full, 2711 *Anno Urbis Conditae* (From the Building of the City).

The Roman Empire was the beginning of our own story of western Europe: but it was also the end of a very much longer story of many ancient races—Egyptians, Babylonians, Assyrians, Persians, Carthaginians, and Greeks. From Augustus Caesar and the Nativity of Our Lord down to nowadays is a mere twenty centuries! By contrast, we can trace into the deepening twilight and dimness of the times before Christ no less than forty centuries of civilized men—men, that is, who could use metals, build and live in cities, and keep some sort of records.

In due course, we shall return to the Romans in whose Empire were gathered up the knowledge and crafts of the more ancient civilizations. Our immediate business is with those civilizations, and what is known of their forty centuries of history; and we shall have something to say of the archaeologists by whose clever digging among ruined cities so much of forgotten ancient history has been recovered.

Before the Smiths

The earliest records of men go back thousands and thousands of years, but they are not written ones. Scattered all over the earth we find stone weapons and tools: fist-hatchets, scrapers, borers, and arrowheads made by men before they found out how to smelt copper and tin and iron out of the rocks, and make metal tools. We find shards of pottery and human and animal bones. What else these early men used of wood, fiber, straw, reed, leather, and cane, has rotted away. So have their woolen woven cloths. We find "kitchen rubbish" of animal bones, shells and ashes left beside their caves and mud huts and dwelling pits which they dug in the earth. Some of these unknown early hunters and fishers were clever artists. In deep caverns of the Pyrenees are marvelous wall paintings of hunting scenes done by the flare of torches by men of these long-lost Stone Ages.

We have learned much, and guessed much, of their lives from what we know of the redskins, of the Negroes of Africa, the blackfellows of Australia, and the Maoris of New Zealand, who were all still living in the Stone Age when white men first came among them. We have many books about them, written by travelers and missionaries who lived among them and learned their languages and wrote them down. This last work has been done on a really grand scale by the Christian scholars of the British and Foreign Bible Society.

Men and women in the Stone Ages were neither stupid nor clumsy. On the contrary, we have seen many of them learn strange new things very swiftly. The redskins of America soon rode and managed the horse that white men took to the New World; Negroes of Zululand whose fathers were Stone-Age warriors have become medical doctors, lawyers, and scientists. English sailors who landed in New Zealand in the early years of last century to cut down kauri pines for masts and spars, traded their iron axes with the Maoris for fresh food: then they saw the Maoris set to work and use the iron axes with skill and gusto in place of their old greenstone axes. Much of the craft of all Stone-Age folk was of beautiful finish.

Imagine being in the place of a Stone-Age man! No decent clothes, no iron tools, no real houses, no roads, no books, no proper lamps, no comforts—just a hut or earth pit or cave, and some sticks and stones and bones and skins and clay. No real knowledge, but very much fear and dread of evil spirits. Man began with nothing, and had to find out everything—and then pass on his knowledge to his sons. When we think of all the things the Stone-Age men discovered, we must admit that they were very clever and resourceful. But after all, some of them were our own ancestors!

They found out the uses of plants and animals and minerals. They began agriculture. They tamed animals and birds. They made the first clay pots. They invented basketry, weaving, plaiting, knotting (knitting) and thatching. They made charcoal. They made the first ships. They twisted fibers into ropes. They dressed leather, and sewed skins together with bone needles. They dug mines for flints, and learned how to shape flints into tools by hammering them and grinding them. Indeed, some of their works were amazingly skillful; like the boomerang of the Australian blackfellow, and the light skin boat of the Eskimo which held many men and could sail the rough ocean; or like the outrigger craft of the South Sea Islanders. A very special case of such skill is shown by the giant stone walls and great roads of the Incas of Peru, built without iron tools.

And we can be sure that among them there were those skilled in the telling of tales of the hunt or of war, men who retold the stories of the past, of strong chieftains and brave warriors, and of the spirits of the trees and rivers, and of the voices that howled in the winds. And the tribes that listened to these storytellers learned to make dances, and took delight in singing or chanting with music of a sort strange to our ears but full of rhythm, sounded on skin drums and reed pipes and clashing boards.

Finally, they themselves brought the Stone Age to an end after taking the first, and therefore the most difficult, steps towards civilization. They discovered metals.

These clever forest folk and river folk in the dawn of history were the brave, nameless pioneers of all our knowledge and power.

The Bronze Age

The word *civilization* comes from the Latin word *civis* which means a city. Civilization is the life of men in cities and towns. Men in cities must have rules or laws to live by, someone to govern them, someone, that is, to see that they agree together and work together; or else someone to make them work together; and they must exchange goods or trade together, because they cannot live crowded together without trade. Only farmers can do this, and even then they live a very poor sort of life. So civilization means not only life in cities but also trade and laws and government.

Men began to build cities in the fourth millennium B.C. This is a short way of saying between 4000 and 3000 B.C. They also began to keep records by writing—not our kind of writing. At the same time, about 3000 B.C., they found out how to make bronze by melting copper and mixing it with a little molten tin to harden it. They also learned to get gold and silver from the earth and shape them into gleaming ornaments. Bronze was their chief material for tools and weapons, but naturally many men went on using stone ones for a long time. The new bronze tools in skillful hands were more reliable, more lasting, and could be resharpened or even remade, and could finish the work in far less time, and far more accurately than stone ones. We should remember that bronze is softer than iron—which explains why bronze swords were shorter and thicker than iron ones; it was very awkward to have a bronze sword bending in the middle during a battle.

About the same time some unknown genius invented the wheel. This enabled loads to be carried with far less effort than on the old sledges. Two-wheeled carts and chariots came into use; and since smooth tracks were needed the first primitive roadways were made. The wheel soon had other uses. The potter used it for shaping his clay, by throwing a lump of clay on a turning disk, and holding his hands against it while it turned. The woodworker used a wheel to make a rough lathe—a tool fixed in a wheel: as the wheel was turned so the tool revolved, and all he had to do was to hold the piece of wood against the tool, which cut through it, or trimmed it. Which man discovered or invented this thing, and which man discovered that, must always remain a mystery.

So the Bronze Age began at the end of the fourth millennium. It lasted for about eighteen centuries until somebody found out how to smelt iron from its ores, and make the long iron swords which were so much stronger than the bronze ones.

All these dates are rough guesses ("estimates" is the dignified word used by scholars), because our knowledge of these far-off events is gained by digging up the ruins of the ancient world scattered in Egypt and the Near East.

With the Bronze Age there enters into History a most important character. He is the smith, the smiter of the fiery metal, the craftsman who works with fire and forge. From the beginning he is a mysterious figure. His craft is kept secret, a jealous secret, almost a magical one. He gives men power by his fine swords and tough armor. He hammers and twists his metal into many shapes. He shoes the horses, perhaps also the oxen who need eight little shoes. His brother craftsmen who work in gold and silver are also clever artists. In one old Greek city there was found a flower of gold set on a silver stalk.

The greatest traffickers in metals were the Phoenicians of Tyre and Sidon. We read in the Bible how King Solomon of the Jews employed Hiram, a skilled bronzesmith of Tyre, to adorn the Temple at Jerusalem with bronze ornaments—huge pillars decorated with chainwork, lilies and pomegranates, and bowls and basins and lions and chariot wheels, all cast in bronze.

Not very long ago there was dug up in France a grand vase of bronze decorated with a molded picture of a chariot and charioteer and horses—and thought by its finders to have been made about 2500 B.C.

The Greeks used bronze on their palaces. The oldest of their poems, which is about the wanderings of Ulysses, gives a splendid description of the palace of a king named Alcinous. It had walls covered with bronze plates topped with blue enamel tiles, and doors gilded all over and hung on silvered doorposts fixed in a bronze threshold! It sounds like a fairy tale. Yet on the ruined stones of another old Greek palace we have found the remains of such bronze plates. When they were new and burnished, they must have reflected gleamingly the flames of the hearth fire around which, after the hunting, the king and his companions sat and feasted, and listened to the songs of the harpers—such as Homer, the blind harper, who made both that poem about Ulysses and another long one about the Ten-Year Siege of Troy by the Greek kings.

So, first, we have the Stone Ages, which run back no one knows quite how far. Then the Bronze Age, which began somewhere about 3000 B.C. When Homer lived is not known exactly, but the Siege of Troy of which he sang happened about 1200 B.C. This siege of Troy was already a dim legend to the Greeks when their own written records began about 800 B.C. King Solomon lived and ruled over the Jews about 950 B.C. Men could write in his days, and indeed for centuries before: but apart from the Bible and the writings of the Greeks (many of which have perished) the written records of ancient times were not known till a hundred and fifty years ago.

These written records are rolls of papyrus found in Egyptian royal tombs, and clay tablets dug up in the cities of Mesopotamia. From these we have learned a vast amount about ancient peoples and empires.

Archaeology

Our forefathers learned their history from the Bible, and from the writings of Herodotus the ancient Greek historian. They knew nothing older than the stories of the Old Testament, such as those of Abraham, Joseph, Moses, Joshua and Samson; and nothing older than the marvelous legends of the

Greeks, such as the tales of Jason and the Argonauts, of Theseus and the Minotaur, and of the Siege of Troy.

To the ancient Greeks, Egypt was a land of wonders like the Sphinx and the Pyramids, and a land of mysterious gods like Isis and Osiris. They knew nothing of its long history reaching back centuries and centuries before their own hardy ancestors came pushing southwards through the mountains to the sunny shores and isles of Greece. Their own old stories told of wars, and of gods, and hero-kings such as Homer sang of in his poems. Beyond these was darkness. They knew nothing of the lovely lost palaces of Crete—nor did we till 1900. They had only a slight knowledge of the glories of the eastern lands of Babylonia and Sumer. When the Greek spearmen of Alexander the Great trudged across the Euphrates plain in 330 B.C., they passed the high mounds of Babylonia in which ruined cities lay already buried by the blown sands of the centuries.

The long ignorance was broken when Napoleon sailed to Egypt in 1799, and conquered it. He took with him a group of scientists and scholars to study its ruins. One result of this was that in 1822 a Frenchman named Champollion began to read the hieroglyphics or priestly writing. Thus the clue to the ancient Egyptian language was found.

Scholars were encouraged to study other ruins of the Near East. In 1845 our own Henry Rawlinson began to decipher the wedge-shaped writing cut in the rocks of Assyria. Layard explored the gigantic ruins of Nineveh in 1846. A German boy named Schliemann believed the tale of Troy to be true. He made his fortune in business, and then spent it in digging up the ruins of Troy in 1870. He found the ruins of not one city but seven cities one on top of another! At the end of the nineteenth century Sir Arthur Evans discovered a lost civilization when he began to dig at Knossos in Crete and found a royal palace. For centuries Crete was the home of a marvelous civilization; yet all the world had forgotten it entirely. Its thousands of tablets remain unread as yet. Was this the palace where Theseus went to slay the dreadful minotaur? Did Achilles really drag Hector's body at his chariot wheels around the walls of Troy? Such questions may be unanswerable, but our discoveries prove that there were some facts behind the old legends. One city was referred to by the Greeks as "golden Mycenae." Sure enough when Schliemann dug there he found great treasures of gold, and quite recently much more gold has been found in its tombs. Quite recently, too, a number of inscribed tablets have been unearthed at Pylos in Greece, the supposed home of Nestor, one of Agamemnon's princes. What is more, an

Englishman, the late Michael Ventris, found out how to read them.

Digging goes on steadily on many sites. The Americans are busy in Athens: the French in Syria: the Turks in Asia Minor. The Egyptians continue to explore their own ruins and tombs. Sir Leonard Woolley made startling discoveries at the city of Ur in Mesopotamia, and equally startling discoveries have recently been made at the neighboring city of Erech. Indeed, this discovery of the buried past goes on in all lands; but the greatest activity is in the lands about the eastern Mediterranean.

Now we know of great empires and nations in all the lands of the Near East. We have thousands of baked clay tablets with records in the languages of the men of Babylonia and Assyria and the neighboring countries. We have great quantities of papyrus with records of the old Egyptian Pharaohs. Whole civilizations, like those of the Sumerians and Hittites and Cretans, have been unearthed by the spade. We call the diggers *archaeologists*, which means men who study very old things. The story they have revealed covers over 4,000 years, and every season's digging adds to our knowledge. But the result is not the easy flowing sort of story like ordinary history. There are gaps and many arguments about dates, and all kinds of questions that men ask in vain—until, maybe, some chance discovery gives an answer. The skill and patience of the archaeologists are amazing. They sift every spadeful of soil, they measure every inch down, they even work with camel-hair brushes to clear earth away from buried objects in order to get them out undamaged. There is no doubt that very much more remains under the ground to be discovered, and that it will be found in time.

Where Civilization Began

The earliest civilizations began along the banks of great rivers in warm countries where the soil is deep and rich, often flooded and plastered over with river mud, and very, very fertile. Such rivers were the Nile in Egypt, the Tigris and Euphrates in Mesopotamia, and the Indus in India.

The ancient cities of Mohenjodaro and Harappa of the Indus valley have only recently been discovered and excavated. Much has yet to be learned of the people who built and lived in them; but we already know that they traded with the men of the great river plains of Mesopotamia, because we have found things in their ruins that could have been made only by the people of the Tigris and Euphrates valleys.

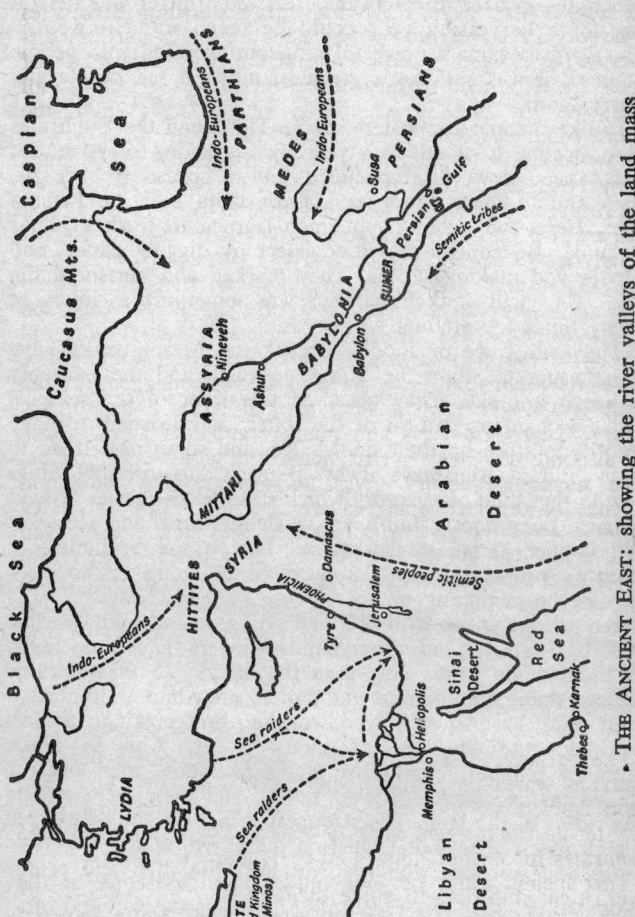

THE ANCIENT EAST: showing the river valleys of the land mass which is contained between seas, mountains, and deserts

Egypt is like a long winding snake with a giant head—a land 600 miles long and 15 miles wide, ending at the sea in a giant delta 100 miles wide made by the many mouths of the Nile. This long, narrow river country was flooded yearly by the melting of the snows in the mountains of Ethiopia, sometimes to a depth of twenty feet. So fruitful was its soil that three harvests a year could be taken up. No wonder that Egypt became a powerful kingdom crowded with people although it was set like a green island in a sea of burning desert sand.

In like manner the waters of the Tigris and the Euphrates were swollen to flood each year by the snows of Armenia, and carried down the crumbled soil to spread it over the plain and to push it out as a great delta into the Persian Gulf. Here, too, as in Egypt, men learned to work together to guide and control the floodwaters by digging canals and ditches and making sluices. They marked and measured the land. The yield of their harvests was sometimes as much as eighty times the amount sown.

The abundance of food in Egypt and Mesopotamia gave men leisure to study the things on earth and the heavenly bodies in the sky. They observed the order of the seasons, and the changing pattern of the stars. They learned to make records to store up their knowledge, and so to pass it on to their children. Men have always been curious to know things —with that kind of curiosity which still makes us peer around corners, open doors, find out how things work, and see what will happen if we do so-and-so. This is the beginning of science, just as doodling on a piece of wood or bone or clay is the beginning of art.

Knowledge grows with skill and skill grows with knowledge. Men have always had clever hands—fingers that think. Some of them made better pots than the others: so they became potters, doing nothing else, and pottery grew into an important craft. And so also with woodworking, brickmaking, leatherworking, and the rest of men's trades. And as crafts grew in number, commerce increased. Some men became skilled in the control of river floods, and these were among the rulers of the land. The strongest men were the rulers, but the strongest always depended on the advice of the cleverest: kings and warriors won renown; but wise men and priests were their ministers to guide them.

Very early men wondered how the world had been made, and how men themselves had been created. They wondered at the thunder and the lightning, at the sudden mysterious illnesses that struck them down, at comets that blazed in the sky and darkness that came at noonday when the sun was eclipsed. They came to believe in "unseen powers"—gods of the grain, of harvest, of light, of the rivers. These they tried to picture in the only way they could by making idols; and tried to please them in the only way they knew by offering them the best things they had—grain, animals, even human beings. The sun was worshiped as a god. He made the earth to bring forth the harvest, but he also smote men by day with his merciless heat. In nearly all places the dead were buried with food and furniture for their use in the next world. And, as we might expect, the mighty men, the kings and nobles, were given rich tombs full of furniture and great treasures for their afterlife. We find kings and priests very early in the records that we dig up. Their grave furniture, when we find it, shows what marvelous craftsmen lived in those distant times.

In Egypt men used a picture writing that we call *hieroglyphics*—a Greek word meaning the "priestly writing." They wrote on papyrus sheets, stuck together end to end, and rolled them into a scroll. The dry sand and rainless climate of their country has preserved fragments of masses of these papyrus records from complete decay. We dig them up from the ruins of old cities—sometimes from the old rubbish heaps of the cities.

The men of Mesopotamia wrote on soft clay in *cuneiform*, or wedge-shaped writing, so-called because each impression was made by pressing on the clay with the triangular end of a stick. Different groups of wedges made different letters. This writing, because it is on clay tablets, is indestructible. Thousands of the tablets have been found and read. And if anyone today is so hasty as to think that these long-forgotten men and women of far-off antiquity do not matter to him, let him know that we reckon our days in hours of sixty minutes each of sixty seconds because that was the way the ancient Babylonian astronomers worked it out.

This is a mighty link with Babylon. If ever we begin to feel rather superior to those strange folk we can remind ourselves also that on some of their queer baked clay tablets scholars have found examples of square roots, and even logarithms—things that are likely to puzzle youngsters today when they learn mathematics.

Egypt of the Pharaohs

For three thousand years the narrow land of Egypt was ruled by dynasties of Pharaohs. The word *pharaoh* means the "great house," and was used as the ruler's title; his personal name was far too sacred to be uttered by human lips. It is a pity that the Bible does not give the name of the Pharaoh who employed Joseph, or the one who made the Jews build and toil for him, because historians are still in doubt about it. They know the names of the Pharaohs, but they can only guess at the dates of Joseph or of Moses.

About 3500 B.C. Upper Egypt (the Valley) and Lower Egypt (the Delta) came under the rule of one Pharaoh named Menes. About 3000 B.C. the Pharaohs began to build huge pyramids of limestone blocks to hold their tombs. The Great Pyramid of the Pharaoh Khafre covers a dozen acres of land and rises to 800 feet, a man-made hill, piled up with immense labor, yet built to exact measurements. Near it the Sphinx was cut from the rock in the shape of a gigantic sitting lion bearing the face of Khafre. Other Pharaohs of this early time built a long line of lesser pyramids.

From about 2500 B.C. the power of the Pharaohs lessened and that of the great nobleman increased, each ruling his own lands as he pleased: and from this time the Pharaohs, their great palace servants and priests, and the lords were buried in pomp in tombs cut in the rocks that bordered the valley. Our abundant knowledge of ancient Egypt comes from these tombs: from the lively colored wall paintings of the burial chambers, and from the rolls of papyrus which were buried there. We know of the craftsmen's skill in glassmaking, in the carving of gem stones, in ivory-inlay work, in gold and silver work, in pottery. We find the embalmed bodies of the dead (the mummies) wrapped in linen fabric woven as finely as silk. We see the sort of boats in which they rode on the Nile, or journeyed down the Red Sea, or on the Great Sea to the Syrian Coast to fetch cargoes of cedar wood for their houses and furniture. We read in the rolls of their knowledge of surgery, and of mathematics. We learn of their elaborate arrangements to control the floodwaters of the river, and of their laws, and their taxes. We read of their beliefs, of the gods they worshiped—of Ra the sun-god, of Osiris the god who died every year (like the grain harvest) and was every year born again (like the grain from the seed); and we learn how they came to believe that Osiris would judge the souls of men after death, weighing the good deeds against the evil ones.

While we can easily reconstruct the luxury and pleasure of their lives passed in delightful houses and bright gardens under a blue sky, we must always remember those multitudes who have no memorials, but who made the pleasant lives of Pharaohs and nobles possible. A swarming population lived in crowded villages of stone and mud huts. Most of the folk were poor peasants whose toil brought each year the rich harvest, so long as the wise men and overseers worked out the calendar, foretold the floods, measured the fields, and planned the watercourses.

A mysterious invasion from Asia by tribes called the Hyksos or Shepherd Kings interrupted this long peace. The event is obscure, but it occurred about 1800 B.C. and the invaders appear to have brought the horse with them. Of the strife that followed we know nothing, but when the intruders were expelled there appears a line of warlike Pharaohs, ruling from Thebes, high up in the valley. These Pharaohs have horses and war chariots, and they lead armies *out* of Egypt. One of them, Thutmose III, conquered all Syria and placed garrisons in it. The Egyptians had an empire. They built vast temples and palaces in and about Thebes. The Temple at Karnak was built with giant columns all carved about with pictures and inscriptions. In the Valley of the Tombs nearly at the edge of the desert are the graves of these later Pharaohs and of their chief men, buried in the splendor of gold and cedar and ivory, but nearly all discovered and plundered of their riches by unknown robbers long ago.

Of these imperial Pharaohs Ikhnaton is remembered because he tried to change the religion of Egypt from the worship of the sun and of Amen and Osiris, the old gods, to the worship of One God of all, a God who cared for every created thing. A hymn to this god reads like our 104th psalm, "O Lord, how manifold are thy works; in wisdom hast thou made them all." But as soon as Ikhnaton was dead—and he died young—the old gods resumed their sway over men's minds. His successor, Tutankhamen, is now famous, not for what he did, but because his tomb lasted undisturbed by robbers until 1922 when it was discovered and opened by Mr. Howard Carter, and men saw the shining splendor of a Pharaoh's tomb exactly as it was when sealed up at the burial.

The Pharaohs who followed continued to lead armies up into Syria, but they met there the chariots and cavalry of a new power—that of the Hittites. For a while the Pharaohs and the kings of the Hittites shared the mastery of the Near Eastern lands.

Lost Empires of the Ancient East

The name of Uriah the Hittite, captain of King David's bodyguard, meant little to us until archaeologists began digging up the ruins of Hittite cities in Asia Minor. The Hittites were a powerful people able to make war against Egypt and

Babylonia. From the clay tablets found in Hittite ruins we know that they had a high respect for law and justice, and were fair and merciful. Moreover, they seem to have taken delight in the telling of tales for their own sake, or, as we should say, in "literature." They have an added interest for us because we begin to think that the Greeks—to whom we owe our civilization—owed a good deal to them. Like the Greeks they were Indo-Europeans.

This name of Indo-Europeans brings us to the question: Where did everybody's ancestors come from in the beginning?

There is no sure answer. But we can trace peoples and tribes on the move in early times, and then try to follow them back to some starting place. One such starting place was Arabia. From here came all those peoples, like the Babylonians, Jews, Amorites, Phoenicians, and Aramaeans, who spoke a Semitic type of language. They came at long intervals of time, not all at once. It seems as if the tribes of the desert and semidesert multiply until there is not enough land or food, and then, when a vigorous leader arises, they break out upon neighboring lands.

Another starting place was in the great grasslands of farther Asia, north and east of the Caspian Sea. From here came our own ancestors. From here came all those peoples who speak an Indo-European language. Some went into India; others into Persia; others, Hittites and Mitanni, into the nearer parts of Asia; others called Phrygians and Greeks into Asia Minor and Greece; others called Gauls into Asia Minor, North Italy and finally France (once called Gaul); others called Germans into Central Europe; still others called Slavs into the great European Plain. This list itself shows how they moved— slowly westward over thousands of years, the first families, groups and tribes swinging southwards toward the warmer lands and the Mediterranean Sea. The Hittites appear in the nearer East about 2000 B.C.: the Gauls entered Italy more than a thousand years later! When a whole people were on the move they moved slowly.

Our story is at present concerned with the Near East only. Between Arabia and the pasture lands of remoter Asia beyond the Caspian there is a mass of mountainous country from which the rivers of Tigris and Euphrates flow down through the plains of Mesopotamia to the Persian Gulf. All this tract of rugged mountain, desert fringe, and smiling plain was the scene of the mingling and conflict of these two groups of peoples—Semitic and Indo-European. It was filled with cities and men, temples and trade, craftsmen and priests; with multitudes of toiling peasants; with herdsmen; with conquerors and their armies on the march; with sieges and the noise of battle, and crowds of captives and slaves. Over two thousand years of it! Today it is a graveyard of lost empires. Like a graveyard it has its silent monuments: giant mounds, each of which is the tumbled ruin of a city. As the old houses and walls of stone and mud brick fell down, or were thrown down, the sites were raked level and new houses built on top. So the height rose; and when the final destruction came and the city was left desolate, the wind and rain beat upon it and smoothed it to a high mound which keeps its forgotten relics of far-off things—pottery, beads, ivories, ornaments of gold and silver, trinkets, and inscribed tablets and sculptured stones. These things we dig up today.

We know of cities on the plain of the Lower Tigris and Euphrates from before 3000 B.C., whose men used copper tools, plowed the fields with oxen, and used rough wheeled carts. They wrote a wedge-shaped writing, or cuneiform, on clay tablets. They made canals which, as in Egypt, carried the floodwaters through the land. Each city had its own god and its own king who was also the priest of the god. The temple which rose high above the city was built of mud brick, square and massive, with each side leaning slightly inward towards the top, on which stood the holy place of the god. Flights of steps ran up outside from the ground to the summit. Such temples, like the pyramids of Egypt, needed careful planning and the employment of thousands of men—perhaps slaves— to construct them.

We can see from the lines of grim spearmen sculptured on their stones that these early Sumerian cities of the plain went up to war against each other "when kings go forth to battle" in the spring of the year. Perhaps the quarrels were over boundaries. The tablets record the strange names of their kings, and we can make out a good deal about their beliefs and what they knew. An excavation of the city of Ur, the place Abraham came from, showed traces of a mighty flood which must have covered all the plain. It also revealed the grave of a princess at whose costly burial a whole court full of attendants, guards, and maids-of-honor were sacrificed in order to accompany their mistress to the world after death. The furniture and precious metalwork buried in this amazing tomb are of unsurpassed quality in design and make. One of the noticeable things about these early civilizations is that, as soon as craftsmen find out how to work in wood or copper or gold or stone, they quickly reach a superb standard of excellence. We see that civilization is made by hands.

We do not know where these Sumerians came from. We do know that about 2500 B.C. a man of mark named Sargon, a Semitic chieftain, led his bearded spearmen southwards into the plain and made himself master of all the lands east and west between the mountains of Persia and the Mediterranean Sea. His fame endured for centuries. The enormous heaps of clay tablets from his time show us a world in which men kept careful accounts, scholars studied mathematics, and children did exercises! We read of charms and spells to please the gods or frighten away the many demons and evil spirits. And there are stories of ancient heroes and of the creation of the world.

About 2000 B.C. a new race of Semites whom we call Amorites entered and became overlords of the plain, and ruled it from Babylon. We have records of their greatest king, named Hammurabi. We have his letters in which he sends orders to his officers and governors—all on baked clay, and in clay envelopes. We also have an inscribed stone with his great code of laws, many of which remind us of those of the Jews, such as the one about taking "an eye for an eye, and a tooth for a tooth." They tell us also of the rules for buying and selling goods and houses, for the payment of craftsmen, and for the borrowing of money, and repayment of debts. So, here was a rich and prosperous empire with many cities and many temples, priests and scribes and king's servants and lords, workers and farmers and merchants, all keeping one law, and obedient to one sovereign king. It was an extensive empire, and relied for its transport on donkeys —just as many parts of the Near East did until recent years. We might call it a donkey civilization. We might also call it a clay civilization. Houses and writing tablets were of clay. Even the bales of the merchants were sealed with tags of clay, all properly stamped with the owner's name.

About 1800 B.C. this Babylonian Empire fell into a state of weakness and decay. There were invasions from north and south. The Hittites entered the lands of Asia Minor and northern Syria, where they began to build up a great power, and another Indo-European nation of horsemen called Mitanni made their kingdom on the Euphrates. These peoples introduced the horse into the ancient East, where he was first known as "the ass of Asia." The Mitanni did not hold their power for very long, but they lasted long enough to make alliances with Egypt and to upset the old Babylonian Empire. We must always remember that the coming of a new people did not mean the wiping out of the older inhabitants. There was conflict always; but the result was usually a gradual mingling.

From the south Semitic peoples called Aramaeans swarmed up from the desert borders of Arabia and set up city kingdoms, of which the most famous is Damascus. We read of this kingdom in the Old Testament, where it appears as the ally of the Northern Jewish kingdom. These Aramaeans spread their language throughout the Near East so thoroughly that the Jews were still using it in the time of Our Lord. Other Semitic peoples had established great trading cities at Tyre and Sidon on the Syrian coast, and they are familiar to us as the Phoenicians, the sailors and merchants whose ships carried their wares to Spain and, perhaps, to Britain. The best-known of Semitic races are the Jews. When they entered the Holy Land is not certainly known yet: the Bible and the results of digging do not tally. We may not be far out if we think of 1500 B.C. King David lived about the year 1000 B.C. By his time the Hittite power had vanished: but he was not troubled by any Babylonian power.

The Babylonian Empire decayed. The Mitanni disappear from the records. The Hittites and Egyptians fought each other to a standstill. And then the Hittites themselves were overthrown by the Phrygians, an Indo-European race who entered Asia Minor. These newcomers were part of a greater migration of races into the lands of the eastern Mediterranean. About 1400 B.C. the whole scene is troubled with armed men under chieftains: there is war and destruction. Some of them sailed against the coast of Egypt whose Pharaoh recorded that "the isles were troubled, and no land withstood them." The newcomers were from the north, and brought disaster to those they found living around the eastern Mediterranean.

But in Babylonia a new power was rising: the power of the lords of Assur. They had always been there. With the fall of so many great nations they stepped into the leading place, and created the military Assyrian Empire.

The Sea Power of Crete and the Land Power of Assyria

The peoples who troubled the isles and drove out the officers of the Egyptian Pharaohs were the ancestors of the Greeks. They had most likely been on the move since about 2000 B.C. across Asia and into Asia Minor and Greece. They took to the sea. They destroyed a civilization of whose existence we ourselves were quite ignorant until sixty years ago!—the Minoan civilization of Crete.

The first lord of the sea was King Minos of Crete. So said the Greek legend, and we did not understand it, until, in 1900, Sir Arthur Evans opened up the mound of Knossos in Crete and found the ruins of a palace of unbelievable magnificence. Its hundreds of tablets were in an unknown script, but it was clear that this "Minoan" civilization ran back for many centuries. Wall paintings of great artistic power and beauty show women dressed in flounced skirts and men in loincloths and high boots! There are the most vivid scenes of bullbaiting, and wonderful floral decorations. The architecture is most impressive: great halls, grand stairways, and a perfect maze of cellars for storage. This discovery turned our attention to the giant fortifications of Mycenae and Tiryns on the Greek mainland in which Schliemann had found treasures of goldsmiths' work and fine pottery that now appeared to be of the Minoan type.

Here was an empire that had been utterly forgotten. It fitted in well with the Greek legend of Minos, but there remained a puzzle.

Mycenae was the famous city stronghold of Agamemnon, who led the Greek kings against Troy. This is the story told by Homer. But we cannot make the times fit together. It seems that someone lived and ruled in Mycenae before Agamemnon. The old Greek saying that there were great men before Agamemnon is right. Our puzzle is, Who were they? Perhaps, some day, we may find out from the inscriptions on the clay tablets of Crete and Mycenae which we are just beginning to read.

The general picture seems to be as follows. Knossos in Crete fell to unknown enemies about 1400 B.C. and the power of its lords over the islands of the sea came to an end. The palace was abandoned and given to the flames—from the marks of the burning we can even tell which way the wind was blowing at the time. At about the same time the Pharaoh Rameses drove back some desperate adventurers, "seafarers," from his coast. These men bear familiar names —Sardinians, Sicilians, Philistines. These last, who appear as soldiers in large plumed helmets, were said to have come from Crete. They landed on the Syrian coast and built five cities for their lords—the lords of the Philistines against whom Saul fought and with whom David was friendly; and they gave their name to the whole country—Palestine, or the land of the Philistines.

How long these troubles lasted we do not know, but long enough for all memory of Crete to be lost among men; long enough to make a break in the continuity of civilization. These were the dark ages when records failed. The historic Greeks whose ancestors had done these things, "fair-haired Achaeans" and Dorians sacking and burning cities, only told the tale of Troy. We should like to know what really happened, and also why it was all forgotten.

So the Philistines of the old Jewish story turn out to be men akin to the Greeks, and the legends of the two most gifted races of antiquity, Jews and Greeks, meet in these shadowy times.

The historic Jewish story is caught up with the story of the Assyrian Empire.

High up on the River Tigris on the edge of the stony hill country was the city of Assur, whose men, a Semitic folk, found themselves for centuries on the warring frontier of great races—Babylonians, Mitanni, Aramaeans, Hittites. They learned a lot from all these, and like so many border people they became skilled soldiers. They rose in power soon after the Babylonians began to weaken, but their rise was slow at first. We find them trading throughout the East, and they appear as a small but vigorous nation of peasants and merchants. Then, under a line of clever and merciless soldier-kings, they swept all before them, conquering Babylon and marching victoriously down to Egypt. Sargon—who took his name from the older conqueror of centuries before—Tiglath Pileser, Esarhaddon, and Sennacherib, led their terrible armies everywhere, their bowmen, their horsemen and chariots, and their great battering rams with which they overturned the walls of cities. They were not content with the yearly raids made by earlier emperors like those made by Arab chieftains for plunder; they subdued and destroyed and placed officers and garrisons in captured towns. They built an organized empire by cruel conquest. A Jewish prophet described them: "The horseman lifteth up both the bright sword and the glittering spear: and there is a multitude of slain . . . and there is no end of their corpses."

These merciless Assyrian kings lived in the eighth and seventh centuries B.C. Like all such monarchs they were great builders. In fact they lived in supreme luxury. They made their capital at Nineveh, a dazzling city of palaces and temples shining with colored tiles and adorned with giant sculptures. On the walls unknown artists carved lively hunting scenes. The gardens were filled with rare plants from all their lands, and supplied with water brought by an aqueduct thirty miles in length.

The Assyrian Empire suffered a change of masters in 612 B.C. when the Chaldeans, another Semitic people from the south, seized the government. These Chaldeans were talented and merciful. To their wise men we owe much of our earliest knowledge of the stars. Nebuchadnezzar, the greatest of the Chaldean rulers of the Empire, rebuilt Babylon. It was he who captured Jerusalem in 597 and carried away the Jews into captivity by the waters of Babylon.

Only sixty years later another people seized power. This time they were Indo-Europeans, the people we call Persians.

With the Persian Empire we enter that tract of history which is told in the books of the ancient Greeks and Romans. It is the tract of history which our ancestors knew before the archaeologists began digging up the far-off past. It is the tale of the three great empires—the Persian, the Greek, and the Roman—one after the other, in that order. The end of the tale is that the Romans took over all those lands which had been mastered first by the Assyrians, then by the Persians, and then by the Greeks; and so brought all the peoples of the Great Sea under one rule in East and West; and all the world paid tribute to Caesar. We are the children of the Roman Empire.

The Babylonians, Hittites, Mitanni, Cretans, Assyrians, vanish as separate peoples. Their descendants are no doubt with us today, but their glory and their works are gone, to be forgotten entirely or turned into legends.

Two other peoples played great parts in that story which our ancestors studied: the Jews and the Carthaginians. The Jews have given us our religion. They founded no material empire, but they still survive as a talented and vigorous race, and they have kept their own history in their sacred writing —our Old Testament.

The Carthaginians were conquered by the Romans. No Carthaginian writings have come down to us, and Carthage is a waste place on the African shore of the Great Sea, and no man knows who is descended from its proud citizens. Persians, Jews, Greeks, and Romans still exist today—not, indeed, unchanged after so many generations and so many troubled centuries.

The Persians

In 538 Cyrus the Persian seized the throne and empire of the Chaldean kings.

He was a noble captain of men, a merciful and wise ruler. He did not enslave multitudes or lead them under the lash or destroy the wells of water as the bloodthirsty Assyrian kings had done. It was Cyrus who sent back to Jerusalem the gold and silver vessels taken as spoils of war by Nebuchadnezzar: and it was he who let the Jews, then living in captivity, return to their homeland in Judea to rebuild the Temple of their God in Jerusalem. His conquests led him as far west as the Greek cities of Asia Minor; but these looked on him as a friendly tyrant not as a cruel conqueror.

His son, Cambyses, led an army across the north of the desert lands behind the Lebanon Mountains, down the fertile coastland of Syria and Palestine, and across the southern desert of Sinai into Egypt, which he conquered for the Persians.

The next powerful king was Darius I, who reigned from 522 to 486. Under him the Persian Empire reached from India to the borders of Ethiopia in Africa, and to the coast of the Black Sea in the north. A good look at the map will do more than pages of reading to give an idea of this huge block of empire, once the cradleland of ancient civilizations, and now strewn with ruins.

Darius I was rightly named the "King of Kings." He ruled over "a hundred and twenty provinces" according to our Bible. His Empire held a crowd of races speaking many tongues. His ships, manned by Indians, sailed from the Red Sea to India; and, manned by the navigators of Tyre and Sidon, to the western Mediterranean. His army was made up of regiments from all kinds of peoples, some of them half-savage, with a fantastic variety of weapons and dress and headgear. At its head were the Immortals—Ten Thousand of the young men of the noblest families of the Persians, under the King's special command.

The Persians were handsome, sturdy folk, warlike, courageous, and fair-dealing, and very proud of their ancestry. Their subjects worshiped all kinds of gods and idols and devils, and were great believers in magic. They themselves believed in a god of light and truth and creation whom they called Ahura-Mazda. This god was constantly at war with the god of evil and lies and destruction, called Ahriman. It was the duty of all believers to help Ahura-Mazda in his everlasting war by living a good life, doing justly, and telling the truth. It was this religion which made them deal kindly with the Jews who also believed in a God of righteousness.

Darius and his successors ruled their empire by building roads, long paved highways linking up east and west and north and south over huge distances. A royal road ran from Susa to the Greek city of Ephesus—1,670 miles away: another road led into Egypt; yet another was made across the wild mountains of the east far into the Indus valley of India. Along these roads went the horsemen of the royal mail service, the king's messengers, the trading caravans, and the royal court itself as it journeyed from city to city.

The Persian kings had several royal cities and palaces. They lived in great state and pomp in these. A royal house was furnished with marble columns and cedar wood, and ornamented with goldwork, ivory, ebony, silver, and precious stones such as carnelian and lapis lazuli, all worked and put in place by craftsmen from far and near, Egypt, the Greek cities, Tyre, and the eastern mountains. The walls were covered with enameled pictures of winged bulls and lions after the old Babylonian fashion. There were many rare tapestries and curtains: in the Book of Esther we read how the king made a feast in his palace in the court of his garden, "where there were white, green, and blue hangings, fastened with cords of fine linen and purple to silver rings and pillars of marble; the beds were of gold and silver, upon a pavement of red and blue and white and black marble."

The provinces of the Empire were called *satrapies* because they were governed by *satraps*, men whom we should call viceroys. These satraps gathered the taxes, did justice, and raised armies for the king. They did not trouble the peoples so long as they paid their taxes and remained loyal. They did not force them to worship this or that god. And Darius and his successors took care to have their satraps watched to see whether they carried out their duties properly.

This Empire was, therefore, something new in history, a very welcome thing in place of the older empires of conquest and terror and the worship of bloodthirsty gods. An excellent thing to remember the Persians by is the phrase which describes the training of their boys—"To ride, to shoot with the bow, and to tell the truth."

The Greeks

Who were the Greeks? Dim legends and archaeology join to give a picture of peoples coming south and bringing tumult and disaster to whatever men lived about the Aegean Sea. The memory of Minoan civilization was lost, nor did any man remember what lords ruled in golden Mycenae, the mighty stronghold above the Argive plain.

The Greek poet Homer sang one grand epic poem about an incident in the ten-years' siege of Troy by an alliance of Greek princes led by Agamemnon of Mycenae: and a second poem about the homecoming of the Greek princes and the wanderings of one of them named Odysseus. These events happened *after* the destruction of Crete, and *before* the beginnings of recorded Greek history. They float "in the air," so to speak, and we cannot find the key which will lock them into known historic events. They are like the tales of King Arthur and his knights which tell of things *after* the fall of Rome but *before* the beginnings of recorded English history.

All the picture we have, then, of the coming of the Greeks is this: somewhere about 1800 B.C. their ancestors began to move south through the passes of the mountains into the

Balkans and into Greece where their descendants possessed the coasts and the islands of the sea. They were known to the later Greeks as "fair-haired Achaeans," and Ionians, and Dorians. Later Indo-Europeans moving farther westwards descended into Italy and Gaul, and later still a great multitude moved into the German lands. We have to imagine all these vastly scattered peoples seeking new pastures, new homes, year by year. Since we ourselves are among their innumerable descendants it will be interesting to note what scholars have guessed about their mode of life in antiquity before they began their wanderings—say, about 3000 B.C.

They spun and wove and wore loincloths and simple overgarments. They kept oxen, pigs and geese. They had ox yokes, plows, and wheeled wagons. They made an unleavened bread. They got drunk on fermented honey. They lived in wattle huts with wind openings or windows. They were horsemen. These dimly perceived clansmen swarming slowly towards the Mediterranean world with herds and wagons from their Asiatic pastures, had tamed the wild horse, and they brought him into the ancient civilized world. He is, indeed, one of the chief actors in our past. For his coming changed the scene. From his docility and power came the horseman of Assyria, of Persia, of Greece, of Rome. The armed horseman, the *knight*, was the master of men until the invention of artillery. We can see the impression made on men's minds by the coming of cavalry in the words of the Hebrew prophet Nahum, who writes of "The noise of a whip, and the noise of the rattling of the wheels, and of the prancing of horses, and of the jumping chariot."

Nahum was speaking of the Assyrians. Horses and chariots play a part in Homer's stories of the Greeks and Trojans.

When we first perceive the Greeks of recorded times they are living in cities all independent of each other. Each city and the farms around it formed a separate state called a *polis*. Sometimes a city sent out a band of its citizens to found a daughter city elsewhere, and this daughter city was quite independent of the other, although naturally tied to it by bonds of kinship. In the eighth and seventh centuries B.C. we find Greek cities throughout Greece, on the islands, on the coasts of Asia Minor and the Black Sea, on Sicily and the Italian coast, on the shores of Africa, and even on the French coast—at Marseilles, for instance. Although all were independent, their citizens looked on themselves as one race and regarded all non-Greeks as "barbarians"—men whose speech was to them meaningless noise. For them the world was divided into Greeks and barbarians.

Though they never learned to live in large states like the

ancient empires of Asia or modern nations, no people have ever been more keenly interested in politics—a word which, as you may have guessed, means "that which concerns the *polis,* or city." The ways in which they governed themselves were various. Sometimes they had kings, as at Sparta; sometimes one strong man made himself a tyrant doing as he pleased—and sometimes he was a good tyrant. Sometimes the noblemen ruled, and this was called an *aristocracy*. Sometimes all the citizens took part in the government. This was easier then than now because the cities were small enough for all adult men to assemble together to discuss things, as they did in Athens. The wisest of the Greeks, Aristotle, saw that all sorts of government can be either good or bad according to the way men behave to each other. Perhaps no men have ever thought so clearly and expressed their thoughts so well in politics as Aristotle and Plato.

Each city could reckon its years from its own foundation, but all Greeks counted their dates from the Olympian Games, which were held every four years and in which competitors from far and wide took part. They were an open-air people, living and disputing in the market place, inquisitive and energetic. Their athletic and religious meetings were held in vast open-air stadiums and theaters. The theaters were built of tiers of stone benches in great half-circles on a slope or hillside, and on these benches thousands of spectators could see and hear the actors and the priests performing below. Their dramas were not mere entertainment but religious spectacles, plays about the heroes of old, and the fates of men, and the influence of the gods. Their stories were taken from the old Greek legends. Their great festivals were accompanied by athletic games at famous places—Delphi, Corinth, Olympia. Torchlight processions led by priests heralded the events, which included foot races, discus and javelin throwing, leaping, and horse and chariot races. The winners received garlands of olive or laurel and won the honor for their city. If they were lucky their prowess might be sung by a great poet like Pindar.

Living in cities by the sea, the Greeks were also fine seamen and thriving merchants. They also made good soldiers; many of their young men took service as hired troops with Egypt and the Persians.

The most astonishing thing about the Greeks was the marvelous skill of their architects, their potters, and their sculptors. The Parthenon, the temple of the goddess Athene that stands in the clear air high over Athens, is still one of the most beautiful buildings in the world. Today it is merely of gray stone with a faint reddish tinge. In its first splendid days it gleamed with color and was adorned with masterpieces of sculpture and bronze work. The pottery of the Greeks is so perfect that each vase seems a work of nature not of man. Equally astonishing is the beauty of Greek poetry and the wisdom of Greek philosophy. The dramas of Aeschylus, Euripides, and Sophocles are still read as among the greatest ever written; the Greek philosophers are still studied for their wisdom. "In all branches of learning," said the Roman scholar, Cicero, "the Greeks are our masters." His statement, made in the first century B.C., is still true today. They did not have our science, but our science is founded on what they thought about the earth. Everyone who learns Greek knows that the Greeks had one great advantage: their language was itself a thing of superb beauty and clarity.

We judge any people by their best. And the best of the Greeks remains unsurpassed. But we must remember that there were a lot of Greeks, and that plenty of them were treacherous and deceitful and quarrelsome—particularly quarrelsome. But they were, perhaps, the most gifted race the world has ever known.

This is why we are so much interested in the question: Who were the Greeks?

The Glory and Decline of the Greek Cities

In 490 B.C. the Greek cities of Asia Minor rose in revolt against the Persian king Darius, and were helped by Athenian soldiers. Darius sent an army to take Athens, but when it landed from its galleys on the plain of Marathon, the Athenian spearmen under Miltiades defeated it decisively.

Ten years later a new Persian king named Xerxes mustered a multitudinous army from all his dominions and marched it across the Hellespont into Europe over a bridge of boats. He then marched northward into Thrace and then down upon Athens. At the same time he sent a great armada of 1,200 war galleys to the Greek coast. The Athenians were forced to leave their city, which was soon burned by the enemy, but a Spartan army stood ready to come to their help. Since the war of Darius ten years before, the Athenian statesman Themistocles had built up a very strong Athenian navy. This navy now came into action. From the cliffs above the bay of Salamis, Xerxes and his court watched the Athenian ships destroy his armada in a fierce all-day battle. The loss of his fleet led Xerxes to return to Persia, leaving a strong army behind to winter in Greece and resume the war in the spring. But the next year the Spartan general Pausanias routed this army at Plataea.

The Athenian navy at Salamis, and the Spartan army at Plataea, saved Greece from becoming part of the empire of the Great King. Xerxes, the King of Kings whose empire stretched from India to Egypt, and whose armies were in number as the sands of the seashore, failed to subdue the Greeks. One story of the war must always be told: the story of King Leonidas of Sparta and his band of Three Hundred devoted men.

On the long march into southern Greece the vast army of Xerxes had to cross the mountains through the pass of Thermopylae—the Hot Springs. This pass was held by Leonidas and his spearmen, supported by a thousand Thespians.

The land to the north of Thermopylae was full of the Persian armies—all the warriors of Asia and the East— cotton-clad Indians, Bactrian archers, Arabs in flowing robes, African blacks in leopardskins, and a host of others in all kinds of outlandish garments, and with all kinds of weapons from horn-tipped spears to great iron-studded clubs; and there was cavalry armed with lances and bows; and at the center of all the famous Median foot soldiers in leather coats and trousers, wearing felt caps and carrying spears and wicker-work shields. Around the king himself there went the Ten Thousand Immortals, a picked bodyguard of young Persian nobles.

Xerxes in purple robes sat on a golden chair and saw his men go to the attack. Leonidas and his Spartans and Thespians held the pass easily, bringing down the Medians in that fifty-foot way with their long, heavy Greek spears. Then the Immortals attacked. But by the end of the day the pass was still untaken. The next day was a repetition of the first.

A Greek of those parts offered to show the Persians a secret path over the mountains whereby they could come behind Leonidas. In single file the Persians followed their guide down the rough track through forests as black as pitch, over boulder-strewn places, and along watercourses—a mere goat's path. It was the long mysterious frou-frou of their feet rustling the fallen leaves that the Spartans heard in the night and wondered at the sound. By dawn a host of the enemy was behind the pass.

Leonidas and his men stayed on. They moved out to where the pass widened and waited for the renewed attacks. They fought and fought and killed great numbers of the barbarians, including the brothers of Xerxes himself. When their spears broke they used swords. When these failed they fought barehanded. The last few rallied at the end in the narrowest part and there fell together. By this time the Immortals were on their way to Athens. But Leonidas and his men had kept faith. Such devoted courage sprang from discipline and from that intense patriotism of the best Greeks for their own city. It was a patriotism not bred in huge Asiatic empires.

After Salamis and the other victories the city of Athens under the leadership of Pericles became the center and glory of the Greeks. Its citizens rebuilt their homes and their temples, which were adorned by the marvelous sculptures of Pheidias. Aeschylus, Sophocles, and Euripides wrote plays for the public theater, plays which are still read and performed today. Plato, the philosopher, taught his pupils in a grove called the Academy, and among his pupils was Aristotle, who became as renowned as his master. Above all, the Athenians prided themselves on knowing how to lead the best of lives as free men. One of the finest speeches ever made was that of Pericles when he spoke of those who had died in the Persian war. "Our city," he said, "is open to all and we never drive away a foreigner or stop him from seeing or learning anything. We are lovers of the beautiful, yet we have simple tastes. We use riches not for show, but as we need them. To be poor is no disgrace: the true disgrace is to be poor and do nothing to help yourself. We look upon any man who is not interested in our city as a useless person. We think before we act, but we do act. I would have all of you day by day to fix your eyes upon the greatness of Athens until you become filled with the love of her: and then reflect that her power has been made by men who knew their duty and had the courage to do it."

But, alas! the Athenians who had taken the lead against Persia soon compelled the lesser Greek cities to pay taxes into her treasury, and even made war upon them. Then in 431 a war broke out between Athens and her allies and Sparta and hers. It lasted for twenty-seven years, bringing misery to thousands. This Peloponnesian War (a long name but worth remembering) was, in fact, a civil war; for the Greeks were one race and thought of themselves as one race, although they never learned to act together for long.

During the Peloponnesian War thousands of Greeks took to soldiering and went abroad to fight for the Egyptians or the Persians or the Carthaginians. They became mercenaries, men who hired their spears and swords for pay. In one of his books, Xenophon the Athenian has left us a finely written story of the retreat of Ten Thousand Greeks from Babylon across the wild hills of Armenia to the shores of the Black Sea. These Ten Thousand had joined the army of a Persian prince named Cyrus, and when he was killed they found themselves friendless and abandoned in a foreign country.

They escaped the only way they could—Arcadians, Athenians, Thebans, men from many cities—trudging steadily for months through the mountain passes and bleak uplands, starving, frostbitten, stumbling in snowstorms, fighting rear-guard actions against hostile tribes, and at last winning their way home.

The Greek cities had never had a supreme leader, but they never lacked for men who sought adventures abroad. Very soon these men found a leader in the person of the Macedonian prince, Alexander.

Alexander

The Macedonians were a tough mountain folk, akin to the Greeks of the cities. Their king, Philip, turned them into a nation of soldiers, well-drilled and marshaled in wedge-shaped bodies *(phalanxes)* of spearmen. When he died, having made himself master of all the northern lands of Greece, his son Alexander succeeded to the throne. Philip had admired the civilization of the Athenians, and had employed their great philosopher Aristotle as the tutor of his son. Whether this had anything to do with this son's becoming the wonder of the world, no man can say.

Alexander was twenty at his accession.

With his father's army under its skillful generals he crossed the Hellespont into Asia, and speedily conquered Asia Minor, Syria, and Egypt. Then, marching into the lands of the two rivers, he routed the Persian king, Darius II, at Gaugemela near Nineveh. The Persians were no match for the heavily-armed Greeks massed in their phalanxes, with Greek cavalry sweeping forward on each wing. Only a century earlier Xerxes had invaded Europe—and failed; now the Greeks, under their young, handsome, and athletic king, had won all the East.

What he did next remains without parallel in all history. He led his army eastward across the highlands of Persia into Afghanistan and Turkestan; he wintered among the savage hill tribes of Afghanistan; in the spring he invaded India, descending the long, winding passes of the Himalayas into the Punjab, whose princes he subdued. He returned by an arduous march through the parched wastes of Baluchistan, leaving behind him a fame and a memory of "Iskander" that did not fade for centuries; for Alexander was not merely a superb general and conqueror; he had learned to govern and organize men and affairs; he showed a farseeing wisdom. Never has there been such a captain, or such an army. But,

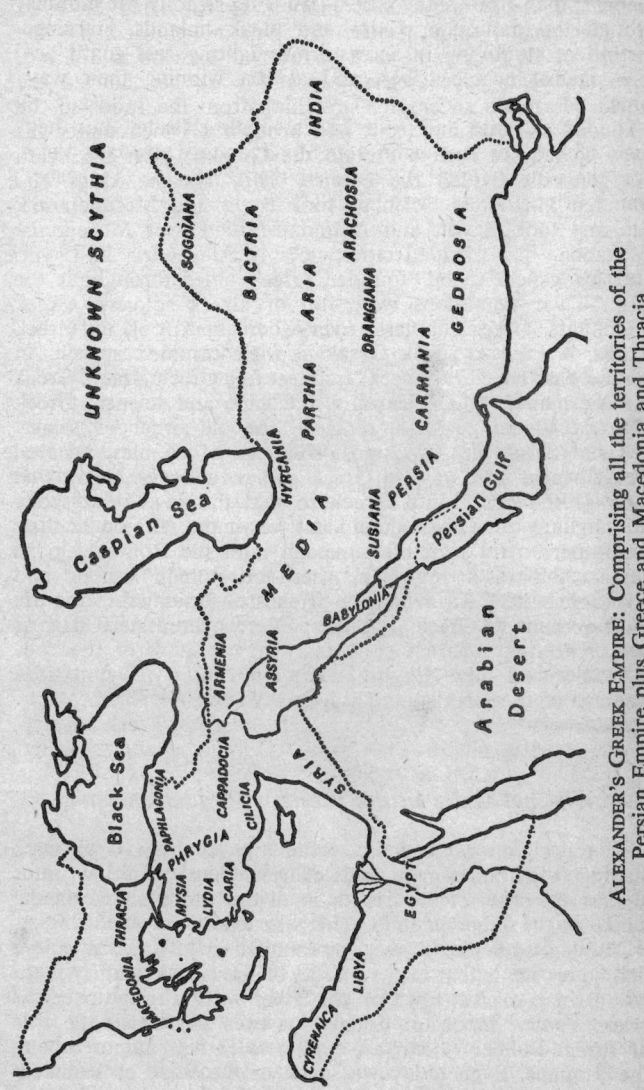

ALEXANDER'S GREEK EMPIRE: Comprising all the territories of the Persian Empire plus Greece and Macedonia and Thracia

then, never has there been such a race as the Greeks. What Alexander might have done more than this, had he lived out the normal span of life, can only be guessed. To the dismay of his peoples he died of fever at Babylon in 323 B.C.

In ten years of ceaseless war and work he changed the world. He made an empire stretching from the Indus to the Nile and the Adriatic, and had brought all men under his sway to admire and to imitate the Greeks. After his death his generals divided the empire. They became kings and founded kingdoms: Seleucus took Syria and Mesopotamia, Ptolemy took Egypt, and Antigonus ruled over Macedonia. Alexander had founded cities, notably Alexandria in Egypt, and his generals, too, founded Greek cities throughout the East. Their dominions were full of Greek soldiers, Greek merchants, Greek scholars. Everywhere men took up Greek habits, learned to speak Greek as their common speech. In all the eastern cities Greek architecture, Greek dress, Greek athletic games, Greek learning, medicine and science, Greek philosophy and customs, replaced the old order of things. Even some of the Jews, most stubborn of peoples, adopted Greek ways, took part in Greek games, and even translated their sacred books into Greek so that the Jews who spoke no language but Greek should not forget the religion of their forefathers. And so it all remained until the Roman legions came. And so it remained after the Roman legions had conquered the East. When the friends of Jesus wrote his life they wrote it in Greek. For ten centuries the eastern half of our civilization was a Greek one.

No wonder that English schoolboys used to study the writings of the Greeks, and still do.

Seafarers and Cities in the Western Mediterranean

In the eighth century B.C., when the Assyrian kings were leading their horsemen and chariots and battering rams against the cities of the east, a small town took shape on the banks of the Tiber in Italy. This was Rome.

The legend is that Rome was founded in 753 B.C. What we had better say is that in the middle of the eighth century there was a small market town on the Tiber with a bridge over the river: a very important bridge, for ever afterwards the title of Bridge-Builder (*Pontifex*) was held in high honor among the Romans. Even today we speak of the Pope of Rome as the *Pontiff*. That cluster of huts and dwellings was a refuge and a market, or *forum*, for the Latin-speaking farmer who could there trade his grain and animals for the bronze and iron weapons and tools which he wanted.

This was the beginning of Rome. We have many records of the eighth-century Assyrians and the east, but few of the western Mediterranean into which Rome's river of Tiber empties itself. Of the tribes who lived in the western lands we know almost nothing; of the seafarers from the east and the cities they founded for their trade we do know a little.

First, there were the Phoenicians, seamen of Tyre and Sidon, rich, adventurous, secretive, guarding their knowledge of the seas from strangers. They were the pioneers sailing west for trade and gain. At home on the Syrian coast they handled the trade of Asia and Egypt, and their craftsmen were renowned for their metalwork. Abroad, they planted a city which they named Carthage (Newtown) on the shore of Africa opposite the island of Sicily. They also built cities on the coast of Sicily and Spain, one of them out beyond the Mediterranean at the mouth of the Guadalquivir, a place called Gades. Probably the natives of Spain worked the copper and tin mines for their benefit. Probably they sailed into the Atlantic to the Scillies and Cornwall, and they sent ships down the West African coast. What they discovered they kept to themselves. For very many years the western Mediterranean was their sea, and the Greek skipper who dared to sail there did so at his peril.

The Greeks from the Greek mainland and the cluster of islands in the Greek seas were their rivals. Greeks founded cities in South Italy, in Sicily and on the south coast of France—Syracuse, for example, and Marseilles.

The long shores of the western Mediterranean were a new world to these mariners. Both the Phoenicians and the Greeks traded with the natives for metals and hides, giving them in return woven cloth, pottery, and ornaments. And as they sailed and rowed always in sight of land from one landmark to another, they came to anchor at the towns they had founded where the cargoes waited for them, and where parleying took place with the less civilized folk from upcountry.

There was one people with a civilization who also sailed the seas and traded their wares. But these lived in a western land, the tumbled country between the Appenines of Italy and the sea, north of Rome. They were the Etruscans. They lived in a dozen or so cities and were ruled by lords or kings just like the Philistines of the Old Testament. They have left many memorials of themselves; for they buried their dead in great chambers cut in the rock, and placed furniture and goods for them for their use in the afterworld of death. They carved inscriptions in Greek letters, but we cannot yet read the words. The language is strange to us. They were excellent craftsmen, metalworkers and potters. Their bronze and gold work is lovely to look on; and their pottery only less beautiful than that of the Greeks. They knew how to build the arch—which the Greeks did not. They used horses and chariots. They have left pictures of hunting and feasting, and they seem to have been fond of music. Where they came from in the beginning is not yet known—maybe from the north and east. Because they were powerful neighbors of the Latin tribes, and because their kings ruled in Rome for over two hundred years, much of their skill and customs passed into Roman life. They gave the Romans their long war trumpets, their purple robes, and the bundle of rods tied about an ax (the *fasces*) which was a symbol carried before Roman magistrates. Many famous Roman families were descended from this mysterious race, and Roman writers wrote books about them—which have, most unfortunately, been lost.

The Etruscans can therefore be reckoned among the founders of Europe.

The tales of ancient Rome tell how the city grew and how the people thrust out their Etruscan kings, the Tarquins, somewhere about 500 B.C.: and next, how the city was taken by the Gauls in 390 B.C. By this time the light of history is growing brighter and we begin to have a more flowing story.

The Gauls, a barbarian people, were on the march across Europe from the east. Some of them had a long while earlier invaded and settled down in Asia Minor, in the part afterwards called Galatia. By 400 they were north of Italy, and in 390 their warriors came down the Alpine passes into Italy, where they attacked the Etruscan cities and then took Rome, all Rome, that is, except the citadel. The old story is that the sacred geese kept in the temple cackled when they heard the stealthy approach of the enemy, and so roused the Romans who repulsed the attackers. But the Romans had to pay a huge ransom to buy back their city, before the Gauls consented to retire to the fertile plains of the Po valley in north Italy. Their kinsmen meanwhile were traveling farther west into what is now France and what was, in consequence, called Gaul.

By this time the Romans were making their city well known. They learned much from the Greeks and the Etruscans. They built ships and traded on the sea. They used money. They took over the Greek alphabet, which they skillfully changed to suit their own language, and this, in time, was passed on to all the peoples of the west. This book that you are now reading is therefore printed in the Latin, or Roman, alphabet.

AROUND THE GREAT SEA

The Romans fought many wars with their neighbors, and they appear in their old stories to be very much the same as our own Anglo-Saxon ancestors—farmers and warriors: men who tilled their farms and went out to meet their enemies in battle, a brave, hard-working and vigorous people, with a very strong sense of duty.

The really extraordinary thing about the Romans was their way of governing themselves.

After the expulsion of the Tarquins, Rome was ruled by a senate or council of elders, and by *two* men called consuls. These consuls acted together as kings, doing justice and making laws with the consent of the senate; and the two were equal in power. Each of them could, in fact, forbid any act of the other one. In wartime they led the army in turn day by day—which sounds rather more awkward than it was in those days of hand-to-hand fighting and single-day battles. It was, of course, easier when the two consuls were friends. But this is the main point: the consuls were changed each year, others being elected to take their place. In this way the Romans thought to save their city from ever being ruled by a tyrant. The nearest thing we have to a consul is the mayor of a city.

It was the senate of nobles that possessed the chief power. Once a senator, always a senator; and the senate included all those who had ever been consuls. There has never been anywhere in all history a body of men more skillful in government than the Roman senate at its best. Listen to what the writer of the Jewish history of the Maccabees says in our Bible: it tells us what was thought of the senate by men who were only too well acquainted with kings and their great ministers.

"None of them [that is, the Roman senators] wore a crown, or was clothed in purple, to be made great thereby. They made for themselves a senate-house, wherein three hundred and twenty men sat in council daily, consulting always for the people, to the end that they might be well-governed."

That is a grand compliment.

How the Romans Spread upon the World

From 390 B.C., when the Gauls took and plundered Rome, the Romans were for many years at war with their neighbors, Samnites, Umbrians, and Etruscans. They enrolled their citizens in legions with centurions at the head of every hundred men, and these citizen-soldiers, led by the consuls for the year, mastered all central Italy. The steadfast and simple patriotism of the Romans is revealed in their tale of Cincinnatus, whom they called from his farm to lead them when they were hard-pressed in the war. He did lead them to victory. Then he returned to his farm. Again, when the Romans were warring against the Greek cities of South Italy, the Greek King Pyrrhus from the mainland of Greece came to the help of his kinsmen. Pyrrhus tried to bribe the Roman leader, Caius Fabricius. Fabricius, who, like Cincinnatus, was only a poor farmer, refused the bribe. But when a slave belonging to Pyrrhus offered to poison his master if Fabricius would pay him to do it, Fabricius promptly wrote to Pyrrhus telling him of the plot. These stories—and there are many such—explain why the Romans earned men's respect and trust. The thing the Romans prized above all other things was *virtue*, that is, all the qualities that make a good man and a good citizen: courage, duty, honor, loyalty, love of one's home and kinsmen. This is why, today, we still study Roman Law, and why today the laws of many people are based upon Roman Law.

While the Romans were spreading their power throughout Italy, Alexander the Great was spreading Greek power throughout the East. That King Pyrrhus was among those who shared his Greek Empire after his death. Men have often wondered what would have happened if Alexander had lived long enough to meet the Romans in battle. But the fight for the mastery of the western Mediterranean was fought out by Rome with a far different foe—Carthage, whose merchant princes held Sicily, Sardinia, and parts of Spain. Just as Persians and Greeks had striven for the dominion of the East, so Romans and Carthaginians strove for the dominion of the West.

The Carthaginian merchants were immensely wealthy. They spoke a language like Hebrew, but all their writings have perished. It is remarkable that nearly all we know of them comes from the records of their bitterest enemies, the Romans. Their grand city of Carthage was the trading center for the long caravans from the African countryside, and for the swarms of merchantmen coming from the sea through a narrow canal into the great artificial harbor of Carthage within the city walls. On the Great Quay were unloaded the Spanish silver, the wines, cloth and spices of the East, and the tin ingots from the islands beyond the straits of Gibraltar. The Carthaginians ruled over a mixed populace—Egyptians, Gauls, Greeks, Libyans, Spaniards, Sardinians, and dark-hued Numidians. The god of Carthage was the Baal of our Bible: in times of stress and danger, human beings were burned alive, even first-born children, to persuade Baal to give them victory. Their army, apart from a select body of young nobles, was a mercenary one made up of many races, Greek, Gaulish, and Sardinian foot soldiers, and the swift and cunning horsemen of Libya. The Carthaginians knew the seaways better than the Greeks did; they were first-class pilots and mariners, but rich enough to pay other races to fight for them on land.

Sicily, like Belgium, has ever been a place where rival nations meet and fight out their wars. In Belgium it has been Germans, Frenchmen, Spaniards, and British; in Sicily it was then Greeks, Carthaginians, and Romans. When the Greek King Pyrrhus was forced out of Sicily he cried out: "How pleasant a land am I leaving to Rome and Carthage!" That pleasant land became Rome's; for the Romans built themselves a strong navy, learned by disasters how to fight at sea, defeated the Carthaginians and drove them from the island. Rome was now mistress of all Italy and Sicily, and her armies had captured Sardinia. Moreover she was now the triumphant naval power of the West. The men of Carthage dreamed of revenge. They had to, if they were to keep their trade on which their life depended. Such was the position in 220 B.C.

Fifty-three years later, a talented Greek historian named Polybius, living as an honored guest in the house of a Roman nobleman, wrote: "Is there anybody so idle in mind, or so ignorant, that he does not want to know how almost the whole world has been taken by the city of Rome within the space of fifty-three years?" He answered his own question in a long and brilliant history.

This is the outline of what happened, of famous generals, and of amazing changes of fortune.

Among the Carthaginians who dreamed of revenge was a young man named Hannibal. He resolved to try to destroy Rome. He raised an army, crossed into Spain, marched through Gaul, and crossed the River Rhone, transporting his war elephants on rafts made to look like islands. He climbed the Alps, cutting and splitting the rocks of the passes with fire and scalding liquid. He descended into the Italian plains with his mercenaries and elephants. He destroyed three Roman armies, and stirred up the peoples of Italy against Rome. Instead of assaulting Rome itself he plundered the countryside, but for this there was little ease of mind in Rome. The Romans, as was their habit, chose one man to be *dictator*, or supreme ruler, in this dangerous and tragic time, and this man, Fabius, earned fame by avoiding battle, while keeping Hannibal alert and puzzled by constant raids and threats of action. But the two consuls who followed Fabius were utterly routed by Hannibal at Cannae, where the Libyan cavalry rode down eight legions.

Rome still had her ships. Scipio Africanus took charge of a Roman army in Spain, subdued that country, and carried the war to the enemy's gates by invading Africa and forcing Carthage to make peace. Hannibal had been in Italy for sixteen years, long, weary years for the people of Rome. Now he returned to save Carthage, but Scipio defeated him decisively at Zama in Africa in 202. Carthage became a vassal or subject state, obedient to Rome.

Hannibal stirred up the Greeks to make war on Rome. The war-hardened legions defeated the phalanxes of the Macedonians; they defeated the armies of the Greek king of Syria and Asia Minor; and they took Egypt without a blow. All this is what Polybius wrote about in his book: and as to the reason why Rome triumphed, he could see it in that unity and patriotism of the Romans, in the virtue of their leaders, and the wise way they were governed by the senate. The Greeks were, as ever, the most brilliant-minded of men, but they always quarreled among themselves: Rome did not so much fight against the Greeks as among them.

So Rome spread upon the world. But in doing this her own life was transformed into something different from the old-fashioned simple ways. Instead of the humble homes and farms of old there now appeared luxurious houses and great villas. The Romans, who had never been skilled artists or craftsmen, now employed Greeks and Asiatics to build and carve and paint and make beautiful things. Roman soldiers brought back wagonloads of statues and paintings from the East. Rome gathered to herself all the world's trade, and thousands of strangers flocked into the world's capital. Worse than this, the long wars had given Romans a vast multitude of slaves, broken men, prisoners of the war, men born free but captured and branded like cattle, and sold like cattle in the great slave market of Delos. These miserable men filled the households of the nobles, worked in gangs on the fields, and in the mines and quarries. The small household farms were replaced by large estates run by slave labor under harsh masters. All through ancient history the rough hard work was done by slaves, the digging, hauling, cleaning, all the drudgery of manual toil. So terrible was this curse of slavery that the slaves, 60,000 of them, rose in rebellion throughout Sicily and south Italy. It took a Roman army years of campaigning to put them down in one of the most dreadful and merciless wars ever fought.

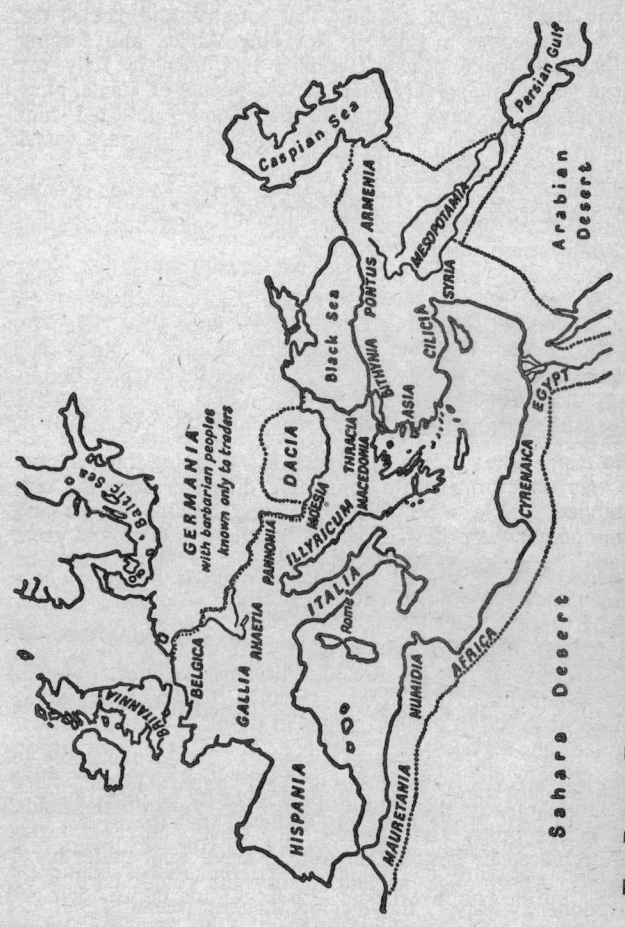

THE ROMAN EMPIRE AT ITS GREATEST EXTENT

Caesar

The long wars had indeed changed the way in which the Romans lived. Rome itself was now crowded with a populace of slaves, runaways, craftsmen, idlers, adventurers from all parts. The rich merchants, moneylenders, and noblemen were growing fabulously rich on the trade opened up by the conquest of Spain, of Africa and Greece. The old-fashioned countryman and citizen with his old Roman virtues and simple ways of living still existed; but he must have felt himself living in a changed world. A clever and wealthy African king who had friends in Rome among the senators summed it all up by saying that money would buy anything in Rome—even justice and honor.

The Roman senate and consuls could not govern such an Empire. Imagine the lord mayor and councilors of the city of London governing Europe! Of course they would try to, and do their best, but it is doubtful if they would remain just the same sort of city officers. Nor was the Roman Empire ready to be ruled by a senate in Rome, or a senate anywhere. Most of the people everywhere were used to being ruled by kings.

This was the odd, almost the comical, thing about Rome: she was the one city whose citizens could not bear kings, yet she conquered the world whose multitudes only understood being ruled by kings whom they looked upon as gods—like the Pharaohs of ancient Egypt, or the oriental monarchs—Babylonian, Assyrian, Chaldean, Persian, Grecian.

There were quarrels in the senate between those who wanted to help the poorer free citizens, and those who disliked any changes. Those men became the most powerful who commanded the legions, because the old short-service citizen army of Rome had gone. In its place were legions of regular long-service soldiers whose "home" was their legion, and whose whole loyalty was given to their general. The commanders with the greatest skill or popularity became the most powerful men in the Empire. Of these, Marius was the first, a rough regular soldier who saved Italy from an invasion of the Gauls. Marius championed the poorer citizens against the richer, but he had no wisdom in politics; and he was defeated by Sulla, an aristocrat, and an equally good general, who led the senators. Sulla ruled with an iron hand, making himself dictator. When he had finished reshaping the government and laws as he thought fit, he retired into private life. That was the Roman way.

Sulla retired. He with his legions had been master of the mistress of the world. Now there were two consuls, as usual, and several hundred senators, and a world to be governed.

Three men shared power, a *triumvirate*: Pompey, one of Sulla's generals, and a very fine one; Crassus, a multimillionaire senator; and Julius Caesar, a member of a distinguished family, who had held several appointments in the government of Rome. Caesar was a scholar and orator.

Julius Caesar was given command of the province of Gaul on both sides of the Alps. Like all Roman senators he was expected to take command of an army when ordered to. The millionaire Crassus was sent suddenly to command the legions against the fierce Parthians in Persia, and there met his death. This was part of the old Roman virtue—the obligation of arms. But what Rome saw now she had never seen before: Caesar, turned forty before his first independent command, led his legions to the conquest of *all* Gaul right up to the Rhine; and he showed a skill, a military insight, and a firmness of purpose worthy of the great Alexander—on whom, it is said, he modeled himself. Caesar found time to make expeditions into Britain, and his own story of his wars in Gaul is read every day in our schools. It is a remarkable book. Caesar was a remarkable man. His energy and personal charm bound his officers and legionaries to him. The only man like him in history is Napoleon.

Having conquered Gaul he marched on Rome in spite of an ancient law that no legions should approach nearer the city than the little River Rubicon. To cross the Rubicon was to defy the senate and the people of Rome. Caesar crossed it, and when Pompey opposed him in the name of the senate, he drove Pompey from Italy.

He crossed to Spain to capture some of Pompey's troops there, then to Greece, where he defeated Pompey at Pharsalus. Then he pursued Pompey into Egypt where he spent some time making sure of its loyalty. Then he cleared all his opponents out of Asia Minor and Africa. In a few years he had fought around the world—Gaul, Italy, Spain, Greece, Egypt, Asia, Africa—always victorious. Of course every soldier who served under him was for him heart and soul.

Julius Caesar was one of those rare persons, again like Napoleon, skilled in both peace and war. Returning to Rome he made himself dictator for life. The senatorial party was alarmed, jealous and indignant. But Caesar carried on with his enormous plans and projects: the reformation of the calendar; the rebuilding of Rome; the building of roads; the ending of bribery and fraud in the government. He planned to conquer Germany beyond the Rhine, over which river he had once flung a bridge during his Gaulish campaigns.

And he also planned to set out for Persia to avenge Crassus.

Caesar was master of the world.

On the Ides of March 44 B.C. a group of senators led by Cassius and Brutus stabbed him to death. They could not bear to see Rome ruled by a tyrant.

Caesar was soon avenged. His general, Mark Antony, and his nephew Augustus, defeated and killed the conspirators at Philippi in Macedonia. These two might have divided the mastery of the world between them, but Mark Antony fell in love with Cleopatra the queen of Egypt, and wasted his time. Augustus defeated the ships of Mark Antony and Egypt off Actium. Julius Caesar had intended Augustus to be his heir; now Augustus took the name of Caesar—*Augustus Caesar Imperator*—Emperor of the Roman World, the first of many such for very many centuries.

The title Imperator means *he who commands*: the emperors were those who commanded. They all took the title of *Augustus* and the title of *Caesar*. They never took the title of *Rex* (King), but they took one title which is very familiar to us: *Princeps*, which means *First*, that is, First Citizen. We know this title under the more romantic form of Prince.

Citizens of No Mean City

Julius Caesar left his mark on the world as no other man has done. Scores of Roman emperors who followed him took his name of Caesar for a title: each of them became a "Caesar," that is, a supreme ruler of men. And other races borrowed the title. The Persians turned it into Shah, the Russians into Tsar, the Germans into Kaiser.

Julius was indeed a remarkable man. But his fame and memory owe much to the fact that he was a Roman. The Romans were remarkable men. They gathered the world to themselves. Their empire stands in history as a place and time into which all earlier civilizations flowed, and out of which all our later civilization has come. There were great Romans before Caesar, and great ones after him: and many of those after him were natives of Spain, of Gaul, of North Africa, of Syria, of the Danube lands. When St. Paul called himself "a citizen of no mean city" he used a phrase that was the boast of thousands of men all over the Mediterranean world. The Romans did something that no other people have ever done: they made those they conquered proud to be Romans. It was their secret.

We get our learning and wisdom from the Greeks. So did the Romans, who looked on the Greek schools as we do on a university, and sent their sons to study at Athens. We get our religion from the Jews, whose religious writings we read every day. The Romans were expert in government and lawmaking. The words we borrow from the Greeks are words of learning—*problem, drama, music, mathematics, logic, philosophy*. Our words for the governing of men are mostly from Latin—*city, civil, council, company, assembly, court, prison, minister, prince, justice, president, senator*. The laws of Europe were written in Latin for many centuries, and our own lawyers used, and still use, dozens of Latin phrases. Of the two greatest systems of law in the civilized world, one is English, the other Roman—which is today the foundation of the laws of many lands. Rome's gift to the world was the gift that the Greek cities never found—the gift of ruling men, of making laws, of doing justice—all those things that hold men together and lead to *peace* and *order* (two more Latin words). The Roman Empire in the second century was a time of almost universal peace in all lands. "The world has peace thanks to the Romans," wrote one Christian bishop. Another writer said "There are no wars, no bandits or robbers, no pirates."

The best of the Romans believed in something they called the *republic*, a word we can best translate as the *commonweal*, or, in common English, the "common good." They always kept in mind the very old Roman idea of virtue, that is, all the good qualities that go to make a good citizen: courage, truth, reverence, family honor, loyalty. And the best of the Romans were fair-minded men who had the good sense to let the peoples they ruled keep their own customs and govern themselves. They could not have won the loyalty of so many races otherwise. When St. Paul feared the jealousy of the Jews and appealed to the judgment of Caesar in Rome, he did so because all men believed Roman justice to be given without fear or favor.

St. Paul tells us he was shipwrecked four times. We have a fine description of the last time in the Acts of the Apostles. There were few hindrances to travel in the Empire, no passports or visas. We have the tombstone of a craftsman who lived in Phrygia which tells us that he made seventy-two voyages to Italy. There are many such records. The Romans cleared their Sea (Mare Nostrum) of pirates, and kept it clear. After the fall of Rome—about 400 A.D.—pirates flourished in that Sea until the eighteenth century. There is a good story of Julius Caesar's being taken by pirates when he was a young man, and held as a captive until his relatives paid a ransom for his release. He played dice with the pirates and told them he would certainly return and hang them all. They must have been rather amused then, but not so much later on when he did return and did hang the lot. The Peace of Rome was on the Sea. Of the continual comings and goings of ships across the Channel to and from Britain we have no record except the ruin of the great lighthouse at Dover, and an inscription or two, such as that to an officer named Aufidius Pantera who was a sort of admiral of the Narrow Seas. His name does not now occur in our history books; but he and his like played their part in safeguarding civilization in the name of Rome.

We read in the Acts of the Apostles how St. Paul journeyed through the cities of Asia and Greece. We know from Roman historians how the legions tramped in their hobnailed boots from one part of the Empire to another. The Romans were superb engineers who knew the value of good roads, and made good roads in every land. They laid down paved highways between drainage ditches, built arched bridges over rivers and streams, drove piles into marshy land to support causeways. One of their finest works was a wooden bridge across the mighty Danube, carried on twenty stone piers. Along their roads were posting stations where horses could be changed, and taverns (*tabernae*) for rest and refreshment. These paved highways remained for centuries, a wonder to the simple countryfolk of the Middle Ages, who sometimes imagined them to be the work of giants—or devils. Many are in use today. Some, and parts of some, lie buried under drifted earth. In England they all led at last to Londinium Augusta, just as the roads and railways do now. In Europe under the Empire all roads led at last to Rome, where was the Golden Milestone from which all distances were reckoned.

If all roads led to Rome at the center, they led outwards to the hundreds of cities which made up that great Empire of cities: to famous markets like Smyrna and Antioch and Tarsus, or Marseilles and Cologne and London; and also to the small countryside capitals like Capernaum of Galilee, or Caerwent in Monmouth, whose walls can still be seen rising from the fields. Between all these cities there flowed an unceasing trade of many races and regions along the vast web of roads. Men made linen garments in the Greek cities from flax grown in Syrian fields. From Tyre and Sidon they sent lovely glassware to all parts of the Empire. In Gaul the potters worked to supply the west with bowls and beakers. Cedar logs from the high forests of the Lebanon Mountains were transported to Rome and Egypt. On the Rhine we have found records of swordsmiths, and in North Italy of armorers. Under the waves off Marseilles, French divers bring up numberless jars of Greek wine from an ancient wreck; and from the shallow seas off old Carthage marble columns and statues from a cargo ship that sank in them two thousand years ago. Lead from Derbyshire and tin from Cornwall were exported to the Continent. Hides and wool and grain in abundance were produced in Gaul and Britain and North Africa for trading overseas. Bales of papyrus were loaded at Alexandria.

A more romantic and remoter trade flowed from the mysterious lands beyond the sunrise. Silks from China reached the Syrian markets after many a dusty and weary month across bleak mountains and toilsome desert. Spices from Arabia, drugs and rubies from Ceylon and the Indies, arrived at the Red Sea ports. The Romans maintained a trading post on the shores of India itself. In the far west their agents knew Ireland. In the north they fetched amber from the shores of the Baltic.

All this traffic filled the long roads in spring and summer and autumn. All sorts of men of all races were to be found in the cities, especially in Rome and the large provincial capitals. Italian vintners took Greek names in order to trade in Greek wines. Syrians and Jews set up business houses in Spain and Gaul. Greek shopkeepers were everywhere. The common speech was Latin, very often a rather battered sort of Latin and often pronounced in strange ways. In the east Greek was the common speech. Non-Romans often took Roman names as Saul of Tarsus did when he called himself Paulus—we have the same sort of thing in the modern world when Negroes are given, or adopt, English or French names. The mixture of races is illustrated very well in the record of the emperors themselves: most of them were not even from Italy, but natives of Spain or Africa or Illyria. One of them was an Arab.

The vast papyrus records of the Empire have perished together with most of its learned books. Our knowledge depends on the spade of the archaeologist, and we are lucky in having so many inscriptions, most of them memorial stones to soldiers of the legions who guarded the imperial frontiers from the Euphrates to the Tyne and from the Sahara to the Danube. Slowly and painfully scholars are piecing together some connected account of the Roman armies, and it is a fascinating job; a tombstone of a British soldier might turn up in Syria, and of a Syrian by the Roman Wall in Northumberland.

Each legion in the early days comprised about 6,000 men, and there were some thirty legions. There were also smaller regiments or units called auxiliaries—that is, additional troops—some of horsemen, some of archers or slingers, some of barbarians taken into the Roman service. In all, at the most, there were some quarter of a million men under arms—none too many to guard a world. The legionaries served for pay and were loyal to their own generals, whom they sometimes hailed as emperors. When they did this, and they often did do it in the third century, the legions fought among themselves. The successful general who became the emperor then rewarded his soldiers with gifts of money. On one occasion a Dutch admiral named Carausius set up an independent "empire" in Britain, and ruled there and issued coins in his own name, until strong forces from Gaul landed and regained the island for the other emperor on the Continent.

Each legion had its special badge and its own sacred standards. It is said that the red dragon of Wales is the badge of a legion handed down through the centuries. Some legions stayed in garrison in one place for centuries, such as the Second Legion Augusta (or "Royal") which was quartered at Caerleon-on-Usk. Caerleon means simply the City of Legion. Sometimes the emperors settled old soldiers in colonies of veterans who became farmers. These colonies were very useful near dangerous parts of the frontier. In Rome itself there was the Praetorian Guard, a sort of imperial guard of picked men. In the later days of the Empire the legions usually stayed in garrison some distance from the frontiers, while along the frontiers—the Wall in Britain, and the line of fortifications on the Rhine and Danube—there were detachments of auxiliaries. If these were hard pressed the legions could come into action.

The backbone of the legions were the centurions, officers in charge of a hundred men—*hundreders* as the old English translators called them. They were not all of equal rank, since in each legion they were graded from the most junior to the most senior centurion: but they controlled the army. They numbered, at any one time, perhaps two thousand. Perhaps we may best think of them as captains. As officers of the supreme commander, the emperor, they represented the might and majesty of Imperial Rome, the mistress of the world. They have their noblest memorials in the Gospels. It was a centurion who said to Jesus: "I also am a man under authority; I say to one man, Go, and he goeth, and unto another, Come, and he cometh." And it was a centurion who stood at the foot of the Cross on Calvary in the world's darkest hour and said: "Truly, this man was the son of God."

Ancient Religions and the Jews

There were many gods to be worshiped, such as Jupiter and Apollo of the Romans, Osiris and Isis of the Egyptians, and the great mother-goddess Ashtaroth of the Syrians. These all had their shrines and their temples and priests. So also had Moloch, the dreadful god of the Carthaginians, to whom mothers sacrificed their children. And every river and stream and woodland glade might have its own special deity. Each city had its own particular god or goddess. The men of Athens gave worship to the goddess of wisdom, Athene, who was regarded as the protectress of Athens. Yet they also worshiped other deities. They even made sure of doing the right thing by putting up an altar to *The Unknown God*. In fact, men willingly worshiped other people's gods, and the gods of the places where they happened to be at the time. The mobs of the cities did not mind strange gods, but they did dislike people who would not worship as they themselves did. Besides all this, the Romans held their emperor in honor as a god, and burned incense before his shrines, which were set up in public places. It was treason not to do this.

The wisest of the Greeks and Romans did not take any of the gods very seriously. To them such worship was nothing more than an old-fashioned and harmless custom followed by mobs and peasants. Some philosophers, nicknamed Cynics, made fun of the stories of the gods. Others, called Stoics, held the gods in scorn, and said that men should disregard whatever fortunes or misfortunes they might send, and that men should live only to do their duty, taking no notice of pleasure or pain. Yet other philosophers, called Epicureans, believed that men should simply enjoy the good things of life, and not worry at all about the future.

Everywhere people were in need of hope and an inspiration. Human life was a hard struggle against illness, ill-luck, and evil. To be poor was bad enough; but every poor man and every captive might fall into slavery. There were many slaves everywhere. Like soldiers despairing in the midst of a battle, men waited for a leader, a saviour and a rallying cry to help them.

One race stood apart from all others, kept united and stubborn by a strong and spiritual religion. They were the Jews.

Many prophets had taught them about the one true God: a God not made with hands, a God who had no single dwelling place: a spiritual God from whom no secrets could be hidden: a God who was from everlasting to everlasting: Jehovah, God of Righteousness and Truth, who commanded his chosen people to keep his laws of mercy and truth. We can learn how the Jews felt about God when we read their poems called the Psalms. Most important of all, Jehovah was a jealous God who did not allow them to honor or worship any other gods. The Jews found it hard to keep this strict commandment when they were surrounded by other races who sang and danced and enjoyed themselves around the gay idols of their gods. These idols were images. Men could think about them easily. It is very hard to think about something you cannot picture. But the great Jewish prophets said that God was a spirit, almighty and invisible.

The Jews were famous in the ancient world and have remained famous to this day. Because of their religion they have not disappeared like their neighbors—the Moabites and Edomites and Hittites and scores of others. No other race has survived as they have done from remote antiquity. Because of their religion they have kept their sacred books, which we know and use today as the Old Testament of our Bible.

So the Jews were stubborn and united. They possessed only one sacred building—the Temple at Jerusalem. King Solomon built the first Temple. This was destroyed by the Babylonians. King Herod built the one that Jesus knew. But the Jews lived on the great highway of trade and war between Asia and Egypt in the midst of mighty empires. They were a small nation. They were enslaved by the Babylonians, conquered by the Greeks, and again by the Romans under Pompey. They were scattered abroad throughout the Roman Empire. Every large city from Alexandria to Marseilles had its Jewish parish or quarter. The Jews in Egypt were settled there for so long that they forgot their language and, for them, the Old Testament had to be translated from the original Hebrew into Greek.

Wherever they traveled and settled, whether in Alexandria or Rome or Athens, they remained a race apart, meeting for prayers and reading of the Scriptures in their synagogues, and thinking always of their holy Temple in Jerusalem. They made pilgrimages to it and gave so much money into its treasury that the gold stored there was worth a king's ransom. They worked hard and prospered because of their family loyalty and strict laws of conduct: and they played an important part in the trade of the ancient world.

The Jews also were eagerly expecting a saviour, or Messiah, who should deliver them from their enemies. An echo of this desire is heard in our own familiar hymn to this day:

> O come, O come, Emmanuel,
> And ransom captive Israel.

Christianity

It was to the Jews of Galilee that Jesus preached his Gospel of love, at a time when the Roman Empire covered all the known world, and when the Jews were widely spread in all its big cities. If any new religion had a good chance of spreading through the world it would be one that began among the Jews.

Our Lord and his followers spoke the old language of Palestine and Syria, which we call Aramaic, but the Jewish sacred writings were in Hebrew, which all the Jewish rabbis could read; and the common language of all eastern lands of the Mediterranean was Greek. It would be interesting to know what language Our Lord used when he spoke with Roman centurions. No doubt to us this mixture of languages sounds rather odd, but it is quite easy, even for unlearned people, to speak two or three languages when they are living among different nations. It is quite common on the frontiers of eastern Europe today.

Greek was the language of traders and of learned men. So it is not surprising that the records of Our Lord's life and of his earliest followers have come down to us in Greek—the Greek of our New Testament. We know that its various books were collected together very early, and were often kept in *book* form, not in the usual rolled-up scrolls of papyrus. Among them is that grand book called *The Acts of the Apostles*, the only book we have which gives such a detailed picture of life in the first century.

The trial of Our Lord took place before a Roman governor, Pontius Pilate. The accusation against him was one of treason to the Empire. Pilate was not sure of his guilt, but to save himself from trouble with the Jews, he ordered him to be put to death. Jesus was crucified because crucifixion was the usual Roman way of hanging criminals—just as our ancestors used to hang thieves at Tyburn gallows near London. It was the most shameful form of death.

The crucifixion took place on a small hill outside Jerusalem a fews years before the Roman legions of Claudius Caesar conquered Britain.

Jesus did not teach men to scorn the world or enjoy the world or make fun of the world, but to love it. All men should love one another and help one another. Jesus taught that love is the strongest thing in life. He ignored all distinctions of rank and learning. He mixed with all sorts of men, and preached to all sorts of men, rich and poor, Jew and Gentile, Greek and barbarian. But we must never forget that he was a Jew and loved the Jews. His first followers were Jews.

His followers called themselves the Brethren. They were first called "Christians" in Antioch, a large and beautiful Greek city on the River Orontes, a city of long marble colonnades and groves of trees, whose people were known for their giving of nicknames.

The Gospel was quickly carried to all quarters. One legend says that St. Thomas took it to India. The desert tribes of Arabia heard it. St. Philip preached it to the blacks of Ethiopia. But the greatest missionary work was done by St. Paul.

He was a true-born Roman citizen of Tarsus in Asia Minor. He had been trained as a tentmaker, for Tarsus was renowned for goat's-hair cloth. He had been well schooled at the university there, and knew something of the learning of the ancient Greeks. He was a devout Jew, a young rabbi studying under the older rabbis at Jerusalem. It was true of him, as of the old Psalmist, that all his delight was in the law of Jehovah. A blinding vision of Our Lord on the road to Damascus, the city that gathered to itself all the routes of the desert, made Paul a Christian. He made three missionary journeys through the rich and populous lands of Asia Minor and Greece, preaching Christ in the Jewish synagogues and in the market places, converting many, causing riots, getting himself arrested, imprisoned, scourged, even fighting with wild beasts in the arena. An old tradition says that he was short and bald, an insignificant looking man. Nothing daunted him. At length, after a riot in Jerusalem, he was arrested by the Romans to save him from the fury of the mob. As a Roman citizen he appealed to be judged by Caesar in Rome: whereupon, safely guarded by strong escorts, he was sent in a merchant ship to Rome. By his wisdom and steadfastness he saved the lives of his escort and fellow passengers when the ship was wrecked off Malta. He lived in Rome for some years. Legend says that he was beheaded in the persecution of Christians ordered by the Emperor Nero, at the same time that St. Peter was crucified.

Archaeologists have found in the ruined cities of Asia Minor—that fair land which became a bleak wilderness—traces of the earliest Christians: tombstones with sad and short inscriptions. Some Christian groups called themselves burial societies, or, as we should say, insurance societies, to escape notice. They met in secret. They were persecuted when they refused to burn incense at the emperor's shrine. The mobs disliked them, and made up false stories about them. In Rome itself the Christians took to worshiping and to burying their beloved dead in miles of underground passages and chambers cut out of the rock beneath the suburbs. We call these places the *catacombs*. In them whole generations of the faithful kept their religion alive; and their walls still hold the earliest Christian inscriptions, their tombs still contain the relics of the earliest martyrs who were put to death in the persecutions.

The old gods of the city and the field were going. There is an idle legend that at the Birth of Jesus all the living creatures of the wild passed on the woeful tidings that their god of the wild—Pan, the goat-footed—was dead. John Milton, the most musical of our poets, has put this into his poem on the Nativity of Christ:

> The lonely mountains o'er,
> And the resounding shore,
> A voice of weeping heard, and loud lament . . .

Indeed, this old fanciful tale does tell us of the amazing spread of the Gospel. It ran like fire in dry grass. Even members of Caesar's household were converted. And we can well imagine with what joy the poor slaves heard the glad tidings of fellowship and love.

But the Jews met their final tragedy.

The Fall of Jerusalem

Among the Jews in Judea were many Zealots or patriots who were determined to shake off the Roman yoke. They could not bear to think that they, the Chosen People of God, should have to pay tribute to a heathen Caesar. They awaited a Messiah to lead them to victory over the Romans. Some of them had hoped that Our Lord would prove to be this Messiah, and they were puzzled and angry when he told them that his Kingdom was not of this world. They wanted war.

In 70 A.D. they broke into rebellion all over Judea, and their bitter feelings made it a merciless struggle which ended with the final destruction of Jerusalem and of the Temple. The Roman general, Titus, brought his legions around the doomed city, and set up his strong engines of war to hurl stones at its walls and towers. The Jews inside starved to death or fought back in sudden sallies, or tried to escape over the walls at night, only to be caught and crucified. Titus did try to spare the Temple. But the Zealots would not surrender even for this purpose and even when their cause was plainly hopeless. They fought to the end; and the end was the overthrow of the Temple and its Holy of Holies. Thousands of wretched Jewish captives were marched off to be sold as slaves, or given to the cities of the Greeks, who made them fight against wild beasts in their arenas for the amusement of the mobs; while on that Hill of Zion where David and Solomon had lived and sung to their God, and where the Temple now lay shattered, the men of the Tenth Legion pitched their tents under the shadow of broken walls.

The Jews went on living in small groups in other cities. Devout rabbis preserved the writings of the Law and the prophets and to this day the old religious life has been kept alive, in spite of centuries of hardship and persecution. In the synagogues of London, Paris, New York, and elsewhere, descendants of Our Lord's people still gather on the sabbath, and still keep the fasts and feasts of the Old Testament. Within the last thirty years they have begun to build their own nation in Judea under the name of Israel. This small state is their "national home," but the greater number of them are still scattered throughout the world.

The Church in the Roman Empire

Jesus and his disciples met together in private houses such as the one at Bethany where Mary and Martha lived, and the upper room in Jerusalem. They were good Jews and did not need what we call a church. All the early Christian meeting places were in the houses of the Brethren, those who followed the Way of Christ. So the earliest Christian church was the "church in the house"; the first Christian services were something like those in the prairie provinces of Canada when the missionaries rode from farmstead to farmstead.

So long as Christians were disliked by the mobs or by the emperors it was not safe to meet in special buildings. When the first churches were built they were fashioned just like the Roman public halls or *basilicas*: that is to say, one large, single room, rounded at one end—that end where the Roman magistrates used to sit in judgment, and where the Christian altar was placed. If the room were very wide the roof was supported on two rows of pillars. Today this is just what we see in many parish churches.

The danger from persecution lasted on and off for three hundred years. At times there were particular persecutions in which scores of Christians were haled off to the Roman magistrates and compelled to burn incense to the emperor or else suffer death. Nero and Domitian persecuted them in the first century, and Diocletian in the third. They suffered also under the Stoic Emperor Marcus Aurelius in the second. But there were no perfectly safe times.

> Mocked, imprisoned, stoned, tormented,
> Sawn asunder, slain with sword.

The words of the hymn are true. No one can know the numbers that died for their faith. Of the first thirty bishops of Rome, for instance, no fewer than twenty-nine suffered martyrdom. That so many of the martyrs were humble folk is perhaps the reason why our records of the early churches are so scanty. A further reason is that very often the written records of the churches were destroyed by Christians themselves to protect one another. When the Roman officials visited a church to arrest its members, someone would burn the lists of the congregation. In any case the whole vast papyrus records of the Roman Empire have perished. The gaps in our knowledge of the first five centuries are lamentable, and the story of the growth and triumph of Christianity is known only in shreds and patches. But that story is the foundation of our modern world.

We do know that, in spite of persecution, the Christians were steadily drawing all men to their fellowships. And this was very true in lands which we do not now think of as Christian countries, namely the old Roman provinces of North Africa.

It was a North African Christian scholar and lawyer named Tertullian, the son of a centurion, who mocked the pagan idolaters. "The images of your gods," he wrote, "are mere nesting places for mice and hawks and spiders. You sell your own household gods, you even pawn them for money. We Christians, men and women, are but of yesterday, and yet we have crowded your cities, your fortresses and camps, your palaces and assemblies, your senate house and your courts: all we have left you are your temples. If we packed up our belongings and departed for some distant land, the solitude and loneliness of your world would terrify you."

St. Peter went to Rome. St. Paul preached in the Greek cities. It was in the cities that the Christian fellowships grew and flourished. The very words "pagan" and "heathen" mean people of the countryside—those who are ignorant of the Christian religion. It was in the big cities of the ancient world that the greatest Christian congregations were soon to be found: and the chief Christian elders or *bishops* in these cities came to be the leaders of the Christian churches. For one thing that the Christians learned from the Jews was the value of unity; they kept in touch with one another. Another thing they learned from the Jews was the singing of hymns and psalms in their worship. Music has always played a leading part in Christian life.

Of the beautiful city of Antioch, whose second bishop, Ignatius, was supposed to have been that child whom Jesus took up and blessed, we have already spoken. Jerusalem, the Holy City, was destroyed by the Romans in 70 A.D. Another city was built there by the Romans over the ruins, and the place remained always a place of pilgrimage for Jews and Christians alike. Then there was Alexandria in Egypt, a city of gleaming white buildings, where all the scholars of the Greek world gathered to study in the libraries and the university. The churches of Alexandria became famous.

Among the ancient Jews there were men who became hermits and holy men living solitary and severe lives in desert places, passing their days and nights in prayer and fasting and contemplation. Many Christians did likewise. From Alexandria there went out into the Egyptian desert a vast swarm of Christian hermits to live among the ruined tombs of the old Pharaohs. These men and women lived by weaving rush mats and baskets. They tortured themselves in the most cruel fashion by floggings and fastings, in order, as they thought, to save their souls by punishing their bodies. They sought to excel one another by suffering just as athletes seek to excel in races. The most celebrated of them was St. Anthony, who died in 356 A.D.

By that year all persecution of Christians had come to an end. The tale of this event spans the Roman Empire from end to end in the life of one remarkable man.

In the fourth century a Roman general died at York. His son, Constantine, was raised on the shields of his soldiers and hailed as emperor. Constantine promised them victory. He led them down through Britain, across the Channel into Gaul, and then into Italy, where he defeated his rivals and marched into Rome in triumph. He was an outstanding soldier.

An old legend says that before his greatest victory he saw in the evening sky a flaming cross with the Latin words, *In Hoc Signo Vinces*—By this Sign Conquer; and that he forthwith set his armorers to work making crosses to fix on the legionary standards. Next day his legionaries won their battle.

That is the legend. The fact is that Constantine did two remarkable things which changed the history of the world.

He made his Empire a Christian one by proclaiming that the Christian religion was the faith of the Empire. From now onwards the bishops of the Church played a leading part in the rule of the Roman world. Constantine and his successors were the heads of the Church in their dominions.

Then he built a brand-new capital city, a *New Rome*, on the shores of the Bosporus where Europe meets Asia. It was a marvelous site in beautiful country with a fine harborage, easy to fortify and to defend. He named it Constantinople, the city of Constantine: and to adorn it he brought statues and trophies from Rome. Large numbers of Roman families migrated to it.

There were now two capital cities. The Roman emperors who followed Constantine and lived in his newly built city made it more and more resplendent with palaces and churches. The greatest church of all was built by Justinian— the Church of the Holy Wisdom, a building of many domes, enriched with precious marbles and gilding and pictures in mosaics.

Just as old Rome was the chief Christian city of the west, so Constantinople was the chief Christian city of the east. Just as the bishops of Rome came to rule the churches of the west, so the bishops or patriarchs of Constantinople ruled the churches of the east. The men of the east spoke Greek. Sometimes we speak of the eastern half of the Roman Empire as the Greek Empire, and of the eastern emperors as the Greek emperors; but they and their people always thought of themselves as Romans. They were very proud of being Romans.

Two great orders of monks replaced the self-torturing hermits of Egypt. St. Basil founded the Greek monks whose lonely monasteries are still to be found on remote island clifftops and in perilous places of the east. Priceless ancient handwritten copies of the Scriptures have been found in them in modern times, like the great Codex Sinaiticus which is in the British Museum. These monks lived in their monasteries apart from the world, under a rule of life which divided their time between prayer and fasting. They were like colleges of hermits.

In the west St. Benedict of Nursia in Italy, who lived from 480 to 543, set down his rule of a monastic life, known as the Benedictine Rule. All kinds of variations on this were made later for different *orders* of western monks, but St. Benedict's Rule remains the foundation of their lives. It enjoins them not to live merely as solitaries or hermits, but as members of a community working together as a community under the strict discipline of an abbot. They were to be obedient, they were to remain single, and they were to give up all their belongings to the monastery. Their robes were to be just rough-spun cloaks, their food plain, their lodging hard.

They prayed regularly, even rising in the midst of the night to attend their chapel and to keep up a ceaseless round of prayer and praise day and night. What makes St. Benedict's Rule utterly different from the eastern one is that it ordered the monks to work for the profit of the monastery, to tend the gardens, to do carpentry, to raise sheep, or copy manuscripts. Through this the monasteries became hives of activity, with beautiful chapels, well-run farms and vineyards, communities with full granges, guest rooms, stables, fishponds, an inn for travelers, an almshouse for the poor and needy. The abbot of a well-run monastery had to be a businessman as well as a spiritual father to his flock. The life of such a monastery is well summed up in the Benedictine motto—*Laborare est orare*, which means "Work is a form of prayer."

St. Benedict taught St. Gregory the Great, who became pope of Rome and was one of the greatest men of his time. But this was after the troubles and destruction had come upon all the lands of the west. St. Benedict and St. Gregory worked amid the ruins of the ancient world.

2

THE END OF THE ROMAN EMPIRE AND THE LOSS OF ANCIENT LEARNING

The Overrunning of the West

In St. Benedict's time the old Roman world in the west was passing away: all the provinces were full of barbarian folk from the northern forests.

If, today, you stand on the tower of the Saalburg in the Rhineland, which was once a Roman watchtower, and if you look northwards, as once the Roman sentinels looked, you will see the country from which the invaders came. With their coming the peace of the world was gone. In its place St. Benedict offered the peace of the cloister, the sheltered place, the quiet of a well-ordered life of prayer and work.

The invaders had been foes of the Romans for a long while. Some of their young men had served in the legions, or in frontier regiments—sometimes, even, under their own chieftains—and they were well acquainted with Roman methods of warfare. In fact, most of the Roman legions were recruited from barbarians, men serving for pay, and faithful to their commanders.

Throughout the fourth century there had been raids and invasions across the Rhine and the Danube. The Emperor Julian, a Greek and a scholar, and a very good soldier, used to spend his winters in Paris reading the works of the Greek philosophers, and his summers in marching and fighting at the head of his legions against the German tribes of the Rhineland. But there came a time when the Roman armies could no longer defend the frontiers.

Our records are few. But one event stands out as a shocking disaster. In the midwinter of 406 a horde of Germans—Goths, Alans, Vandals, Burgundians—crossed the frozen Rhine at Mainz, and swarmed into Gaul. These people knew a lot about the Roman way of life, and wanted to settle in the Empire and enjoy its wealth. The Goths made a kingdom in the south of France and in Spain, where their kings ruled for two centuries. The Vandals passed through Gaul and Spain and crossed into North Africa where they set up a kingdom. Other Goths invaded North Italy and plundered there. A fierce race of Mongolian horsemen, the Huns, invaded Italy and then France (Gaul), under Attila their king. These strange and ugly warriors were defeated by a combined army of Goths and Romans.

In all these "wanderings of peoples" we must always remember that the strife was not just one of Romans against barbarians. We know of many barbarian soldiers serving in the Roman armies who fought bravely to save the Empire from the invaders, and who died fighting bravely. One of the greatest of Rome's defenders was Stilicho, a Vandal, who became commander-in-chief. But the legions disappeared: how and where they broke up we do not know.

The yellow-haired Franks, fiercest and most famous of all the Germans, moved south from the Rhine delta into north Gaul (which became "Frankland" or France): other eastern Franks lived in and beyond the Rhineland itself. These Franks had often been friendly with the Romans, and many of them had served in the Roman armies.

By these invasions the Roman world in the west was utterly changed. Yet there remained great numbers of Roman citizens in the walled cities, living under the old Roman laws, but paying tribute to their new barbarian masters. There were seen, in places, Roman landowners living on their own country estates. One thing we cannot really guess is the *number* of the invaders. We can, however, be sure of their power and the misery and loss they caused. But we must remember two things: (a) the Romans and the barbarians were well known to each other, and (b) that they were of similar races, or "stock," and that they could, and did, intermarry—just as easily as English and Germans or French can intermarry today. The last of the Roman emperors, a mere youngster, named Romulus Augustulus, disappeared. In any case there was no Roman government left. Goths, Franks, Burgundians, Vandals, governed their own districts. The general picture is one of confusion, with the countryside full of runaway slaves, with rebellions of slaves—no man's men, or bandits—a picture of lands where every chieftain kept himself strong and free by the power of his warrior companions. In the cities, behind walls, men were sometimes safer, and in the cities there remained, *on the Continent*, some measure of civilized life.

In 410 when the city of Rome itself was captured by the

THE END OF THE ROMAN EMPIRE

army of the Gothic king Alaric, men felt the worst had happened. Barbarian soldiers wandered wondering (and plundering) through the Eternal City which had once been the mistress of all the civilized world from the Euphrates to the Tyne. It was after this disaster that a learned North African bishop named St. Augustine wrote his famous book, *The City of God*, in which he said that although Rome, the greatest city of the world, had fallen, the "City of God" remained, and was everlasting and unconquerable, because it was built in the hearts of all Christian men and women. "Here on earth we have no abiding city, but we look for one to come."

These events had a startling effect on Britain—that last western province of the Empire.

The Roman garrison of the island crossed the Channel into Gaul to help save the Empire, and it never came back. This "Army of Britain" seems to have been a good fighting force. With its departure Britain became truly a lost province. If our record of events on the Continent is scanty and broken, that of events in this island simply does not exist! We have traces of a migration of Britons into a land called Armorica, which, as a result, became Brittany, and which explains why, today, Welshmen and Bretons understand each other's tongues. The Welsh are, of course, the descendants of the Romanized Britons, and their language contains lots of Roman (Latin) words. They were called Welsh by the barbarian invaders of the island whose word for stranger was "Welsh."

Those invaders were Angles and Saxons, and this island—or the larger part of it—became Angle-land or England. Their coming is not clearly recorded. At least one lot were driven off with loss. Others seem to have landed in shiploads, and the ships' crews under their leaders settled on the east and south coasts. What happened to the Roman fleets of "Tigris boatmen" who were stationed near the Tyne, or of those ships of the Channel guard, we just do not know. We know that, at that time, the Irish kings and chieftains were raiding the west coast. And we know that the British princes were quarrelling among themselves.

Yet it seems pretty certain that the invaders were resisted here more strongly than on the Continent. The Angles and Saxons did not reach the Severn till a century had passed after their last landings! One hundred and fifty miles in a hundred years is slow going. Perhaps there were not very many invaders. We do not know. Somewhere in the wars against them comes the story of King Arthur, and a great battle fought at a place called Badon Hill. Where this was we do not know.

But whatever happened, Roman Britain fell into ruins, and the speech of Roman Britain disappeared, except in Wales. After 150 years of almost unrecorded events "England" appears as a heathen land of small kingdoms—Kent, Sussex, Essex, East Anglia, Mercia, Northumbria, and Wessex. The Welsh are Christians, but Welshmen do not try to convert the English.

So the Roman Empire in the west broke down during the fifth and sixth centuries. For seven generations of men we have only partial records, just bits and pieces of writing.

It was the time when the legions with their centurions and proud standards came to an unknown end, many of them—like the Second Augustan Legion which we last hear of at Richborough in Kent—after five hundred years of existence. It was the time when the immense records of mighty Rome, papyrus records on frail reedpaper, moldered away or were burned; the time when the barbarian soldiers battered down the walls of fortresses with siege engines which the Romans had taught them to use; the time when the war leader put on Roman dress and armor and had the staff of a Roman general carried before him. It was the time when shiploads of Angles and Saxons landed on our own shores and made their homes here, giving their villages the names we know them by today; the time when an unknown chieftain was buried beneath a huge mound of earth in the south of England, known to country folk afterwards as "the grave of the Lord of Plunder." It was the time when the Roman post service and other public services ceased, when public baths, libraries, and theaters were deserted and council chambers and granaries fell into decay. It was a time of violence and sudden death, of burning farms and deserted fields. Gold and silver platters and cups were battered together for melting down, or else buried for safety by their owners—to be found in later ages.

It was a time which not only destroyed old records but left little or none of itself. In the little record it did leave we read of invasions, wars, famines, and of the eastern pestilence which spread like an angel of doom over the world.

> Bright were the castle-dwellings, many the bath houses,
> lofty the host of pinnacles, great the tumult of men,
> many a mead-hall full of the joys of men, till
> Fate the mighty overturned that. The wide walls fell;
> days of pestilence came; death swept away all the
> bravery of men; their fortresses became waste places;
> the city fell to ruin.

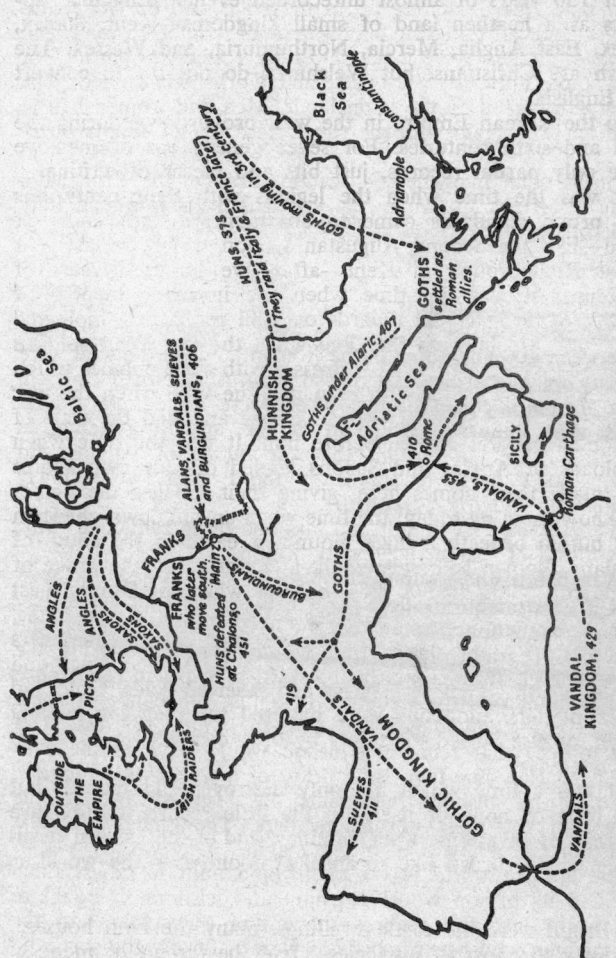

THE BARBARIAN INVASIONS OF THE WESTERN ROMAN EMPIRE IN THE FIFTH CENTURY

That was how it looked to an English harper, singing afterwards as he gazed on the ruins of the Roman city of Bath. Men did not soon revisit cities whose inhabitants had suffered the plague. Weeds sprang up in the villas and on the roads. Bridges collapsed in the floodwaters of winter. Canals and drainage ditches were choked. Ships rotted in harbor, or were sunk. Potteries were left, and workshops ruined. The wilderness spread on the grain lands. Men and women had to begin all over again with the rough hard toil of simple farming.

This is what happened in Britain, France, the Rhineland, Spain, and Italy. In Britain the loss was the greatest; in Italy the least.

Barbarians and Bishops

Between 400 and 600 A.D. the Roman lands in the west were overrun by barbarians. There were Goths in North Italy, in Spain, in the south of France. There were Vandals in Africa. There were Franks in northern France, and Burgundians in eastern France. In Britain the war bands of Angles and Saxons, after fierce resistance by the Britons, were slowly settling and moving westwards.

In these years of tumult and loss one thing remained firm: the Church of Christ, led by its bishops.

Even before the troubles the bishops in both east and west were powerful. St. Basil in Asia Minor ruled his lands like a great Roman nobleman. St. John Chrysostom defied the emperor. St. Ambrose of Milan commanded Theodosius, the last of the great emperors in the west, to kneel in repentance for having caused the slaughter in unjust vengeance of some rebels. If a great soldier and emperor would do this, it is easy to see what renown a bishop would have in the eyes of a barbarian chieftain. As a priest of a world-wide religion, robed in his bishop's vestments, he inspired awe in the breasts of the most unruly invaders. The "magic" of the Christian Church was a strong magic.

The ancient world was a civilization built in cities. Each city had its bishop whose learning and wisdom in booklore and Latin law and records made him powerful. And the sort of men who became bishops were naturally the sort who would have been leading men in the old pagan world—men of character and ability, skilled in government and in controlling other men. Moreover they were leaders of the Christians who, like the Jews, on whose religion their own was founded, looked upon their Church as the center and mainspring of their lives. The Church, the faith, was something they were ready to die for, like patriots dying for a country. No Roman or Greek ever died for his faith in Jupiter or Apollo. Again, the heathen invaders feared other men's gods. The Christians feared nothing.

So, the west was not just a patchwork of barbarian kingdoms. Something was left of the old Roman order: that was the Church. The very name of the district over which a bishop ruled—his *diocese*—was the name, in older times, of a Roman, pagan, division. And there was one very important fact: the bishops all kept in touch with one another, and were thus more able to keep alive the memory and habits of the old civilization.

The renown and power of the popes of Rome were due to their being rulers of that Eternal City whose citizens had once ruled the world. When the slant-eyed, ugly, and bandy Hunnish horsemen swept into Italy in 452 it was Pope Leo who persuaded their king Attila to withdraw them.

The fate of the west in those two dark centuries from 400 to 600 was therefore in the hands of the invading chieftains and the Christian bishops. We must not think of the invaders as savages but as mail-clad warriors skilled in the arts of war. They may be thought of more easily if we remember that the great Roman armies were themselves *mostly barbarians*, and that the newcomers—countrymen of the Roman legionaries—behaved like them, dressed like them, fought like them.

The Goths, first of the German peoples to settle in the Empire, had been made Christians before 400 while they were still in the Balkans. Alaric, who took Rome, was a Christian, though perhaps not the sort that made him welcome to the Romans. He probably was just enough of a Christian to fear the Christian's God and the Christian magic. Unfortunately, the Greek who preached the gospel to the Goths was a "heretic" Christian—a man who taught that Jesus was not a divine person. We can understand the horror with which the Roman Christians regarded the Goths, who seemed almost worse than heathens—just as rebels seem to be worse than ordinary enemies. This heretic form of Christianity had been taught by a bishop named Arius, and, at one time, had been fairly widespread until it was finally quashed by Bishop Athanasius, whose *Athanasian* creed you will find in the English Prayer Book today.

The Goths were "Arian" Christians. The other powerful race of barbarians, the Franks, became Christians after the creed of Athanasius—what we should call *Catholic*.

The Franks who took over the Roman estates and cities

of north France were the fiercest fighters of all the invaders. Their first leader, Clovis, married a Christian Burgundian princess. Through her pleading he became a Christian. With two thousand chosen warriors he received baptism at Rheims in the presence of all the bishops of his cities. In his white robes he stood before St. Rémy, the bishop of Rheims, who instructed him briefly and pointedly how to behave as a Christian: "Worship that which you have burned; burn that which you have worshiped." This was in 496 A.D. Clovis defeated the Arian Goths of the south of France. Soon he received messengers from the emperor at Constantinople giving him the title of Roman Consul: and he put on the purple robes of a Roman consul. Under him and his successors, Gaul became Frankland, or France.

In Spain Romans and Goths lived side by side under Gothic kings.

In Italy a Gothic king named Theodoric ruled over his Arian Goths and his Catholic Romans, and ruled well. Among his chief ministers were many learned Roman scholars, and he did all he could to preserve the old Roman ways of life during his long reign from 493 to 526. But Italy suffered shocking disasters in the "Gothic Wars" that began after his death. These were the result of the attempt of the emperor of the eastern half of the Roman Empire to reconquer Italy from the Goths.

The Emperor Justinian

While the western lands were being overrun, the eastern half of the Roman Empire stood fast. Ruling from their fortress city of Constantinople, the emperors built up a fine army which included squadrons of heavy, mail-clad cavalry as well as archers and other lightly armed men, and they learned to change their methods of fighting according to the tactics of their different enemies. And so Egypt, Palestine, Syria, Asia Minor, and the lands and islands of the Greeks, escaped the ruin that befell the west.

The emperors wore the golden slippers and gorgeous purple robes of the Caesars. They kept the ancient laws of the Romans. In the schools at Constantinople and Alexandria men argued about Greek philosophy and learning. In the hippodrome at Constantinople excited and shouting crowds watched their favorite charioteers driving their teams to victory. The city was full of crowds, idlers, beggars, slaves, craftsmen of many races, and there were plenty of riots between rival parties of "Greens" and "Blues," especially

The End of the Roman Empire

over the races in the hippodrome. But the Empire was rich. On the sea rode its war galleys and its merchantmen with cargoes: and across the lands from the sunrise came the trade of the east. This was the time when some hardy adventurers smuggled the silkworm from far-off China, and so began the silk-farms in the Empire. It was a Christian Empire, keeping vigil over all the most holy places of the Christian Church, the places where Our Lord walked and where his disciples traveled. The bishops ruled large estates and were men of power and authority who preached in all the ancient cities of the Near East.

Throughout the two centuries of darkness and tumult in the west, the eastern or "Byzantine" Empire kept its ordered and prosperous life (400 to 600 A.D.).

The greatest of its emperors was Justinian, who reigned from 527 to 565. It was he who sent armies to reconquer the west. They took Africa in a lightning advance and destroyed the Vandal kingdom there. They also reconquered Italy—but only after twenty years of fierce warfare against the Goths. Italy suffered appalling losses from war, famine, and plague. The ancient historian who records this long Gothic War paints a grim picture of wasted farms and starved peasantry.

But Justinian's chief fame is not in his wars, but in his building and his work for the law. He set skilled lawyers to collect and arrange all the laws of Rome into a *corpus* or body; and this formed the basis for many codes of law still used today. In our universities students still have to study this Roman Law, a fact which reminds us how strongly linked we are to those distant times. Another of Justinian's works remains—the beautiful Church of St. Sophia, or the Holy Wisdom, which still lifts its many domes above Constantinople. The Emperor was a builder of many churches and of fortresses.

His successors kept hold on parts of Italy—Venice, Rome, Naples and the South, and Sicily. Justinian died in 565. Five years later the northern plain of Italy was invaded by a German nation, the Lombards, who came from beyond the Alps, and whose dukes quickly made themselves masters of Milan and other cities. Our name for the northern plain is still Lombardy, although Lombards and their German speech have both long since dissolved into an Italian people together with the Goths and the Romans.

Italy was not united again for 1,300 years!

We have seen that the Christian Franks ruled Gaul and were turning it into Frankland or France; and that the Christian Goths ruled Spain. Britain alone had heathen kingdoms. It is true that the Welsh were Christians, and the Irish had been made Christian by the preaching of St. Patrick, a Roman-Briton: and there was much coming and going of priests and people between Ireland, Cornwall, Wales, and Brittany. But in Kent, in Sussex, in Essex, in Northumbria, in the west and midlands of England, men still worshiped the old heathen gods of the north, Woden and Thor.

Such is the picture we have at the end of the sixth century. Such was the state of the broken Roman Empire when there appeared on the scene two men whose work was to change everything: Pope Gregory the Great of Rome, and an Arab trader named Mohammed.

3

THE BANNERS OF
THE CROSS, OR KINGDOM,
CASTLE, AND CHURCH

Christendom: Pope Gregory the Great

Pope Gregory the Great, who came to St. Peter's Chair in Rome in 590, was a pupil of that St. Benedict who founded the monks of the west. As we have seen, these monks gave their lives to prayer and labor, and their work soon bore fruit in well-kept monasteries, in the copying of Christian books, and in the teaching of the Gospel. It was a good thing in those rough times to have houses which were really homes of light and learning and the true Christian faith.

Gregory the Great took his share, as the chief bishop of the west, in rebuilding a new Christian civilization.

He had been a governor of Rome and knew how to rule men with wisdom and firmness. He wrote books on religion, and he sent letters to his monks and clergy telling them how to run their churches and monasteries. Today we call a certain sort of church music "Gregorian" because that was the kind he ordered to be used. Above all, he sent out missionaries to teach the faith and turn men to Christ. Through this, and because of his wisdom and ability, he became the leader of all the western Christians: and through this, the churches in the different barbarian kingdoms became a Christian brotherhood whose bishops and abbots exchanged letters and visited one another. The west became "Christendom"—a great congregation of Christian folk or a *"Regnum Dei"* (a Kingdom of God on earth). In spite of this, Gregory called himself *the servant of the servants of God*—a marvelous title.

This explains why, in 597, the monk Augustine, with forty others, crossed the Channel and landed near Sandwich in heathen Kent. The king sat on a throne in the open air to receive them. They came to him carrying a silver cross and a board painted with the picture of Christ, and they came singing a Latin litany. The king listened and was converted. He received baptism with all his leading men: and he gave Augustine an ancient church in the old Roman town of Canterbury. Once upon a time there had been Christians in Kent who worshiped Christ in their own homes, as we have recently found out by digging up a Christian Roman house at Lullingstone. Now the new, barbarian men of Kent became Christians, and Canterbury, which is still a very small city, became the seat, or see, of the archbishops of the English Churches.

What followed in England reminds us of the words in our Bible: "The Gentiles shall come to thy light, and kings to the brightness of thy rising." There were many kings and princes in these islands, and within a hundred years they had all heard the gospel, and most of them received baptism. The Welsh princes had been Christians all along from the old days of Rome, but they and their people made no effort to convert their English neighbors who had driven them out of the fairest parts of the island.

There were some exciting happenings during the conversion. The men of London chased out the first Roman monks who ventured up the Old Kent Road. In Yorkshire the high priest of Woden himself led a crowd of heathen folk to destroy and burn the temple of Woden, after he had heard the monk Paulinus tell the Gospel story.

The work of the missionaries from Rome was matched at the same time by the preaching of missionaries from the ancient Irish church. The Irish had heard the gospel in the fifth century from St. Patrick, a Christian Roman, whom they had captured in a slave raid on Britain. An Irish church was built on the island of Iona off the Scottish coast. Now, at the very time that Augustine came into Kent, St. Aidan came into Northumbria from Iona to preach to the Northumbrians. Aidan built his monastery on the island of Lindisfarne off the Northumbrian coast.

The Irish and the Roman priests and monks did quarrel about some points of their religion, but the quarrel was settled without ill-feeling, and all the island moved into the great family of Christendom which the work of Gregory the Great was making possible. A later pope sent a learned Greek monk named Theodore of Tarsus (St. Paul's old city) to become archbishop of Canterbury; and this led to a great increase in the learning of the English churches. Very soon the monasteries, such as Jarrow and York in the north, and Malmesbury and Canterbury in the south, became homes of light and Christian learning. Greek and English and Irish monks and scholars all worked together, and they all kept in close touch with Rome. So the lost province of Britannia was again linked up with the growing Christian civilization of western Europe. One curious difference—which lasted for centuries—was that while in France and Italy the bishops were to be found in each city, in England each bishop ruled the churches of one kingdom or division of a kingdom. In consequence, the English bishops, though few, became rich and powerful men.

These were the golden days of the English churches and the Irish churches. Their buildings were simple wooden structures, but their handiwork in writing, bookmaking, and embroidery was famous throughout Europe. Moreover, Ireland and England sent out their own missioners. Irish saints like Columbanus and Gall traveled into Europe and founded monasteries like Fulda in Germany. English saints like Boniface preached to the fierce Saxons in Germany and many suffered martyrdom there. The story is one of the greatest in our history. Much of it was told for us by the monk Bede of Jarrow, who spent all his life from the time he entered it as a choirboy until the time he died as its librarian, at the monastery there. Bede wrote many works. The grandest was his *History of the English Church*, written in good Latin, and today available in translation to all of us.

Bede died in 735, a hundred and thirty-eight years after the landing of Augustine: his father could have met and spoken with men who had seen Augustine. In that short time the work of restoring England to Christendom had been done. Unhappily, in that short time, something else not so pleasant had happened in the east and south of Europe.

Men from the Desert

The herdsmen of Arabia had always plundered the luckier peoples who lived about them. Life on the thin desert pastures was hard, and it was pleasant, especially in times of drought, to rob the more fortunate folk who lived on fertile earth or in the cities. During the times of the Greek and Roman Empires the cities and fertile lands were guarded by the emperor's troops; and for many centuries Arabian raids had been mere border affairs.

An Arab named Mohammed, born at Mecca in 570, preached a new religion to his fellow Arabs. He taught them to pray to one god, Allah. He taught them to lead sober and strict lives, forbidding them wine and even music. He taught them to help the poor and the oppressed. He taught them to obey their emirs, or leaders. He forbade them to worship idols, or to make images or pictures of any living creatures. To this day Arabic architecture has neither statues nor pictures, but is decorated with lines of color which we call arabesques. He taught them that all true believers in Allah formed one equal brotherhood, but that all who refused to believe were to be made slaves and compelled to work and pay taxes for the true believers.

These Mohammedan Arabs believed in the Old Testament. They gave their sons names like Ibrahim (Abraham), Yakub (Jacob), Yusuf (Joseph), and Suleiman (Solomon). They looked on Solomon as a mighty magician. They accepted Jesus, not as the Son of God, but as a minor prophet. For them there was only One True God: Allah, the Merciful, the Compassionate, the Mighty, the Wise: and only one true Prophet of God: Mohammed, the Apostle of God. Mohammed alone knew the will of Allah which ordained all things in Heaven and Earth, and Mohammed's teachings were written down in one sacred book—the Koran.

The Arabs were skillful horsemen and camelmen, athletic, swift, hardy, and vigorous. They formed strong and dauntless squadrons. Their new religion, a simple and clear one, united the tribes and became a religion of conquest, a fighting creed of scimitar, spear, and sword. Under Mohammed's successors, who were called Caliphs and Commanders of the Faithful, the Arabs were a conquering army. Led by their white-robed, turbaned emirs, these swarthy sons of Ishmael carried war into the Christian lands, killing and enslaving. It was the will of Allah. It was also a very fine thing to leave the sun-scorched desert for the green pastures and groves. The conquerors were fatalists. They believed that all things to come are laid down by the Will of Allah, and are unalterable. And they fought all the better for holding that, if they died in battle, they would go straightway to the paradise of Allah.

A weak and foolish Greek emperor had let the Persians overrun Palestine and Egypt, and so the Arabs found their way of conquest made easier by the lack of Greek garrisons and troops. They were opposed by the Emperor Heraclius, who was trying to undo the mischief caused by his foolish predecessor, but they drove Heraclius back and captured Damascus, the great desert capital where St. Paul had been made a Christian; and Antioch, that beautiful city of colonnades and gardens where the followers of Christ had first been nicknamed Christians; and they captured Jerusalem, which was a Holy City for them as well as for the Christians. They conquered Egypt, the ancient land of the Pharaohs, known for its learning and monasteries. They took Alexandria, a shining city of white marble, and destroyed its vast libraries in which was stored up all the knowledge of the Greek world. It is said that the Caliph Omar who led them remarked that if the books contained what was in the Koran they were not needed; and that if they did not, they were evil.

The Arabs also rode eastward and destroyed the power of those old enemies of Greece and Rome—the Persians. They made Bagdad their chief city. They spread their religion down the East African coast, where they enslaved the natives; and their ships sailed on the monsoon winds to India.

So much for the east. In the west all North Africa with its many Christian towns and villages was conquered. The emirs led their troops westward following the sun, and only halted when the hoofs of their mounts splashed in the waves of the far-off Atlantic. The Christian populations were enslaved. The native Moors of Morocco were made soldiers of Allah. Mosques replaced churches. The works of Rome—temples, villas and amphitheaters—vanished. It was an easy victory.

All this happened before the death of the English monk, Bede, in his beloved monastery of Jarrow.

The First Repulse of the Crescent

From Morocco the Mohammedan armies of Arabs and Moors crossed into Spain, and overran the Peninsula, driving the Christians into the northern mountains. Then they raided year by year deep into France.

We must remember that both in the east and the west what had once been a single empire in Roman times was now ruled by a great number of kings and princes, each with his own warrior companions, each a Christian ruler, but each acting on his own. The half of Christendom had been lost to the followers of Mohammed, and that half held the most sacred and best-loved lands of antiquity. Even the fortress city of Constantinople itself had been threatened. Round the southern frontiers of the Christian lands there lay a wide and warlike crescent of Mohammedan states. And the Mediterranean Sea had begun to swarm with their ships. Only a miracle could check them.

Yearly the tides of horsemen moved on, summer by summer, into France. Then the miracle happened. The Franks of France, those yellow-haired and valiant people who were both Christian *and* warlike, led by their prince Charles Martel—Charles the Hammer—met a host of Arabs and

Moors at Tours in 732, and routed it. The Franks saved France, and, in doing so, saved the west.

Spain and Portugal had yet to be set free. As for the other conquests of the Mohammedans, they stayed under the Green Flag of Allah for twelve hundred years.

Charlemagne

The fame of Charles Martel was exceeded by the fame of his grandson, Charles the Great, or Charlemagne. He enlarged the dominions of the Franks until his power reached from the Pyrenees to the River Elbe in Germany, and from the Atlantic to the River Danube, and to the River Tiber in Italy. In other words, he ruled over an empire which included France, Belgium, Holland, western Germany, and northern Italy. He spent most of his summers in warfare against the Moors of Spain, the Saxons in Germany, the Danes on the Danish border, and the Slavs on the eastern borders of Germany. Yet he found time to encourage learning, art, and architecture; he built a fine minster at Aachen, his capital city, fetching marble columns for it from Rome and Ravenna in Italy. He spoke languages fairly well, but did not master writing. He loved church ceremonies, church music, discussions about religion, and the telling and retelling of stories of his own people. He invited foreign scholars to his court. Of these the most celebrated was an Englishman named Alcuin of York, who reformed the teaching and the church services of the Frankish lands, and made Charlemagne's court a new school of learning for the west. Alcuin came of that happy and remarkable band of scholars and saints of whom the monk Bede wrote in his *History of the English Church*.

The most solemn moment of Charlemagne's life was also the greatest event in the history of the west for centuries. On Christmas Day in the year 800, in St. Peter's Cathedral in Rome, he was crowned "Emperor" by the pope. From that day onwards there were two emperors in Europe: one at Constantinople, the other in the west.

The successors of Charlemagne were called "Holy Roman Emperors"—but not every one of them. The explanation is this. Some years after Charlemagne's death in 814, his empire was divided into three parts—west, middle and east, one member of his family taking each part. From the west, where men were beginning to speak something vaguely like French, comes the kingdom and nation of the French. From the middle part—which was the richest and loveliest—come the Rhineland and Lorraine, and Burgundy and North Italy—all those lands and provinces which Germans and French have always fought about. This Middle Kingdom did not last very long: it broke up into bits and pieces—counties, cities, dukedoms, and so on. From the east, where men spoke German, come the beginnings of Germany. By a series of chances the title of Holy Roman Emperor became attached to this eastern part: and the Holy Roman Emperors were for centuries the chief kings or overlords of all the hundreds of German states and dukedoms. The Holy Roman Empire, while it lasted—and it did last right down to 1806—was practically the same thing as Germany and Austria put together.

In this way Charlemagne's own empire which he made was the parent of western Europe—of France, of Germany, and of the disputed lands between them. The Holy Roman Emperors claimed to be overlords of North Italy—but, in fact, their power always depended on whether the many dukes and noblemen of the German peoples and of the Italian cities were loyal to them. And, in fact, neither the German peoples nor the Italian cities became single united nations until well on in the nineteenth century. The maps of Germany and of Italy for a thousand years (870 to 1870) look like gigantic jigsaw puzzles.

The Franks themselves spoke a German tongue. They were rulers and landowners. Those of them who settled this side of the Rhine in what is now called France (after them) lost their old language and adopted that of the Romano-Gallic inhabitants. That is why modern French is what we call a "Latin" language—it comes from the sort of Latin spoken by the Gauls, who, themselves, learnt it from the Romans. In modern Brittany they still speak an ancient Celtic or Gallic language—one like the Welsh. The Franks who lived on and beyond the Rhine carried on speaking their own German language.

During Charlemagne's reign a new and savage peril threatened Christendom. Charlemagne had fought against the Danes in the "Dane-mark" or Danish border. Now the Danes and the Norwegians began to raid the western coasts, killing, looting and burning. They took Bordeaux in 779; Lindisfarne in 793; and Iona, where they slew sixty-eight monks and took the gold and silver vessels from the altar, in 806. We know these men as *vikings*.

Men from the North

In the Anglo-Saxon Chronicle we can read this entry: "787 A.D. In this year king Bertric of Wessex took Edburga, the daughter of king Offa of Mercia, to wife. And in his days came three ships of the Northmen from the land of robbers.

The sheriff rode down to them, and would drive them to the king's town; because he did not know what men they were. But there he was slain. These were the first ships of the Danish men to come to England."

In other words, the king's sheriff took his men to arrest the strangers, and was killed in a fight on the beach.

For nearly three hundred years the warriors of Denmark and Norway—men of the "viks," or vikings—raided the coasts of all the Christian lands. They destroyed and plundered, at first as ships' crews; later on they moved in large armies under famous leaders. They were heathen and could be mercilessly cruel. Yet they were given to the making of laws and to settling disputes by discussion among themselves. They held valor to be the highest of virtues: and they waited for no man's leadership, for each of them was capable of acting, when necessary, on his own.

Of their religion we can read in their ancient poems. The heavenly stronghold of Asgard, which could only be reached across the rainbow bridge, was the home of the gods, Odin and his wife, Frigga, and his sons Thor and Balder, and also of Loki, the spirit of evil. Odin wandered always in search of wisdom. Thor with his mighty hammer, Mjölnir, made the thunder, and warred perpetually against the giants of the frozen north. Balder, the beautiful god of day, was specially protected by a magic spell of Odin's, but Loki, the evil one, caused him to be slain by an arrow of mistletoe. At the demand of the gods Balder was restored to life, while Loki was chained to rocks until "the twilight of the gods" should come, and all the world of gods and men break up in ruin. Across the "fields of the heavens" there went riding the fire maidens, the helmeted Valkyries, choosers of the slain, who led the dead vikings into Valhalla, the hall of the slain, where every day was spent in battle preparing for the last great conflict which was to take place at the ending of the world. To the vikings both this world and the next were places of strife where only the strong were secure and happy. So their pride was all in valor and strength. Yet they were something more than mere fighters. In the same old poems we find shrewd sayings.

> A man should be wise and not too wise, for the heart of the wise is seldom a glad one.
> Wealth dies and kinsmen die, and a man himself dies at the last; but glory and fame never die.

Such men with such beliefs were a terrible contrast to the Christian folk who were now trying to rebuild the civilization of Europe.

These vikings came south in long open boats, built high at bow and stern, and driven through calm water by from twenty-four to sixty oars. They were made of oak and clinker-built, that is, of long overlapping planks. They were shallow enough to be beached easily. There was a mast amidships to carry a sail. The gunwale was hung with wooden shields. Such vessels were among the most seaworthy craft in the western world until the invention of the steamship in the nineteenth century.

The vikings were born seamen whose raids and voyages took them as far afield as Constantinople and even to America. They settled in Iceland and from there some of them visited the New England coast of America, which they called Wineland. They settled in Russia, in France, in Scotland, in Ireland, and in England: and in all these countries their descendants are living today.

Across Russia they traveled overland down to the Black Sea, dragging their boats from river to river. They had colonies of traders in Russia who exchanged furs and slaves and timber for gold, silks, and armor from Constantinople, which they called Micklegarth or the Great City. In 907 they even laid siege to it with 2,000 ships, but retired when the emperor paid them a large sum of money. Later, the emperor enlisted a number of them in an imperial guard of battle-ax men to protect him and his treasury.

In the west the vikings brought Irish civilization and the Irish Church to ruin with their plundering and murder. In Dublin, Limerick, Wexford, and Waterford, their descendants lived separated from the other inhabitants, and were known as Easterlings, or men from the east, as late as the eleven hundreds. The reason why, today, the extreme north of Scotland is named Sutherland is that in the ninth century it was the "southern land" to the Norwegian vikings who raided it and settled in it.

The vikings banded together in large fleets under renowned leaders and sailed up the French and English rivers. They destroyed Rouen and Nantes. They attacked Hamburg with a fleet of 600 ships. They sailed around Spain and captured Lisbon and Seville.

It was an unhappy time for Christendom, which had lost North Africa and Spain and the east to the Arabs; and now had these fleets of heathen plunderers all along its western coasts.

One exploit of the vikings must be specially noticed here. In 912, under Rollo, a skillful leader, some pirate gangs came to northern France, opposite the coast of Sussex, and settled down there. They became Christians and were baptized. They took to speaking French and adopted the civilization of the French. This was the beginning of the Northmen's-land, or *Normandy*, as we call it. What Normandy and the Normans meant for England and elsewhere we shall see later.

Alfred of Wessex

It was all very shocking, and it brought misery and destruction to Christian cities and farms. In England it brought to an end the golden days of the saints and scholars that Bede knew and loved.

At first the raids were small affairs with fights on the beaches, a few ships' crews against the king's officer and the local farmers. Then about 850 appeared the viking fleets under redoubtable leaders. They pulled their keels ashore, made a camp, plundered the district, seized themselves horses, and rode inland. London was taken and looted. Within thirty years the Danish vikings occupied East Anglia: as the sorrowful English chronicler wrote, they "wintered there." They took York and set up a kingdom of York. They burned the fine abbeys of the fenland, Croyland and Peterborough, and killed St. Edmund, king of the East Anglians, in battle. All the middle and north of England fell to them, and was known as the Danelaw, the place where men lived under the "law" of the Danes.

Only Wessex, the kingdom of the West Saxons, remained free.

At midwinter in 878 they invaded Wessex, riding swiftly into the country from Gloucester. Wessex was caught unprepared at the worst time of the year when there was plenty of stored harvest to loot, but when ways were foul. Alfred the king took refuge in the west in the Somerset marshland at Athelney. With the spring the men of Devon went into action, wiping out a viking fleet that had appeared on the coast. Then Alfred set out and joined the Wiltshire, Dorset, and Hampshire men, and gave battle to Guthrum and his viking host at Ethandune, where, after hours of battle, he broke through their ax-wielding warriors and drove them back to their camp. He made Guthrum accept peace and be baptized, and retreat into East Anglia.

When other Danes invaded Wessex later Alfred and his men were ready. He and his valiant son, Edward, defeated them: and for the last four years of his life he and his people lived in peace. He had won his victories not only for Wessex but for all Christendom. The secret of Wessex was his secret.

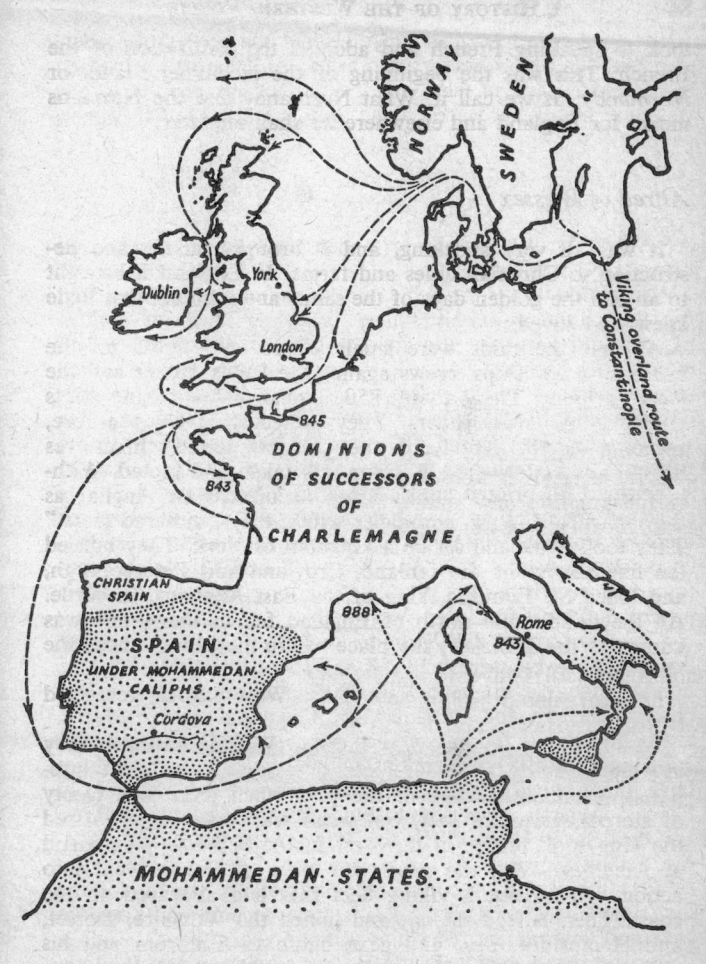

THE TROUBLES OF WESTERN EUROPE IN THE NINTH CENTURY: VIKING RAIDS FROM THE NORTH, "SARACEN" RAIDS FROM THE SOUTH.

1. Viking raids began in 798. Alfred defeated Danes in England 878-901; the Emperor Arnulf destroyed Great Viking Camp at Louvain 891.
2. Saracens overran South Italy in 843; they were driven out by 916.

Alone then of all English kings he had the power of leadership without which bravery is wasted. And his true Christian leadership is seen in what else he did for his people; for he was not merely a warrior-king but the true father of his people.

> The king doth follow Christ, and we the king,
> In whom high God hath breathed a secret thing.

As Alfred himself put it, "No man may do aught of good unless God work with him."

He divided up his royal income for the upkeep of his army, for the payment of his skilled craftsmen such as smiths, masons and jewelers, and for the care of his churches and monasteries as homes of religion and learning. He welcomed foreign scholars and travelers to his court, like the Norseman Othere, who had sailed far north into the White Sea. He studied law. He caused the sons of his noblemen to be educated in English and in Latin. This was a thing unknown in England till printed books appeared six centuries later. He collected manuscripts and had them copied, and some of them he translated himself. He ordered the monks to keep a chronicle of events. This Anglo-Saxon Chronicle, which continued to be written up year by year long after his death, is one of our most treasured possessions.

Alfred withstood the viking armies when all other seacoast lands of the west were helpless, and spent his whole life in a heroic endeavor to save Christian civilization. The queer names of Odda and Ethelnoth, of Plegmund and Werferth, mean little to us today; yet they were just a few of Alfred's good and faithful companions without whom he could not have done what he did, a band of steadfast men whose likeness we can never know, but whose work still endures.

Alfred saved Wessex. His son Edward the Elder, his grandson Athelstan, and his great-grandson Edgar, in the next century (the tenth) reconquered all England, which, for the first time since the Romans left it, now became one kingdom with one government. The long Roman roads were then in a better state than they were in the days of Nelson and Wellington: and we must picture our Anglo-Saxon forebears using them for war and for trade.

One great battle stands out. King Athelstan met a host of Danes, Picts, and Scots which had gathered together against him, and routed them in a conflict that lasted from sunrise to sunset. This took place at "Brunanburgh," a name unknown now, but most likely it was *Birrens* on the Roman Wall by

Solway Firth. The old English harpers sang of the battle, the *Song of Brunanburgh*.

	They clove the broad-shield wall,
Hewed the linden bucklers	with hammered blades;
They, the sons of Edward	in the noble manner
Of their own race	who in the war-rush
Fought for their own lands	against all foes,
For their hearths and home.	The hated ones were struck [down
The Scots warriors,	and the seafarers
Fell fated . . .	The West Saxons pressed on
All that day long	driving in companies
In fierce pursuit	of their hated foemen.

Like the old Greek bards who sang of Troy, the English gleemen sang of the battles fought by their kings. They sang in the hall after the feasting while their lord and his men listened to the deeds of their ancestors. Most of the songs are lost to us; St. Dunstan collected many for his own delight: but they, too, are gone with the dust of ages.

An Arabic Civilization

As the vikings settled down to farm and trade, and as they became Christian, their savagery lessened and they became men of peace like their neighbors. One of their greatest leaders was Canute, who became king of both Norway and England. He was a Christian, and ruled well, and gained the faithful service of Englishmen. And those viking raiders who had settled in Normandy were making themselves some of the foremost Christian knights of the west.

Vikings could be converted. Not so the Mohammedans. Warfare between them and the Christians went on in the east and in Spain. The soldiers of the Greek emperor at Constantinople and the Christian knights of Spain defended the flanks of Christendom. There were pauses, truces, and intervals of peace. There was even trade and occasional friendship between the two sides; for the best of the Arabs were men of high culture and refinement. Many Mohammedans and Christians came to respect each other and learn from each other—as enemies often do. But the religious hostility was always there, ready to break out in open war.

Their amazing conquests had given the Arabs hold of the Greek and Roman civilization of the east: and among the best of them were fine scholars and wise rulers who did not hesitate to employ learned Jews and Christians to advise them. One of these rulers was that Harun al-Rashid of Bagdad whom we know as the caliph of the *Arabian Nights Entertainments*. Another was the Caliph Abd-er-Rahman of Spain.

In the lovely fertile valley of the River Guadalquivir in Moorish Spain, was Abd-er-Rahman's capital, the city of Cordova, a dream city of marble palaces and glittering mosques. It had public baths (just as the Romans had had), libraries, and schools. Its streets were lighted at night, cooled by fountains and conduits of running water, and made fragrant with gardens of fruits and flowers. The Moors were skilled in horticulture and agriculture. They planted vineyards, and grew rice and cotton and sugar. They brought ginger, date palms, bananas, mulberries, and apricots into the land.

They were scholars. They studied chemistry (*alchemy*) and medicine. They had copies made of all the books they could discover, many being translated from the writings of the ancient Greeks. It is said that there were six hundred thousand volumes in the caliph's library! The Arabic scholars wrote books on navigation and geography. They studied mathematics, as a token of which we still call one part of mathematics by the Arabic name of *algebra*. They used "arabic" numbers—1, 2, 3, 4, 5, 6, 7, 8, 9, 0—in place of the old Roman ones—I, II, III, IV, V, VI, VII, VIII, IX, X, L, C, D, M. They were skilled in the knowledge of the heavens, and today we call stars by the names they gave, like Betelgeuse and Aldebaran. The strict teaching of the Koran forbade music, but the caliph and his Moors took delight in it, and in poetry. It was from them that the Spanish Christians learned how to make and sing the ballads and love poems which were taken up later by the troubadours of the south of France.

Altogether a very pleasant way of life and learning. And this was in the tenth century, when England was a battleground of Dane and Saxon, and when the schools of Oxford and of Paris were not even thought of. To Cordova in the time of Abd-er-Rahman came many Christian scholars to gather wisdom at the feet of Mohammedan masters. In truth, the only Christian city to be compared with Cordova was Constantinople. Even mighty Rome of the Caesars was still a half-ruined place where the birds nested in the crumbling masonry of antiquity.

In spite of such things and of periods of peace and amity, the religion of Mohammed and of Christ could not long remain side by side without conflict. The war of the Cross and the Crescent was carried on season by season through centuries of border warfare. The central mountains of Spain still bear the name of Castile—the land of castles—from that long war.

In the Mohammedan dominions stretching from Spain through North Africa to Syria and Persia there were many hidden Christian congregations whom the caliphs left in peace so long as they paid their taxes. A long and lasting truce might have come into being. But it was a matter for great sorrow to all Christians that the Holy Places where Our Lord passed His earthly life should be under Arab rule, even though the Arabs allowed Christian pilgrims to visit Jerusalem. And Christian pilgrims did go there in hundreds.

The Normans and the Great Crusades

During the tenth century, when the kings of Wessex were winning back the midlands and Northumbria from the heathen Danes, other heroic kings were saving Christendom from its heathen enemies in the German lands. The Saxon king, Henry the Fowler, drove back the Danes in the north and the fierce Hungarian archers in the east. His grandson, Otto the Great, destroyed a great Hungarian army in 955. These men shared with the men of Wessex the honor of saving Christian Europe. And the defeated heathen were converted to the Christian faith.

From these dim and perilous times of wild alarms and hardship and suffering we may trace the beginnings of some modern states: the German kings settled fighting men in borderlands or "marks" to protect their kingdom. One borderland settlement was the Dane-Mark (Denmark); another, the East-Mark, was the origin of Austria; another, the Slavonic-Mark, was the far-off beginning of Prussia.

We have seen that Charlemagne, the king of the Franks, took the title of Holy Roman Emperor because he was the protector of Christendom, and was therefore a kind of successor to the old Roman emperors. Now, Otto the Great took the same title, and was crowned with great pomp Holy Roman Emperor at Rome in 962. From that year onwards it was always a German prince who bore the title, and it was the German lands together with North Italy which made up the dominions called the Holy Roman Empire. This arrangement endured till the time of Napoleon in 1806. The Holy Roman Empire, therefore, lasted for nearly 900 years! So what took place in the tenth century was important for many ages afterwards.

In the eleventh century England suffered the great change that altered the island's fortunes—and the fortunes of the world. The descendants of the Northmen began their startling adventures. Those pirate gangs which had settled down on the shores of France (Frankland) in 912, and had given their name to the place—Normandy—became Christians, and, by some unknown magic, they became the most gifted of rulers and soldiers. They conquered the two largest islands of Europe.

How Duke William of Normandy in 1066 crossed the Channel and defeated King Harold Godwinson in the battle by "the hoar apple tree" near Hastings is an oft-told tale. Not only did William conquer England, but he parceled it out, all of it, among his barons, and he even made an inventory of it, a description of its land and wealth, just like a man taking over a new estate. We still have this inventory, which is called *Domesday Book*. This William the Conqueror and his successors made a stronger monarchy in England than had been known in all Europe since the great days of the Roman Empire. Because of this conquest the men of England spoke two languages for over 300 years: the king, the court, the barons, and the churchmen spoke Norman French; the craftsmen and men of the plow spoke English. From the blending of these two tongues came the present-day speech of England and of the New Worlds of America and Australia.

How certain other Normans conquered Sicily is not so often told. A handful of Norman adventurers, led by Roger de Hauteville, mastered all South Italy and Sicily, which they made into a strong Norman kingdom (1050 to 1090). In this island of ancient strife were the descendants of many races—Carthaginians, Greeks, Romans, Arabs. Under the Normans, Sicily became one of the most cultured places of the western world, and made the most of its old advantage as a meeting place of merchants.

Another race of men came into prominence and power in this same eleventh century. The Seljuk Turks from Central Asia made themselves masters of Persia, became Moslems, and took over the leadership of the Mohammedans in the east. Soon they were threatening the lands of the Greek Christian emperor at Constantinople. They had none of the gifts that lead to the wise government of men, but they were vigorous, hardy, and skillful in war; and they came just at the time when Christians and Moslems were beginning to settle down peacefully. And they came at a time when multitudes of western Christians were making pilgrimages to the Holy Land to worship at the Holy Places.

The Greek emperor at Constantinople asked the Christians of the west to help him against the Turks. The pope called for volunteers to deliver Jerusalem from the infidel. The first crowd of volunteers, led by a knight nicknamed Walter the Penniless, set out straightway for the Holy Land. They were mostly poor folk, they had made no preparations, and those of them that reached Asia Minor, a very small remnant indeed, perished there miserably. This was in 1095.

The next year four grand armies of knights from the west met at Constantinople. They were commanded by the princes of the French, including Godfrey of Bouillon, Raymond of Toulouse, Robert of Normandy, and by the indomitable Normans of the house of Hauteville, Bohemond and Tancred. Under the banners of the Cross, and in the splendor of chain mail, they crossed the Bosporus into Asia Minor. Thence they marched and fought eastwards and southwards, suffering hunger, thirst, disease, wounds, and death. Antioch they took after a nine months' siege. Nearly four years after their first setting out, the survivors fought their way across a wooden bridge lowered from a tall siege tower onto the battlements of Jerusalem. They took the city, and then slaughtered without mercy, sparing neither for age nor sex. They then offered Godfrey a crown. "I will not," he said, "wear a crown of gold where the Saviour of mankind wore a crown of thorns." He called himself Defender of the Holy Sepulcher. But his brother, Baldwin, who succeeded him, took the title of king.

So this first, and greatest, of crusades set up a Christian kingdom of Jerusalem, and other Christian duchies and counties, in Palestine. The ruins of the massive castles they built still stand today in gaunt and solitary grandeur on the coast or on the hills bordering the hot desert. Their empty and roofless halls were once the scene of banquets and jousts in the days when their lords raised armies of footmen from the natives and marched out to meet the Turks raiding from the desert frontiers. This border warfare in armor under the fierce heat killed off many of the crusaders. And disease took them. To keep their power they needed steady reinforcements. Their main help came from two famous crusading orders of "military monks"; the Templars, or Knights of the Temple of Solomon, and the Knights of St. John of Jerusalem, who vowed their lives to God's service by fighting the Saracens. But the Christian states of Palestine lacked recruits from the west.

A second crusade in 1147 led by the French King Louis VII and by the Emperor Conrad failed to do any lasting good owing to the quarrels of its leaders: and the Turks found a fine soldier and a ruler of genius in Saladin. He destroyed the main army of the Christian knights in a battle fought

THE LATIN CRUSADING STATES

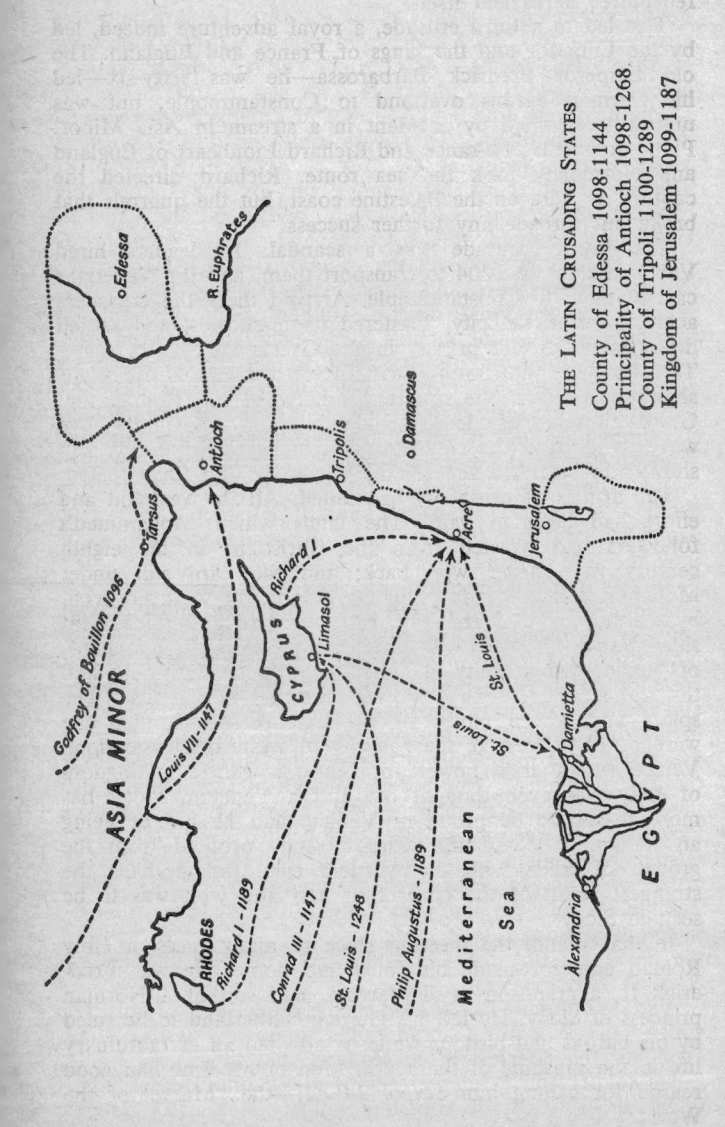

County of Edessa 1098-1144
Principality of Antioch 1098-1268
County of Tripoli 1100-1289
Kingdom of Jerusalem 1099-1187

at the Horns of Hattin. The disaster was such that Saladin recaptured Jerusalem itself.

This led to a third crusade, a royal adventure indeed, led by the Emperor and the kings of France and England. The old Emperor Fredrick Barbarossa—he was sixty-six—led his German barons overland to Constantinople, but was unluckily drowned by accident in a stream in Asia Minor. Philip Augustus of France and Richard Lionheart of England and Normandy took the sea route. Richard directed the capture of Acre on the Palestine coast, but the quarrels that broke out forbade any further success.

The fourth crusade was a scandal. Its leaders hired Venetian ships in 1204 to transport them, and the Venetians carried them to Constantinople. Arrived there the crusaders actually seized the city, mastered its territories, and settled down as dukes and princes in the Greek Christian Empire. This attack by the Latin Christians on the Greek Christians shows how much the differences between the Roman and Greek churches divided Christendom, and what little love was lost between the eastern and western Christians. It also shows how much the zeal for the war of the Cross had abated.

The armies of crusaders had failed. All the vast toil and effort had been in vain. The lands which Mohammed's followers had wrested from the Christians in the eighth century were never won back; and they are still under Mohammedan rule today. But the men of the west did profit by the trading that grew up, since warfare and trade went side by side. The men who profited most were the merchants of Venice, whose city became a wealthy, luxurious, and thriving republic, a naval power "married to the sea." The spices and woven cloths of the east passed through the warehouses of Venice, the gateway of western Christendom. Venice was a great power for centuries before a kingdom of Italy was even thought of: and a Venetian today has more reason to be proud of Venice than he has of being an Italian. True, all the cities of Italy profited from the growth of trade with the Moslem east. But perhaps the strangest result of the contact of east and west was to be seen in Sicily.

In that island, the meeting place of many races, a Holy Roman emperor made his court and home. He was Frederick II, a grandson of Barbarossa, and son of a Norman princess of Sicily. He left his German fatherland to be ruled by his barons and bishops while he adopted an extraordinary life in the sunshine of the south. Men of his time had good reason for calling him *Stupor Mundi*—the "Marvel of the World."

He kept a harem like a Turk, and lived surrounded by Moslem guards. He collected a zoo, and had his baggage carried about on dromedaries. He himself was an expert scholar speaking six languages, including Arabic: and he filled his court with mathematicians, astrologers and physicians—Christians, Jews, and Arabs. He founded the University of Naples. He knew more about the habits of birds than any man of his time and many men since his time, and he put his knowledge in a book written in Latin on falconry. He was a scoffer at the Christian religion and he quarreled with the pope. Yet he made a crusade! What is more, he got possession of the Holy Places by making a treaty with the Moslems—who allowed him to be crowned in Jerusalem!

Frederick's crusade had no lasting effect. His saintly brother-in-law, Louis IX of France, took an army to Egypt and invaded Palestine from there. This expedition failed; and so did a later one made by St. Louis to Tunis in North Africa.

These events were in the thirteenth century, the high peak of what we call the Middle Ages—the years between the end of the Roman Empire and the discovery of America. For three more centuries men spoke of crusades and planned them. The cause of the crusade, as it was called, was dear to many hearts, but leaders were lacking. The kings of the west were too busy making war against one another—like those of France and England. The popes and the emperors were always quarreling. Nevertheless, the war of the Cross did go on. In Spain the Christians fought to recover their land from the Moors. Christian ships in the Mediterranean went ever in peril from Turkish and Arab pirates. The most faithful soldiers of the Cross were the Knights of St. John of Jerusalem. When they were driven from the mainland of Asia, they fortified the island of Rhodes, and became known as the Knights of Rhodes. When the increasing naval power of the Turks compelled them to leave Rhodes, they went to Malta, and fortified that island. And as the Knights of Malta they raided constantly against Turkish shipping, and they withstood all attacks. They were a brotherhood of knights of all nations—a kind of rear guard of Christendom in its retreat from the east and south.

Warfare and Worship: Castle and Church

Our tale of the crusades has carried us into the high centuries of the Middle Ages, those thousand years from 500 to 1500 A.D. which are so named because they run between the ancient civilization of the Mediterranean and the modern world.

Throughout the Middle Ages the lands of the old Roman Empire remained divided into three parts. There was the Eastern Greek Empire of the Balkans and Greece and Asia Minor, all ruled by the Greek Christian emperor at Constantinople. There were the western lands of France, Italy, Britain, Scandinavia, Germany, and parts of Spain: all Catholic Christian countries that looked to the pope at Rome as the head of their church, but all ruled by many kings, dukes, counts, and bishops. Then there were the lost lands of the south and east—part of Spain, all North Africa, Egypt, Palestine, Syria and Mesopotamia, ruled by Mohammedan sultans. *This threefold division runs all through the history of Europe.*

The Christians have never regained the lost lands—except in Spain. This is what it means for us today when we say that the crusades failed: and they failed because the western kings and dukes were too busy fighting against one another.

The German Kaisers, or "Holy Roman Emperors," who ruled over the multitude of German dukes and counts, often marched into Italy to claim their overlordship of the Italian cities there. The Italian cities and Italian noblemen frequently made war on each other: they were quarrelsome and fought for lands or for revenge. England and France were often at war—so often, indeed, in the fourteenth and fifteenth centuries that the campaigns of Edward III and his sons, and those of Henry V and his brothers, are called by historians the Hundred Years' War (roughly, from 1350 to 1450).

These were the campaigns in which Edward III defeated a French army at Crécy, and Henry V one at Agincourt. But for years the English soldiers ravaged the French countryside, working in companies of lancers and bowmen under independent or free captains; and such free companies spread into Italy and even Spain, taking what they liked by force, or hiring themselves out to noblemen and cities. It was then that the English kings held the town of Calais as a fortified outpost across the Channel. The long warfare ended in the defeat of the English royal armies, who were driven from France largely by the marvelous inspiration given to the French by the Maid of Orleans, Joan of Arc.

Of all the western wars this Hundred Years' War created the most misery for the wretched countrymen who suffered so much from plundering and famine that bands of peasants rose in ragged revolt, and were most cruelly put down even by their own lords; for warfare in the Middle Ages was not of nation against nation but of feudal army against feudal army.

A feudal government was quite a simple thing. The king or duke granted lands to his barons and knights, and in return they swore to be loyal to him, and to serve him in war when he called on them for forty days every year at their own cost. The number of men-at-arms they brought with them depended on the amount of land they held. So an army was made up of many contingents of men, each under the banner of their lord. Such arrangements depended on keeping good faith; and the feudal oath of loyalty was a most solemn engagement. If a German Kaiser quarreled with the pope and crossed the Alps into Italy he summoned to his standard all his German dukes and barons, who rode into his camp with their retainers. If an English king like Edward I made war on the Welsh the lords of the realm from Northumberland to Devon rode into Chester or Shrewsbury with their feudal levies—lancers, sergeants, squires and bowmen—and were there marshaled by the king's marshal, himself one of the great earls. If Edward III or Henry V prepared to invade France, the barons and their men gathered at Sandwich or Southampton to embark under their many banners for the short sea crossing. Sometimes a bishop, like the mighty bishop of Durham, would have to summon his men for war against Scots invaders. Sometimes a wealthy town like London or Bristol would raise a fine company of longbowmen for the king's service from among their craftsmen and apprentices. Longbows could only be used by men of strength and sinew and skill who were highly paid for their service.

So wars were made by knights and their men. At first, as in the first crusade, armor was made of flexible chain mail fitting closely to the body; later on the knights wore heavy plate armor, that is, suits made of metal plates cunningly shaped by the armorers, and skillfully hinged at the joints of shoulder, elbow, and knee. By the fifteenth century the knights were completely encased in metal from top to toe, and even their horses carried armor. Their horses were in fact more like shire horses than modern cavalry mounts, and an advance of heavily armored knights was a ponderous affair. The change may be illustrated by two contrasted pictures: the first of the crusading knights in chain mail scaling the siege tower to clamber onto the walls of Jerusalem; the second of fifteenth-century knights of the English civil War of the Roses, unhorsed in the shock of battle, burdened with their plate armor, and stumbling awkwardly and helplessly along—an easy capture.

This cumbersome armor which made speed impossible proved such a handicap that it soon dwindled to helm and back and breast pieces, and sometimes thigh pieces. All these, save the last, survived as part of the dress of our own dragoons and of the French cuirassiers at Waterloo in 1814.

The use of guns in the later Middle Ages helped to make armor less effective. The word artillery means missile weapons, and once meant bows and arrows. In the ancient world it meant the great catapults which hurled massive stones against city walls. During the Hundred Years' War gunpowder was used to discharge round stone balls from cast-iron bombards, a hit-or-miss business. In the records we find mention of the king's *gonnes* (forerunners of the Royal Artillery) and we can be sure that such *gonnes* frightened as much by their noise and smoke as by the damage they did. Their most telling use was in the siege of castles and cities; bombardment could breach the walls; and as guns were improved, so more and more they were used as siege artillery.

Cities were walled in the Roman Empire, and castles were then built along frontiers. In the Middle Ages castles abounded in all places. Their massive walls were made to withstand long sieges, and towers and angled walls overlooked the gateways and approaches, enabling archers to shoot down attackers. Winding stairs, easier to defend than to attack, gave access to the upper stories and roof. A moat of water made direct assault very difficult. One way of approach was to throw forward, or rush forward with, bundles of withies to fill the moat—a most unpleasant undertaking when sharp eyes were sighting yard-long arrows at you from the narrow stone slits in the high walls. To take a castle needed scaling ladders, siege towers, battering rams, guns. Unless taken by surprise, a castle was fairly safe. It contained storehouses, stables, and garrison quarters. Within the main buildings were the kitchens, larders, the armory, the sleeping rooms, the great hall, and the chapel. Somewhere in the courtyard would be a smithy. Somewhere, also a well—often protected by a tower built above it. The towers were often built so that each could be defended on its own whatever happened to the rest. Taking a castle was, therefore, often a series of sieges. Once the drawbridge was up and the enemy appeared, life in the castle was hard and vigilant. But in peaceful days life must have been pleasant enough. There was plenty of company; for a castle was more than a fortified residence of baron or knight. It housed a large community of people whom it sheltered and fed.

Before the Normans conquered England, castles were made

of wood, like the fortified palisades of Africa and America. In the Greek Empire men had kept the knowledge of fortification in stone from the days of Rome, and when the crusaders went east they learned much about castle building. In Syria they built magnificent castles like those of Askelon, and of Krak des Chevaliers on the edge of the desert. And when they came back similar castles rose all over the west. Along the Rhine on the hilltops above the vineyards rose the strongholds of the German lords, those Rhineland castles whose ruins now add to the pleasure of the tourist. The Spanish lands were full of castles built during the interminable border warfare against the Moors. In the eastern "Mark" of Germany, and in the Welsh "March" of Britain rose the castles of the border barons who lived always on guard against old foes, and whose fighting men were trained in a hard school: which is why the Welsh marcher-lords and the barons of the Prussian Mark have played such an important part in the stories of their countries. The northern border in Britain abounded in castles, such as Alnwick and Berwick and Norham. But the castle was a feature of every medieval landscape, and of most medieval cities. London had its famous Tower; Paris, its Bastille.

The story of warfare between men is a dismal one, yet it is unhappily a part of human story, and like all human stories it has its tales of virtue and self-sacrifice, as well as of untold suffering. The tale of the Middle Ages centered upon its castles. Naturally, no king or baron could ever win a war by sitting down in his castle; he had to march out and seek his enemy and fight his battle in the open. But it was from their castles that kings and barons governed the kingdoms.

Churches, like castles, were a part of the medieval landscape. Every village had one. Large towns had many—Norwich, for instance, and London, which had a church in nearly every street; and what a clangor of chimes its bells made when they rang out over the tiny houses clustered beneath their steeples! Besides the churches and cathedrals there were monasteries in both town and country. Some, like Fulda in Germany, Cluny in France, and Monte Cassino in Italy, were of very ancient foundation. They had their chapels and churches where the ordinary people could go to worship; and, like the castles, they were centers of work and marketing, and sometimes small towns grew up around them—as in Bury St. Edmunds and Peterborough. Many London names remind us of churches and religious houses: St. James's, St. Martin's, the Temple, Austin Friars, Westminster, and so on;

and the same is true of other cities where parishes took their names from the churches, like those of St. Antoine and St. Germaine in Paris.

The story of the Middle Ages is largely the story of the churches. They kept men in mind of that other kingdom to which all belonged: the Kingdom of God on earth.

In the lay kingdoms of England and France and other lands, a man's rulers were the lord of the manor, the lord of the county (a count, or an earl), and finally the king—Harry or Philip or whatever his name might be. In the spiritual kingdom a man's rulers were the parish priest, the bishop, and finally the pope at Rome.

The two kingdoms were mixed up together; for the bishops were also lords of the realm because they held lands just like the knights and barons. Such bishops as those of Cologne and Mainz and Durham were, indeed, rulers with all the pomp and powers of princes. At their bidding men sprang to arms and armies assembled, and their houses were palaces full of retainers and hosts of servants. Bishops everywhere were king's counselors, for they had learning and were experienced and able men. Some were saints; some were great scholars, writing books in Latin, about philosophy, religion, and law; all of them had to manage large estates with treasurers, bailiffs, and stewards.

So also had the abbots of the monasteries. The Benedictine monks continued to follow the Rule of their founder. Other, and later, orders of monks copied this Rule but made it stricter, by having more fasting or more meditation and prayer, more silence, and more solitary hours in their cells. Of these later monks, the Cistercians built their houses in waste places: hence we find the ruins of their monasteries in the north of England, which was then sparsely populated, and which led them to become sheep farmers and wool traders. The Carthusian monks, who were renowned for their deep piety, have left their name in the London Charterhouse near Smithfield—a form of the word which somewhat resembles the name of the place where they started—Chartreuse in France.

The monks stayed at home working and praying apart from the busy world of men. The friars founded by the Spaniard St. Dominic, and the Italian St. Francis of Assisi about the year 1200, lived in the busy world preaching and working among the people. They took vows just like the monks, to be poor, to live unmarried, and to be obedient to their superiors. St. Dominic meant his followers to preach the Gospel and defend its truth against those who would mislead people by false doctrines. They wore black robes, and their house by the river in London became known as the Blackfriars. Dominicans often became personal chaplains or confessors to kings. Another house in London was named the Gray Friars after the gray-robed Franciscans.

St. Francis believed that not riches only but any possessions endangered a man's soul. He was the apostle of poverty. He left his father's cloth business abruptly one day and became a beggar, wearing a coarse gray gown and asking alms to repair an old ruined chapel in the woods. His neighbors thought him mad. But his sincerity and goodness convinced them that he was no ordinary man, and he soon gathered a band of devoted followers whom he called "little brothers," and to whom he gave inspiration in a Christian life of self-denial and love. No man, outside the Gospel, loved more. He spoke gaily of Sister Sleep and Brother Death. His command was that given by Our Lord: "Provide neither gold nor silver, nor brass in your purses, nor scrip for your journey, neither coats nor shoes." His disciples went barefoot, singing on their way, living on crusts and dregs of drink—friends of all the world and gay minstrels of God's love for men. They sought out the foulest slums and butcher's shambles in which to dwell and build their simple huts. But like the picked regiment of an army they drew the most able and devoted recruits. Talented men joined them: they became famous and wealthy: they taught in the universities: and their simple huts soon gave place to fine stone buildings.

We are used to public buildings of all kinds today in which councils and conferences meet; and they are neither castles nor churches. In the Middle Ages castles and churches and abbeys were the only "public" buildings. Only in them could the king meet his counselors or gather the great lords of his kingdom. In the great hall of his castle, or the chapter house of a cathedral, or hall of an abbey, he discussed the government of his realm. His counselors were nearly all churchmen: and most of the members of the House of Lords were bishops or abbots.

The king's council was a very old-established thing. It dated, in England, from Saxon days: and it included anyone whom the king was pleased to call to it. In the thirteenth century a new form of meeting came into existence. This was based on the idea that one man could represent his fellows, those of the same rank and occupation as himself. Since all the knights of the land could not conveniently meet together, nor all the citizens of all the towns, nor all the clergy, the king called their representatives to meetings (*parliaments,* or discussions) at Westminster, or Oxford, or Gloucester, or wherever else he happened to be. There they

THE BANNERS OF THE CROSS

gathered, and there the great lords gathered, the knights and the citizens making the "Commons" and the others the "Lords"—names still in use today. Two knights were selected by the knights of each shire, and two citizens by the citizens of each town. They brought with them the complaints of their shires and towns about injustices, and these complaints, or petitions, were read by the clergymen who formed the king's learned clerks. Following this it was easy for the king to have laws drawn up to deal with the wrongdoing and injustices. Then he asked the parliament for a grant of taxes, generally to help him pay for his wars.

Such parliaments took place in the summer months, and never lasted very long. They were only called when the king thought fit. The knights and citizens paid their own expenses, and often found it very irksome to attend. One of the points we must notice is that the church had its own parliament, which it called *convocation* and which granted the king taxes. Throughout all parliamentary business the bishops and abbots took a leading part, sometimes in their own cathedral or monastery buildings.

Such parliaments, in various forms, were also called together in France and Spain. In the Church there were many occasions when representatives gathered together to discuss affairs. But it was only in England that such representative parliaments continued to be called right down to the present day. Edward I used these words: "What concerns everybody should be discussed by everybody." The English lords and king's ministers got used to this; and other things helped the English parliaments to survive. In our own times the English parliament has been called the "mother of parliaments," because other nations have copied it. Englishmen were lucky to live in an island and so escape invasion; they were lucky to have a single strong monarchy of kings who believed in strong and just government; they were lucky in obtaining a great charter of liberties from King John (Magna Carta); and in having a good sense of law.

The two kingdoms, the earthly one and the spiritual one, sometimes clashed. The popes owned lands in Italy and kept courts like kings: and the church had its own system of law. Popes and kings sometimes quarreled bitterly. If a pope excommunicated a ruler, that is, placed him outside the communion of the Christian church, the ruler's subjects were no longer bound to obey him. They could rebel with the approval of the church, and this could make things very awkward for him. When Pope Gregory VII excommunicated the Holy Roman Emperor Henry IV, Henry was forced to beg the pope's forgiveness, which he only obtained after crossing the

Alps and waiting for three days outside the castle of Canossa where Gregory was staying. We cannot imagine any great ruler—or even a prime minister—doing this today.

The worst result of such quarrels came in the fourteenth century, when some French knights seized the pope because he and the French king were quarreling. As a result of this, the popes moved to Avignon in France, where they lived for many years. Then some cardinals in Rome elected another pope there, and, to the disgrace and scandal of all true Christian men, there were two popes each claiming to be the true one, and each condemning the other. This sorry state of affairs was later brought to an end, but not before it had lessened men's respect for the Church.

In spite of these deplorable disputes, men did feel that they were all members of one church and one civilization. This can be made clearer if we remember that in the Middle Ages an Italian priest could become a bishop in England, and an Englishman could be a learned teacher in the University of Paris. The universities of the west were then really international, each of them having students from all nations. The Church was international, and its language was Latin—spoken by all educated men.

One of the most frequent causes of dispute was, Whom should a bishop obey—the king, because he was a landowner, or the pope, because he was a minister of God's church? One such dispute is famous because of the tragedy it led to. When Henry II of England, a vigorous and hot-tempered king, quarreled with his archbishop of Canterbury, Thomas Becket, four knights, thinking to please Henry, murdered Becket in the cathedral at Canterbury. Henry humbled himself, and even let himself be scourged by the monks of the cathedral; and Becket's shrine became a notable place of pilgrimage.

Castle and Church dominated the Middle Ages. The knight and the priest, the monk and friar depended, however, upon the work of thousands of humble farmers and craftsmen whose homes were of timber and clay. But all men were helpless before famine and diseases which struck them down mysteriously. A man might become a leper and be shunned by his fellow men. Life was short, and death a frequent visitor. Most dreaded disaster of all was the plague or pestilence, never absent for long. In 1348 it swept across the whole of Europe in a "Black Death," wiping out whole villages, and killing one in every three of the people.

The protection of the castle and the comfort of the Church were very real things to these forefathers of ours. And now we shall learn something of their lives by going with a band of them to that same shrine of Becket's at Canterbury, in the company of Geoffrey Chaucer, the first of English poets.

Pilgrims to Canterbury

Geoffrey Chaucer, a servant of the English King Richard II, spent his days collecting the customs duties or taxes of wool on the quays of the Thames, or else in looking after the building repairs and furniture of the royal palaces. His evenings he spent in retelling old tales, writing them down in poetry which we can still read, although the language is a little old-fashioned.

In his book of the *Canterbury Tales,* written about 1400, we have a picture of the men and women of his day making a pilgrimage to the shrine of St. Thomas Becket at Canterbury. They were a more mixed crowd than we should find going out together on holiday now; but pilgrimage made all men equal.

On the south side of London Bridge, in Southwark, was the Tabard Inn. From its courtyard on a bright, showery April morning the pilgrims set out, all on horseback. Harry Bailly, the innkeeper, went with them; for in those days the innkeeper was really a host who welcomed travelers as his guests, and sat at board with them. Bailly was a right merry man, bold in speech and wise. It was he who suggested that each pilgrim should tell a tale to beguile the journey. They all agreed—and so we have the book.

The Miller led the way, playing them out of the town on his bagpipes. He was a burly man, short-shouldered, broad, and thickly built, who could break through a door by running his head against it! He wore a white coat with a blue hood. After him followed the others.

There was a Knight, a "very perfect gentle knight," whose sober-colored doublet was rust-stained where the coat of mail had pressed against it; then a Squire, the son of the Knight, a lusty bachelor with curly hair and gaily embroidered clothes; then a brown-faced Yeoman in green, with a sheaf of peacock arrows at his belt, and a great bow in his hand. Then came a Doctor of Physic, or Medicine, whose cloak was of red and sky-blue stuff lined with silk, and who knew the causes of all illnesses whether they were "hot or cold or moist or dry"; a Sergeant of the Law, grave-faced and learned, and dressed very plainly; a Merchant with a forked beard, wearing a Flemish beaver hat and elegant boots; a jolly, red-faced and white-bearded Franklin, or farmer, in whose house it "snowed meat and drink"; a Cook who knew how to make good "blank-manger"; a Clerk of Oxford—or student—whose nag was as lean as a rake, and who spent all his scanty pence on books which he kept by his bed; a Shipman of the barge *Maudelayne* of Dartmouth—a sunburnt mariner who knew all the coasts from Hull to the Mediterranean Sea, and, in coarse-spun clothes, now rode his horse awkwardly as a sailor would.

After these there followed a yellow-haired Pardoner with his wallet full of parchment pardons from Rome; then a Summoner, a church officer who summoned men to church courts of justice—his face was blotched and pimply in spite of the ointments he used, and probably because he often got drunk. The next was a Maunciple, whose job it was to buy food for a college of lawyers. Then came a spindle-shanked Reeve in a blue coat with a rusty sword at his side. Then a lady, a dainty and trim Prioress named Madame Eglantine, who would weep at seeing a mouse in a trap. After her was another lady, a "Wife of Bath," buxom and bold, rich and much-traveled. She had had five husbands, one after the other, and had outlived them all; and she could weave cloth as skillfully as any Flemish weaver.

Then came a Monk who loved hunting more than he loved singing in chapel, and a Friar who did his singing in taverns where he cadged money from people. By contrast, then, came a poor Village Parson who really loved his people and taught them truly the word of God: and with him was his brother, a Plowman.

At the end of the procession came a group of city craftsmen—a Haberdasher, a Carpenter, a Dyer, a Weaver and a Tapestry Maker, each one dressed in the livery, or uniform, of his craft guild.

Geoffrey Chaucer gives us most of the sorts of men and women to be met with in the Middle Ages. Great barons and bishops, of course, journeyed with their own bodies of household servants. When the earl of Oxford rode into London to lodge in his house in Warwick Lane, eighty gentlemen dressed in Reading-tawny livery rode before him, and a hundred stout yeomen followed after him, wearing the Oxford badge of the blue boar embroidered on their coats. When the bishop of Hereford rode to London his retinue needed fifty-one horses.

As for the king, his royal progress was made with heralds and couriers, and long wagon trains, and the whole of his court. It was a great sight to see these processions go by.

Let us leave Chaucer's merry pilgrims jingling cheerfully down the Old Kent Road on their way to Canterbury, and turn to speak of the lives of some of them.

Knights and Chivalry

A true Christian knight defended the Church and helped the poor and the weak: he was courageous in battle, and kept faith with his liege lord: and he opposed all wrongdoing and injustice. He was chivalrous, that is, he had the virtues of knighthood. At first he was a young squire who waited at his lord's table, groomed his lord's horse, and carried his lord's weapons. When he became a knight he was girded with a sword, fitted with gilt spurs in place of his old silver ones, and he received a buffet or blow on the shoulder with a naked sword. Sometimes he laid his arms on an altar in church, and kept a vigil by them all night. His shield and his surcoat which covered his coat of mail, bore his own badge or device, and he adopted a motto or perhaps inherited one. He was then ready to prove himself a valiant knight in battle or in tournament. He took as his example the great heroes of the past—Alexander, Julius Caesar, Charlemagne, Arthur, Godfrey of Bouillon.

Above all he was a Christian knight. In the great days of the big crusades he "took the Cross," or went on crusade with Richard Lionheart or St. Louis. Though the great days of the crusades were over, he could, if he wished, still fight the Turk by joining the Knights of St. John of Jerusalem, or he could fight the heathen Prussians by joining the Knights of the Sword in East Germany. There were other orders of knights, or orders of chivalry, founded by kings and princes. Edward III of England founded the Order of the Garter; Henry IV of England founded the Order of the Bath; Philip the Good, duke of Burgundy, founded the Order of the Golden Fleece. These were all fellowships or brotherhoods of knights with rules and regular meetings and a special chapel or church for common worship.

The men of the Middle Ages were much given to forming brotherhoods or fellowships.

City Craftsmen

Another sort of fellowship, a humbler one, was the guild of craftsmen. A guild consisted of all those in one town engaged in one craft or *mystery,* such as baking, brewing, candlemaking, or carpentry. Among the wealthiest guilds of London were the goldsmiths who acted as bankers, and the drapers who made fortunes out of the woolen trade. These craft guilds in London (and elsewhere) often quarreled with one another over their share in the government of the city.

In Chaucer's day the grocers and fishmongers had a feud with the drapers and the mercers and the haberdashers. This sort of quarrel often led to rioting among craftsmen and their apprentices, with broken heads and punishments by the magistrates.

The master craftsmen of each guild regulated the quality of the work and the hours of work, and they punished guildsmen for doing shoddy work or giving short weight. Shoemakers who made bad shoes were forced to wear them strung around their necks in public. The guilds fixed prices to be charged. They acted as insurance societies, giving money to the widows and orphans of fellow craftsmen. They had their own livery, their own hall, and they worshiped in common in some nearby church. Some crafts had their own patron saint, like St. Hugh for the shoemakers. Each guild controlled the entry of the boy-apprentices who were to live in their master's house for seven years in order to learn the secrets of the craft; and they examined the apprentices' work, by which, in the end, they became masters of their crafts. Indeed, they were masters of bakery or leatherworking just as certain other learners became "masters of arts." If an apprentice were very lucky, like Dick Whittington, he also married his master's daughter, and became Lord Mayor! Every city in Europe had its craft guilds.

Many cities had markets, and a few had fairs, which were yearly markets made of wooden stalls or booths set up for the purpose. Stourbridge Fair near Cambridge was held each year and lasted for three weeks, and merchants came to it from all parts of Europe. Nottingham held a Goose Fair. London had its own famous St. Bartholomew's Fair, held under the walls of the great priory of St. Bartholomew, and opened in state by the Lord Mayor himself each year. Such fairs drew the crowds, and, of course, the catchpenny cheapjacks, the jugglers, the fortunetellers, and that familiar sort of quacks who still offer pills and medicines to cure all illnesses. Quarrels and disputes in these fairs were settled in special law courts set up in the fair ground, and very suitably called the Courts of Piepowder, which is to say, the courts of the dusty feet. What we call a fair today is just the amusement part of these old yearly markets.

The old love of pageantry was well provided for by the guilds. Each one in London took its share in keeping watch and ward within gates; for then there were no policemen, and the streets had to be guarded against robbers and the houses against fire. One of the grandest sights was that of Midsummer Night when the Marching Watch of all the companies of the guildsmen paraded through the streets which were lit by lamps and gay with flags and flowers, and all set with tables of cakes and gingerbread for the feasting afterwards.

Every summer the guildsmen gave plays from platforms on moving wagons that stopped at certain regular places where the waiting spectators could see play after play in turn. The scenes were taken from the Bible. The Shipwrights acted Noah's Ark, and the Goldsmiths did the Adoration of the Three Kings at Bethlehem. The same dresses were used from year to year. At York, Judas Iscariot was always clad in yellow garments, and Our Lord in white sheepskin and red sandals. Herod was always shown as a great boaster and blusterer; and the scene of Noah and his wife was treated in a comic way. These craft or mystery plays kept the Bible stories before the eyes of people who had no books, just as the pictures and sculptures in the churches did. Our forefathers were as fond of dressing up and play acting as we are.

Lawyers and Clerks

Chaucer's Sergeant of the Law belonged to one of the Inns of Court in London. Lawyers, like other folk, lived in fellowships, and the Inns of Court were colleges where they stayed and dined and studied together under strict discipline. They studied mainly English law. In the University of Paris the lawyers studied mainly Roman law. It is one of the most important things about England that her people kept their own special sort of law. The Roman Civil law was studied on the Continent, and is the origin of much European law today. Besides these two systems of law there was a third one, Church Canon law, which was used in the Church courts of justice.

Chaucer does not include a judge or a justice of the Royal Court among his pilgrims because such a grand and frightening person was too high and mighty to go riding in such a fashion. He had his own attendants. He could be seen by evildoers when he sat alone, or with one or two of his fellow judges, on the bench of the court, clad in scarlet robes with white coifs or wraps over their learned heads. It might be in Westminster, or in some county town like Warwick or Norwich, where the Sergeants of the Law argued out a case before them. When the King's Justices arrived at a county town to try all the people who had done wrong since their last visit, many of the inhabitants were very scared men, for the King's Justices were stern and very searching.

Besides the Sergeant-at-Law there was a Clerk of Oxford

with Chaucer's cavalcade of pilgrims. He was what we should call an undergraduate. The London Inns of Court were never a university. Abroad, it is true, lawyers were trained in the law schools of universities like Paris, or Bologna and Salerno in Italy. England had but two universities, Oxford and Cambridge. In Europe there were many, some of them renowned for special studies: at Padua, for example, there was a school of medicine, and many Englishmen went there to study. A university was not a building nor a place but a body of teachers and pupils. It was quite common for students to go wandering from one university to another to learn from famous masters. These wandering scholars were lively fellows, mostly poor and carefree. They obtained a permit from a bishop to beg their way. We still have many of the Latin songs they sang as they trudged the roads or sat in wayside taverns.

They were "clerks" or clerics—the words are the same: and they became clergymen. Because they were the only readers and writers (of Latin—the chief language used in writing) anyone who could read and write was called a clerk. And so to this day a clerk is a man who earns his living by writing. Most of their reading and writing was about religion. The highest form of study was called *theology*, or the study of the things of God. Besides the Latin Bible, the work of St. Jerome made a long time before in the fourth century, and known as the "Vulgate," there were many books written by the early Christian bishops, such as St. Clement and St. Augustine. These were called the Fathers of the Church. Then there were the Latin writings of the great university teachers, of whom the greatest was St. Thomas Aquinas. The ancient Greek writings of Aristotle had been translated in part into Latin, but were not very well done. Still, Aristotle's teachings were held in great honor, as the wisdom of the chief philosopher of the ancient world. Some knowledge of his writings came to the Christians through the Arabic translation, made by Mohammedan scholars.

Some scholars studied astrology, which was supposed to foretell the future by the movements of the planets and the constellations. Some tried to find a "philosopher's stone" which would turn base metals into gold. A few rare scholars, like the Friar Roger Bacon of Oxford, did study optics and mathematics. Many of the Arab scholars were clever mathematicians. Of course, the main drawback to study was the difficulty of getting books, since every book had to be written out entirely by hand.

One handicap to the progress of learning was the widespread use of Latin for all purposes. It was the language of all learned men. Church services were said and sung in it. Royal proclamations were made in it. Charters and laws were written in it. Scholars used it in their arguments. Some fine books were written in it, like the beautiful book called *The Imitation of Christ* by Thomas Kempis. But when all learned men use a language which is not their own native one, we cannot expect many great works.

But by 1400 there were an increasing number of books of devotion, of romance, of chivalry, and of poetry in the ordinary, everyday languages of western Europe. There had always been ballads and songs. A few of these we still have left, but a great number must have perished. But by the end of the fourteenth century there were books written in Italian, in French, and in English. In Italian was Dante's grand poem of the *Divine Comedy*—a Vision of Hell, Purgatory, and Paradise. In French there were the *Chronicles* of Jean Froissart about the knights of France and England in the Hundred Years' War. And in English there were those same *Canterbury Tales* of Geoffrey Chaucer, of which we have spoken.

Tucked away in monastic libraries there were old writings in Anglo-Saxon and Old French which no one read. Hidden in oak chests and boxes there were old Anglo-Saxon charters and laws. We know these things now. Whether any inquisitive monk or clerk ever managed to read them then, or whether anyone bothered at all about them, we do not know.

Farmers

Of the rest of Chaucer's pilgrims we may make three groups: the Plowman, Miller, and Reeve; the Parson, Monk, Friar, Pardoner, and Summoner; and the Shipman.

The plowman kept the whole world going. He lived in a hut framed of timber, filled in with wattle and daub, and thatched with straw or reed. His food was coarse bread, bacon, butter, cheese, milk, honey, ale, fruit, and nuts, all provided by the work of his own family or neighbors. His clothes were made of homespun wool made by the women. His footwear was homemade of wood or leather. He wore a smock. Such light as he needed came from rushlights fixed in a lantern. Oil lamps and candles were luxuries. His single-roomed dwelling gave shelter to his cattle and lambs in the biting days of winter—a partition being made by a beam across the hut. He slept in a wooden box filled with straw. From the hearthstone, the center of every house, the smoke of a wood fire, which was always smoldering, escaped through a hole in the roof.

There was much working together between the men of the village, both in farming and in exchange of goods and labor. The blacksmith, the carpenter, the shoemaker, the weaver, and the miller were all to be found in the village—or in the next one. Over all ruled the lord of the manor, who lived in his wooden hall of two or three rooms, with barns and granges nearby. Of course, if the lord of the manor happened to be a rich lord, he might live in a castle or a fortified manor house of stone or brickwork. All the villagers paid some tribute to him by working for him, or by payments of corn, eggs, fish, honey, or the like, or by both methods. The lord of the manor might, indeed, be an abbot, in which case the work and the payments would be given to his steward, who managed the abbey lands.

For convenience there was a common-sense division of labor: one man minded the swine in the woods, another looked after the cattle, another the sheep. Every farmer could graze his cattle and sheep on the common land, send his pigs into the woods, and cut and gather firewood. His best friends, the oxen, were the chief beasts of burden. They were small, slow, patient brutes; and to plow up unbroken ground it took eight of them, yoked together two and two, and driven by a long oxgoad.

The horse carried men to war and on pilgrimage. It was a noble animal, fit for crusades and chivalry, and the horseman was the lord over his fellow men. He was the knight. The sheep clothed men and kept craftsmen busy and made woolen merchants wealthy. But the lean, small, bony ox was the breadgainer. He worked unceasingly under the yoke across the acres with his master guiding and goading. He was the farmer's best friend, pulling plow and harrow for centuries, helping to shape the land. "What profit has he of all the heavy clods that he has upturned with the plowshare?" These words were written in the first century B.C., by the Roman poet Vergil. We can answer the question by calling him "Brother Ox"—as St. Francis might have done—and by remembering him with thankfulness.

Villagers owning two or three oxen each worked together in the plowing. Their lands were divided into single-acre strips—each acre being 22 yards wide by 220 yards long, a furrow-long or furlong. These strips were made in three "fields," and a field in those days was not a small, hedged piece, but a large stretch of open country. One field was left fallow each year as pasturage for the beasts, and to recover its goodness. Each farmer might hold some thirty strips, which were scattered about among the strips belonging to his fellows, so that everyone got his share of the good and bad ground.

In summer life was pleasant enough. In winter, owing to the lack of fresh food and of the many green vegetables which we cultivate today, things often went hard. There was great risk of cattle dying for lack of fodder, there was great risk of sickness, and always great risk of fire. At all seasons, should the weather be bad and the harvest poor, there was a risk of famine.

For utensils the villagers had wooden platters, coarse pottery, knives, and drinking horns; for furniture, stools and rough tables. Farming skill was shown in plowing, sowing, harrowing, breaking clods with hammers, reaping, threshing, winnowing, garnering the grain, and grinding it into flour. There were other skills: thatching, hedging, splitting staves for hurdles, scything, sheepshearing, felling timber and trimming it with the adz. In monasteries and towns there were men who could make chain mail, jewelwork, enamelwork, brooches, rings, buckles, pins, swordhilts; who could carve in timber and stone. Baking, brewing, tanning, milling, weaving, smithying, were common tasks. Where osiers lined the streams or grew in water-logged meadows, men made baskets and plaited rushes. Dwellers in the fens spent their time in fowling, and learned how to cut and stack peat for fuel. In the Forest of Dean and Sussex Weald men dug for iron, in Derbyshire and the Mendip Hills for lead, in Cornwall for tin. Saltworkers collected salt from the brinewells of Cheshire, and the salt was carried across country on packhorses along tracks that came to be known as "saltways." In the woods, which abounded, the charcoal burners worked at their lonely and wonderful art of stacking vast heaps of twigs, covering them with sods, and charring them for days on end so slowly that there was never the least spurt of flame; and building for themselves small huts of branches in much the same way as the men of the Stone Ages had done.

To simple folk in nearby hamlets the great monasteries were houses of wonder and help. To the people elsewhere the only witness of the Christian religion was the parish church in which the priest hallowed the bread and wine at Mass; in which folk were married and had their children baptized at the font; and by which their fathers and mothers were laid to rest in the churchyard—God's acre. Relics of old heathendom remained, charms and spells, magic amulets bought from peddlers, bonfires lit on St. John's Eve, a belief in witches, and in the little folk. But the churches were the centers of village life. Feasts were held in them at which great quantities of cakes and ale were consumed.

Clever boys were taught their letters sitting in the porch beside the priest. The good priest, like Chaucer's one, was the leader and comforter of his people.

These farming folk were unlettered, ignorant of history or geography. They lived hard lives. To them the parish priest told the story of Jesus, the carpenter's son of Nazareth. It was the story of a poor child born in a manger, of a wandering preacher who spoke in parables of sowers, of men falling among thieves, of vineyards, of wedding feasts, of unjust stewards, of salt and leaven, of harvests and shepherds, of prodigal sons and husbandmen. As they listened they understood these things in their own way by the simple everyday happenings of their own lives.

The Church

The Church was the center of all men's lives. They paid taxes, or "tithes" to it, sometimes in the form of grain—and we still have the huge tithe barns in which the tithe grain was stored. There were Church courts of justice, which dealt with shipwrecks, with disputes about wills, and about marriage. The Church supplied skilled lawyers and clerks to do the king's business, and nearly all the great ministers of the kings in the Middle Ages were bishops. Men made pilgrimages to Rome, to Jerusalem, to the shrines of St. James at Compostella in Spain and of St. Thomas Becket at Canterbury, and of Our Lady at Walsingham in Norfolk. But in their own life the Church was their guide and comforter. The powers of evil might attack them, but the saints listened to their prayers, and the souls of the righteous men were in the hand of God. Every man on his deathbed wanted to hear the voice of the priest saying the sacramental prayer. Those who could do so left money for priests to say masses for the welfare of their souls, and these masses were said daily by chantry priests in the cathedrals and churches.

From this life of Christian religion came the cathedrals and the great monastery buildings.

The problem of roofing a wide span was solved by the round arch of the Romans. This grew into the dome or vault of the Emperor Justinian's churches—particularly of his marvelous Church of the Holy Wisdom. After this the grand churches in the west became Romanesque, that is, built of long rows of round arches holding up a round, vaulted roof. Many Italian and Rhineland minsters are in this style, and the Normans used it. Its chief impression is one of massive grandeur.

THE BANNERS OF THE CROSS

The effect of what we call the "Gothic" style of building is just as grand but more amazing. The style was first used in the church of St. Denis near Paris in 1140. We can see it today in the Sainte-Chapelle in Paris, and in the cathedrals at Orvieto, Chartres, Westminster Abbey and Salisbury—to give only a few examples. The builders made much use of pointed arches, which, rising in clusters from each pillar, spread and crisscrossed to make a framework of stone ribs upon which were laid the stone ceiling slabs. The sides of the huge vaults of slender stonework were pierced with windows of stained glass. It was all like "a stone cage with films of stained glass suspended in the void, a marvelous jeweled lantern." In place of the old solid buttress, or prop, outside its walls, a Gothic building used a flying buttress. The amount of work done by the busy masons and their men was enormous: every single stone had to be measured and cut and hoisted into place—hundreds of tons lifted high and poised skillfully upon those slender pillars and walls. But many other craftsmen were busy before the work was finished, and every art of man was called upon for its adornment.

The story of Christ was carved in stone, painted on the walls, and set forth in the colored windows. The masons carved quaint carvings of heads and faces, and beasts and angels and devils, on the ends of the stones that happened to project from the walls. They covered the west porches with statues of prophets, priests, kings, queens, saints, patriarchs, and even with whole scenes of the Day of Judgment. Even the buttresses carried fretted and carved pinnacles and had niches for saints. Carpenters, glaziers, smiths, painters, weavers, goldsmiths, and silversmiths all gave of their best work; for the chief end of every craft was to adorn architecture. Carved wooden rood screens and choir stalls, heavy stone canopies fretted as fine as lace, wrought-iron railings and gates, tapestries with blazing golds and purples and greens and blues, vessels of silver and gilt, pictures and colored patterns on the walls—all these lit by the easy light of a multitude of wax candles gave men a sense of the mystery and awe of their religion. And often the sound of their footsteps was hushed to a rustle by the swathes of dry rushes, green and brown, strewn upon the stones.

Mass was said every day, and the kings and barons attended; in fact, the word "mass" came to mean a time of day as well as a sacrament.

The singing, accompanied on organs, was in plain song, the melodies of which followed the rhythm of the Latin words. A beginning was made with part singing, in which two or more voices sang together but not on the same notes. An

Englishman named John Dunstable invented the art of writing parts for different voices singing different notes and moving along independently of one another—from which has developed all our modern music. At the end of the Middle Ages music developed very rapidly: one Dutchman actually wrote an anthem for 36 different voice parts!

Seamen and Travelers

There is not the least doubt that they had a very different sort of singing on board the barge *Maudelayne;* sailors were always a good singing race, and the men of Dartmouth in Chaucer's time were no exception. West-country seamen were among the hardiest. Chaucer's Shipman was a bold fellow like his fellow townsman, Harry Pay, who went to war against the king of Spain on his own account.

Another group of towns deserves mention for ships and seamen: the Cinque Ports. These were Dover, Romney, Sandwich, Hastings, and Hythe—to which Winchelsea and Rye were added later. They had to provide ships fully manned for the king's navy. The Cinque Ports were so important that they had their own special courts of justice to punish robbers and shedders of blood, and to raise taxes to build sea walls. At their full strength they could turn out some 57 ships with 1,300 mariners. The vessels were of oak, barge type, single-masted, carrying one sail, and fitted in wartime with a forecastle and an aftcastle and fighting top on the mast. Their size was reckoned in tuns—that is, the number of tuns of Bordeaux wine they could hold. These were the ships, painted and pennoned, that carried the English kings, Edward III and Henry V, and their knights and archers across to Normandy.

These were all islanders. The greatest sea powers of the Middle Ages were Venice and the German merchants of the Hanseatic League.

The merchants of Venice fought the Turks and also traded with them. They bought furs, hemp, carpets, silks, gems, precious metals, coffee, sugar, spices and drugs from the Greek merchants of the Black Sea and from the Arab dealers of Syria and Egypt. Westward their tall-masted galleons rode into Southampton Water and the Thames to exchange their goods for English wool, hides, and tin. The network of their rich trade from Venice reached overland across the Alpine passes to the cities of South Germany and the Rhineland; and on the way the precious spices had to pay duty to many a robber baron whose castle frowned down from a hilltop a bowshot above the highway along which the train of pack horses passed. No wonder that eastern spices cost a fortune in the markets of Antwerp or Cologne, or Paris or London.

Eastward the Venetian trade reached across the sea—that Great Sea of the ancient world—to the broad lands of the ancient east, and to the Red Sea across the valley of Egypt. Camel, donkey, and horse caravans traveled through the mountains and plains of Asia: Arab ships flew before the monsoon wind from the Red Sea; and so came to India and the East Indies, and even to the ports of fabulous Cathay. Indeed, a few adventurous Christians had traveled to these outlandish places.

We know of friars who went as missionaries to the Tartars. The first of them went in 1250, not so long after St. Francis founded his Little Brothers. And between 1250 and 1350 these hardy venturers made their way in the name of Christ across desolate, snow-swept plains to live with Tartar horsemen and shepherds. They often rode for three days on end without seeing a soul. They slept in the open or in miserable huts. They lived on sodden mutton and mutton broth and drank fermented mares' milk. One of them, after riding 5,000 miles, came to the Great Khan's court at Karakoram, where everyone soon got drunk on rice wine and where, marvelous to say, he found a silversmith of Paris, one Master William, who had been captured in a Tartar raid and was now working in silver for the Khan! Later on, friars, whose journeys are known to us, reached China itself going by sea from the Persian Gulf, and they founded friaries in the Far East, and even in Pekin at the court of Kublai Khan.

The best-known story is of the travels of the merchants of Venice named Polo. They set out in 1260, Nicolo and his brother Maffeo. They learned to speak the Tartar language and made friends with Kublai Khan, who sent them back with a request for 100 Christian priests. Nothing came of this, but they returned to China with Nicolo's young son, Marco Polo. The three climbed over the "Roof of the World" (the Pamirs and the high tablelands of Tibet) and they reached Kublai Khan's court after three and a half years of travel.

This was in 1275. Marco and his father and uncle found favor in the eyes of the Tartars and traveled as their ambassadors all over the East. They returned home bearing golden tablets, or passports, to ease their journey through Asia, and they arrived at Venice in 1285, coming by sea to Java and then to the Persian Gulf. No one believed their tale until they ripped open their rough Tartar sheepskins and out tumbled rubies and sapphires! Marco told his story at length, and this story is one of the greatest travel books of all time.

We are more fortunate than the men of Marco Polo's time, or of Chaucer's time, because all of us can read his book. The only persons who could read it then were those lucky enough to get hold of a handwritten copy.

But to return to Venice, the city of marble palaces whose doge, or duke, went through the ceremony of marrying his city to the sea by flinging a ring into it. Venice could count her ships by the hundred—galleys, galleasses, galleons—and by their might she was the proud mistress of the Mediterranean. Her rulers were her merchants and she governed a dozen cities in North Italy, besides keeping settlements in the Greek islands. Her sons were rich, lavish, and splendidly dressed. Her buildings were adorned with bronze statues, gorgeous colored mosaics and marbles, serpentine and porphyry stone. She was a city of canals and lagoons—"made very beautiful in the midst of the sea" like ancient Tyre. The reports of her ambassadors whom she sent to all foreign princes and kings are among our best historical records.

Chaucer's Shipman knew their ships. He also knew well the northern seamen of the Hansa towns, a great fellowship of merchants living in the Rhineland and Baltic cities. These men traded in timber and furs from the winter lands of the north, in salt and stockfish, in Swedish copper, and in woolens. Like the Venetians they were also bankers and lent their money to kings like Edward III of England, who wanted it to pay for his invasions of France. They kept "factories" or fortified branches in foreign cities, where their agents lived almost like monks under strict discipline, with the gates barred to all outsiders. In London, where their factory was called the Steelyard, they were known as Easterlings.

Just as the Venetians knew the enemies of Christendom in the eastern Mediterranean, so the Hanseatic seamen and merchants knew the heathen men of the Baltic plains where the German order of crusaders—the Teutonic Knights, or Knights of the Sword—fought against and won lands from the barbarous Prussians.

The wars of the Cross and the adventures of seamen changed the fortunes of western Christendom during the century after Chaucer—the greatest century of adventure and discovery, of crusaders and mariners: the fifteenth century.

The Wars of the Cross

The wars of the Cross were fought at each end of the Mediterranean: in Spain, and in the lands of the Greek Empire.

THE BANNERS OF THE CROSS

The crusaders from the west never regained a footing in Palestine after the failure of the third crusade, in which Richard Lionheart took part. The power of the Mohammedans grew and grew and threatened the Greek Empire more and more. All the valor and wounds and suffering of the Christian kings and knights came to nothing because they quarreled, and because they were not supported from home. The men of the western kingdoms grew tired and lost interest, having other business to see to. *The danger was not close to their own homes.*

By contrast, during the whole time of the peril, from the eighth century to the fifteenth, the men of Spain had no need to travel abroad to make the crusade; for all that time the war of the Cross was at their doors. They fought against the Moslems in order to regain their own lost country.

In the fifteenth century the danger was close enough to the heart of the dominions of the Greek emperor at Constantinople.

The end of it was that the enemy conquered all Asia Minor, the land where St. Paul had preached the Gospel, the land where the very first Christians had met for communion in their humble houses, the land in which stood the shining Seven Cities to whose churches St. John had written his great Book of Revelation—the last book in our Bible. And the simple peasants of Asia Minor became Moslems, as they are to this day—men and women whose ancestors belonged, perhaps, to those earliest Christian churches.

Worse than this, far worse, the Turks crossed into Europe, rode through the Balkans, and reached the mighty River Danube.

This was a shocking disaster. Christian nations of shepherds and farmers, men of the hills and plains, came under their lords to fight for the Cross: Serbians, Albanians, Hungarians, and Poles strove hard to turn back the invaders. They failed. Many farseeing men in the west tried to rouse the kings and barons and churchmen to a new heroic effort to make a final crusade. No one stirred. Kings and barons were too busy fighting each other.

The End of Constantinople

John Justiniani, a nobleman of Genoa and a famous soldier, brought his two ships into harbor at Constantinople in January 1453. He and his seven hundred men, well-armed and wearing brazen breast pieces, joined its defenders who held the walls against the Turks. Some noblemen and soldiers of Venice were already there, fighting "for the honor of God and the honor of all Christendom." The emperor of the Greeks made John Justiniani his commander-in-chief.

For the tired men who stood to arms along the city walls, this was part of the endless war. It had been going on for ages past, and looked like going on for ever. These nine thousand Christian soldiers—Greeks, Genoese, Venetians—were holding back an enormous army of seventy thousand Turks. Behind them in that rich city on the Bosporus were treasures of art and learning of a thousand years: mansions, churches, palaces, libraries, sculptures, paintings, mosaics. The people were crowding the churches to pray for deliverance from the enemy. Many of them were quite sure that a miracle from Heaven would save the city.

The walls were majestic but old. When the huge Turkish gun, the "Taker-of-Cities," was fired, the earth shook, a deafening roar filled the air, and a hundredweight of stone cannon ball was sent crashing against the ancient masonry, which crumbled under the mighty blow. The plain in front swarmed with the hordes of Asia, and these were not only rough peasants and wild horsemen but also skillful, brave and well-disciplined troops. The Christians threw back attack after attack. They resisted the onrush of the bashi-bazouks, fierce Asiatic cavalry. They resisted the onslaught of the picked regiments of Janizaries who were sent forward under the eyes of their sultan, with orders to scale the walls or die in the attempt.

The Turks had begun to threaten the city in the autumn of 1452. Now it was May. Still, as the anxious days passed and Justiniani's forces watched and waited and fought, there came no sign of reinforcements from the Christian nations of the west. Yet this was the war of the Cross of Christ against the Crescent of Mohammed: the war in which all Christian Europe had at one time or another taken part. Now, these Greeks and their few allies fought on alone in that dreadful springtide of 1453.

The city stood like an island in a sea of foes, a Greek and Christian city. Nine thousand brave men, mostly Greeks with a handful of Venetians and Genoese, manned its defenses, standing to arms in that endless struggle which had first broken upon, and sundered, the Christian world seven hundred years earlier.

So the Turkish guns opened, and the walls shook under the blast, and the soldiers of the sultan rushed to the assault. A gap was blown in the wall beside one of the gates. Even this was stoutly held by the Greeks and Venetians. Then some Turks passed unseen through an unguarded postern gate, and got behind the defenders. Soon the tall white felt hats of the Janizaries were seen on the walls, and great numbers of the enemy, clambering over their dead comrades, poured into the approaches to the city. John Justiniani, wounded and in sharp pain, was forced to retire to one of his ships, where he later died of his wound.

The last of the emperors, Constantine Palaeologus, rode in his armor with a band of chosen companions into the gap by the gate. There he died fighting a host of Turks. It was a somber and fitting end to the age-long story of the Caesars and emperors of Rome, that the last of them should not survive the final wreck of the Empire.

Amid the tumult the citizens crowded along the waterfront to escape by sea; but only a few got away in the Italian galleys. The Turks were about the streets, killing and looting, and when they saw there was no serious resistance, collected herds of miserable captives to sell into slavery.

Mohammed II, Commander of the Faithful, rode through the streets to the magnificent church of the Holy Wisdom (St. Sophia). There he ordered his *mullah*, or preacher, to climb into the pulpit from which, for hundreds of years, the bishops of Constantinople had preached the Gospel. The *mullah* summoned the faithful to prayer. The faithful were now the victorious soldiery, hotfoot from their plundering and killing. The prayer that rang out in a strange tongue was the cry: "There is but one god, Allah; and Mohammed is his prophet."

The sultan was himself a highly educated man, and he was not unmoved by the fall of this great and renowned city. When he saw the palace of the dead emperor after it had been looted, he paused and quoted from an old Persian poet: "The spider has woven her web in the Imperial palace, and the owl has sung her watch song on the towers."

Such was the end of Christian Constantinople. It now became "Stamboul," a Turkish possession. But the war went on. It had to go on if Christendom itself was to be saved. The Venetians kept their war galleys at sea. The valiant Knights of St. John of Jerusalem held the island of Rhodes as a sea fortress. The horsemen of Hungary and Poland and the hardy hillmen of Serbia kept the Turks south of the Danube. But upon the captured and half-deserted city came the terrible blight that fell on all places under Turkish rule: for the Turks knew how to destroy but not how to build.

All the ancient and beloved lands of the Christian east— Egypt, Palestine, Asia Minor, and now Greece—were under the Green Flag of the Prophet. And they remained so for the next four hundred years, most of them—and they were all once civilized, prosperous and full of cities—in a state of profound ignorance and continuing decay. It is one of the saddest stories on earth.

The Fall of Granada in Spain

In Spain the Christian knights were victorious. The kings of Castile and Aragon captured Seville and Cordova in the thirteenth century. When Constantinople fell, only the small kingdom of Granada was in Moorish hands. This was attacked and taken in 1492 by a great Christian army in which were some English and French knights. When the gates of Granada were opened to the triumphal entry of King Ferdinand of Aragon and his wife, Queen Isabella of Castile, a banner of the Cross was raised on the highest tower of the Alhambra palace: and the victors sang a solemn *Te Deum* of thanksgiving and praise.

From these old tragic events came many things that affect the world today. Spain and Portugal have people of Moorish blood now, and their languages contain many words of Arabic origin. More important than this, the Christian soldiers of the Peninsula were filled with a burning zeal for the cause of the Cross, and they were hardened by their long crusading wars. They had hoisted the Cross over the mosques of Granada. They were very soon to raise it high in many strange lands, some of them under strange stars, thousands of miles over the seas.

Southward Ho

When the fishermen of Portugal looked to the west and south over the long Atlantic rollers, they were standing at the world's end. So were the Irish fisherfolk on the wild west coast of Ireland. There was also a land's end in Cornwall, another in Brittany, and another in Spain. But there were islands beyond the sunset—or so the stories said. They even had names: Antilha, Brazil, St. Brendan's Isle, the Isle of the Seven Cities, the Isle of Sheep—all somewhere out in that far west over the waters. The men who sailed in search of these either came back with no tale to tell, or else the ocean took them for ever. All the Atlantic coast, was, indeed, the end of the known world in the west. Beyond there was nothing but the salt sea.

But the south was another matter. Strange exciting tales

THE BANNERS OF THE CROSS

came from the south to the crusaders of Portugal who captured Ceuta in Morocco from the Moors in 1415.

The Moors told them of a green fertile land of Ghana far away across the Sahara desert, where on the banks of a big river (the Senegal) there lived many people. This river, it was said, was a branch of the famous Nile of Egypt. Those who reached it could sail up it and come to the mysterious Christian empire of Prester John, the man who was both priest and king, and who lived in the east beyond the Mohammedan lands.

One rich and powerful prince was deeply stirred by the news. He was Henry of Portugal, brother to the king, and head of the Portuguese order of crusaders—the Order of Christ. Prince Henry made up his mind to conquer Ghana, and make it Christian, and rule it with the knights of his Order. He had money enough to employ mapmakers, astronomers, and learned Jews, and to build ships and pay for the voyages. He sent caravels to sail along the African shores. His men felt their way southwards, voyage by voyage, past the sandy, barren beaches and the rocks. Every adventure won a little more knowledge for the next attempt. It was very slow going.

After years of endeavor his captains reached Rio de Oro, which was a good thousand miles from home—not a bad achievement for small, half-decked ships holding 30 men each, most of whom were scared by fears of burning heat and terrible sea monsters. The nights at sea must have been full of terrors.

So far the coasts had been infertile, desert or half-desert. But the Portuguese managed to land and capture some Negroes to bring home and sell as slaves for work on the farms of Portugal. On one voyage alone they took over two hundred of the wretched blacks.

At length, in 1445, a fleet of six caravels, flying the banners of the Cross, came to the Senegal River and saw the green forests of Ghana, or, as the Portuguese pronounced it, "Guinea." They brought back some slaves and the news that they had discovered the way to Prester John. Another fleet took colonists to the Azores, or "Hawk" Islands. Very soon, Prince Henry's men were fetching home African ivory and Guinea gold dust.

Before he died in 1460 the prince knew that his dream had come true.

The merchants now took up his work because there was money in it. Farther and farther south went the ships; past the Ivory Coast, past the Gold Coast, past the Niger River; then under new stars to the mighty Congo River. Ports were built in Guinea as trading posts for gold, ivory, and slaves. And all this voyaging was kept a close secret, the utmost pains being taken to keep the charts from falling into the hands of other nations.

In 1486 Bartholomew Diaz sailed past the Congo and then stood out to sea to the southwest. That is, he sailed out into the open Atlantic. The westerly winds caught him and drove him back; and when he again made a landfall the coast was on his north!

Without knowing it he had sailed round the Cape of Good Hope, and was now off the south of the African continent. He would have sailed on, but his men were unwilling to risk it. So he turned homeward, and this time he saw the cape which he named Cape Tempestuous (Cabo Tormentoso). It was the king of Portugal who gave it the name of Good Hope—one of the grandest names ever given to a cape.

Beyond Good Hope

The next voyage was a mighty adventure. The two ships were named after archangels—the *Gabriel* and the *Raphael*. They were stoutly built, square-rigged, three-masted vessels. At each end they rose high out of the water and carried fore and aft castles. Each was equipped with twenty guns. Each was about 100 tons burden. Bartholomew Diaz had designed them from his experience, but Vasco da Gama, a gentleman of the royal court, commanded them.

With a small caravel and a store ship, they moved down the Tagus, the river of Lisbon, the wind filling their sails, on which were the large red crosses of the Order of Christ. They carried stores for three years. Before going on board the crews attended a solemn service of blessing and farewell in Lisbon cathedral. Now, as a throng of relatives and townsfolk, many in mourning, watched from the shore, the tiny fleet drew off into the ocean and towards its adventure. The king's standard flew from the *Gabriel's* masthead: trumpets were blown, flutes and drums sounded. On board, the officers stood arrayed in armor, among them the captain-general, Vasco da Gama, a man whose ancestors had fought against the Moors, and who himself had grown up by the sea, full of tales of the sea, and skilled in knowledge and experience of sea voyaging: a strong, firm-set man of ruddy visage: brave, determined, inflexible, and—to his enemies—cruel.

Slowly the ships moved to the limits of sight, and then sank below the western horizon on that summer day of July, 1497.

The first part of their voyage was the well-known run to Cape Verde and the Sierra Leone coast. Then there followed a wide sweep through the South Atlantic which brought them to South Africa, where they captured a Bushman—whom they clothed—and afterwards joined in dancing with some Hottentot savages. Later, they dropped anchor at a place they called Natal because it was Christmas Day, and there they beached and scraped their ships. There, also, some of the crews showed signs of the horrible disease of seafarers called scurvy.

Three months later, after sailing steadily up the coast northwards, they came to Mozambique, where da Gama's interpreters talked with Mohammedan Arabs. Here they saw flying fish and coconut palms. A month later they were off the fine harbor of Mombasa, where they defeated an Arab attempt to capture or wreck them. Next, they came to Malindi, where they saw Arab trading vessels from India, and got an Arab pilot to serve them. He guided them on a monsoon wind across the Indian Ocean to the Malabar Coast of India.

They anchored off Calicut in May, 1498, fourteen months after setting out from Lisbon. The Hindu ruler welcomed them, but the Arabs were hostile. "What have you come here for?" asked one of them. "In search of Christians and spices," replied a Portuguese. They stayed off Calicut for three months, during which they saw all the wealth and variety of an Indian trading town: the coconut palms and pepper vines, mangoes, bananas, and lemons; the peacocks and mongooses, parakeets and monkeys; the elephants at work; the market wares of copper and brass, swords and knives; silks and cottons; tortoise shell, ivory, emeralds, rubies; camphor, cinnamon, sandalwood, nutmeg; copra. And they mingled with the motley crowds of Hindus, Chinese, Negroes, Malays, Persians, Arabs. Vasco da Gama was carried in a palanquin. His seamen traded their own trifling goods for market keepsakes. At length da Gama weighed anchor and turned homeward, knowing two things very well: first, that a rich trade was possible with the Indian princes; and secondly that the Arabs who controlled the coastal markets were bitterly hostile to his Christian expedition.

The return took a year. A thunderstorm so damaged the *Raphael* that she had to be beached and burned. But the *Gabriel* rounded the Cape of Good Hope with a fair wind and made a good voyage to Guinea and the Tagus, in which river she cast anchor at last in August, 1499.

It had been an amazing voyage, the greatest ever made till then. Portugal had discovered a private way to the vast treasure house of the Orient. No wonder then that the Venetian ambassador at Lisbon sent the news posthaste to his masters in Venice; for the Venetians lived on the handsome profits of the spice trade with the Arabs of Egypt.

The next venture of the Portuguese in 1500 was one of thirteen ships. The third voyage in 1502 was of twenty ships, again under da Gama, who put to death every Arab he caught, and bombarded Calicut. A later Portuguese commander, D'Albuquerque, slaughtered 6,000 Mohammedans in Goa. So the soldiers of the Cross were revenging themselves on their enemies, without the mercy of the Cross. In this hard and cruel fashion did the Portuguese set up their power in the east, and in a short time their forts and trading stations reached as far away as China.

For over a hundred years the Portuguese had the east to themselves, lords of the Indian Ocean and the China Seas.

Sunset Islands and Strange Empires

These men of Portugal, and their rivals the merchants of Venice, lived in an age of marvels. Even before Vasco da Gama reached India the soldiers of Spain were streaming westward over the long Atlantic waters. They also sailed under the banners of the Cross.

The thing happened in this way. A Genoese pilot named Christopher Columbus was employed by the Portuguese in their Guinea trade. He was an experienced seaman who had also sailed north as far as Iceland. Moreover, he nourished a wild ambition: this was to sail to the west, not in search of any island of the sea, but to reach Cathay (China) and Zipangu (Japan) and the Spice Islands, to which places he could take the Gospel of Christ. He was quite sure it could be done, and asked the kings of Europe to help him with ships and men. The king of Portugal was too busy with his own eastern voyages. The English king, Henry VII, considered the matter. The monarch who did help him was Queen Isabella of Castile. She and her husband, Ferdinand of Aragon, were the rulers of Spain.

So, on August 3, 1492, Columbus sailed from Palos in Spain in the *Santa Maria* and two tinier ships with crews which included jailbirds forced to go on a venture which appalled most free mariners. On September 9, Columbus left the Canary Islands and made for the unknown west. By the twenty-first of that month his crew were mutinous with fear. The wind held steadily from the northeast and they saw no hope of a return. There was nothing in the world but the sea and the sky and the sound of their voices and the noise of the tackle. Their captain–pilot threatened them, reasoned with them, and deceived them about the distance they had already come.

By October 11, they were ready to murder him. Late that day land was sighted; and on the next day they went ashore. At last, Columbus thought, he had found a western sea route to Asia, and was even now standing on an island of Zipangu. In reality he was on one of the Bahamas, and the Indians who offered him gold and trinkets, cowering before him and his men as if they were gods, were Carib Indians. After exploring among the West Indian islands Columbus returned home, arriving back at Palos on March 15, 1493. His second voyage, six months later, was an armed expedition of 1,500 men in seventeen vessels. This was a crusade: the soldiers who had just driven the last of the Moslems from Spain were setting out to conquer and convert a new world. They settled the islands of Puerto Rico and Cuba. They forced the wretched natives to work in the gold mines; they baptized them; they hunted them with dogs if they ran away; they flogged them to death.

Columbus never knew that he had stumbled upon a new world. It was another Italian pilot named Amerigo Vespucci who first wrote of the "New World" he had seen: and men took to using the word "America"—meaning the land described by Amerigo.

What, then, had become of Cathay and the Spice Islands? The question was soon answered. From a mountaintop in Panama some Spaniards saw a new ocean flowing beyond the New World.

By now, however, the Portuguese had themselves discovered America. Running before the northeast trade winds and then tacking across the southeast ones, their pilots saw the coast of Brazil in 1500. A pilot from the Portuguese service who had visited the Spice Islands by sailing around the Cape now took service with the king and queen of Spain. He was Ferdinand Magellan. In 1519 he crossed the Atlantic to Brazil, sailed south, passed through the long straits that now bear his name, and entered that new ocean—the Pacific. He was killed by natives in the Philippine Islands, but his ship, the *Victoria*, held on to Borneo and the East Indies, and then round the Cape of Good Hope, and arrived home in 1522, with eighteen men left alive out of the 272 who had set out three years before. Magellan's feat of circumnavigation far surpassed the dreams of Columbus; not only was the western seaway to Asia revealed, but the great globe itself had been encompassed.

The soldiers and priests of Spain had found a new world of vast size, abounding in gold and silver. From the West Indian islands they sailed to the mainland. What they did there almost passes belief. They struggled through the deadly, fever-haunted swamps and across the forested mountains of Darien. In 1519 Ferdinand Cortés mastered the ancient empire of the Mexicans. He burned his boats after landing, and advanced inland with 600 men. With these he conquered the Aztecs who ruled the land, and he took their capital city, and hung the Cross of Christ in the high place of their temple where the Aztec priests had sacrificed human beings. The gold he captured, the treasure of the Aztecs, had been heaped up for over 700 years. This feat of arms was outdone by that of Francisco Pizarro, who, in 1531, with only 160 companions overthrew the mysterious empire of the Incas of Peru. These people had learned to build gigantic palaces of stone and to construct long roads without iron tools or even a knowledge of the wheel, and they used precious metals for common utensils, as we use iron or clay. Every detail of their lives was planned by their rulers, their lands rearranged each year, their food carefully shared out, even their marriages fixed on the appointed days. There was no want—and, until the Spaniards came, no excitement. To ransom their king from Pizarro they filled a room with bars of gold.

In Florida hundreds of Spanish soldiers perished in swamps and forests. Of one expedition of a thousand men only 300 survived after a four-year trek to Mexico. On another occasion one man alone reached the Pacific coast out of the 600 that set out, and he only did this by joining a tribe of Indians. In truth the Spanish soldiers searched all this huge continent for cities of gold and fountains whose waters would give men everlasting youth. Their simpleness seems childish to us now, but their endurance was heroic.

The work of the Spanish churchmen was no less heroic. Many of them did all they could to help the unfortunate natives. It was at their suggestion that African Negroes were brought in to work the sugar plantations—because the Negroes were a tougher race. The work of the churchmen is still written large and clear on our maps. If you look there you will read names like Vera Cruz (the True Cross), Trinidad (Trinity), San Salvador (the Holy Saviour), and dozens such. To many devout priests, monks, and nuns, the new world was a grand missionary field, and side by side with the cruelty and greed of the soldiers we find true Christian charity and kindness. The earliest accounts of the natives of the Indies and of the mainland come down to us from the patient study of Spanish monks.

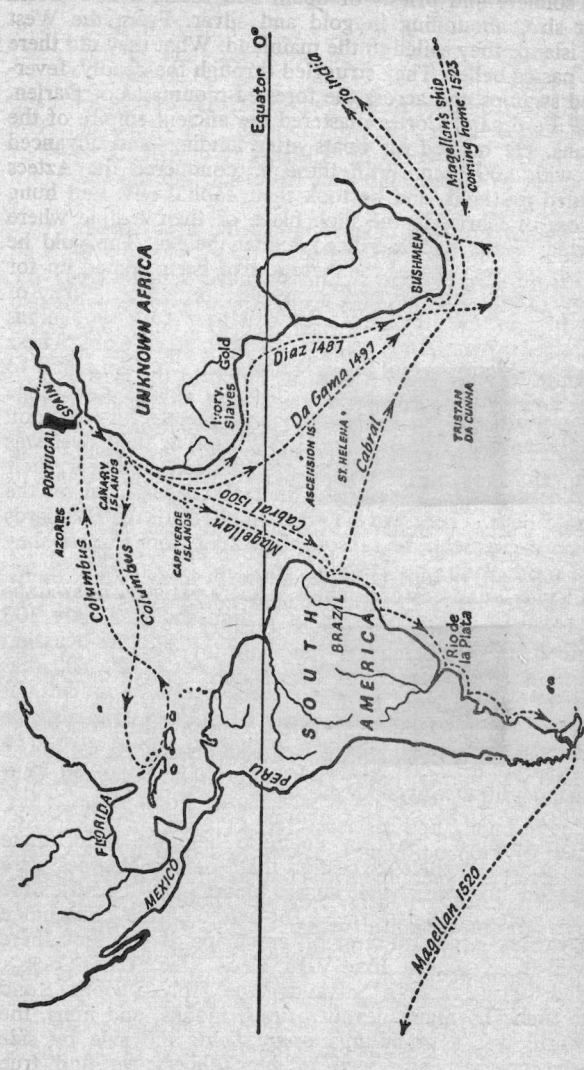

THE SPANIARDS AND PORTUGUESE DISCOVER THE SOUTHERN WAYS OUT OF THE ATLANTIC OCEAN: The northwestern and northeastern ways (or passages) are icebound

The World Enlarged

These were great changes, greater indeed in that single lifetime—1453 to 1530—than we could find in any other eighty years.

The Greek Christian Empire with its treasures of a thousand years has gone under the Mohammedan tide of victory. The Turk is in Europe, where he will stay in one of the loveliest cities on earth. Worse than this, his armies are on the banks of the Danube.

The men of Portugal have found their way by sea to Asia, and Lisbon grows rich on the spice trade. They have found the coast of Brazil. The Spaniards have sailed across the Atlantic, and their pathfinders are on the way to New Mexico and California. Their ships have sailed around the earth. The banners of the Cross wave over Peru and Mexico, over Portuguese forts in West Africa, in India, in the East Indies. Gold is flowing into Europe, Guinea gold and Spanish gold. Spices and muslins, dyes and silks, come to Europe by sea.

The ghastly slave trade in African Negroes has begun in the west. In the east the Mohammedans have been trading in Negroes for centuries.

Greeks, Turks, Venetians, Moors, Portuguese, Spaniards—these have played leading parts during these eighty years, with long-lasting results. Other events with long-lasting results were taking place in the Italian cities and in Germany, and we shall pass to these in the next chapter.

Meanwhile, in England a merchant of Venice lived in Bristol. His name was John Cabot and he had traded to Arabia for spices. Now he fitted out a ship at Bristol with a Bristol crew, and sailed westwards. He nourished much the same idea as Columbus, and like him he discovered a strange land. This was in 1497—the year of da Gama's voyage. Our forefathers could give it no special name. They called it the New-Found-Land, and so it still is. Thereafter, the hardy fishermen of England, Wales, Biscay, and Brittany took their small craft every year up to the shores of Newfoundland to bring back codfish, salted for Europe. Those nameless fishermen were the most skillful seamen in the world, working by day and night, in mist, icy wind, and tumultuous seas.

Africa circumnavigated: the Asiatic East revealed: a New World of America opened up: all in a lifetime! Only by reading old travelers' tales can we share at all in the astonishment of the pioneers as they saw the volcanoes of the Andes, the forest of the Appalachian Mountains, the mangrove swamps of Africa, the jungles and temples of India, the Burmese pagodas, the crowded, noisy Chinese towns, the silent spaces of the ocean. A thousand new sorts of rock, of animals, insects, fish, birds, and plants waited for the geologist, the zoologist, and botanist to study.

Somewhere, maybe, in idle tavern gossip in the ports, or on a lost chart, or kept fast secret in a king's cabinet, there was news of a still undiscovered continent. Let us call it (as the Portuguese did) "The Southern Land of the Holy Ghost" or "*Terra Australis.*" At least one Portuguese ship reached this last of continents to judge by the long brass guns she left on its northern coast.

So medieval Europe lost its frontiers. The deserts of the south and east had been outflanked by seamen, and the ocean of the west had been navigated by seamen.

The Seaways

Throughout the story that follows there is a new trade at work, the trade of the men that go down to the oceans in ships. Day and night, year in and year out, the ships and the men that man them and sing in them cross the oceans to America, Africa, India, China, and, at last, to Australia and the islands of the Pacific. Day in, day out, they carry the Old World to the New, and keep open the rich trade with the Far East. Civilization as we know it could not last without this unceasing labor and peril and loss of seamen. Like the toil of the farmers, it often goes unheeded because it is unseen by the multitudes of people in the great cities. Many, unhappily, have been the

> Drowned old wooden hookers green wi' drippin' wrack,
> Ships as never fetched to port, as never came back . . .

but ships and men have never been lacking to keep open the seaways.

The first exploration of the oceans was made possible by the discovery of the mariner's compass, and by a rig invented by unknown shipwrights between 1400 and 1500. The rig consisted of three masts carrying some half a dozen sails which skillful seamen could trim so as to beat up against contrary winds. They were no longer at the mercy of the winds. The compass was a needle–magnet swinging on a pivot above a marked card; its exact origin, like that of other medieval inventions—paper, gunpowder, arabic numerals, parliaments, printing—is unknown. Together with the *astro-*

labe, an instrument for finding latitude by taking the height of the sun and stars, it enabled a pilot to keep his course with reasonable accuracy in the open seas. For longitude, men had to make a rough calculation by reckoning their speed with the help of an hourglass. In the eighteenth century such a calculation was made more exact by using a ship's *chronometer* (a timekeeper, or "watch") and by using tables of nautical times and places made by astronomers.

Because of these inventions and the adventurers who used them, trade passed from the Mediterranean to the Atlantic, and later to the Pacific: and the nations of Europe spread their people, their way of living, their laws, their customs, their religions, and their wars, throughout the world.

4

THE REDISCOVERY OF ANCIENT KNOWLEDGE

Three Civilizations

What we call the Middle Ages were the centuries from the fifth to the fifteenth, from 500 A.D. to 1500 A.D. These are the centuries between the world of the ancient civilizations and our own times. They began with the breakdown of the Roman Empire in the west when the Caesars and their legions disappeared and cities decayed, and learning and crafts were forgotten. That was when the Franks and Goths, Burgundians and Saxons, entered the western half of the Roman Empire, and settled down in it under their kings and dukes.

The eastern half of the Roman Empire continued under the Greek-speaking emperors at Constantinople, the strong fortress and beautiful city built by Constantine at the entrance to the Black Sea, where Asia and Europe come closest together.

The Franks and Goths, Burgundians, Saxons, and other such folk from the great northern forests, became Christian, and did their best to imitate the civilization of ancient Rome. But very soon, far too soon, strong and skillful enemies seized all the lands of Asia Minor, Mesopotamia, Syria, Palestine, Egypt, North Africa, and Spain. These enemies of the Christian nations were the Mohammedan Arabs.

The great wars of the crusades were wars to recapture the lost lands, which were not only fertile and fair, but had been the homes of ancient learning and of the earliest Christian congregations. The flag of Mohammed flew over the places where Our Lord walked on earth, and where his disciples had preached the Gospel.

As we have seen, the Christians did recapture Spain after

long centuries of border warfare. And they did lodge their armies of knights in Syria and Palestine for a few years. But the crusades failed to drive the Moslems back: and in the fifteenth century the Christians lost Constantinople. With its loss the Roman Empire in the east vanished.

Throughout the Middle Ages then, there were three civilizations: the Greek Christian one centered at Constantinople; the western, or Latin, civilization of Italy, France, Spain, Portugal, Germany, and the British Isles; and the Arab, or Moslem, civilization ranging round the south of these others from Cordova in Spain to Bagdad on the Euphrates.

Below the three civilizations lay the ruins of the ancient world of pagan Greece and pagan Rome, forgotten, crumbling away. Whole cities had disappeared. Cyrene, in Roman Africa, after being blasted away by an earthquake, remained a mere tumbled ruin of broken marble columns and shattered walls. Other towns in Africa were hidden under the blown sands of the desert. In England, only the rabbit and mole could visit the foundations of Silchester, the city of the Atrebates, left desolate and buried by drifting earth and rotting vegetation. Some bridges remained, and the long straight roads, falling into decay, and founderous from winter floods. There were the stupendous remains of huge aqueducts like the Pont du Gard in France, striding across the country; deserted, grass-grown amphitheaters; triumphal arches with sculptured walls; forts and castles in the frontiers of the Rhineland forests or along the Great Wall of Hadrian on the high moors of Northumbria. The city gates of York and Lincoln, the walls of London, the three-storied "Black Gate" of Trier where once lived the Roman governor of Britain—these and hundreds of other monuments might remind men of the engineering skill of the Romans, even if they were only used as quarries for building stone or for making lime. Often the peasant gazing at the walls of Richborough or Caister with wondering eyes imagined them to be the works of giants! The plowboy turned up a bronze brooch or a pot of coins, the gravedigger discovered a pavement of colored stones—and his children had them to play with!

Besides all these broken relics and ruins there were other remains of far greater importance, but equally neglected. In the libraries and cellars and vaults of monasteries and churches old books and manuscripts lay moldering. The papyrus ones perished entirely, as paper will. The parchment ones were forgotten. These books were the writings and records of the Greeks and Romans—histories, poems, plays, letters, speeches, books of travel, science, mathematics, engineering and agriculture.

THE REDISCOVERY OF ANCIENT KNOWLEDGE 133

The only books cared for by the Christian scholars of the west were the Bible and religious writings of the Church Fathers like St. Augustine, and university teachers like St. Thomas Aquinas. Why should any man bother himself with the books of heathen Greeks and Romans? St. Augustine himself, who had lived when the old pagan books were plentiful, said that the only book needed by Christians was the Bible.

The Moslem Arabs had, of course, no use for Latin or Greek, or for any books save their own sacred one, the Koran, which held the teaching of Mohammed. Nevertheless, there were among them keen and curious scholars who studied astronomy, medicine, and mathematics, and who knew something of the works of the Greeks; and who had had handed down to them the wisdom of the Magi of the East—the knowledge of the stargazers of Chaldea and the knowledge of numbers from the wise men of ancient India. From such clever Arabic scholars the men of the West came to know a little of the teaching of Aristotle, the Greek tutor of Alexander three hundred years before Christ. Aristotle's many books summed up much of the knowledge of the old world. But a Christian scholar who read a Latin translation of an Arabic translation of Aristotle's Greek writings was by no means reading exactly what Aristotle wrote!

As for the history of the ancient world, to the men of the Middle Ages it was a glorious jumble of tales of heroes and emperors, all far-fetched happenings and magic.

Such was the state of things in the west during the Middle Ages.

The country folk everywhere labored with their oxen on the strips of grainland. The craftsmen of the towns gathered themselves into guilds for work and worship and charity to one another. The landowners or knights were the armed horsemen who swore faith to their kings and princes and followed them in battle, going on crusade or fighting among themselves. Merchants ventured on land and sea buying and selling their wool and woven cloth, and wine and hides. The world was a small one for them. The ocean closed them in on the west, the dark forest in the north. Only the Arabs could guess what lay over the deserts of the south. Only a few travelers passed into remote Asia along the spice and silk roads.

Over all men and amidst all was the Christian Church with its marvelous cathedrals, its great monasteries, its learned (and ignorant) clergy, its monks, its friars, its law courts and taxes, its many universities formed for the study of the things of God and the purpose of God's creation.

Of the wisdom and learning and craftsmanship of the

ancient world of the Greeks there was practically nothing known in the west. In Constantinople men spoke Greek, not as the ancients had done, but with some changes of sound and words. In Constantinople a few scholars did know and study the ancient speech, which was also used by the nobly born ladies of the emperor's court. And in Constantinople there was a multitude of old books. The Christians there, of the Greek Church, however, were just as indifferent to the old writings as those of the Latin or western Church, and there was not much love lost between the two groups of Christians.

On such a slender thread hung the chance of keeping in existence the records of the ancients.

Such was the position in the fifteenth century when the Portuguese were sailing into the southern hemisphere along the mysterious shores of Africa; when the Mohammedan Turks under Mohammed II stormed into Constantinople; and when Columbus took his frightened crew into the Caribbean Sea.

The Search Begins

When at last towns began to grow rich by trade; when men had learned to build in stone and make beautiful work in iron and wood, to weave lovely tapestries, to build ships of size; when life had become a little safer, a little less hard and toilsome, less watchful for savage enemies, more lawful; then did a few scholars begin to take an interest in old books, old coins, vases, and statues left by the ancients.

This was in Italy, the land where the old civilization had flourished most, where its remains were most clearly to be seen. The cities of Italy were the first to grow fair and rich in trade, cities like Florence, Bologna, Padua, Venice, Perugia, Milan, and great Rome itself. The Italian craftsmen were amazingly skillful in all types of work (as they still are): and they strove to outdo one another in the excellence of their craft. In the fifteenth century they were fast approaching the finest work done of old by the Greeks and Romans: and it was natural that they should begin to admire the relics of the past with a craftsman's delight.

One of the first men to begin the quest for the lost treasures of antiquity was Petrarch, who lived in the fourteenth century (1307–1374). He wrote poems in Italian and was therefore interested in words and their use. He tried to write Latin as Cicero, the great Roman statesman, had written it. And this

The Rediscovery of Ancient Knowledge

led him to Greek. Cicero himself had declared that, "In learning and in every branch of literature the Greeks are our masters"; for Cicero, like all educated Romans, knew Greek. So, in imitating Cicero, Petrarch was led to the Greeks. He traveled in Italy and France, and went to Greece and even to North Africa to look for books and coins and inscriptions. He was trying to discover that lost world of beauty and learning which had been hidden for centuries. One of his grandest treasures was a book he could not read—Homer's Greek poems on the fall of Troy and the wanderings of Ulysses. "The memory of the great deeds, even the very names of the ancient Greeks and Romans, fill me with delight." This he said: and this was true of those who followed him.

They were many: monks, scholars, priests, bishops, popes, artists, merchants, bankers, and dukes in all the cities of Italy.

When a Greek from Constantinople named Manuel Chrysoloras settled in Florence and began teaching Greek, crowds of people thronged to his lectures. One student of law who attended them made this excuse to himself for neglecting his own law studies: "Wilt thou refuse to be taught about Homer, Plato, and Demosthenes; about all those poets and writers of whom such wonders are related?" Other Greek scholars followed Chrysoloras, many of them glad to leave Constantinople, which was threatened by the Turks. They came with their books, Greek books. One of them brought 238 volumes! Rich merchants of Florence and Venice sent agents to Constantinople to buy Greek books there. Pope Nicholas V began collecting the great library which is still housed in the Vatican where the popes live, and gathered together no fewer than 5,000 books.

Just before the capture of Constantinople in 1453, a large number of Greeks fled into Italy. Even after the capture of the city there still remained many books in its libraries: and even a hundred years after a German ambassador to the Turkish sultan boasted that he had begged and bought whole wagonloads of Greek books and parchments ready for shipping to Venice.

The search for ancient books was now carried on everywhere. The lost works of many ancient authors were found in single copies, and brought to princes or bishops or merchants who paid handsomely for them.

The Renaissance

The Greeks were the wisest of the ancients. It is no wonder that their wisdom took captive the men of the fifteenth century. Because Plato, the Greek philosopher who wrote about Socrates—the wisest man in Athens—had once taught his pupils in a garden called the Academy, men founded "academies" in the Italian cities where lovers of learning might meet together. The writings of Plato were treasured like religious books. Pico della Mirandola burned a lamp before a shrine which he had dedicated to Plato. Even Erasmus, the Dutch scholar, a more level-headed man, asked "Saint Socrates" to pray for him. One cardinal of the Church advised his friends not to read the Latin Bible because its style was bad compared with the lofty Latin used by Cicero. Another cardinal said that no one could understand the Gospels without reading the works of the Greek Aristotle.

This "new" learning was, in fact, the rediscovered learning of ancient Greece: it was a "renaissance," which means a rebirth. And *Renaissance* is the name that historians have given to that time. It was at its height in the city of Florence under the rule of Lorenzo de' Medici from 1469 to 1492; and in Rome under his son, Pope Leo X, from 1513 to 1521. But for half a century bishops, nobles, and merchants in all the cities were its patrons.

It did not begin and end with books. The ruins of Rome were ransacked for inscriptions and statues. The sculptor Donatello actually disguised himself as a laborer and wandered about with pick and shovel to unearth ancient masterpieces, but found none; and was soon forced to earn his living as a goldsmith. When the famous statue of Laocoön was found buried near Rome, its excavation was carried out by the great artist Michelangelo, and its transport through the city was like the procession of a conqueror. The streets were gay with flags, bells were rung and cannons fired, while the crowd cheered and threw flowers. Coins, medals, bronze urns, vases, figurines, came in shiploads from the Greek islands to Venice where they fetched high prices from collectors. Artists who decorated the walls of the churches and houses thought nothing of introducing the pagan gods into their pictures of scenes from the Bible! and of course, being in Italy, men prided themselves as descendants of the ancient Romans. Some wore togas like old Roman senators. One pope claimed with a boast that he was descended from the Emperor Nero.

Apart from all the excitement and odd behavior of some people, a great deal of real hard work was done. Many scholars spent long lives in the study of Greek grammar and the understanding of the Greek poems and plays and histories. We owe much to their patient work which made all later study possible. And besides this scholarship and learning there were in Renaissance Italy an astonishing number of great artists.

Michelangelo could carve huge blocks of marble swiftly and accurately into the most wonderful statuary the world has ever seen. Leonardo da Vinci would wander the streets for hours looking for "faces" as subjects for his brush. He painted pictures of matchless beauty. Both these artists were many-sided in their genius. Michelangelo was also a poet and an engineer. Leonardo studied music and mathematics, and designed flying machines and quick-firing guns. His life reminds us of Plato's words: "The man who follows wisdom ought not to love one kind of labor but all kinds."

The Renaissance widened men's interest in all that men have done and can do. Their studies were in human beings: and they were therefore called *humanists*.

The first great years of the Renaissance were in Italy. But it spread to the other lands of western Europe, and scholars elsewhere became "Grecians" and humanists, in France, in Holland, in Germany. The feet of Englishmen had often trodden the long roads to Florence and Bologna and Padua in the past centuries when they wandered as students singing their Latin songs. Now they journeyed as torchbearers of the new learning, visiting Italy to bring home to England the reborn wisdom of the ancient Greeks. Among them was Thomas Linacre, the founder of the Royal College of Physicians, and John Colet, who founded St. Paul's School in London. It was not long before Greek was being taught at Oxford and Cambridge.

Books were multiplied. Rich collectors paid scriveners to write out the works of Plato and Aristotle and the rest. The humanist discoverers of so much forgotten learning did not intend that it should be lost again. But we should still be copying all our books by hand but for a man named Johan Gutenberg, who lived in the German city of Mainz.

Printing

Gutenberg invented his printing press about 1450. Before his day, men had for a long time known how to print—that is, make an impression—on wax or clay with a carved seal. And they had begun to cut pictures and letters on blocks of wood, to smear the blocks with ink, and make simple printed pictures by pressing them onto pieces of paper. The sort of paper we know, not papyrus.

Papermaking had been going on for some time. It was learned by our ancestors from the Arabs who may have got it from the Far East; and its manufacture was at once a simple and a highly skilled job. Rags of cotton cloth were cut up and teased into shreds, then made into a liquid pulp like thick milk, whitened, and poured out on to trays to dry into thin white films—of paper. Gutenberg printed his books on paper.

The point of his invention was that he made movable "type" of metal which could be arranged in words, lines and pages, held tightly in a frame, and then inked over so that sheet after sheet of paper could be pressed down on it.

We are so used to printed books that we cannot imagine the world without them, nor without paper. When Cosimo de' Medici of Florence made his library he ordered books from his bookseller, who thereupon employed 45 scribes to copy 200 different books by hand. It took them 22 months. The Englishman Sir John Paston paid his scrivener two pence for copying one leaf of a parchment manuscript. The best handwriting in jet black ink on ivory parchment is much more beautiful to look at than print; and, in fact, many of the early printed books were ugly. One Italian nobleman refused to have a printed book in his library. He went on paying a large staff of copyists to make his books.

What a grand chance the first printers had—all the books in the world were waiting for them! Within fifty years the invention had been set up in all the western countries, and the books were no longer crude. New and clear and well-designed type was in use. Gutenberg had printed a Latin Bible. In Italy, Aldus of Venice printed a great series of Greek and Latin classics. The early printers were themselves writers and scholars.

William Caxton, an English woolen merchant living in Bruges, learned there how to print, and brought his press to England. He set it up at the Sign of the Red Pale by Westminster Abbey, where he worked with astonishing industry. The first book printed by him here can be described by its own colophon or last words:—

Here endeth the Book named the Dictes and Sayings of the Philosophers, emprinted by me, William Caxton, at Westminster, the year of Our Lord MCCCCLXXVII [that is, 1477]. Which book is late translated out of the French into English by the Noble and puissant lord, Lord Anthony, Earl of Rivers.

Caxton's many books included *The Golden Legend of the Saints,* and Chaucer's *Canterbury Tales.*

Printed books increased the desire for booklearning and made men eager to gain the knowledge that can come from books. The printing presses enabled many scholars to read the works of the Greeks and Romans who would otherwise not have seen them. Printing, in fact, was the invention that not only preserved the old writings but also made possible the spread of new knowledge, as it was gained, throughout the world.

Paper and print came along just in time to save what remained of the wisdom of the Greeks. And since the first printers printed many books in English, French, German, and Italian, men began to study their own languages as well as Latin and Greek. And they began to write books in their own languages more and more, although scholars continued to use Latin as a sort of international language.

Earth and Heaven

Most men believed the earth to be flat. Learned men, however, had for a long time believed that the earth was a globe, around which the sun circled. The Italian poet Dante, in his wonderful poem of the *Divine Comedy,* had pictured Hell as a nine-circled pit under the earth; Purgatory as a steep mountain rising out of the southern seas; and Paradise as a place beyond the nine moving spheres of the sky. These spheres were like transparent globes that turned round one inside the other.

Nearly all scholars thought that the sun went around the earth. But there were a few who believed that the earth went around the sun. One of the old Greek philosophers had thought this. Leonardo da Vinci thought that the earth was a star like other stars. The man who proved that the earth revolved around the sun, and turned around and around as it went on its path, was Nicholas Copernicus, a Pole who was a Catholic priest and studied in the universities of Cracow, Bologna, and Padua. He wrote a book about it after studying mathematics and astronomy.

Very slowly his ideas became known. Other men carried on his work and proved him to be right, and began mapping the universe of planets and stars.

It may well be said that the sailors, the scholars, the artists, and the scientists of the Renaissance gave men a new earth, a new learning, a new sense of beauty, and a new heaven.

5

THE GREAT KINGDOMS OF THE WEST AND THE NEW WORLD OF AMERICA

Principalities and Powers

The characters in this part of the story are kingdoms and states; and the three great kingdoms of the west were Spain, France, and England—which became Great Britain in 1603 when King James of Scotland succeeded to the throne of Elizabeth I of England. These three kingdoms had long ocean coasts, and they strove against each other for trade and overseas possessions. They were the kingdoms that gained most in wealth from the discovery of America and from the opening up of trade with Africa, India, and the Far East.

Two smaller states were also busy with trade and colonies: the kingdom of Portugal and the republic of Holland, both on the coasts of Europe.

Inside Europe, with no ocean coasts, were the powerful dominions of the Austrians and the Turks—both containing many races of men.

The rulers of Austria, which is itself a very small place, wore the ancient crown of the Holy Roman Empire because they inherited the pomp and powers and majesty of the emperors of the Middle Ages, who themselves pretended to be the Christian successors of the Roman emperors of the ancient world. The Austrian Holy Roman Emperors were overlords of the multitude of kingdoms, dukedoms, counties, cities, and bishoprics of Germany, but found it hard to keep them in order. Strong German states like Bavaria, Saxony, and Württemburg did more or less as they pleased. Nevertheless, the Holy Roman Emperor did possess a legal authority over them. Besides being the traditional rulers of the Germans, the emperors were also kings of Hungary, where the Magyars lived, and, in consequence, had the task of defending Europe from the Mohammedan Turks. They also ruled over the Bohemians, whom we now know as Czechs.

The sultans of Turkey tried to control a huge empire stretching from the River Danube to the Euphrates and the Nile, founded upon the manifold ruins of ancient civilizations, and now moldering away to desert and waste.

Eastward, spread over the great European plains, were the Prussians, a borderland race of hardy knights and landowners, nurtured in warfare—like the Welsh marcher-lords of the Middle Ages in this island; and beyond the Prussians were the gallant, Catholic Poles under their own king. Farther off, a very long way farther off, was the kingdom of Muscovy around Moscow, which was the beginning of modern Russia. Our own merchants began to trade with the Muscovites after two adventurers, Willoughby and Chancellor, had sailed into the White Sea, whence Chancellor journeyed overland to the colorful court of Ivan the Terrible.

Italy remained a land where each city looked after its own fortunes; where men regarded themselves not as Italians but as Romans or Venetians or Florentines or Genoese. The midmost part of the peninsula was ruled by officers of the popes.

We have called these nations and kingdoms "characters" as though we were writing a play. We might go on to say that the play had two main scenes: the first, Europe, where kings fought for power and lands—Austria against the Turk, Austria against France, France against Spain, Britain against France, and so on; and the second scene, the oceans and the New World, where Spain, France, and Britain strove for trade and colonies.

The kingdom which took the leading part in *both* scenes was France. France was a sort of pivot on which the fortunes of the western world turned. The French had been the leaders of the Christian nations against the Mohammedans in the crusades—so much so that, to the Arab and the Turk, any westerner was a "Frank." The French remained the leaders of western civilization in modern times. In the seventeenth century French manners, French fashions, French literature, French learning, were models for all Europe to copy. French was the language in which nations spoke to one another, the language of ambassadors and of peace treaties —right down to our own century. It was the polite and civilized tongue even of the German courts and of the Russian noblemen. To imitate the dress and manners of the French was the mark of an educated and polished man.

Many Churches in Place of One

When Columbus first sailed to America, in a Spanish ship, the rulers of Spain were Ferdinand of Aragon and Isabella of Castile. By their marriage these two united Spain into one kingdom, made powerful and rich by American gold. By the fortunes of other marriages, their grandson, Charles V, inherited not only Spain and the Spanish possessions in America, but also the crown of the Holy Roman Empire. He ruled over Austria and Hungary, and the German states (including what we call Belgium and Holland), and Spain, and Spanish America. No king had ever been in such a powerful position—or such a difficult one. Trying to rule Spain and all the Empire at once was far from easy even in ordinary times. Unhappily for Charles V, who was a fair-minded man, it was during his reign and in his dominions that a revolt took place against the teachings of the Church. Because he was emperor he was the natural protector of the Church.

The Greek word *schism* means a separation or a split, and is used in talking of religion. The great schism of the sixteenth century, known as the Reformation, was the work mainly of two remarkable men: Martin Luther and John Calvin.

The state of the Church was bad. There were far too many slack clergy and too many easygoing monks. Too many churchmen in high places were only interested in getting lands and money for themselves and their relatives. Good men everywhere wanted to see the Church made better, and some small reforms were made here and there. In Spain the clergy were ruled strictly. In Italy groups of pious men set good examples of the Christian life by prayer and almsgiving and visiting the poor and sick. In England a few decayed monasteries were turned into schools. But the chief trouble was in Rome itself. The popes were not always all they should be. Some of them were just like ordinary princes heaping up treasure for themselves, their nephews—and, in some cases, their children. Some were scholars—good scholars, maybe, but bad churchmen. But of course, if the popes and the Church were not as good as they should be, the princes and noblemen of Europe were equally bad. Lots of people had grown careless and, as we say, worldly. Not so very long before the time of Charles V there had actually been two rival popes, one in France and one in Rome. This sorry state of affairs had been ended by councils of churchmen, and, if anything, the Church was getting a little better. Still, it was bad enough to worry good men like Sir Thomas

More, the great lord chancellor of England, and his friend Erasmus, the Dutchman who was one of the greatest scholars of the time.

Long, long, ago the Church had made all the races who settled in the lands of the old Roman Empire feel they were members of one great Christian society in spite of their different languages and kings. Now men began to feel otherwise. A man of Venice had once said, "Let us be Venetians first and Christians afterwards." Now the time was near when men might say, "Let us be Frenchmen, or Germans, or Englishmen first, and Christians afterwards." They were thinking more of being patriots than of being Christians.

Even if this had not been so, and even if the Church had been in a good state, there would still have been arguments and squabbles over religion; for the invention of printing gave the Bible to all men to read. The Bible is not an easy book to understand, and different men find different meanings in its teaching.

This, then, was the position when Charles V was doing his best to rule half Europe.

Martin Luther, the son of a German miner, was born at Eisleben in 1483. Being a clever boy he was given an education in grammar along with a great deal of whipping to keep him at his books—and at the age of eighteen he entered the University of Erfurt, where he took his M.A. degree in 1505, and became a priest. He then became a teacher at the new University of Wittenberg, where his earnestness and mastery of language drew men's attention to him. He was devout and devoted to the Church.

Two events altered his life, and in consequence the lives of millions of other people. First, he made a journey to Rome in 1511, and was dismayed at the shocking want of piety and decency there among the swarms of clergy. Secondly, he quarrelled with a friar named John Tetzel.

Tetzel traveled about selling pardons to make money for the pope—just like Chaucer's Pardoner. A man truly sorry for his sins would never mind giving money to the Church; but these pardons were offered for sale to all and sundry like cheap medicines or pies. You paid your coin and received forgiveness for your misdeeds. The idea was good; the way it was carried out was bad. Tetzel beat a drum to draw a crowd. "God willing," said Luther, "I will beat a hole in his drum." What he did was to write down 95 statements or *theses* against this trade in pardons, and nail the parchments to the church door—the usual place for public notices, as it often is now. This began a fierce argument. And many men took Luther's part.

The Great Kingdoms of the West

Luther was clever and honest. For a long time he was worried by doubts and fears, until he came on the text, "The just man shall live by faith alone." This was like a great light shining in his darkness. What need was there, he thought, for these pardons, for sacred relics of the saints, for pilgrimages, for pomp and show, for the great wealth of the clergy? In 1520 he made an address to the noblemen of Germany in which he attacked the pope's claim to be head of the Church. "Every Christian man," he said "can know and judge of his own religion," and so there was no need of priests to stand between God and men, because men could be guided by their own Bibles and their own consciences.

This was defiance of the pope, and therefore of the emperor. In 1521 Luther was ordered to attend a "Diet," or meeting of the Emperor's Council, at Worms, to answer for his conduct. Standing before Charles V and the nobles and bishops of the Holy Roman Empire in all their pomp and majesty, he refused to take back one word of what he said. He had superb courage. He expected imprisonment and death—and death by burning. He was, however, made an outlaw—that is, left for anyone to kill; but he found refuge in the castle of the ruler of Saxony, a nobleman who liked him, and who was too strong to fear Charles V. In this castle Luther began his grand translation of the Latin Bible into German, which is now one of the treasures of German literature. Luther was a poet, a master of language, and his Bible made hundreds of men believe in his teachings.

Luther's ideas continued to spread in Germany and Holland and into England. But he was not a leader to organize a new church. There were, by now, many others who preached against Rome and the popes. Among them, standing out above all, was John Calvin.

He was a much younger man than Luther, being born in 1509, the son of a French lawyer, and trained to become a lawyer himself. The study of law makes a man's wits sharp and keen. Calvin was still a young man when he published in 1536 *The Institutes of the Christian Religion*, an extraordinary book which laid down a full scheme of church government and belief. This became the strong foundation of a new Calvinistic church, one ruled by pastors and elders, a severe and very strict church, far stricter than the old one of Rome. The Calvinist congregations believed that they were the chosen people of God. When the Catholics—as the men of the old Church were now called—persecuted them, they persecuted the Catholics. It was all rather cruel and dreadful, but when men begin taking sides they often grow to hate each other without reason.

For many years John Calvin ruled his own church in Geneva, whence scores of pastors went out to spread his teachings. In France they were known as Huguenots, in England, as Presbyterians.

The popes and their clergy might hope to win back some of the Lutherans to the old religion someday. But only swords and guns could prevail against Calvinists: and they could use swords and guns themselves, as the Catholics found.

The popes of Rome and the Calvinists of Geneva were bitter enemies.

The result of all this was that a large part of the German people, and of the Dutch, became Lutherans, and still are. A large number of Frenchmen became Calvinists or Huguenots. In both Germany and France there were fierce wars between Catholics and Protestants—wars which only made each party more bitter against the other.

The pity of it was that there were good, true, and pious men among both; and that what sort of Christian teaching a man believed became mixed up with what nation or kingdom he belonged to. Just at the very moment when the men of Europe were going out to meet the natives of America and Africa and Asia for the first time, instead of going out as fellow Christians they went out as different sorts of Christians who hated one another.

"Bluff King Hal"

Henry VII of England, a "prince sad and serious and full of thoughts," who was reigning when Columbus discovered America, lifted his kingdom out of the baronial riots and battles of the Wars of the Roses to peace and prosperity. For twenty-four years Englishmen enjoyed his firm and merciful rule. He checked the power of the barons, and encouraged the merchants' trading abroad; and by thrift he left the royal treasury full when he died—a most unusual thing for any king to do. When this gray-eyed, reserved, and cautious monarch died, his son succeeded him as Henry VIII, 1509.

The new king was eighteen, and gay and handsome, fond of tennis, hawking, and archery, a keen musician, and something of a scholar. He liked pleasure and good company, and was hearty and good-natured unless thwarted: and for eighteen years his court was merry with feasts, tournaments, banquets, masked dances, and revels by torchlight and candlelight at Richmond and Greenwich. Henry had a faithful and wise servant in Cardinal Wolsey, his lord chancellor. Wolsey, indeed, was one of the last great princes of the

Catholic Church in England, with five hundred persons in his household, gentlemen and lords as well as yeomen and grooms. When he spoke, under the king's favor, his voice was the voice of England. As lord chancellor he was the "keeper of the king's conscience"; as cardinal he might hope to become pope some day. Yet he had started life as the son of an Ipswich tradesman. No subject of any English king ever lived more sumptuously, nor toiled harder at his master's business.

Henry was deeply attached to the Church. He wrote a book denouncing Martin Luther and his teachings. He had no use for rebels of any kind. Yet it was not long before he himself was denouncing the pope.

His queen was a Spanish princess, Catherine of Aragon, and their only child, Mary, was the delight of his eye; but he did want a son to succeed him, and he did fall violently in love with Anne Boleyn, a lady of the court. When, however, he asked the pope to grant him a divorce, and the pope refused, Henry renounced the pope's authority. He would allow no matter of conscience or policy to stand in his way once he had made up his mind; and from being a good-natured companion he soon became a willful tyrant. He made himself head of the Church, arranged his own divorce, and married Anne, packing poor Catherine and Mary off to live in poverty in the country. The new queen bore him a daughter, Elizabeth, and was soon afterwards beheaded at Henry's orders on a charge of making love to other men.

These events brought disgrace and death to many men. Wolsey was dismissed and arrested and died of grief. The devout friars of Greenwich and the Carthusian monks of the London Charterhouse, who opposed the divorce, were flung into the Tower dungeons where they rotted to death. Sir Thomas More, the wisest counselor of his time and the noblest of men, was beheaded for not changing his lifelong loyalty to the Church. The saintly Bishop Fisher of Rochester was likewise executed. Thomas Cromwell, an ambitious adventurer who had once served in Wolsey's household, was given power to seize all the monasteries, with their money, treasures, and lands. This he did, and sold them for the king's profit. Some abbots were hanged. Most of the monks were treated fairly. But when the men of the northern counties rebelled against this wanton destruction of their ancient religious houses, Henry put them down with merciless severity. The king's wishes were law; he who opposes the royal will is a rebel; and rebels deserve death. It was all as simple as that!

All this suffering and upset came from the king's desire

for a divorce, and from his spoiled and imperious nature, which, as Wolsey had noted, would allow nothing to stand in the way of his desires. In fact, Henry was singularly unlucky in his matrimonial adventures after he had packed Catherine off to the country in disgrace, and beheaded Anne Boleyn. He married four more times. His next wife died in giving birth to a weak boy—the much-longed-for son and heir, Edward; the fourth wife, a German Protestant princess, turned out to be rather plain, and was at once pensioned off; the fifth, known to everyone else as a flighty girl, captivated Henry by her youth and charm, and was soon beheaded for making love to other men; and the sixth, a widow, looked after him and outlived him. Henry does not appear such a majestic or wise man considered as a husband. When he died he left a queerly assorted family of three children by different mothers—Princess Mary, a Catholic; and Princess Elizabeth and Prince Edward, both brought up as Protestants. Henry was never a Protestant. He still hated Luther and all his works. He was just Henry, making his own decisions about religion. He punished Protestants for denying the truth of the Catholic faith, and punished Catholics for denying that he was head of the Church. Only Henry was right. What the mass of Englishmen thought we cannot know: most of them kept a wise silence. The most striking thing about Henry's quarrel with the pope was its timing. It happened when the Protestant teachings of Luther were gaining converts in Cambridge and elsewhere, and it helped to make more difficult any reconciling of the old and new forms of worship and belief.

In the short reign of the boy King Edward VI, who was guided by Protestant noblemen, the Lutheran teachings spread more widely; and there was further plundering of the churches, tearing down of rood screens, seizing of plate and vestments, burning of old books, and a general destruction of good handiwork in wood and stone. Some men became rich; a few schools were founded; the wealth taken was not given to the new Protestant church. Generally speaking the poor suffered, as they did when the same lords who plundered the churches robbed the small farmers of their lands to make sheep runs—lords described shortly by one nobleman as "men sprung from the dunghill."

When the devout Catholic princess Mary Tudor succeeded Edward in 1553, the people acclaimed her joyfully. She had been brought up in the Old Church (which was hardly a fault in her) and she was a real royal princess, daughter of the popular Catherine of Aragon. But her young life had been blasted by her father's cruelty. She who might have been a happy and gracious queen, had been spurned, impoverished, even threatened, for over twenty years. She did not increase her popularity when she married Philip of Spain in Winchester Cathedral; nor when she ordered the persecution of scores of Protestants who were burned at the stake. She was, indeed, a gentle and kind-hearted woman in all affairs save in this matter of burning Protestants: and there is no doubt that her persecution did much to make the Catholic cause thoroughly disliked. When she died, childless, in 1558, Elizabeth, her sister, succeeded her.

Elizabeth I was the daughter of that Anne Boleyn for whose love Henry had broken with the pope. She took up her father's position as head of the Church in England, and she reissued her brother Edward's Prayer Book for all her subjects to use. Under her, England was officially a Protestant land. But she was something more than a Protestant queen. Like her grandfather Henry VII, she proved to be "a wonder for wise men." She ruled for forty-five years amid perils and plots, and by her force of character she made her reign legendary.

Bibles for Plowmen

Out of this turmoil when mean-minded men were hacking away the carved stone and woodwork, and plundering shrines, destroying what they would never have the skill to replace, there came two of the noblest books ever written in the English language.

The Prayer Book was largely the work of Thomas Cranmer, whom Henry VIII made Archbishop of Canterbury. Many of the prayers were translated from old Catholic ones in use at Salisbury, but only a master of words could have put them into such memorable sentences:

O God, from whom all holy desires, all good counsels, and all just works do proceed; Give unto thy servants that peace which the world cannot give; that both our hearts may be set to obey thy commandments, and also that by thee we being defended from the fear of our enemies may pass our time in rest and quietness.

Poor Cranmer was burned at the stake at Oxford by Mary Tudor; for he was not only a Protestant but had, at Henry's command, divorced her mother. Cranmer had this magical gift of phrase—a gift which has caused his prayers to sound ever since in all places where English is spoken.

And wherever English is spoken men treasure the English

Bible. In its final version it was made in 1611 by a number of learned Greek and Hebrew scholars and issued as King James's Bible. Most of these scholars were old men who had listened to the Latin of the old Bible, and who were brought up on the magnificent simplicity of early Tudor English. Their translation, indeed, rested largely on the work of William Tyndal, who, in the reign of Henry VIII, had set himself to make a version that every plowboy could read. This is his rendering of Isaiah, Chapter 35:

But the wyldernes shall rejoyse, the waste grounde shalbe gladde, and floorysh as the lylye. She shal floorysh pleasauntlye, and be joyful, and ever be geving of thankes more and more. For the glory of Libanus, the beuty of Charmel and Saron shal be geven her. These shal knowe the honoure of the Lorde, and the majestye of our God. And therfore strengthen the weake handes, and comforte the feable knees.

Say unto them that are of a fearful hert: be of good chere and fear not. Behold your God commeth to take vengeaunce and to rewarde. God commeth hys own self, and wyl delyver you. Then shal the eyes of the blynde be lightened, and the eare of the deaf opened. Then shal the lame man leape as an harte, and the domme mans tounge shal geve thankes.

This is Tyndal. The 1611 version is in all our hands today, and can be compared with this. Tyndal had to escape secretly to the Low Countries to carry on his work unmolested by the king's officers—although Henry VIII afterwards issued an English Bible for his subjects to use. Tyndal suffered death for his Protestant faith, being strangled and burned in 1536 by orders of the Emperor, Charles V.

What the Bible has done for the English language is beyond the power of any man to express. Its words and phrases have become part of our speech. Into no other language has the vivid, pictorial quality of the Hebrew and the simple clarity of the Greek been so skillfully carried over. For multitudes it has been the only book worth reading. For many it became their history and geography as well as their religion. They absorbed the history of the Jews as if it had been the record of their own heathen ancestors.

The Century of Spain

In the sixteenth century the greatest power in the world was Spain. Her history had been strangely unlike that of the other western lands. Like them she had formed part of the

THE GREAT KINGDOMS OF THE WEST

Roman Empire; but long before that her mines and fields and ports had been worked by the Carthaginians from Africa; and after the downfall of Rome she had been conquered by Mohammedan Arabs and Moors from Africa. For centuries most of the country lay under this alien rule, cut off from the mainstream of Christendom until the Christian kings and knights of the north and northwest began their long war which ended in the final victory of Granada.

Now, Spain was growing richer and richer on the gold and silver of America. This she owed to the heroic voyage of Columbus. And while her stately galleons each year were blown homeward by the trade winds across the Atlantic, her viceroys governed the Netherlands with the help of the famous, well-drilled Spanish infantry; for through the lucky chances of royal marriages Philip II of Spain was also lord of the Low Countries. The knights and soldiers of Spain kept their watch by the mouths of the Rhine as well as along the shores of the Caribbean Sea.

All through the sixteenth century the strife between old Catholics and new Protestants increased in bitterness. The Spaniards were Catholics. Their Dutch subjects were largely Protestants, as also were the people of England and the Scots. The Irish remained Catholic.

In 1588 Philip II, whose armies were encamped in the Netherlands, sent a grand fleet or *armada* to invade and subdue England. This expedition was the climax of a drama whose earlier acts took place in Scotland, in the Netherlands, and in the New World of America.

Mary Queen of Scots

The Stuart kings of Scotland were related by marriage to the Tudors of England, and Elizabeth, the last of the Tudors, was childless. When James V of Scots died suddenly in 1542 he left a baby daughter, Mary, who was thereupon taken to France by her French mother; and there at the age of seventeen she was married to the French king. When he died two years later, in 1560, she returned to Edinburgh, a widow of nineteen and a Catholic. Her distant Protestant cousin, Elizabeth I of England, had been queen for two years. The sister realms of England and Scotland were, in fact, "queen-doms."

Mary Queen of Scots is one of the tragic queens of history. She did not get on well with her Protestant lords, and she lacked wise and capable advisers. She married again, this time a featherheaded young nobleman named Darnley. Lord Darnley became madly jealous of Mary's secretary, an

Italian named David Rizzio, and led a ruffianly group of companions to murder Rizzio in her presence. A year later, Darnley, lying ill at Kirk-o'-Field, a house near Edinburgh, was blown up by gunpowder and killed. The man suspected of this murder was the Earl of Bothwell, and when Mary married Bothwell, she too was suspected, and the lords rose in rebellion against her. She fled into England to seek the protection of Elizabeth. Elizabeth did protect her by keeping her in a castle under strict guard.

Mary was twenty-five, and her beauty was already a legend. She was a Catholic. She was also heiress to Elizabeth and might possibly become queen of England. Elizabeth did not know what to do with her. For twenty years Mary remained under guard, moved from castle to castle, a prisoner. Meanwhile the Scots Protestant lords brought up Mary's baby son, King James VI of Scots, as a Protestant.

The divisions and quarrels between Catholics and Protestants widened and deepened. Because all sorts of Protestants were preaching all sorts of doctrines, the Italian and Spanish bishops, all Catholics, met in a Council at Trent in Austria to make decrees about the Catholic faith and Catholic worship. In Spain the Church court of inquiry called the *Inquisition* was set up to examine men and women who were suspected or known to be heretics—believers in non-Catholic doctrines. Such people, if they proved stubborn, were handed over to the king's officers to be burned. Thousands of Jews and Protestants were burned at the stake. The Inquisitors were busy wherever the Spaniards held power.

A Spanish soldier named Ignatius Loyola founded the Society of Jesus, the Jesuits, whose purpose it was to defend the Catholic religion against its enemies. The Jesuits were a remarkable body of men, sternly trained and sternly disciplined, and taught to obey without hesitation the commands of their superiors. They differed from all existing religious orders. They lived in the world, not in a cloistered monastery. They wore no distinctive dress. They were permitted to follow ordinary callings in craft or commerce. Like the begging orders of the friars, the Society of Jesus attracted men of first-class ability. Some of them practiced deceit and intrigue to gain their ends, but their ranks included saints and heroes as well as plotters and politicians. They were forbidden to enter England under penalty of death, and some were put to death. "Jesuits were to be found under every disguise, and in every country; scholars, physicians, merchants, servingmen; in the hostile court of Sweden, in the old manor-houses of Cheshire, among the hovels of Connaught; arguing, instructing, stealing away the hearts of the young, animating the courage of the timid, holding the crucifix before the eyes of the dying . . . They were found in the depths of the Peruvian mines, at the marts of the African slave-caravans, on the shores of the Spice Islands, in the observatories of China . . . they preached and disputed in tongues of which no other native of the West understood a word."

The Council of Trent, the Inquisition, and the Society of Jesus were the means by which the Catholic Church sought to regain the Protestants to its faith. There were wars of religion in which Protestant Christians and Catholic Christians killed each other. They began in Germany: and before 1570 the Catholics and Huguenots in France had fought three civil wars.

Christendom was divided against itself and there were no signs of peace. But Christendom still had its ancient foes. In the south the fleets of Ottoman Turks were threatening to sweep Christian ships from the Mediterranean. Angered by the attacks of the Knights of St. John whose galleys plundered the Moslem traders, the Grand Sultan of the Turks, Solyman the Magnificent, laid seige to the island of Malta in 1565. For over three months the Knights endured continual attacks, but they held their forts and saved Malta. In 1571, Don John of Austria, in command of Spanish and Venetian galleys, destroyed the Turkish fleet in a resounding victory off Lepanto. Cervantes, the Spaniard who wrote the story of Don Quixote, lost his hand in that fierce fight. The other nations of Christendom were too busy with their own affairs to join in the Turkish war.

What was Queen Elizabeth of England to do with Mary Queen of Scots, whose cause might lead Catholic gentlemen to plot and rebel against her? The Inquisition and the Jesuits were making a Catholic *counterattack* on the Protestants, and Mary was the Catholic heiress to the English throne.

English seamen in the Narrow Seas knew all about this Catholic counterattack. A few miles from the mouth of the Thames the viceroys of Philip II of Spain were doing their best to destroy the Protestants of the Low Countries.

The Dutch

The Lowlands, or Netherlands, about the mouths of the mighty River Rhine and its companion river, the Maas, were settled during the Middle Ages by the Dutch, who, as one historian put it, "plucked up" their land from the sea. By ditches and dikes and channels they learned to control the flow of fresh water and sea water among the saltings and islands of their coast. They were subjects of the Holy Roman Emperor, Charles V, and they passed, at his abdication, into the hand of Philip II of Spain. In the northern provinces the new Protestant teaching made very many converts.

The time was bitter with religious dispute and persecution. In France the Catholics, encouraged by the queen mother Catherine de' Medici, carried out a sudden and treacherous massacre of French Huguenots in Paris on St. Bartholomew's Eve, 1572. In England Elizabeth I feared that she would be assassinated by Catholic gentlemen who wished to put Mary Queen of Scots on the throne. In Spain the Inquisition was searching out and condemning Protestants and Jews. Philip II resolved to stamp out the new religion in all his dominions.

He sent his renowned infantry to the Netherlands to quell the Protestant burghers in the Dutch towns clustered along the waterways. Though they laid the towns waste they could not extinguish the Protestants. In 1572, when some Dutch seamen, "Sea-Beggars," captured Brill, a small coastal town, the revolt blazed up fiercely; and fishermen, shopkeepers, craftsmen, farmers, and merchants became heroes, fighting against an army that was not merely Catholic but foreign as well. When the town of Leyden was besieged, its defenders cut the dikes, giving back to the sea their hard-won fields. The Spaniards sacked Antwerp and slew 8,000 of its people.

By 1579 the Duke of Parma, Philip's captain-general, managed by sheer terror to win back the ten southern provinces. The northerners called in the French to aid them: but the French were as unpopular as the Spaniards and Antwerp suffered again, this time from a "French fury" of destruction. The Dutch hopes were further shattered in 1584 when a madman assassinated William, Count of Orange, the leader of their resistance to Philip.

Help could only be expected from England where Elizabeth I and her cautious ministers, Cecil and Walsingham, were anxiously watching and waiting on events. Some of the plots uncovered by the spies of Walsingham included the use of Spanish troops to put Mary Queen of Scots on the throne. Even Don John of Austria, the victor of Lepanto, played with the idea of rescuing the unhappy Scots queen.

Since Elizabeth's people were islanders, events came to depend on the doings of the English seamen.

The English Seamen and Drake

The effect on England of the overseas discoveries was profound. The western ocean, which had once been a barrier of illimitable waters, was now a highway of adventure beckoning her sons away. From now on, ships and seamen fill the foreground of her activities. With the ocean went peril and heroism.

They that go down to the sea in ships, and occupy their business in great waters; these men see the works of the Lord, and his wonders in the deep. For at his word the stormy wind ariseth which lifteth up the waters thereof. They are carried up to the heaven, and down again to the deep.

These words in the Hebrew psalm were written of the Mediterranean; the Elizabethan seamen knew them to be true of vaster and stormier seas where

> . . . the seaman's whistle
> Is as a whisper in the ear of death,
> Unheard . . .

and the response of the seamen can be given in Sir Humphrey Gilbert's words:

He is not worthy to live at all, who, for fear of danger or death, shunneth his country's service or his own honour, since death is inevitable and the fame of virtue immortal.

Gilbert, in 1583, went down in the 10-ton *Squirrel* in a storm off the Azores, crying cheerfully as his ship plunged into a wild trough of sea, "We are as near heaven by sea as by land." Sir Richard Grenville, seven years later, fought his ship, the *Revenge*, at Flores in the Azores, against fifty-three Spanish galleons for fifteen hours before surrendering to die on an enemy's deck, a marvel to the grave Spanish dons.

Such were the seamen of Elizabethan days, and of them all the greatest was Sir Francis Drake. To the Spaniards he became a legend, and his name "El Draque" a word of fear. In one of his visits to the Spanish Main he saw the Pacific and vowed he would sail it. In 1577 he set out from Plymouth in the *Pelican* with four consorts. They made the Brazilian coast and then threaded the straits of Magellan. Two small ships had already been abandoned on the South American coast. Now in a stupendous storm of wind and rain, the little *Marygold* went down with all hands, and the *Elizabeth* made for home. Drake sailed on alone, raiding the Spanish American cities of Valparaiso and Lima, and capturing the *Cacafuego*, a treasure galleon from which his young Devonshire crew cheerfully transferred "13 chests full of royals of plate, 80 lbs. weight of gold and 26 tons of silver." He held on northwards till he rested his men on the Californian coast, which he named New Albion. Then he sailed westwards again to the Moluccas (the Spice Islands), and afterwards rounded the Cape of Good Hope. Three years after his departure the men of Plymouth saw his ships coming in to anchor, and that night there were many tales told in the west-country port.

In 1585 he took a fleet of twenty-five ships to Spain and the Spanish Main, raiding Vigo, San Domingo, and Cartagena. Drake was at war with Spain on his own account.

The Spanish Armada

The long drama was nearing its climax. In 1586 Mary Queen of Scots was accused of plotting against Elizabeth. She may have been innocent, but was condemned, and was executed at Fotheringay Castle in 1587. There was now no hope that a Catholic would succeed to the English throne, since Mary's son, James VI of Scotland, was a Protestant.

In 1587, also, Elizabeth allowed her favorite, the Earl of Leicester, to take a force of English volunteers to the aid of the Dutch.

Philip of Spain made his decision: he would invade and subdue England and then settle with his rebellious Netherlanders. For more than a year he collected ships and stores and gear from all the ports of Spain, Portugal, and Italy, spending the gold and silver of the New World without stint. Drake, for whom the English frontier was always the enemy's coast, destroyed thirty-seven Spanish ships in Cadiz harbor. In spite of this setback Philip kept his shipyards, smithies, and arsenals busy, and persevered in what was to him a holy war. The zeal of crusaders burned in the hearts of his *hidalgos,* and his ships bore the names of Our Lady, the Apostles, and the Saints. At Dunkirk he had waiting an army of 30,000 infantry—Italians, Germans, Flemings, Spaniards, all ready with flat-bottomed boats for their easy transport as soon as the great armada came from Spain.

Elizabeth and England watched and waited. At Tilbury was the royal army under the Captain of the Yeomen of the Guard, Sir Walter Raleigh. The seamen took their stations: Wynter and Seymour off Kent, Howard, Drake, and Hawkins at Plymouth.

On July 19, 1588, Philip's armada was sighted off the Lizard, 130 ships sailing in a vast half-moon formation before the prevailing wind. The Plymouth squadron slipped out and got to windward of the Spaniards, and captured two of them.

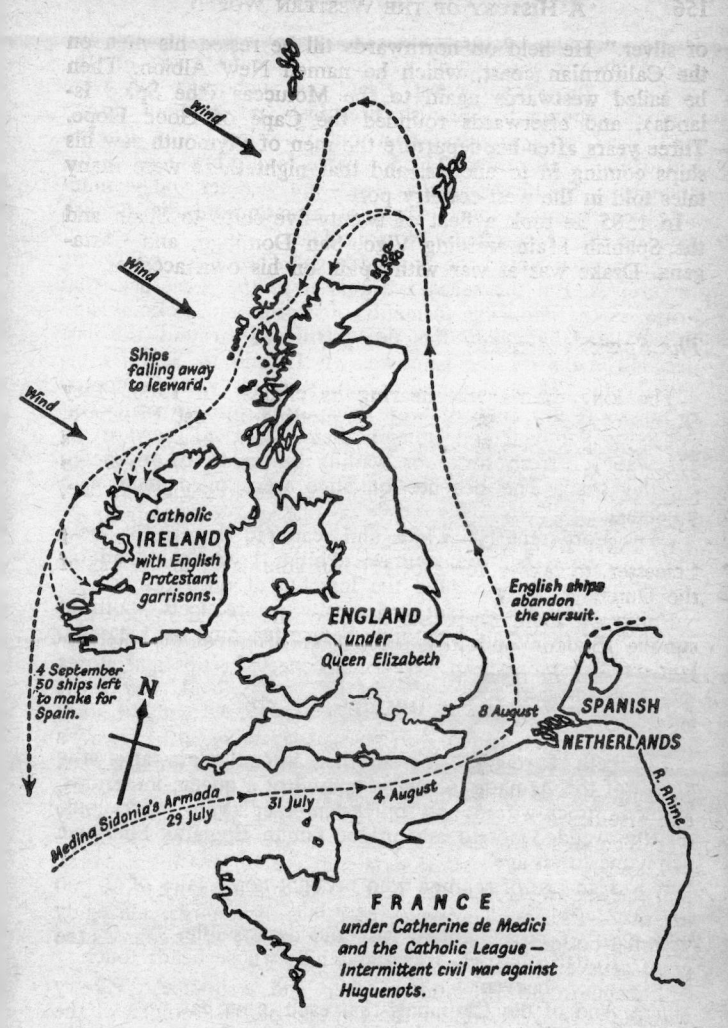

THE SPANISH ATTEMPT ON ENGLAND 1588

On July 23 and 25 there were engagements off Portland and the Wight, as a result of which the galleons made for the shelter of the French coast. From this anchorage they were driven in panic by English fireships, and as they turned northward, still a grand fleet but disordered, the English squadron pursued them. The Spaniards fought bravely—all the chivalry of Spain was in that fleet—but weather and seamanship were against them. Short of ammunition, the English gave up the chase off the Norfolk coast.

Where now would the Spaniards go? They disputed among themselves. But the seas gave answer in the great gale that arose. After enduring torments of storm and sickness and thirst, less than half the fleet struggled around the last dreaded rocks off the southwest of Ireland to Spain. Nine ships were sunk or captured in battle: the rest were foundered in the northern seas or were cast away on the wild west coasts of Scotland and Ireland, their exhausted crews dying for want of fresh water or wading ashore to be murdered by the Irish. The beaches of Sligo were piled high with wreckage.

"The Lord sent His winds and scattered them." Elizabeth thus expressed her thankfulness. Philip II of Spain had his own heroism: he accepted the loss but at once resolved to try again. He did in fact prepare two more fleets—both of which were destroyed by storms before reaching the Channel.

Elizabethan England

Elizabeth I reigned for another fifteen years after the defeat of the Armada, a true nonpareil of a queen, imperious, learned, quick-witted and quick-tempered, vain, capricious, thrifty: wedded not to any prince but to England. She gave her name to an age.

It was an age of seamen who brought home tales of

> antres vast and deserts idle,
> Rough quarries, rocks and hills whose heads touch heaven . . .
> And of the Cannibals that each other eat,
> The Anthropophagi, and men whose heads
> Do grow beneath their shoulders.

Parson Richard Hakluyt collected narratives and notes of all the voyages he could, and published them in 1600 in an epic book of maritime adventure, *The Navigations, Voyages and Discoveries of the English Seamen*. The Queen's own kinsman, the Earl of Cumberland, sailed his ship, the *Malice Scourge*, many times to plunder on the Spanish Main. William Adams, a Limehouse pilot, went with Dutch ships to Japan, where he settled down for the rest of his life as nautical adviser to the Mikado.

Strange and unknown regions of the world were familiar topics on Thameside. Any London tavern would yield a mixed company of seafarers. The man with the gaudy kerchief around his head is back from the Levant; his ship had a brush with Barbary corsairs off Gibraltar. The sunburnt man with puckered eyes has spent a year on a slaver between Guinea and the West Indies. Another is in the pay of the wealthy Muscovy Company; his ship lies in the river with a cargo of train oil and timber. He can tell of Northern Lights on Russian snows, of uncouth Laplanders wrapped up like bundles of fur. The two younger men speaking in the same soft west-country accents that Sir Walter Raleigh uses at court have come off Thomas Cavendish's ship after a voyage around the world with the loot of a Spanish galleon on board. For the rest, they are in the coastwise trade, and maybe some of them have sometimes slipped across to Holland to help the Dutch. The sea was certainly calling the islanders away. The Elizabethan Age saw the beginnings of their great adventure of trade and empire.

It was an age also of great poets and playwrights. Edmund Spenser wrote his famous poem of *The Faerie Queene*, but every courtier could make good poems. At the Globe Theatre in Southwark, citizens, apprentices and law students could see the plays of William Shakespeare. They could watch Shylock the Jew demanding his pound of flesh from Antonio the *Merchant of Venice*; or Bottom the Weaver of Athens transformed by magic into an Ass-Head, and making love to Titania, queen of the Fairies; or the fat knight, Falstaff, hiding in a basket of foul linen to escape the wrath of the husbands of the *Merry Wives of Windsor*; or enjoy the plays that showed the kingly pomp and pageantry of the Wars of the Roses. Sometimes the players took a play to the Queen's court as they did with *Twelfth Night*. And they often toured the country, acting in great houses like Wilton in Somerset.

London was a small place. There were swans on the Thames, and rose gardens in the Strand, and cherry orchards in Bermondsey. What we call the East End was open country with oak trees and farms. Hay wagons lumbered daily into the market, and cattle were driven to the shambles. Country villages like Islington and Camberwell were a short stroll from the City. City men were never far from countrymen, plowmen, harvesters, threshers, and thatchers. In the villages on summer evenings there was dancing to pipe and tabor, and play in the nine-men's morris. In some parts there was wrestling, and coursing of the hare. And there was a sort of "hunting football," played all day across wide stretches of country, in which men could use cudgels and even go on horseback! Peddlers, like Autolycus in Shakespeare's play, wandered with their wares. No doubt they called at the new manor houses, those red-brick and timbered houses with tall, twisted chimneys, set in ornamental gardens with terraces, clipped hedges, smooth lawns, covered alleys and seated arbors. Like the villagers, the lords and ladies must make their own amusements. After supper the music books were handed round for the singing of madrigals for many voices in different parts. Elizabethan England could boast very many musicians such as John Wilbye and William Byrd, whose songs were sung to a lute accompaniment.

After the company have ceased to sing, the candles are put out, and soon all have gone to bed. The house is quiet. In such a house King Oberon and Queen Titania enter with their fairy train, in Shakespeare's *Midsummer Night's Dream*, to guard it and tidy it.

> Through this house give glimmering light
> By the dead and drowsy fire.

The mortals have sung their songs and gone to rest, and the embers in the great hearth flicker and die to cold morning ashes.

In 1603 the lonely mistress of that larger household of England was drawing near to her end. She had been queen for forty-five years and was the last of her family. She had outlived friends and enemies. Her ministers, Walsingham and Burghley, were dead. Philip of Spain was dead. On March 24 the great Queen herself died at Richmond. Instantly, upon the news, Sir Robert Catesby was on horse riding hard for Edinburgh to greet the Scots king James VI as James I of England.

An age had come to an end.

A New Century

For the first time in their history Scotland and England were a united kingdom under one king, a Stuart. But James I who came riding south in 1603 was not the only new royal actor on the scene. In France the wars of religion were ended by the victories of the Huguenot champion, Henry of Navarre: and when he became King Henry IV in 1594 and turned Catholic, he let the Huguenots worship as they pleased.

THE GREAT KINGDOMS OF THE WEST

In Spain the industrious and zealous Philip II had been succeeded by the easygoing Philip III: he and his grandees continued to rule their American empire and to draw great store of gold and silver from it; and they continued to rule the southern Netherlands (the "Spanish Netherlands"). The Dutch of the northern Netherlands had won their freedom from Spain, and quickly showed themselves skillful, bold, and enterprising.

The beginning of the seventeenth century was indeed the beginning of a new age of oceanic commerce and religious wars.

Cradled by the sea from which they wrested and defended their fertile coast lands, the Dutch proved to be a nation of seamen and merchants. They drove the Portuguese from the Spice Islands and set up their own factories and settlements in the East Indies, where their empire lasted till 1946. They earned the nickname of the "wagoners of the world" because they carried cargoes for all peoples, and Amsterdam became the port of Europe. They carried slaves from West Africa to the West Indies, and sugar from the West Indies. They made a settlement in New York (first called New Amsterdam) and engaged in the American fur trade. They planted a small colony at the Cape of Good Hope which was the beginning of the Boer settlement of South Africa. Their pilots searched the South Seas, discovered Tasmania, and sighted Australia. All this they did in fifty years. As a result of their trade their cities throve and their burghers built themselves fine houses. Holland flourished. This was the great age of Dutch art: the famous artist, Rembrandt, was born in 1607. Although the smallness of Holland prevented the Dutch from becoming one of the most powerful nations of the west, they played a leading part in the fortunes of the west.

The Dutch filled the seas with their argosies, but the English did not lag far behind. A group of London merchants sent a convoy of ships to the east in 1600 which returned with a handsome cargo of pepper in 1603: and from this venture grew the powerful English East India Company and the British dominion over India. Other English merchants adventured to Africa and the West Indies, to Turkey and the Levant, and to North Russia. Both Dutch and English traded in the Baltic.

The two nations were soon jealous rivals in trade, and later in the century their navies fought three stubborn and rather terrible wars in the Narrow Seas—without, happily, engendering any lasting bitterness or hatred. The world was wide enough for both.

There was bitterness and hatred in plenty in the wars of

religion. That which began in 1618 in the German lands lasted till 1648, a Thirty Years' War, in which Catholics and Protestants laid waste the countryside, sacked towns, destroyed and ravaged—and all to no purpose; since in 1648 the strife ended in a stalemate—each ruler, great or petty, king, duke or baron, was allowed to settle the religion of his own lands. Thirty years of savage warfare retarded the progress of civilization throughout Germany, which remained a patchwork land of hundreds of states under the vague authority of the Hapsburg emperors at Vienna who governed Austria and Hungary. Italy was spared the religious wars, but remained divided into small states. The Venetians still controlled most of the trade of the eastern Mediterranean, but this trade declined in volume after the opening of the Cape route, and the republic of Venice sank slowly from her one-time power and wealth.

The new united kingdom of Great Britain also suffered from a religious war. But in Britain religious quarrels were tangled up with political ones about the powers of king and of parliament. The kingdom of France also experienced a new political adventure.

To understand the contrast between these two kingdoms is to understand the history of the west for the next two centuries.

The Contrast: Britain

Ever since the thirteenth century the kings of England had called parliaments from time to time to advise them and to grant taxes so that the king's government could be carried on. Changes in the law were made by "acts" of parliament, agreed on by the king, by the lords and bishops, and by the knights of the shires and burgesses of the towns. The lords and bishops sat in the House of Lords; the knights and burgesses, who were elected to represent the country yeomen and the town guildsmen, sat in the House of Commons.

The quarrels of the Stuart kings, James I and his son Charles I, with their parliaments, were quarrels between kings who believed in their own divine right to do as they pleased, and their subjects, who believed that kings should keep their word and keep the laws of the land. When the lawyer, Sir Edward Coke, opposed James I in some matter, James exclaimed: "Then I am to be *under* the law—which it is treason to affirm." The stout-hearted Coke answered: "Yes, sire; under God *and* the law." James and Charles quarreled with their parliaments over money: Should the king tax his

The Great Kingdoms of the West

subjects without their consent? The Stuarts were unlucky because the value of money was falling in their reigns, and they needed more of it. Neither of them was tactful in dealing with men or skillful in choosing counselors. But it was a bitter and deeper quarrel about religion that led to the Civil War.

Protestants were not united like Catholics. Most men were content to abide by the rule of the bishops, and to use the Prayer Book of the English Church. But a very active and strong minority, nicknamed "Puritans," objected to both bishops and Prayer Book. They disapproved also of pleasures such as maypoles, morris-dancing, sports, and theaters: some, as Lord Macaulay has said, may have disliked bearbaiting not because it gave the bear pain but because it gave the spectators pleasure. These men were "independents"—every man free to interpret the Scriptures by the light of his own knowledge and conscience. They could not leave the Church except by emigrating to America—which many of them did in 1620 and afterwards. But they could not reshape the Church to their own desires unless they abolished the bishops.

Bishops were not only pastors of their people but also servants of the king, officers of the Church of which he was the head. They were powerful men. They could arrest and try men in their own courts of justice, and fine them and imprison them in their own prisons. One Puritan had his ears cropped for writing a book against bishops. Another suffered in the same way for condemning stage plays; this extraordinary man (who was a lawyer) also condemned Magna Carta merely because a bishop had helped to make King John sign it. The Puritans included some very odd people: and the bishops were not all saintly. It was unfortunate that Charles I, a serious, upright, kind, and considerate man, and more devoted to the Church than any of England's other monarchs have ever been, was entirely lacking in the art of managing men.

Puritan gentlemen, powerful in parliament, demanded changes in the Church. Charles resented this so much that he tried governing the country without parliament for eleven years (1629–1640); during these years he raised taxes of all sorts on his own, and he let Archbishop Laud of Canterbury persecute the Puritans. Laud, a good but fussy man, set out to make everyone worship as the Prayer Book directed, and he even hoped to spread the Church of England in all parts of the world, wherever the subjects of his king happened to live. When, however, he thrust a Prayer Book on the King's Scottish subjects in the northern kingdom there was immediate trouble. The Scots were Presbyterians with a set worship of their own devised by John Calvin, and their

Church was strong and united. They rebelled: they raised an army and invaded England.

Charles could not persuade his lords to help him, and was forced to summon a parliament. After two years of bitter dispute, the Puritan leaders in parliament tried to get control of the county militias. Charles rode to Nottingham and called all loyal men to rally to his standard. Parliament was divided, some members declared for the King, some against. Many deplored the threat of war. Some who disliked the bishops disliked still more the idea of taking up arms against their lawful king. "I have no reverence for the bishops, for whom this quarrel exists," wrote Sir Edmund Verney—and he was the royal standard-bearer.

The civil war that followed, 1642–1648, was a half-hearted affair to begin with, and might have resulted in the King's victory but for two things: (1) the Presbyterian Scots army, and (2) Oliver Cromwell. Alarmed by the failure of their hastily raised regiments of blue-coats, yellow-coats, red-coats, green-coats and purple-coats, against the Cavaliers who rode for Charles, the leaders of the Puritan parliament made a solemn league with the Scots and brought them in against the King. Next, they reformed their musketeers and pikemen into a "New Model Army" led by gentlemen and noblemen used to arms. Oliver Cromwell, who had raised his own fervent and godly troop of horse in the Eastern Counties, was one of the New Model officers, and soon became its general-in-chief. He was a soldier of genius. In the New Model were many fanatical zealots who listened to the exhortations of their field chaplains before carrying their pikes into the battle, and who regarded themselves as the chosen men of God warring against the Amalekites and idolaters. There was never an army like them. They were invincible soldiers. One of their enemies described them as "an army whose sobriety and manners, whose courage and success, have made it famous and terrible all over the world." When the New Model routed the royal army at Naseby in 1645, Charles surrendered.

That should have ended the war. But when parliament tried to disband the army, the army refused to be disbanded, and Cromwell expelled most members of parliament, leaving only a "rump" of Puritan independents in session. Cromwell and the army took charge of the island. Cromwell proceeded to quell royalist outbreaks and to defeat the Scots, who had no love for independents and much affection for a Stuart king. The Rump and the army officers condemned Charles I to death. He was beheaded in Whitehall, his scaffold strongly guarded by files of pikemen.

Ireland and Scotland were royalist. Cromwell made a

merciless campaign in Ireland, and then defeated the Scots. Large numbers of Irish and Scots were sold into slavery in America and the West Indies. Large numbers, specially of Irishmen, joined foreign armies in Europe.

These were dreadful things, but never approached the bloodshed, famine, pestilence, and destruction in Germany in the Thirty Years' War.

The army made Cromwell Lord Protector of the "Commonwealth," which he ruled through a dozen major generals. So much for the rule of parliament! Abroad, Cromwell's army and navy fought against Spain, the "Archenemy," the fleet capturing Jamaica, and the army defeating the Spaniards by push of pike at Dunkirk. His navy, under his "generals-at-sea," Monk and Blake, warred against the Dutch treasure fleet under the muzzles of the shore guns at Tenerife in the Canaries.

It was Cromwell's turn to keep the fanatical part of the Puritans in order. Even he could not do this. The parliaments he called were useless, and he drove them out. He was lonely, feared, and hated. Royalists plotted his death; Puritan extremists abounded; "Levelers" in the army tried to abolish officers, and were shot; "Fifth-Monarchy Men," self-styled troopers of the last earthly monarchy (the kingdom of God) who respected no man's authority, unfurled the banner of Judah on the outskirts of London, and had to be rounded up. Some men wanted to wipe out all the laws and replace them by the Book of Deuteronomy.

Cromwell kept his head. And he was no kill-joy. He had a fund of common sense and practical wisdom, or he could never have been a great commander. This wealthy gentleman from the Fens came to his great place by his military genius guided by "faith and matchless fortitude." His fame at home was but a shadow of his fame abroad. When he died at Hampton Court in 1658 of a tertian ague, his soul passing in a storm of wind and rain, some said it was a sign from God, and others that the Devil had come for his own. Men could not be lukewarm about Cromwell. He was the first commoner in Europe to raise himself to the rank of a monarch by his genius.

The island had lost both king and parliament. It had created a professional army, and a powerful navy. But most men were heartily tired of the rule of the army and the rule of the "saints." In 1660 General Monk brought Charles II over to Dover as king, on a tide of universal rejoicing. Parliaments, bishops, and the Prayer Book were all restored. But the bitterness was going out of the religious strife, and Charles was clever enough to rule for twenty-five years without serious political quarrels. There was persecution; independents, or nonconformists as they were now called, were forbidden to teach or enter the universities, or worship except in family circles; and they were barred from taking any part in government. But as time went on, they found ways of getting around these restrictions.

Strangely enough, when James II, Charles's brother, tried to brush aside the law of the land, it was not the Puritans who opposed him but seven bishops of the Church. He tried them for treason and his judges acquitted them. In 1688 the lords of parliament invited James II's son-in-law, William of Orange, to come and restore the laws. James fled. William became William III and reigned jointly with Mary II, his wife —king and queen by the Grace of God and *by the consent of parliament.*

The Contrast: France

During the seventeenth and eighteenth centuries Great Britain became a parliamentary monarchy. This island was ruled in turn by two Stuart kings, Oliver Cromwell, two more Stuart kings, a Dutch king married to a Stuart queen, another Stuart queen—Anne—and then four German Georges; for when Queen Anne died the great parliamentary lords offered the crown to the German ruler of Hanover. Leaving out the last of the four Georges, we have listed ten rulers. During the same time that these ten governed Britain, France had but three kings—Louis XIII, Louis XIV, and Louis XV, all Frenchmen. While Britain became a limited monarchy, France became an absolute one under these three Bourbon kings.

When Henry of Navarre was assassinated by a madman in 1610, his son Louis XIII was only nine years old. The chief minister of state was Cardinal Richelieu, a man of energy, resolution, courage, and clear intelligence, more regal in his manner and actions than the king he served. The cardinal had one purpose: to make Louis XIII the most powerful man in France, and to make France the most powerful country in Europe. He destroyed the political powers of the great nobles, demolishing their castles, and sending some of them to the block. He found that Huguenots practically ruled certain cities and districts; so he besieged the strongest of their cities, La Rochelle, and took it by force. He placed in every region royal officers called *intendants* whose duty it was to carry out the royal commands. Under his guidance France prospered at home and abroad: industries flourished and farmers thrived; the University of Paris was reformed and enlarged; trading companies sent fleets to Madagascar, Senegal, the West Indies; and thousands of peasants from Normandy and Poitou were settled in Canada (where their descendants still live). The royal army was increased to 100,000 men. The naval ports of Brest and Le Havre were established, and ships of war built for the ocean and for the Mediterranean. In order to advance the power of his royal master to the natural frontiers of France—the Rhine, the Alps, and the Pyrenees—Richelieu made wars against the Hapsburg rulers of Austria and Spain.

He died in 1642. His king, Louis XIII, died in 1643.

Louis XIV, a child of five, succeeded. Another churchman succeeded Richelieu, the Italian Cardinal Mazarin, not a grand figure like Richelieu, but still clever, energetic, tenacious, and determined. He continued Richelieu's work, in spite of riots and revolts by nobles, citizens, and lawyers— revolts known as *La Fronde*, which lacked a real leader and which ended in famine and pestilence. Mazarin, patient and subtle, survived this period, regained his power, and, when he died, left his king, Louis XIV, absolute master of France. Louis XIV took no one minister, but ruled for himself, choosing his servants from humble folk—sons of merchants, tradesmen, and grooms. The great nobles had no part in the government of France. Louis XIV reigned supreme for over fifty years, from 1660 till his death in 1715.

Louis XIV and his son, Louis XV, reigned between them for over a hundred years, from 1660 to 1774; and the best way of describing the history of Europe during these years is to look upon them as the "Century of France."

With her eighteen millions of people, her fertile farms, her forests and vineyards, her clever mechanics, her intelligent townsfolk, France was the leader of civilization and the keystone of Europe. And the riches and power of France were at the command of one man—the King. Louis XIV was the *Roi Soleil*, the kingly sun, about whose resplendent throne the court and the nation moved. Among his ministers were Louvois, who created a fine regular army, Vauban, famous for his skill in military engineering, and Colbert, an expert in finance and commerce. Colbert fostered manufactures by welcoming foreign craftsmen and regulating industries; he developed overseas trade and colonies by setting up East and West India Companies. He increased the navy so much that in 1680 it could muster nearly 300 ships.

The greatest monument of Louis XIV's reign was the Palace of Versailles, built at enormous cost between 1669 and 1710. In the midst of orangeries, flower gardens, lawns, shrubberies, artificial lakes, tree-shaded avenues, and alleys adorned with statues and fountains, rose the vast edifice which housed the king, his ministers and officers, his courtiers, musicians, players, huntsmen, and guards, and the army of servants and lackeys employed in its upkeep. In its mirrored and gilded saloons and galleries, men gambled away fortunes, planned wars, conducted state business, watched the comedies of Molière or the tragedies of Racine, or listened to Lully's operas. Their wigs, their satin coats, their lace cuffs, their elaborate manners, gave them the look of actors rather than of men in ordinary life.

Both Vauban and Colbert were aware of the fair prospect of overseas trade and settlement. Louis XIV preferred to use his power in making war against the Hapsburgs, for the sake of obtaining frontier fortresses like Lille and Strasbourg. And he did damage to the trade and industries of France by persecuting the Huguenots, many thousands of whom fled into England and Prussia, giving those lands the benefit of their skill and intelligence.

Under Louis XIV and his successor, Louis XV, French armies marched into the Low Countries and the Rhineland, where they fought against Dutchmen, Germans, and Austrians. But all Europe took France as its exemplar: the French language and French customs were used everywhere in polite society.

The contrast between the two kingdoms of Britain and France in their political life was to continue: and the two kingdoms were for many years at war in the eighteenth century with important consequences for them and the world. But before we follow this theme, we must see what was happening overseas in the New World and in the east.

Westward Ho

The first English colony in America was Virginia, the "Old Dominion." Sir Walter Raleigh began sending settlers to the Virginia coast, but none of his settlements lasted. Some London merchants took over his idea and despatched settlers in 1607 to the James River. They were not a well-chosen body of men: and idleness, ignorance, and quarrels nearly brought the infant colony to an end. Its savior was Captain John Smith, a brave and boastful soldier of fortune, who saw the need of hard work and of making friends with the Indians. After some very lean and difficult seasons Virginia began to prosper, with tobacco as its main crop, and by 1635 its population numbered about 6,000.

THE GREAT KINGDOMS OF THE WEST

By that year the American continent, which already had a New Spain, possessed also a New England, a New Netherlands, and a New France.

New England was founded by religious exiles who sought a land where they could worship as they liked. Some Puritan families from the eastern part of England got leave of the London merchants to settle on the Virginia coast. Actually they landed a long way north; a hundred of them—the "Pilgrim Fathers" (with mothers and children as well)—crossed the Atlantic in the *Mayflower*, whose stout-hearted London mariners landed them in Plymouth Bay. This was in the autumn of 1620. During the first winter, half of them died from hardship and illness. But they were a determined folk, and under the leadership of William Bradford, who ruled them until his death in 1657, the pilgrims became a colony of farmers, fishermen, and fur traders.

A larger and richer New England settlement was made at Boston by the English Massachusetts Bay Company in 1628. By 1642 its townships and villages held more than 16,000 settlers, Puritans who could worship just as they wished to, but who stopped Quakers and others who differed from them from worshiping as *they* liked. The only place in America then where freedom of worship was allowed to all Christians was Maryland, a small Catholic colony founded by Lord Baltimore in 1631 and named in honor of Charles I's queen, Henrietta Maria.

Virginia in the south and New England in the north were the twin foundations of the later United States; but whether they were rich tobacco planters or Puritan farmers the settlers took with them the speech, the songs, the customs, and the laws of seventeenth-century England. This is why Magna Carta belongs to American history as much as it does to English, why trial by jury and the English Common Law exist in America, and why the sheriff and his men in the United States acted in the same way as the sheriffs and their men in old England. We might say that American history begins in Anglo-Saxon England and crosses the ocean in the sixteen-hundreds!

South of New England were the New Netherlands; north, about 300 miles away beyond forests and mountains, was New France.

The Dutch planted their colony of New Amsterdam on Manhattan Island in 1609, and since the Dutch were keen merchants this settlement soon became one of the chief centers of the Indian fur trade. With a great many changes, it is now, under the familiar name of New York, the largest commercial center of the United States.

New France differed from all other colonies in lying some 800 miles away from the ocean. The map will explain this: first, the Gulf of St. Lawrence River is as large as the English Channel; secondly, Montreal is a port a thousand miles from the Atlantic. In 1608 Samuel Champlain from Normandy founded a colony at Quebec. Here the old-fashioned manorial life of old France was reproduced, the peasants working on their lords' lands and paying dues in money and goods to their seigneurs. And, of course, New France was Catholic. Champlain's voyages took him well into the Great Lakes. The men of New France made friends with the Huron Indians, among whom French Jesuit priests did heroic missionary work. Many of the French settlers became expert in the fur trade of the far north.

These tiny settlements of English, Dutch, and Frenchmen were made on the shores and waterways of a mighty land whose dense forests of hemlock, oak, spruce, cedar, and birch stretched immeasurably inland, threaded only by silent streams and narrow Indian trails. The forest was everywhere like a green sea. But winter changed the scene, "sealing the fountains, fettering the streams, and turning the green-robed forests to a shivering, naked wilderness," where the only sounds in a cold, starving world were the "whistling of the northeast wind and the hungry cry of the wolves."

The redskin of old time roamed this land in search of hunting grounds, enduring terrible hardship, suffering and inflicting savage cruelties, yet at times wildly generous. He was a child of the forest with a code of behavior utterly unlike that of the palefaces. He would listen for hours to long speeches, squatting in council with a grave patience worthy of some senator of an ancient civilization. Yet he was also the hideous, naked savage, plastered with ocher and soot, treacherous and merciless, a scalp-hunter whose tomahawk and firebrand were used against the lonely frontier farms.

In the great West were prairies where herds of buffalo roamed, rivers which flooded wide plains or were lost in tremendous gorges, deserts strewn with fantastic cacti, vast chains of mountains, and fierce Indian tribes unknown and unsuspected. On this side of the Mississippi the continent was dominated by the Iroquois, or Five Nations, who preyed on the other tribes, and whose birch-bark lodges were scattered across the path of the white men coming from the sea.

Later in the century, in Charles II's reign, a group of Cavalier gentlemen founded Carolina—named after Charles; and William Penn, the Quaker friend of Charles II, founded his Quaker colony called Pennsylvania with its capital city

THE GREAT KINGDOMS OF THE WEST

at Philadelphia—the "place of brotherly love"—in 1680.

By the end of the century the European colonies in America reached for over a hundred degrees of latitude from the River Platte to Hudson Bay.

In the south were Jesuit Fathers ruling the Indians of Paraguay and guarding them from all contact with the outside world. There was Portuguese Brazil with its sugar and tobacco fields worked by Negro slaves. There were the old Spanish colonies, all governed from Spain through her viceroys in Peru and Mexico, whose duty it was to send precious metals to Madrid, and whose olive groves and vineyards were destroyed for fear they should compete with those of Spain.

In the Caribbean Sea were the wealthy and populous West Indian Islands, English and French, thriving by the trade—and the smuggling—of sugar, molasses, rum, cotton, and logwood. There, also, were the haunts of the buccaneers whose motley crews joined together under Henry Morgan in 1671 to sack the Spanish city of Panama.

On the mainland of America, north of Spanish Florida, were the English colonies: southern planters living in spacious houses, with their Negroes toiling on the rice fields of Carolina or the tobacco fields of Virginia; more Negroes coming in a steady stream from West Africa, terror-struck from the ghastly suffering of the middle passage across the Atlantic; West Indian smugglers slipping quietly into Charleston harbor; German Protestants, "Pennsylvania Dutchmen" from the Rhineland; French Huguenot refugees in New York alongside of the rich "mynheers" or Dutch fur traders with their households of black slaves; homely, peaceful Quakers in Penn's colony and in New Jersey; Puritan congregations in Boston excited over a witchhunt; New England farmers, hard-working, thrifty, independent; Connecticut seamen and Nantucket whalers; Newfoundland fishermen, temporary settlers for the season, from Biscay and the west of England; backwoodsmen treading the first trails into the Allegheny and Appalachian Mountains; and everywhere in the forests the redskins—the Mohawk allies of the Dutch, the Tuscaroras and Yamasees on the borders of Carolina, and the Hurons raiding the farms of Maine and New Hampshire as allies of the French in Canada.

And the French were not confining themselves to Canada. La Salle, one of their governors, explored the rivers and waterways all the way from the Great Lakes to the Gulf of Mexico, where he proclaimed Louis XIV to be king over the territory of "Louisiana."

As for the far north, Charles II gave it to the gentlemen of the Hudson Bay Company under Prince Rupert, his nephew; and the company's agents lived lonely lives in the frozen northland, bartering guns, sugar, tea, blankets, kettles, and axes for the furs of the beaver, racoon, otter, and fox, brought year by year to York Factory by the Indian trappers in their canoes.

A new world of America, all transplanted from old Europe, was coming into existence, the work of countless, unknown hands.

Sultan and Tsar

Spaniards, Dutchmen, Frenchmen, and Englishmen had broken through the western seaward boundary of Christendom and were adventuring, to their own profit, beyond the wide waters of the Atlantic. Other nations were shaping the destinies of Europe on its eastern, or landward, side, where Turkish sultans from their palace by the Golden Horn ruled over the thousand ruined cities of antiquity; where German knights kept their castles and governed their estates carved out of the sandy wastes of Prussia in the time when that land was a "mark" or frontier fortified against the heathen; where the Catholic noblemen of Poland ruled their peasants scattered in villages over the plains, and counted among their subjects a great number of Jews; where the plains on this side of the Carpathians were the home of the Hungarians, men of the strange Magyar speech, peasants and nobles, whose king was the emperor of the Holy Roman Empire; and where, hundreds of miles farther east, a Christian prince held his court at Moscow.

The Turkish Empire held a great variety of races. Its merchants were Armenians and Greeks, its scholars were Arabs and Jews, its sailors were Greeks. Its learning and poetry were borrowed from the Persians and Arabs. Its soldiers were Anatolian peasants from Asia Minor, its picked regiments of Janizaries were recruited from kidnaped Christian children brought up as Moslems. The Turk himself was master of these, and many others, and taxed them. He did little else. He stabled his horses in the crumbling market places of Rome's lost towns, he prayed to Allah in Rome's lost churches turned into mosques, he took what he liked, doing nothing to improve, or rebuild, or irrigate, or clean the watercourses, active only in the arts of war. But his reliance on the will of Allah made him a formidable fighter in the long war of the Cross and Crescent.

Owing to the disunion of the Christian peoples the Turk had stretched his power over the races of the Balkans, over

Rumanians, Bulgarians, and Serbians. He overran Hungary. In 1683 his warrior host was at the gates of Vienna. The kings of the west did not move. But in that campaign the Moslem tide was turned for good; for John Sobieski at the head of the gallant Polish nobles and their levies drove him from Vienna and saved the city. In 1697 the Austrian Prince Eugene overwhelmed a Turkish army at Zenta. Venetians and Hungarians maintained the war until in 1699 the sultan gave up all claim to the overlordship of Hungary. From this time onward, the Ottoman Empire was on the defensive. But the presence of the Turk in the Balkans continued to be a problem—the *Eastern Problem* of Europe.

From this time also there was a new power to champion both the Christians and the Slav nations whom the Turk still held in subjection. This new power rose on the plains of Muscovy, its ruler was the tsar of the Russians, and its people belonged to the Greek Church. The travelers and merchants of the London Muscovy Company knew its markets, and its tsar, Ivan the Terrible, had sent his high-booted and bearded ambassadors to the court of Queen Elizabeth I. For a long time it had been subject to Tartar horsemen and paid tribute to the chieftains of those Asiatic hordes. Now it was roughly wakened from its backwardness and easygoing ways by a young giant, the tsar Peter the Great (1689-1725), "regenerator" of Muscovy.

Peter visited Holland and England where he worked as a laborer in the shipyards of Zaandam and Deptford and learned all he could of the habits and crafts of the West. On his return to Russia he began with tremendous energy, almost with frenzy, to change all Russian life and work. He brought in foreign advisers and experts to help him. He built a new capital, a "window-opening on the west," at St. Petersburg (Leningrad), a brand-new town built in a swamp at a dreadful cost in laborers' lives. He built ships and cast cannon. He punished opposition and revolt with scourging, torture, and beheading, often using the ax himself and making his judges do likewise. He was absolute master of all men in his dominions, and his intention was to make Russia a European power.

After his death the work went on more slowly. Russia began to take some part in the politics of eastern Europe. She came into conflict with the Turks on the shores of the Black Sea and with the Swedes on the shores of the Baltic. These two seas were her outlets; but the Black Sea could be closed by the Turkish forts at Constantinople, and the North Baltic Sea was frozen in winter. Behind Russia there lay to the east the interminable woods and plains of Siberia, and to the south the steppes and deserts and mountains of Turkestan. The new power had as much uncharted territory to the east and south as the new colonies in America had to their west. Russia under the tsars remained a despotism, and her people continued to live in their village communities under the rule of the landowners. In the new capital the Russian courtiers and noblemen imitated the life of the cultured aristocracies of France and Germany.

The Russians did not learn or understand the political ideas of the west about freedom and self-government. Nor did the people of the brigand state of Prussia, which also grew in power at this time.

The Protestant duke of the Prussians, Frederick William (1640–1688) kept a large army, and strengthened his power by welcoming as settlers many French Huguenots driven out of France by Louis XIV. His son adopted the title of King of Prussia. But it was his grandson, King Frederick William I (1713–1740) who turned Prussia into an armed state. He was an uncultured, brutal, military maniac. He kept a standing army of eighty thousand men, many of them kidnaped foreigners flogged into submission; and he filled his treasury by melting down the royal plate, selling the royal jewels, abolishing the court, and cutting down the pay of his personal servants to mere pittances. All that mattered in the kingdom of Prussia was money, population and soldiers—especially soldiers.

Britain Against Louis XIV and Louis XV: 1689–1748

In 1689, when William III became king of Great Britain on condition that he maintained the laws and the Protestant religion, King Louis XIV was the absolute ruler of France. In 1789 the contrast was as sharp: His Britannic Majesty George III ruled by the advice of his lords and commons in parliament, while Louis XVI did as he pleased. In truth, the contrast went deeper than this. England had one law, and Scotland had one law—Westminster law, Edinburgh law. In France there was a profuse variety of laws from province to province: and it was the monarchy that held the country together. No wonder that many Frenchmen looked on the British form of government as a model one; or that a pope remarked that the continued existence of the French monarchy was a miracle.

Between 1689 and 1815 these two countries were at war with each other for over seventy years.

France was the strongest military power and Britain the

strongest naval power. No age since Rome had seen such a sustained military effort as that of the armies of France, which reached its climax in the victories of Napoleon. No previous age at all had seen such a display of naval power as that of Britain, which enabled her to keep 150 great warships at sea, reached its climax in the victories of Admiral Nelson, and gave the command of the oceans to Britain all through the nineteenth century.

In her wars with France, therefore, Britain sought the help of powerful military allies on the Continent—usually of the Austrians whose Hapsburg monarchs were old rivals of the Bourbon kings of France.

Dutch William was crowned king, as William III, but many men, especially in Scotland and Ireland, kept their loyalty to James II; and it took William some hard fighting to defeat the "Jacobites" in Ireland. Thousands of Irishmen took service in the armies of France, where they formed Irish Brigades and acquitted themselves with great valor. James II, and his son James Edward ("James III"), and his grandson Charles Edward ("Charles III"), kept their "court" in France as guests of the French kings; and for half a century there was always a chance that their followers might cause trouble in Britain. Secret Jacobite agents came and went: and no man could be sure how far inland the cry of a "wildfowl" on Romney Marsh might travel before the dawn—to what remote manor house as a signal for invasion or uprising! William III was equal to the game. He knew that he was necessary to the great lords who had given him the throne. He had great courage, fortitude, and patience, though outwardly cold and unenthusiastic. He was content to be a parliamentary king so long as he could obtain British help in his endeavor to check the power of Louis XIV.

He joined the island's regiments to his own Dutch army and led them through seven successive seasons of warfare against the marshals of the French King in the Low Countries. A fine soldier, stubborn and tenacious, even heroic in his disregard of his chronic asthma, he endured stoically the hardships of camp and field. He never won a decisive victory but never suffered a bad reverse. The field of Neerwinden was typical: Marshal Saxe was victorious but lost 10,000 men in the battle.

A peace was made in 1697, but war began again when Louis XIV accepted the throne of Spain for his grandson. Unfortunately for Louis, William died while he was preparing for war—unfortunately, because Queen Anne, who succeeded William, made John Churchill, Duke of Marlborough, her commander.

Marlborough was a soldier of genius. By patience and tact he kept the allies together. He had imagination and military insight, and, while enforcing discipline, was most careful for the comfort of his men, who had the utmost confidence in their "Corporal John." In 1704 he marched secretly and swiftly to the Danube, where he joined the Austrian General Prince Eugene and shattered the French army at Blenheim. This and his other famous victories of Ramillies, Oudenarde, and Malplaquet were high points in a whole series of brilliant maneuvers which forced Louis XIV to make peace. Things had not gone so well in Spain, where the allied army under the French-born Earl of Galway was beaten by a French army under the British-born Duke of Berwick at Almanza in 1707. The allies were not liked in Spain. So at the peace in 1713 Louis XIV's grandson kept Spain. To balance this the Spanish Netherlands were given to Austria in order to keep the power of France in check.

At sea, Admiral Rooke had destroyed a French fleet off La Hogue, and another at Vigo where he took eleven million pieces-of-eight from the Spanish treasure ships. It was Rooke who captured the old Moorish fortress of Gibraltar in 1704. Throughout the two wars the British squadrons kept the seas safe for the troop transports.

Queen Anne and Louis XIV died and the scene changed; for in 1714 the great lords invited the Protestant Elector of Hanover, the German George, to be George I of Britain; and in 1715 the new French king was a mere boy—Louis XV. There followed a long period of peace of twenty-five years, owing to the policies of the bluff Norfolk squire Sir Robert Walpole, who was the first prime minister in Britain, and the aged and talented Cardinal Fleury, who governed France for Louis XV. Both believed in peace and the encouragement of trade and industry, both saw little profit in war, and under each their respective countries grew rich and prospered.

George I was succeeded by George II, and Louis XV came to manhood and took the government into his own hands. Cardinal Fleury died and Walpole was driven out of office by a clamor for war against Spain, a war which was quickly merged into one against France. In 1740 the Austrian emperor died leaving his throne to a daughter named Maria Theresa. In 1740 also the savage old king of Prussia died, leaving his crown and his fine army to his clever son, Frederick II, who promptly seized the rich Austrian province of Silesia from the young queen. The French went to the help of Frederick against Austria, while Britain took sides with Maria Theresa, and, of course, did it by attacking the French.

THE GREAT KINGDOMS OF THE WEST

The Continent was soon astir again with armies; and this war of the "Austrian Succession" saw British and Hanoverian regiments under George II fighting their way out of a difficult situation at Dettingen in 1743. Later, it saw George's son, the incompetent Duke of Cumberland, beaten more than once by Marshal Saxe, whose French army included the redoubtable Irish Brigades of Jacobites. It is hard to say whether Britain has gained more from the gallant Irishmen who have fought for her than lost from those equally gallant ones who have fought against her. The British admirals Anson and Hawke defeated French fleets; and hostilities between French and British forces took place in India and in North America. But after much marching and countermarching in Austria, Bohemia, Silesia, the Rhineland, and the Netherlands, the war came to an end in 1748 in stalemate. All conquests were given back—all, that is, except the first shameful one of Silesia made by Frederick of Prussia.

Of more immediate concern to Englishmen and Scotsmen was the Jacobite rebellion of 1745.

While the court of St. James's was listening to Handel's *Te Deum* for the King's victory at Dettingen, Stuart agents were busy planning an invasion of England. This was found to be too difficult without French participation on a large scale, but the debonair and brave Charles Stuart—Charles Edward, the Young Chevalier—sailed for Scotland where he landed with seven followers. Within two weeks he was at the head of two thousand highlanders, mostly Macdonalds. The clans continued to gather around him and he entered Edinburgh, where he was proclaimed as Charles III. Then, brushing aside a lowland force, he marched south. Eight thousand clansmen crossed the western border. They piped themselves through Carlisle in brave style, and, climbing over windswept Shap Fell, were welcomed in "loyal" Lancashire. Charles went at their head, dressed "in a Scotch plaid, a blue-silk waistcoat with silver lace, and a Scotch bonnet." On December 4, when the highlanders reached Derby, the gamble looked like succeeding. Charles was all for going on to London, but his Scots lords, disappointed by lack of support from any English noblemen, advised a retreat. They turned and trailed back the way they had come.

George II's English and German troops assembled under Cumberland in the Midlands, and followed. Three months later the two armies met in a snowstorm on Culloden Moor.

Displaced by the Atholl brigade from their usual post of honor on the right of the battle line, the Macdonalds held aloof until the Mackintoshes and others had all but destroyed themselves in gallant and desperate attacks on Cumberland's triple lines of infantry. The success of a highland onset depended on its first fierce rush. When the Macdonalds did engage, it was too late to save the day—the last Jacobite army was breaking up fast. Two Irish captains led Charles off the field. Cumberland's men remained in possession of it.

Prince Charles escaped through the loyalty of his friends, the poor highland men and women. Cumberland, aided by the Campbells of Argyll, hunted down and executed rebels, burned cots and crops, and seized cattle. Parliament abolished the feudal powers of the clan chieftains and forbade the wearing of the tartan and the plaid cloak. The Jacobite cause was finished. Charles Edward lived until 1788, with nothing to do but drink. His younger brother, Henry—"Henry IX" to the Jacobites—became a Catholic priest and a cardinal, and died in 1807, the last of the hapless Stuart line.

One result of this "Forty-Five" rebellion was, strangely enough, the strengthening of the British royal army; for the government encouraged the raising of highland regiments. No words are needed to pay tribute to the glorious record of these since 1750. Indeed, not only the army alone, but every part of British national life, has been enriched by the contributions of the Scots since the middle of the eighteenth century.

In the larger war, of which the Forty-Five was a lively incident, British sea power again proved its worth in keeping the seas safe for transports and trade. But while British sea power could decide events overseas in the east and in the New World, it could not force a decision in Europe without the support there of a strong military ally.

The Seven Years' War

All the king's horses and all the king's men in France and Britain could now return to their barracks—guards, dragoons, carabiniers, fusiliers, grenadiers, and the rest of them—drilling and parading in jack boots or white gaiters, in bearskins or tricorn hats, with pigtails nicely set in flour and grease. The war in Europe was over.

But not in India, where the rival East India Companies traded, or in America, where the settlers competed for a continent.

There was no strong native power in India, and Dupleix, the French governor of Pondicherry, saw a chance of increasing his power by taking part in native politics in the Indian state called the Carnatic. In 1751 he helped to place a new Indian ruler, or nawab, on its throne; and an army of Indians laid siege to Trichinopoly, where the old nawab had taken refuge. These events alarmed the British Company's men at Madras. Robert Clive, a young clerk, led a handful of native soldiers, or sepoys, and seized Arcot, the ancient capital—a shrewd stroke; for it drew off the horde that was besieging Trichinopoly. Clive held Arcot against odds for fifty days, and then drove the Indians away. In 1752 he took Trichinopoly and restored the old nawab. After this, both Dupleix and Clive returned home, the Frenchman in disgrace, Clive to be made a colonel in George II's army.

These operations in the crumbling forts of south India were trifles compared with the events in the American forests. The French from Canada had explored the waterways, and for a long time their trappers and officers had been active all along the rivers from Canada and the Great Lakes to the French settlement in Louisiana: and their activity was extremely unwelcome to the British colonials in the coast states.

In 1749 a scouting party from Montreal proclaimed Louis XV to be king of the lands about the Allegheny River. In 1754 the French built Fort Duquesne where the Allegheny and Monongahela flow together. This menace far inland brought Major George Washington and his Virginia militiamen into the wilderness west of Pennsylvania, where they ambushed a French detachment. That volley of musketry, breaking the silence of the forest, began a war for a continent.

In 1755 General Braddock set out to take the fort. His rangers cleared a twelve-foot track though the forest, and his two thousand redcoats and militia advanced a hundred miles in a month. They forded the Monongahela in brave style to the sound of fife and drum. They were then ambushed in the forest by French and Indians, and half of them fell to the shots from unseen enemies, Braddock being mortally wounded. The disaster had a bad effect on the reputation of the redcoats among the colonists and the redskins. Although Sir William Johnston's friendly Indians and his New Englanders beat off a surprise attack in the north, the situation was bad. The French threatened to isolate the British colonies, and Washington was trying hard to hold off the redskins, whose savagery had been let loose along the frontier farms from New York to the Carolinas.

It was at this moment that war began again in Europe. Maria Theresa, who was determined to win back Silesia, planned with France, Russia, Saxony, and Bavaria to attack Frederick of Prussia. Becoming aware of this, Frederick forestalled her by marching a large army into Saxony, which he proceeded to treat as his own land. This time Great Britain, as an enemy of the French with whom her sons were already

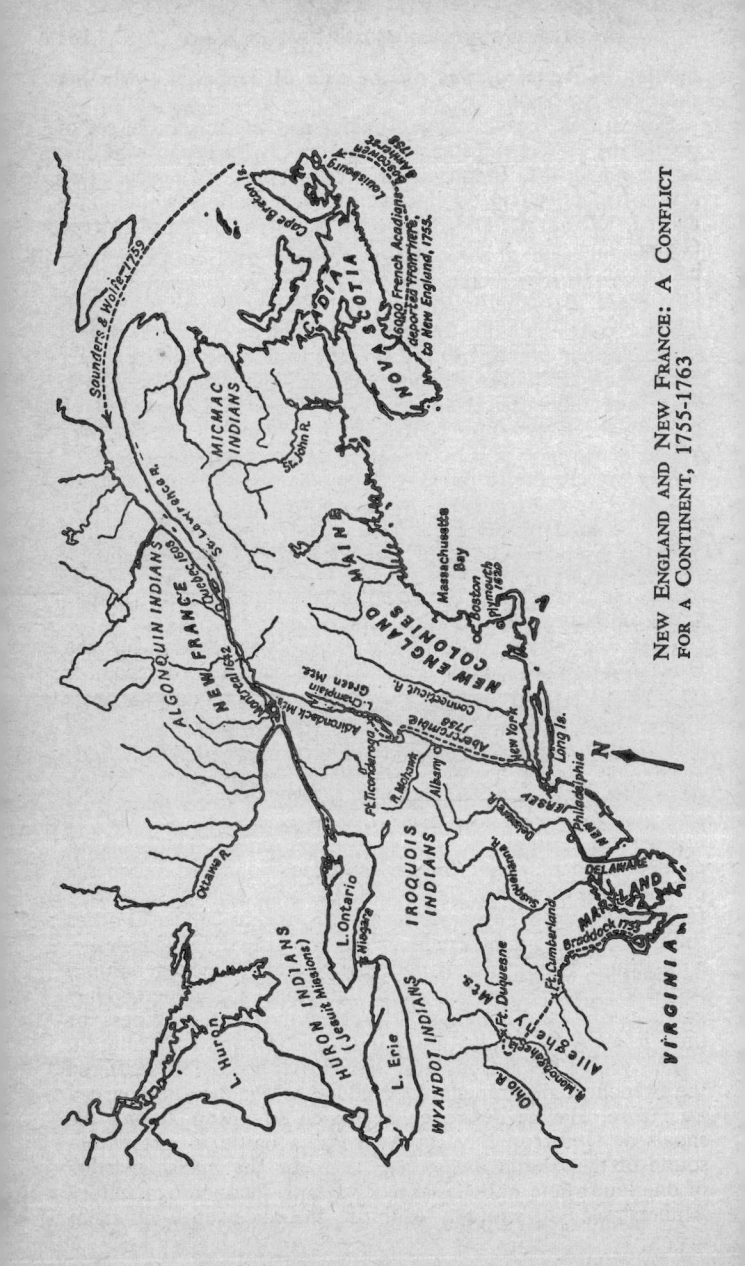

New England and New France: A Conflict for a Continent, 1755-1763

fighting in America, was on the side of Frederick—whether she liked it or not.

For Britain the war began badly, and the miserable set of politicians at Westminster shot Admiral Byng because he had not stopped the French fleet from seizing Minorca. This action had no effect on the enemy: and matters would have drifted into a muddle, if public opinion had not forced George II to let William Pitt manage the war. Pitt did not believe in half-measures. He galvanized the fighting services into aggressive action. He put a hundred and fifty ships of battle into commission. His aim was simple. It was to reduce France to the level of a second-rate power, to wipe out her fleets and capture all her overseas possessions. He arranged to defend Hanover and protect the Netherlands by paying vast sums of money to Frederick, and by sending some British regiments to the Continent. His main effort was to be on the seas and overseas.

Admirals Holmes, Anson, and Hawke gained the mastery of the Narrow Seas. Osbourne sealed up the Mediterranean, and captured the French Admiral Duquesne in his flagship. Boscawen carried General Jeffery Amherst's army to Louisbourg, the fortress that protected the seaward gate of Canada: and Louisbourg was assaulted and taken.

Then the attack on Canada began. Advancing up the Hudson–Mohawk route, 20,000 men under Abercrombie embarked on Lake George. The spreading flotilla with countless oars dipping into smooth water moved north between the forests of the Adirondacks and the Green Mountains. When they disembarked, Abercrombie made a frontal attack on Ticonderoga, where Montcalm's troops were entrenched on a ridge between swamps, protected by a *chevaux-de-frise* of felled trees. The attackers fell in scores under the musketry of the defenders, and the newly raised highland regiments of Gaelic-speaking clansmen suffered very heavily. It was a foolhardy action. Meanwhile British troops under Forbes followed warily along Braddock's old trail to Fort Duquesne, with drums tapping night and day to hold the long column together. They arrived to find the place abandoned. They garrisoned it and renamed it Fort Pitt. In the fullness of time it grew to be the great industrial town of Pittsburgh.

The year 1759 was a year of victory. Boscawen shattered the French Mediterranean fleet off Lagos. Rodney bombarded Le Havre. Hawke destroyed a French squadron among the shoals of Quiberon Bay. In America, a battle fought within sound of the roaring Niagara Falls made the British masters of one land route into Canada. By taking Ticonderoga Jeffery Amherst secured another. A third—the sea route—led them to the crowning victory. Admiral Saunders took General James Wolfe and his army up the St. Lawrence, the Thameside skippers of the packed transports picking their way through the uncharted waters with superb skill until they anchored before the astonished citizens of Quebec. When Wolfe decided to pass his army up a narrow goat track from the water's edge to the Heights above, it was the seamen who hauled up the guns and stores. On the Heights, the French and British armies met to decide the fate of Canada. Both Montcalm and Wolfe were killed in the battle that gave the British possession of Quebec. When Amherst arrived in the spring of 1760 Montreal surrendered. All Canada was British.

So the war stood when George II, on a visit to Hanover, called for and drank his morning chocolate, and then dropped dead.

This was a decisive event; for his grandson, George III, who disliked William Pitt, replaced him by a minister who made peace. Pitt's plans continued to bring victories even after his resignation. When Spain entered the war, British expeditions promptly captured her possessions of Havana and the Philippines. At the peace in 1763 these were given back, but Spain ceded Florida to Britain; and with this land and Canada, Britain now held *all* the North American continent east of the Mississippi. In South India, to which both countries had despatched squadrons and soldiers, Sir Eyre Coote defeated the French at Wandewash and Pondicherry, 1760. The French kept their trading stations on the Indian coasts, but lost their hopes of power over the native states. Instead, victories over native armies, by Clive at Plassey in 1757 and by Munro at Buxar in 1764, made the London merchants masters of Bengal.

So the French lost an empire, and the British gained one.

We left Frederick of Prussia with his army in Saxony in 1756. He ended the war with a sadly devastated kingdom but still kept his hold on the province of Silesia!—the land about the possession of which the continental war had begun. Frederick had won victories over the Austrians at Prague, over the French at Rossbach, and over the Russians at Leuthen: but he had also suffered many defeats. For six years he did not see his own capital of Berlin, which was taken by his enemies. His task against the great powers was a formidable one. Pitt's money helped him, and so did the campaigns of the Hanoverians and British in the west against the marshals of Louis XV, but only a little. His salvation came at last from the death of the Empress Elizabeth of

Russia; her successor, Catherine, was not hostile to him, and withdrew her forces from the war.

Frederick was a great soldier, cool and indomitable, and his courage in the face of such great odds won the world's admiration. He believed firmly in the overwhelming attack delivered against a weak flank—an attack conducted by his disciplined infantry and the shock of a massed cavalry charge. More often than not it carried all before it. But there were times when, even to him, all seemed lost. He was careless of lives, not least of his own life. Outwardly determined and even harsh, he possessed a sensitive nature, and was passionately devoted to the welfare of his people. He inspired confidence and devotion in return in his people and deserved their name for him of "Great"; not only for his military skill, but for the work he did in restoring prosperity to their stricken land after the war. He rebuilt the wasted towns, encouraged trade and industries, and restocked the desolate farms. He made his people toil hard, but he protected them from cruel landowners, and began an orderly system of education. He ran his kingdom like an army, requiring obedience and order and hard work, but insisting on fairness and toleration and duty.

Hitherto, Austria had been the leader among the German states. From now onward there was a rival power in the disciplined and ordered kingdom of Prussia.

Man and the Universe

One way of getting to know our surroundings is to look for some real thing that we hope may be there, such as gold. Many men in the past often spent their lives looking for magic substances such as a *philosopher's stone* whose touch would turn base metals into gold, or an *elixir of life* which would give its owner everlasting youth. They heated, and boiled, and dried, and crumbled up, and distilled, all sorts of fantastic mixtures; and sometimes they did make useful discoveries by accident. They were known as *alchemists*. They were like men seeking a fabulous city, and not seeing the flowers at their feet.

The second way of getting to know our surroundings—by looking at what is actually there—has been followed by thousands of humble people: by the country folk who distinguished and named all wild plants and creatures; by the craftsmen, smiths, tanners, glass-blowers, cutlers, watchmakers, brewers, and so on, who discovered all sorts of useful and interesting facts about the materials of their crafts.

And these also often made discoveries by accident. Civilized life was made possible by their manifold knowledge and skill; and education (which is the means we use for preserving civilized life) used to be a training in one or other of these skilled crafts.

The knowledge of the scientist is founded on that of the craftsman; and sometimes scientists do really look for a special thing—like a cure for malaria. But the pure scientist is moved by sheer curiosity. His knowledge comes from the pursuit of truth for its own sake, and might properly be called the fruit of idleness—the reward of watching spiders instead of digging the garden, or of gazing at the night sky instead of getting enough sleep to do tomorrow's work well. He is the onlooker of the universe. He does not care whether his knowledge is useful or not. He just builds up a picture of the world: and by his searches (called by the imposing name of "researches") he begins to learn that the world is a more marvelous place than any dream of magic can make it.

The heaps of facts so discovered must be linked together into a pattern or scheme if they are to be understood and remembered.

Scientific knowledge is kept in order by theories and hypotheses. Signs of order, or (to borrow and misuse a word from the statesmen) signs of "law," show themselves in the return of the seasons and the movements of the heavenly bodies. "Thou hast appointed the moon for certain seasons and the sun knoweth his going down." The sages of old Chaldea and priests of Egypt knew a lot about astronomy, and the Greeks learned from Chaldea and Egypt both astronomy and mathematics. The Greeks made the greatest advances in the knowledge of the universe ever recorded before our own times and the advances in our own times are based on the leap forward in knowledge which came from the rebirth of Greek wisdom at the Renaissance.

The Greek notion that the planets and stars were fixed in invisible spheres turning about, one inside the other, was taken over by Christian scholars: Jerusalem was the center of the earth, the earth was the center of the planetary system, and man was at the center of the universe. Toward the end of the Middle Ages many men of acute minds were not satisfied with this. In 1543 a Polish churchman, Nicholas Koppernik (Copernicus), who had been trained in Italian universities, published a book entitled *De Revolutionibus*. This suggested that the earth spins on its axis like a top while it circles about the sun in company with the planets. Copernicus found this out with the aid of three sticks of wood fixed together to make a sighting instrument. His was indeed a rare genius. His discovery was confirmed by the Italian Galileo (1564–1642), who improved the newly invented telescope with which he saw the landscape of the moon, and the satellite stars which spin around the planet Jupiter. His researches into the motions of the heavens were confirmed again by the tireless nightwatches of the Dane Tycho Brahe, and by the painstaking mathematics of the German Johann Kepler. Science is international.

The facts and theories of astronomy, and of all the sciences, cannot be described without the help of mathematics, which is a kind of exact language. Fortunately, in the seventeenth century great progress in mathematics was made by four gifted Frenchmen—Desargues, Descartes, Fermat, and Pascal. Mathematics is international.

It was a seventeenth-century Englishman who crowned the work of all these men. Isaac Newton (1642–1727), the son of a Lincolnshire farmer, entered Trinity College, Cambridge, where he became a Fellow in 1667. A book picked up at Stourbridge Fair had turned his mind to mathematics. By the time he was twenty-three he had discovered the binomial theorem, and was working away at a method of reckoning since known as the *calculus*. He gave much of his time to the study of light. He cared little for fame, so little that his masterpiece, the *Principia* (written in Latin so that all scientists could read it!) was published only through the persuasion of his friend, the astronomer Halley.

Newton's genius was an outstanding combination of mathematical and practical ability, both of the highest order. His theory of gravitation linked up all the known facts of the puzzling world in one grand system, including every moving thing from a speck of dust to a comet, from a playing top to a planet. Notice his modesty. He said of himself: "I do not know what I may appear to the world, but to myself I seem to have been only a boy playing on the seashore, and diverting myself in now and then finding a smoother pebble or a prettier shell than ordinary, whilst the great ocean of truth lay all undiscovered before me." The poet Alexander Pope summed up Newton's work in a famous couplet:

> Nature and Nature's laws lay hid in night:
> God said, "Let Newton be!" and all was light.

But Newton's own words are the nobler ones: they describe the true scientist who knows how little he knows.

What of the earth and all things in it? Aristotle had said that all things were made of four elements—earth, air, fire, and water; and each of these might be hot or cold, wet or dry. The real nature of substances remained a mystery even in Newton's time. Wax, iron, sand, sulphur, salt—what sort of scheme could possibly put these and all the other millions of things in any sort of order? Hundreds of facts were known, and the magnet (the loadstone, or magnet iron ore) was being studied: Queen Elizabeth's physician, William Gilbert, experimented with this. Van Helmont of Brussels (1577–1644) studied vapors and made up the word "gas," which has become such a household word since. Glauber (1604–1668) gathered a large number of facts about the preparation of various substances. Robert Boyle (1627–1691), in his book *The Sceptical Chymist*, threw doubts on the system of Aristotle and on many more recent speculations—as a skeptical chemist should do. It was he who first suggested the true nature of an element—a substance which, however much divided, remains the same substance, and out of which no other sort of substance can be got; it never turns out to be a compound or a mixture. Cavendish (1731–1810) and Priestley (1733–1804) and Lavoisier (1743–1794) proved that air and water are not elements but composed of other substances, and Lavoisier demonstrated that however much any matter may alter its shape (that is, turn into a gas or a liquid) it always weighs the same. In 1808 the Cumberland Quaker, John Dalton, summed all these advances up in his atomic theory of matter—that all matter is composed of atoms; that all the atoms of each element are of the same weight and nature; and that when elements join to make compounds like common salt, for example, their atoms join together always in the same pattern or proportion. Dalton's theory did for the matter around us what Newton's had done for the invisible forces around us. The universe was falling into order.

Of the unseen powers or forces, that known as electricity was investigated by many scientists, who learned how to control it, conduct it through wires, measure it, and harness it for use. The names associated with this continuous progress are those of Benjamin Franklin, Galvani, Volta, Ampère, Faraday, Ohm, Clerk-Maxwell, and Lord Kelvin.

What of man himself, and of living things? The anatomist Andreas Vesalius (1514–1564), student at Louvain and Paris, and a professor in the celebrated schools at Padua, published at Basle in 1543, a month after Copernicus's book, an important work entitled *De humani corporis fabrica* (Of the working of the human body). Following this, anatomy and surgery made steady but slow advances until William Harvey (1578–1657), who had also studied at Padua, published his epoch-making book, *De Motu Cordis* (Of the movement of the heart), in which he described the circulation of the blood. This discovery laid the foundation for all future work; and just as the telescope had extended the study of the skies by bringing the infinite a little into man's vision, so the invention of the microscope in northern Italy, about 1650, opened up new realms, especially in biology, by bringing the infinitesimal a little into human vision. All living creation was brought into one great scheme by the theory of evolution and natural selection put forward by Charles Darwin in 1859, in his book *The Origin of Species*.

Another approach to "Man" was indicated by John Locke in his *Treatise on the Human Understanding*, 1690, which was an attempt to study the human mind. This had been started by the Greeks. It is still being pursued by modern psychologists.

Only a history of science can tell the full story of discovery, which has been continuous since the Renaissance. Its history in Britain is largely reflected in the records of the Royal Society, founded by a charter of Charles II in 1662. Its earliest members included Boyle, Wren, and Newton; and it has since included nearly every British scientist of note.

The American Revolution

The French danger to the American colonies had been removed by the Seven Years' War. And the danger from redskins had been checked by the defeat of Pontiac, an Indian chief who led a conspiracy of many tribes against the British garrisons. But garrisons of soldiers were still needed, and so was money to pay for them. An English minister, George Grenville, persuaded the Westminster parliament in 1764 to pass a Stamp Act, ordering the colonists to buy and stick stamps on legal documents, which was a common and simple way of raising revenue. When the colonists protested and chased away the tax collectors, the Act was withdrawn. But other taxes were placed on glass, paper, and tea: and then, when the colonists refused to buy such goods, withdrawn from all but tea. These "on-and-off" tactics occupied six years.

The Americans objected to being taxed without having a say in the government. This is such a sacred principle with us today that it is difficult to understand the men who governed Britain and America in the eighteenth century. The parliamentary government of Great Britain had become a make-believe one, in which very rich men bought and sold seats in the House of Commons. To such men as George

Grenville and his fellows, none of them very intelligent, the Americans were George III's subjects in the same way that the peasants of Sussex or Norfolk were. But the colonists were free men in the sense that English farm laborers could not be: they breathed the freedom of a new, prosperous, and vast land: they could wander in forests unclaimed by any landlord. And, in any case, while it might be sensible to pay taxes to a king, it could never be sensible to pay taxes to a parliament elected by somebody else.

There were other quarrels about the smuggling among New Englanders, which the British tried to stop but which was as popular among New Englanders as it was among the men of old England. In 1772 the Rhode Islanders went as far as burning a small British warship which was engaged on the prevention of smuggling.

The final mischief came in 1775, when Lord North let some tea ships sail to America with the price of the tea reduced, but the tax kept on it. This looked like a shabby commercial trick, since the very powerful English East India Company badly wanted to sell off its large stocks of Indian tea. A party of Bostonians, tricked out like Indian braves, boarded the tea ships and pitched their cargoes into the harbor. The Westminster politicians replied by closing the port of Boston and putting the colony of Massachusetts under military rule.

By now Americans from all the colonies were consulting together, for the quarrel had dragged on for eleven years; and at a congress at Philadelphia they appealed to King George III and to the people of Britain, asking to be treated as grown men who might have some say in their own government.

The best men at Westminster—Lord Chatham, Edmund Burke, Charles James Fox—were for listening to the appeal. Burke proclaimed that if Britain treated her colonists well "no force under heaven would be of power to tear them from their allegiance." He might have been speaking to ignorant barbarians, for all the good his words did.

The dispute drifted into war, not a real war between peoples, not even a civil war, but a war between a handful of politicians at Westminster and the American colonists.

It began at Lexington, where American militiamen ambushed some British troops in 1775. Later, when General Gage ordered his soldiers to capture a height called Bunker Hill, they did so most gallantly by a frontal assault—and suffered a thousand casualties in doing it.

Congress made George Washington, a gentleman of Virginia, its commander-in-chief. His thankless job was to form

The Great Kingdoms of the West

an army from volunteers of the separate thirteen colonies; to feed it, get it paid, munition it, clothe it, drill it, discipline it, and find good officers for it; and then use it against some of the best professional troops led by brave officers experienced in European wars. That, in spite of cold, hunger, lack of co-operation, lack of officers and supplies, Washington managed to keep an army in being, is proof of his genius. The British army was reinforced by 30,000 German mercenaries hired to fight. But Washington and his men knew the country, and most of them were good shots.

On July 4, 1776, the Continental Congress issued its famous Declaration of Independence, mainly the work of Thomas Jefferson, a Virginian aristocrat:

> We hold these truths to be self-evident, that all men are created equal, that they are endowed by their Creator with certain unalienable Rights, that among these are Life, Liberty, and the pursuit of Happiness. That to secure these rights, Governments are instituted among Men, deriving their just powers from the consent of the governed. That whenever any Form of Government becomes destructive of these ends, it is the Right of the People to alter or to abolish it, and to institute new Government, laying its foundations on such principles, and organizing its powers in such form, as to them shall seem most likely to effect their Safety and Happiness.

There was nothing in this unacceptable to men whose grandfathers had turned James II off the throne because he governed badly. This Declaration spoke the language of freedom. The men who governed Great Britain did not. Nor did they know much about making war.

For the conquest of America (even if this were desirable) three things were needed: the command of the seas *at all times;* strong military bases on the American coast; and large forces of troops to hold down a scattered people. In fact, the war was so unpopular in Britain that it was hard to find recruits.

The plan for 1777 was for General Burgoyne from Canada to meet General Howe from New York. Burgoyne set out through the forests. Howe also set out—but, not having heard of the part he was expected to play—he sailed south for Philadelphia! The result was that Burgoyne was forced to surrender to the Americans at Saratoga Springs, outnumbered, surrounded, and short of supplies.

This was heartening news for the men with Washington now watching Howe. They needed encouragement. The next winter saw them encamped in wooden shacks in Valley Forge, blanketless, barefoot and ragged. Only Washington's great spirit kept them together. But Lord Chatham on the other side of the Atlantic shared the same spirit: "If I were an American," he said, "as I am an Englishman, while a foreign troop was landed in my country, I would never lay down my arms—never, never, never!"

The Americans received plenty of help after 1777. France, Spain, and Holland all declared war on Great Britain. Against these enemies the British navy did great deeds, destroying a Spanish fleet off St. Vincent, and a French one in the West Indies. But the only fleet at hand off the American coast when Lord Cornwallis with his army arrived at Yorktown and was besieged by Americans and French volunteers, was a French squadron. So he was forced to surrender, and the war was over.

The peace which was signed at Versailles in 1783 recognized the independence of the United States of America.

In 1783 this was little more than thirteen rather quarrelsome colonies, led and pushed along by some very able men. In 1787 these men drew up a Constitution, which joined them all into a *federal* Union, with an elected President, an elected Senate to represent the separate states, and an elected House of Representatives to represent the people as a whole. This was something entirely new in politics. The first President was George Washington, the second John Adams of Massachusettes, the third, Thomas Jefferson.

So the eldest-born of Britain's many children set up house, and a great new adventure began. So for now we must leave it; leave the small societies of bustling New York, of learned Boston, of fashionable Charleston, and Quaker Philadelphia; leave the southern planter and his slaves, the northern farmer, and the New England fisherman; leave the French Huguenot, the German Protestant, the Massachusetts Puritan; leave the backwoodsman plying his ax in the clearing, the trapper, the hunter, the missionary, the redskin in his wigwam. But before we do so, we should take one look back at those slow-moving, covered wagons pulling out on the trails up and across the mountains into Kentucky, Ohio, Illinois, and Indiana. They are the forerunners of the West.

Britain had lost her first overseas empire—the old one whose ways of speech ran back to the English of Shakespeare's day. By a strange chance, this loss is linked up with the birth of her second overseas Empire.

During the American War, thousands of Americans who did not want to break away from Britain migrated by land and sea into Nova Scotia, into New Brunswick, and into the Kingston peninsula among the Great Lakes. Here they formed an English colony of "Upper Canada," and their coming changed Canada from a purely French settlement to a twofold settlement of French and British. This was the beginning of the later Dominion of Canada.

The other event is picturesque but not so respectable. We had been in the habit of sending convicts to America. Naturally enough, the United States hardly wanted us to go on with the practice. Captain Cook had recently discovered the fertile shores of New South Wales, and it was suggested that the convicts might be sent there. Perhaps the beauty of the place would help to make them good men. So, in 1787, Captain Phillip, R.N., sailed with 700 convicts for the South Seas, and he landed them at Sydney in January, 1788. They were the first Britons to make their homes in Australia.

The transported convicts did not become the ancestors of the Australian nation: but their settlement made the southern continent a British possession, and also revealed the possibilities of that faraway land to free, adventurous men.

The Wealth of Nations

The tale of wars in the eighteenth century must not lead us to think it a turbulent time. The tall grenadier and the dashing dragoon in their handsome uniforms were professional soldiers whose code of conduct taught them to respect civilian life and property. Army made war against army, not —as nowadays—nation against nation. Wars decided the destinies of peoples, making, for example, the French Canadians British subjects; but warfare did not bring civilized life into ruin. The century was an age of good manners even in war. There is a story of a French captain so well-mannered that, at the beginning of an engagement, he begged his enemies to fire first. In the midst of their wars Frenchmen and Englishmen still traded together. Battles were, in fact, infrequent events; most places enjoyed peace all the time.

So much had the discovery of new lands and the progress in arts and crafts done for mankind, that western civilization was more varied and prosperous than at any time since the Caesars of Rome. Of course, there were shocking blemishes and sufferings, cruel punishments of criminals, and a hideous trade in black slaves—but nothing as beastly as the popular slaughter in the arenas of the ancient world; and no dreaded barbarians threatened to swarm out of untracked forests beyond the frontier. Many centuries of law, of town life, of peaceful custom and habit, were bearing fruit. The fierce wars of religion were over. Thanks to commerce the necessities and luxuries of life were abundant. Think of the colliers laden with Tyneside coal creeping down the North Sea to the Thames; or the fine French sugar ships making for Bordeaux from Gaudaloupe; or the East-Indiamen homeward bound with spices, tea, and oriental wares; or the Levanters coming up from the Mediterranean with fruits and wines and silks. The wealth of the world was flowing into the west, and for the comfort of western nations unseen multitudes toiled under tropic and subtropic skies.

The craftsmen of the west had brought their own work to a high pitch of excellence, and the things they made are treasured today in museums, in old houses, and in the hands of dealers: fine glassware and porcelain from Dresden and Limoges; Gobelin tapestries from Paris and silks from Lyons; lace and brocaded cloth; silver and gold plate—cups and jugs, salvers, goblets, bowls, and cutlery; wrought-iron and cast-iron work from Sussex—railings and firebacks; clocks in tall wooden cases and watches of amazing accuracy and finish; Louis XV and Georgian furniture—cabinets, wardrobes, sofas, Chippendale and Sheraton chairs, all of mahogany inlaid and patterned; and fans, snuffboxes, buckles, miniatures, mirrors, and trinkets of all sorts. Some very fine fonts of type, like the Caslon, Baskerville, and Bodoni, were designed for printers to use in the books they published—books bound in full calfskin. Books and libraries were multiplied beyond the wildest dreams of those old monks who had so lovingly handled their own few volumes in the Middle Ages. Even in homely farmsteads the furnishings were of admirable, as well as practical, design—fourposter beds, settles, Windsor chairs, dressers, and the copper bowls, pewter mugs, and ironware of the kitchen. The farmer's wagon showed the loving care that went to its making, and was a delight to the eye. Perhaps the grandest work of men's hands was the great ocean sailing ship, tall and three-masted, with every part of her the result of generations of experience among shipwrights.

The eighteenth century was, indeed, the age of superb work, the end of a long heritage of craftsmanship, before the coming of machinery.

For the first time since the Greeks, whose aim it was to lead the good life in beautiful cities, men now began to plan parts of their cities and adorn them with public monuments, to give pleasure to the eye and dignity to life. They ceased to be satisfied with the homely, huddled, and higgledy-piggledy towns of their forefathers, and thought of architecture as the supreme art of building cities—what we now call town planning. From this came the terraces of

THE GREAT KINGDOMS OF THE WEST

Brighton, the Place de la Concorde and Place Vendôme in Paris, the squares of Bloomsbury, the quays at Bordeaux, and the crescents of Bath and Cheltenham. All this is not surprising when we reflect that every man of education was brought up on the classics of Greece and Rome, and all public inscriptions were done in Latin—not often, alas! in the perfect lettering we find on Roman monuments. Architects drew inspiration from the ruined buildings of antiquity. What the Greeks would have thought of eighteenth-century wigs we can only guess!

In France the royal ministers had the great highways repaired so that coaches could travel comfortably and regularly; and they dug canals linking all the important rivers, and making it possible for goods to be waterborne from the Atlantic to the Mediterranean. In Britain too a beginning was made with the repair of roads and the digging of canals; but the tale of this will be more conveniently told later in our story—as will the tale of the beginning of mechanical inventions. For a long while travel was sufficiently difficult to make each large city a sort of "capital" of its own district. Edinburgh was truly the center and head of the Scots Lowlands; Norwich, the center of the woolen industry of East Anglia; Bristol, the second largest port in the land; Bath, rebuilt and revived as a health resort, was crowded with a fashionable rout of well-to-do folk who sought to be cured of their gout by its medicinal waters, and amused themselves by gambling at cards. Exeter and York were centers of local society. What we know as industrial towns were few. Sheffield pursued its ancient craft of cutlery, and Birmingham resounded with the ring of hammers on anvils turning out small brass and iron goods—"brummagem" wares. Middlesborough and Birkenhead did not even exist.

It was in the eighteenth century that the "capital city" of the country—as we know it—came into existence: a kind of magnet drawing more and more people to itself every year. Paris, which held some 700,000 persons, began already to dominate France—much more than London dominated Britain. This increasing power concentrated in a capital city was the mark of the increasing power of the monarchies and of their governments. It has gone on increasing ever since, as nations have become more and more like armies controlled from one headquarters—have become, in fact, "great powers."

The London that Shakespeare knew perished in the Great Fire of 1666 in the reign of Charles II. The timbered and thatched houses blazed like an inferno and left it a smoking ruin. From its ashes there arose a new city of brick and stone, adorned with the many steeples of Sir Christopher

Wren's new churches, and crowned over all with the dome of his masterpiece, St. Paul's. The new city, together with its neighbor of Westminster, was now a *metropolis*. The royal court at Kensington; the parliaments at Westminster; the Inns of Court where the lawyers were trained; the town houses of the nobility; the offices of the trading companies of the East and West Indies, Russia, Africa, and Hudson Bay; the new Bank of England and the Stock Exchange—all these made London the center of society, government, law, politics, trade, business, learning, fashion, news, and the arts. In Queen Anne's time it contained one tenth of the population and its river was crowded with ships carrying three quarters of the kingdom's trade.

Even in the eighth century the monk Bede had described London as "the market place of many nations resorting to it by land and sea." A thousand years later it was the same: Daniel Defoe in 1724 saw in the Thames "above Two Thousand Sail of All Sorts of Vessels that really go to Sea." Ratcliffe Highway, where the mariners lived, was the threshold of the gateway of the world. Its men took the tall ships downstream on voyages lasting for whole seasons, to return on some flood tide with West Indian sugar and molasses, China tea, Virginia tobacco, African ivory and mahogany, Russian furs, and muslins and coffee from the east.

Such a trade could not continue without a good coinage and a sound banking system. In both Britain and France the old, battered, clipped and debased coins were replaced by new ones—the splendid silver shilling and golden sovereign in Britain, and in France the silver crown *(écu)* and the gold louis. Banking, the business of borrowing and lending money at a profit, was a very old art carried on by goldsmiths and pawnbrokers. The new banks helped traders by issuing banknotes, which were promises to pay so much money on demand: and traders could use these notes in place of coins— so long as they trusted the banks. In fact the shortage of gold and silver for minting into coins made it hard to carry on business without this paper money. From Defoe's time men began to buy and sell shares in trading companies, and the shares were traded on stock exchanges according to set rules. We still do this. At its beginning this "Prodigious Paper Commerce," as Defoe called it, led to the ruin of hundreds of people both in Britain and France, who bought shares in sham companies or for harebrained schemes. Nowadays the price of shares is printed daily in the newspapers.

Newspapers began in the seventeenth century, and the first London daily, the *Daily Courant*, came out in 1702. It was quickly followed by a whole flock of *Posts, Packets,*

The Great Kingdoms of the West 195

Registers, and *Mercuries.* One of the latter enjoyed the largest circulation of its time. This was the *Mercure de France*—a proof of the influence of France in the century when, as Frederick the Great said, "with a knowledge of the French language, a man could travel everywhere." The most famous paper in the world, the *London Times,* began in 1785.

News and trade need to be discussed. In Queen Elizabeth's days men met in taverns like the Mermaid, where Shakespeare and his friends gathered. In Queen Anne's days men of fashion took sedan chairs, while the more modest clergymen or scholars walked, to their favorite coffeehouses. There were scores of these. The wits and scholars met at Will's; the clergy at Child's; the aristocratic gamblers at White's or Almack's. Lloyd's has become famous all over the world, for it was at Lloyd's coffeehouse that the ship brokers met. Many old fraternities and clubs still used the taverns—the Fellowship of Parish Clerks, for instance, who probably talked knowingly of psalm-chants and pew-rents over their ale and their long churchwarden pipes.

There were, unhappily, less pleasant resorts, hundreds of them in the alleys and byways—gin shops where idlers and rogues drank themselves drunk for a few pence. Among them one might espy the desperadoes who had waylaid the Islington coach the night before. There were no policemen. Gone was the old-time watch and ward; instead, only a few old watchmen called the time. It was not till 1750 that Henry Fielding, the wise Bow Street magistrate, formed his band of Bow Street Runners to chase and arrest criminals. A London mob —or a Paris mob—was a fearful and unsavory thing. City slums were not new: but in the eighteenth century, as in ancient Rome, they were disgracefully numerous and overcrowded.

The honest citizen, desiring crowds and pleasant company, could listen to David Garrick acting in Shakespeare's plays at Drury Lane Theatre, or to Handel's operas at Covent Garden; or he might have enjoyed the lively tunes of John Gay's *Beggar's Opera* at Lincoln's Inn Fields. He could, on a fine summer evening, take a cushioned wherry across the Thames, and stroll about the lamplit pleasure gardens of Vauxhall to the strains of music—on one memorable evening, to the sound of Handel's Fireworks Music celebrating the peace of 1748.

Yet London was still small enough for him to wander afoot into the countryside—to Paddington, or the meadows of Chelsea, or the leafy lanes of Camberwell: and close to the north and east were the woodlands of Enfield and Epping.

Most men in all the western lands were peasants, and time and change did not work so fast with them. But new methods of farming and new crops were tried out in Holland, and were the cause of much change in parts of Britain. In some parts, indeed, Piers Plowman still drove his ox teams afield as in old times, but experiments with crops and the breeding of beasts had begun a real revolution in agriculture. In the sixteenth century, when it had been more profitable to keep sheep than to grow grain, many rich men had hedged their lands to make money from wool. In the eighteenth century hedging and enclosures went on at an increasing rate—not for the purpose of keeping sheep, but to grow selected seed and breed selected cattle—to improve the yield of grain and the new root crops, and to increase the size of the beasts— things that could never be done on the old intermingled acre-strips. Wealthy landlords paid for acts of parliament to permit them to enclose the old acres, and with them, too often, the meadows, the village greens, the commons, and the wasteland. All too often the poor tenants were forced out to become landless laborers: even if they kept their small holdings they lost the commons where they had kept their cows and the waste on which they had fed their pigs. By constant hoeing, by manuring, by draining the fields, by spending great sums of money, the rich farmers did wonders. They began the kingdom's famous breeds of cattle. They turned the landscape into its present familiar checkerboard appearance of hedgerows and fields, which distinguishes it from the older-fashioned open-field country of the Continent. The process went on well into the nineteenth century. The disappearance of the small landholder was a disaster. Like so many improvements the revolution in agriculture was a good thing done in a bad way.

Throughout the land were the Elizabethan manor houses of red brick, mellowing with age; and also the newer, enormous piles of the wealthy eighteenth-century noblemen—places like Blenheim Palace, Stowe, and Castle Howard. In these they enjoyed their leisure hours, and collected great stores of furniture, books, paintings, and pottery, and kept armies of servants. The ruined castles of an earlier nobility frowned down at Chepstow and Bodiam and a score of other places, giving a romantic contrast to the plaster, pillars, and pediments of the new classical buildings. The vestiges of Rome still showed at Uriconium, Lincoln, and elsewhere, and earthworks of prehistoric man were being discussed by the newly formed Society of Antiquaries. Here and there a few moldering walls revealed the site of a monastery built by the ancestors of the men and women who lived both in the lordly houses and the village hovels.

Cathedrals and churches were neglected and dusty. Many churches were furnished with high family pews in which the squire could keep his table, his sofa, and even a fireplace, and snore there with his favorite dog at his feet during the service. The Church was not in a flourishing state. It had never regained the wealth plundered from it by the king and the lords, and in the eighteenth century its bishops and clergy did not show much zeal. Some parishes went without pastors, some bishops never visited their dioceses except on rare occasions. It was all very comfortable and easygoing and spiritless.

Zeal returned with John Wesley, an Oxford scholar and clergyman who believed in the Gospel message and commandment. He traveled thousands of miles on horseback in all parts of the land, preaching and praying and exhorting the people to mend their lives. The pulpits of the Church were denied to him, and many clergy treated him with scorn. He organized his followers into a Christian community, and because he was a great organizer that community remains today among us. With his brother Charles, a hymnwriter of genius, he brought back to religion something of the fervor that had been lacking ever since the Middle Ages:

> Jesu, Thou art all compassion,
>   Pure, unbounded love Thou art;
> Visit us with Thy salvation,
>   Enter every trembling heart.

This was emotional, popular, even exciting. Cornish tin miners, Lancashire folk, Midlanders, the Welsh, all caught eagerly at the new revelation of hope and faith. They certainly needed both. The reformed Protestant church had never struck deep roots in the life of the west, whose people wanted a richer religion. In the villages of Wales—named after the Welsh saints of the Dark Ages—now arose new chapels of Bethel, Salem, and Ebenezer, around which the life of the people revived. Wesley's preaching affected all the kingdom: in the life of Cornwall and Wales it has been as much a forming influence as the Presbyterian teaching of John Knox in Scotland.

Wesley gave to many poor and humble folk a new dignity and a new moral purpose based on more lasting values than politics or commerce. And there were other men, moved more by reason than by religion, who wanted to improve the fortunes of mankind. "The empire of reason," wrote the scientist Joseph Priestley in 1791, "will ever be the reign of peace." Toward the end of the century both reason and religion were needed badly; for there was then beginning a revolution in the way men and women lived. Above the coal fields of Wales and the Midlands and north, and along the streams of the Pennines, were new factories. Villages were growing into crowded slums. There were blast furnaces reddening the skies at night. The landless laborers were crowding into the new industries to live unhealthy lives in dingy streets, far different from the age-long natural life of the countryside when even a poacher living in a hut could be happy and healthy. All the wisdom of statesmen, all the wisdom of employers and clergy, would be needed to preserve the true wealth of the nation—the lives and the welfare of the people.

The fates were proffering new gifts to men. Medicine was emerging from magic; science from alchemy and astrology; engineering—which had begun to change the face of the world—from the handicrafts. The knowledge and invention of ten generations since the Renaissance were giving new opportunities for the betterment of human life. And never before were so many men anxious to make things better—to reform the laws, set free the slaves, help the poor, teach the ignorant, and bring light and life into all dark places.

Unfortunately, the world has seldom been ready to profit from the discoveries of its wise men. Here, ready, were the inventors; here, ready, were the reformers who wanted to act in the name of reason and of compassion. Across the prospect of this common-sense and Christian charity there swept a tornado of unreason and hatred: it all began in the sacred name of freedom. It began in France in 1789, and convulsed Europe and the world for twenty-five years.

6

THE FRENCH REVOLUTION

The Revolution

While Captain Phillip's convicts were settling down on the other side of the world in their new and strange Australian home, the ancient kingdom of France came to a violent end: and in its downfall it shook the world.

Government, laws, and taxes in France were clumsy and unjust. So they were in all the German and Italian states. Some German rulers actually sold their young men as soldiers to other kings, and some were fantastically mad. But France led the world in learning, in arts and science, and in the civilized ways of life; and the French king, Louis XVI, was a decent and good-natured man.

It is possible for a country to be wealthy and prosperous while many of its people are poor and needy. So it was with France, where the peasants lived as their ancestors had lived in the Middle Ages. They paid heavy taxes to both the king and their lord of the manor. They worked on the lord's domain. Their hard-won grain fed his pigeons and rabbits, which they were forbidden to snare. Their grain was ground at his mill, and their grapes trodden in his winepress. They could not sell a beast, or marry, without paying him a fee. They were serfs. But there were plenty like them in other lands.

We in Britain can consider ourselves lucky to have been conquered and ruled by strong Norman and Plantagenet kings who were masters of all men, and gave all men duties to perform; who summoned parliaments to help them govern; and whose law—the royal law—was carried throughout the length and breadth of the land by stern and fearless judges before whom *all* men quailed. In France in 1789 there were still provinces with their own laws. Imagine finding in eighteenth-century England a province called Mercia or Wessex with its own laws! Many Frenchmen admired the British system of government, and many had been deeply stirred by the American Declaration of Independence, made by British citizens who revolted rather than pay a trivial tax—because they wished to be free to have some say in their own affairs. Many Frenchmen, also, had spent their lives denouncing the power and wealth of the Church in France: some hated the Church and clergy with a fierce and burning hatred.

Louis XVI ruled all France from Versailles, and his power was absolute. He chose his own ministers as he pleased. There was no parliament or assembly, and none of the nobles, or *seigneurs,* who should have been the leaders of France, had any say in the government. Instead they idled their time away as courtiers, or stayed in their châteaux. Yet they were privileged: although they paid no taxes they had no duties. In Britain all men had for centuries been trained in the arts of governing, or *of being governed:* in France men had no such experience.

In 1789 Louis XVI, being hopelessly bankrupt, called together an elected assembly of nobles, clergy, and commons—the ancient three estates, or Estates-General, of the French kingdom, which had not met for 180 years. They met now at Versailles, where the nobles and clergy in their robes and the commons in sober black made a brave show at the opening ceremony, and all was hope and high expectancy of good reforms of taxes and government. A long wrangle about the method of voting caused the Third Estate (the commons) to assemble on its own and turn itself into a National Assembly with the task of reshaping all the government and laws of the land. There was plenty to discuss, especially by men who had no experience of affairs; and while the Assembly talked the people of France did what they liked.

In many districts the peasants attacked and burned the châteaux, and many noblemen and their families left France. In Paris a mob forced its way into the old prison fortress of the Bastille, and, being a mob, cut off the heads of the innocent soldiers who guarded it, and paraded them on pikes. Most Parisians were quiet and peaceful, but this mob of some thousands of rascals ran riot without opposition. A courtier told Louis that what was taking place was not a revolt but a revolution. His words were true. In London George III had recently put down a roaring drunken mob with a regiment of footguards. No one in Paris was strong enough to take action. The unruly citizens set up their own city government, and raised companies of a National Guard which took for badge a red, white, and blue cockade—the *tricolor* of the Revolution. The mob did not lack powerful supporters from among the wealthy and educated. The King's cousin, the Duke of Orleans, earned his nickname "Egalité Orleans" from his encouragement of the baser elements of the populace.

The French Revolution

In the midst of endless debates on everything, the National Assembly issued a Declaration of the Rights of Man, asserting that all were free and equal. Everyone became a "citizen": just that and nothing more. A mob trailed out to Versailles and brought the King and his family to live in Paris in the Tuileries Palace. The Assembly followed him, and continued its debates amid the excited clamor and agitation of the capital, where political clubs were noisy with orators, and where all sorts of parties and men published newspapers. Henceforward, the mob and fanatics of Paris led the kingdom.

Noblemen and royalist exiles *(émigrés)* gathered in the Rhineland and asked the kings of Europe to stop the revolutionaries. When the Assembly ordered all clergy to become civil servants under the French government, most of them refused. This attack on the Church gave deep offense to many moderate men. Louis XVI himself, who, so far, had been half-hearted about most things, took flight with his family secretly to the German frontier. His coach was stopped and he was recognized just short of the frontier, and when the news reached Paris, many of the revolutionaries clamored for a republic—the king would desert his people, would he? Then down with the monarchy! Long live the sovereign people!

When the National Assembly, having at last drawn up a system of government, dissolved itself, it forbade its members to sit in the next assembly. This meant that no one with any practical knowledge of government was to take part in the next government, and all was to be started again. This extraordinary decision gave the wild men of the Parisian clubs their chance. The next assembly declared war on Austria.

Lawlessness and disorder increased. The German Duke of Brunswick, encamped in the Rhineland, warned the French that he would destroy Paris if Louis XVI were harmed. The Paris mob set up a republican city government called the Commune, and its leaders invited all peoples to rise up and destroy their kings. The Marseilles men marched in singing a new song—the Marseillaise. A mob attacked and murdered the King's Swiss Guard and ransacked the Tuileries. Louis was imprisoned. Brunswick crossed the frontier. Gangs of ruffians went around the prisons killing the royalists who had been crowded in them. By a chance in the slow sort of campaigning of those days the Prussians were checked in a gun duel at Valmy, and began to retreat. The revolutionaries ordered a general conscription of able-bodied men to form new armies, and hurried them to the frontier. What they lacked in training they made up for in dash and enthusiasm. They reached the Rhine, and overran the southern (Austrian) Netherlands.

In Paris the tragedy of the King moved to its end. He was tried, condemned, and guillotined in January, 1793. The revolutionaries called on peoples everywhere to rise against their kings, and encouraged them by declaring war on Britain, Holland, and Spain.

In four years the oldest kingdom in Europe had been turned into a raging people at war with all other kingdoms—at war, too, at home; for after the attack on the Church and the killing of the King, there followed large royalist rebellions in the provinces against the godless republican government in Paris. The peasants of Brittany and La Vendée, led by their seigneurs and priests, were not easily put down. These perils and the insane and bitter jealousies and suspicions among the parties in Paris led to a Reign of Terror. A Committee of Public Safety sent thousands of men and women to the guillotine—aristocrats, defeated generals, royalists, spies, personal enemies denounced by their neighbors, criminals, and, in fact, anyone unlucky enough to be accused. Most of the victims were poor people. Among the notables to suffer were most of the leading revolutionaries, like Danton, who were entangled in the vast webs of suspicion; and also men of note like Lavoisier the chemist, and Chénier the poet. Among them also was the unhappy Queen, Marie Antoinette—contemptuously known as "the Austrian woman." It was a nightmare of arrest and summary execution. Daily the tumbrils rolled through the streets with their quotas of condemned. In all this the dominant figure was Robespierre, who stayed in power untouched while his colleagues perished. The Terror only ended when he himself was attacked, knocked down, and bound by a group of men and hurried off to the scaffold.

There were many others as bloodthirsty as Robespierre whose fanatical spirit drenched Paris in blood; but there were many also, like Carnot, who worked day and night to raise, equip, and train the new armies.

These armies of conscripts, leavened by the men of the old and excellent royal army whose artillery was the best in Europe, were the children of this strange and violent revolution. The army of the north, named the Army of Sambre and Meuse, was a host of men learning order and discipline on the battlefield in the face of danger—the only ordered and disciplined thing to come out of the frenzy of France. Under such stringent conditions it was only natural that the new armies should be finding good young generals, men like Hoche, Jourdain, and Moreau, accustomed to require loyalty, discipline, and obedience of their troops—virtues long absent from Paris.

Napoleon and the British Navy

Among the scores of general officers appointed by the French Republic was a young Corsican, Napoleon Bonaparte, one of Louis XVI's artillery officers, well trained in the profession of arms. When a mob rose in the streets after the fall of Robespierre, he blew it away with his gunfire—the first man to disperse a Paris mob since 1789. Unlike the rest of Frenchmen of his day, Napoleon always took decisive action when he had the power; and the Republic gave him the power by creating a great army, after it had declared the beginning of a reign of peace!

Napoleon himself was one of the two tremendous forces in the history of the Revolution. The other was the British Navy.

Since the days of Drake that navy had gained strength, skill, and experience. Blake taught it how to maneuver and fight in squadrons, and its tasks in all the seven seas had hardened it to the highest pitch of seamanship and discipline. As soon as the French Republic declared war the British fleet came into action. In 1794 Lord Howe defeated a French fleet in the Atlantic on the "Glorious First of June." British armies landed in the Low Countries were useless. In any case they were too small. But the navy swept French commerce from the seas and captured French overseas possessions—and also the Dutch possessions when the French overran Holland. It was in this way that Trinidad, Ceylon, and the Cape of Good Hope became British.

In 1796 Napoleon was given command of an "army of Italy," and revealed his military genius in a brilliant campaign. Within six weeks of starting he had crossed the Alps of Savoy and driven the Austrians from Lombardy, a feat of arms that showed up the better because his fellow generals, Moreau and Jourdain, had failed against the Austrians in the Rhineland and Germany. But Napoleon did much more than this. He carried the war up the Tyrolean passes into Austria, and was only sixty miles from Vienna when he forced the emperor to make peace. Then he set to work to turn North Italy into republics dependent on France, a task in which he showed his fierce energy and organizing talents. Venice, the renowned and proud mistress of the Adriatic, gateway and guard of Christendom, ceased to be an independent state. Like the rest it was subordinate to France.

At sea the British Admiral Jervis destroyed a combined French and Spanish fleet off St. Vincent, and Admiral Duncan defeated a Dutch fleet off Camperdown. These victories against the allies of the French were gained in spite of serious mutinies of British seamen against low pay, foul quarters, rotten food, and brutal treatment by some captains. The mutineers, however, did keep their warships in good fighting trim ready to sail against their country's enemies. They did obtain some betterment of their conditions.

Meanwhile Napoleon was winning fresh laurels in a distant land. He sailed to the Nile (missing the British fleet narrowly), and there overthrew with ease the Egpytian army in a battle fought beneath the pyramids, after which he set his scholars and scientists to survey and collect Egyptian antiquities. His fleet lay at anchor in Aboukir Bay until Admiral Nelson sailed in and blew it to pieces. Napoleon then marched his Frenchmen up into Palestine, where his grenadiers were repulsed in their assault on the walls of Acre, largely owing to the help given to the Turks by Captain Sidney Smith's naval gunners. This made Napoleon abandon whatever project he may have had of eastern conquests, and when he got back to Egypt, he left his army and sailed secretly to France. There he found all in confusion and threatened with defeat, 1799.

A new coalition, of Russia, Austria, and Britain, was in being against France. Napoleon made himself First Consul after the old Roman fashion—old Roman fashions being much in favor during the Revolution—and, working sixteen hours a day for months on end, he brought some order into the government. Then, marching swiftly over the Great St. Bernard pass he caught an Austrian army at Marengo and shattered it. Moreau defeated another Austrian army at Hohenlinden, and again Austria was forced to accept peace.

In 1802 the stalemate between the military genius of Napoleon and the naval power of Great Britain was recognized by the Peace of Amiens.

The peace was merely an armed truce. Napoleon reoccupied Holland and Switzerland, and sent his troops into George III's kingdom of Hanover. The same year he crowned himself Emperor of the French in Notre-Dame Cathedral in the presence of the pope whom he had brought to Paris to conduct the ceremony. Then he resolved to conquer Britain. At Boulogne lay his army of invasion, and five other armies were strung out along the coast of Europe from Hanover to Brest, all under his most trusted commanders. The British blockading squadrons rode in all weathers for long months off the harbors of Europe under experienced British admirals —Cornwallis, Collingwood, Nelson; and the Channel was alive with British sloops and frigates. Volunteers in the United Kingdom sprang to arms ready to meet the invader with pike and musket; fishermen off the southeast coast could see the French practicing their embarkation in flat-bottomed boats; beacons were piled high on the Downs ready to flame into warning, and false alarms set farmers and cattle moving inland! Coastal forts were repaired or built. But again the event proved to be a seaman's job.

There followed one of most celebrated sea campaigns ever fought by the British Navy, and one of the most skillful of land campaigns made by Napoleon.

Napoleon needed warships to protect his troops while they crossed the Channel. At last, in 1805, his Admiral Villeneuve, harbored in Toulon, eluded Nelson's blockading fleet, and sailed away to the French West Indian island of Martinique. Nelson, at fault, sailed off eastwards to Egypt, thinking Villeneuve had gone there. Then he doubled back to Gibraltar, and then made for Martinique to find that Villeneuve was on his way back to the English Channel. Nelson made such good speed that he was soon on Villeneuve's heels, running for home waters: a long chase, indeed, as Captain Keats of the *Superb* well knew, for his ship was old and foul and slow— "a lame duck lagging all the way." Nelson slipped a fast frigate ahead to London with the news. So, when Villeneuve arrived in the Channel he found a fleet under Sir Robert Calder barring his way, and without engaging he fell back on Coruña.

This ended Napoleon's hopes of invasion.

The French Emperor now displayed his extraordinary military genius. By clever staff work he moved all his armies without confusion into Austria, four hundred miles away, where they arrived after rapid marching, and concentrated before the Austrians were fully aware of what was happening. They captured one Austrian army at Ulm, and defeated a combined Austrian and Russian army at Austerlitz. There was never a soldier like this Corsican! He forced Austria again to peace, and gave Hanover (which belonged to George III of Britain) to Prussia. Such was the land war which shattered the third coalition against France, and ended William Pitt's hopes. Pitt was a sick man and died a month after Austerlitz. But he lived long enough to learn that all fear of invasion had passed.

Six weeks before Austerlitz Englishmen learned a new name—the name of Cape Trafalgar on the Spanish coast. Villeneuve with a French and Spanish fleet was caught off this cape by Nelson and his "band of brothers" and overwhelmed. Nelson and Collingwood, leading their weather-beaten ships in two lines, broke up the enemy's squadrons, passed through

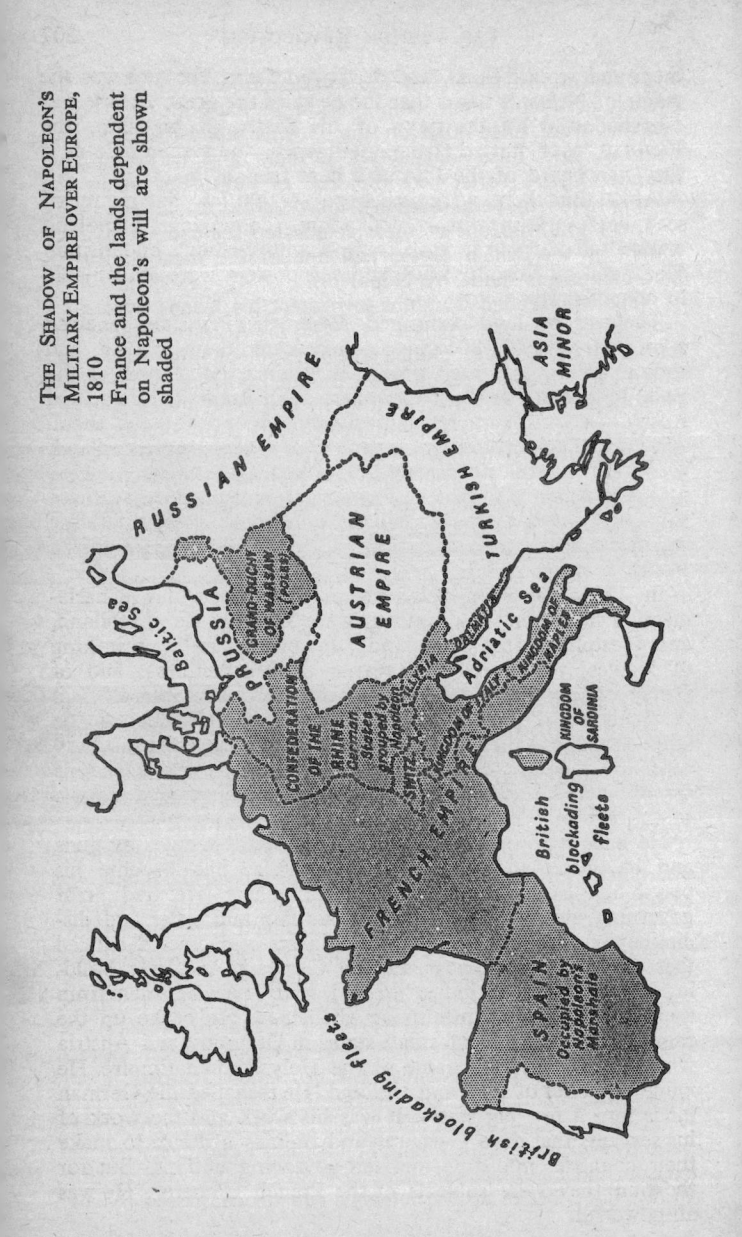

The Shadow of Napoleon's Military Empire over Europe, 1810
France and the lands dependent on Napoleon's will are shown shaded

THE FRENCH REVOLUTION

them and around them, and destroyed them. Yet such was the magic of Nelson's name that the news of the great victory was overshadowed by the news of his death on his ship, the *Victory*. "Men started at the intelligence, and turned pale as if they had heard of the loss of a dear friend."

After this there were no more sea battles, but plenty of sea work, transporting, blockading, convoying. Napoleon ordered all Europe to stop trading with Britain: and Britain blockaded all Europe. Land and sea powers were still unable to come to grips.

The war on land continued. When the Prussians renewed it on their own in 1806 Napoleon defeated them at Jena, and rode in triumph through Berlin. He gained the support of the Poles by promising to set them free from Russia, Prussia, and Austria—countries which had divided Poland between them. After this he fought Russian armies at Eylau and Friedland. Then, meeting the Russian tsar on a raft in the River Niemen, he made a pact with him. The two potentates agreed to share Europe between them. Napoleon dominated the west; the tsar was to be his partner in dividing and controlling the civilized world.

In 1808 Napoleon ruled an empire larger than Charlemagne's had been. His brothers were kings of Italy, Holland, and Westphalia (the Rhineland); his brother-in-law was king of Naples; the rulers of Bavaria, of Württemberg, and of Baden were married to his kinswomen. He himself had divorced his first wife and married the daughter of the emperor of Austria. The young and rather reserved artillery officer of Louis XVI had become an emperor who made his friends and his marshals dukes and marquises and counts of the new nobility of his new empire.

He had imposed his will on princes and peoples by guns and bayonets; and thrones and dynasties had become his playthings. But he was no mere conqueror. He had great governing ability, and a passion for law and order and discipline in peace and war. His engineers and officers carried these ideas into backward lands of Germany and Italy, building roads, fostering industries and trade, rousing men from their long habits of unthinking obedience. He broke up the ramshackle collection of small states in Germany and Austria which went under the name of the Holy Roman Empire. He made republics of Italy and Holland. He reshaped the German lands into a few big states. It was his work and the work of his servants that gave Germans and Italians a desire to make their countries into free and self-governing nations. But for the time they were subjects of the French Emperor. He was all-powerful.

Napoleon: Spain and Russia

Only Great Britain kept up the war. She seized French merchantmen and blockaded the coasts of Europe. These things her incomparable navy did. But she could not make successful war without allies in Europe. Napoleon provided these by his invasions of Spain and Russia.

In 1808 he deposed the king of Spain and put his own brother, Joseph Bonaparte, on the Spanish throne. No one could say that Napoleon ever neglected the fortunes of his own family. The Spaniards, a proud and independent nation, rose in arms, town by town and village by village, and defeated and captured a large French army. Napoleon himself then marched his veterans into the peninsula and entered Madrid. Thence he was drawn away to the north where a British force under Sir John Moore threatened his communications with France. He hurried his cavalry across the bleak mountains after Moore's regiments, who fell back to the coast, doing seventeen miles a day through blizzards of sleet, while the Light Division held off the French pursuit. A final stand at Coruña, in which Moore was killed, enabled the British to get away in the waiting transports. The campaign was comparatively small, yet it does illustrate the advantages of sea power. Napoleon had already gone back to France, leaving Spain to his marshals.

These had to deal not only with the stubborn and hostile nation whose fighting qualities were legendary, but with a British army under Wellington based on the splendid harbor of Lisbon. Even before Moore's defeat at Coruña, Wellington had commanded an expeditionary force in Portugal, and had checked a French army at Vimeiro. Now he defeated them again at Talavera in 1809. This battle, indeed, was a small affair compared with the main war in Europe, which the Austrians had restarted, and which lasted just three months before Napoleon, after two furious battles at Aspern and Wagram, forced the Austrians again to make peace.

Spain continued to be a scene of savagery and terror. Spanish peasants fought a guerrilla, or small war, of sudden attacks on outposts and detachments. For years Napoleon had to keep five separate armies there under his marshals, in a land where "large armies starve and small ones get beaten"; a land whose enraged people captured, tortured, and killed French stragglers and foragers. So successful were the Spaniards that it took two hundred horsemen to escort one French courier in safety. Marshals in neighboring Spanish provinces often got news of each other's movements only by way of Paris! Yet Spain had no government. Spaniards only knew that Frenchmen had no business to be living and looting in their homeland. So they made war in the only way they could—piecemeal, savage, revengeful.

All this time Wellington kept his small but tough British army based on Lisbon, which he protected by long fortified lines of earthworks, fallen trees, and gun batteries. The French army, watching him, had to camp in a wasted land while he and his men enjoyed plenty—supplied by his ships. When at last the French were forced to retreat, he followed them in 1811, and won a series of fine victories at Fuentes d'Onoro, Albuera, Ciudad Rodrigo, Badajoz, and, on July 22, 1812, at Salamanca.

On the day of Salamanca, a Grand Army under Napoleon was already in Russia marching eastward. His horsemen had led the way, crossing the Niemen on June 23. The infantry and guns followed in clouds of dust over the endless plain, half a million men—French, Germans, Italians, and Poles.

The Russians fell back, leaving a waste land for the invaders; but they stood to battle on the River Borodino on September 6. That day a courier rode into the French camp with news of Salamanca. Both ends of Europe were aflame with the Emperor's wars! Napoleon dislodged the Russians, but lost thousands of men doing it. The columns resumed their long march. At last Napoleon entered Moscow. The city was deserted, a ghost city of silent streets. Somehow the place was set on fire, and its wooden houses blazed fiercely while the Emperor's troops waited, hungry, dispirited, ragged, and losing the bonds of discipline. A month later Napoleon sounded the retreat, and just over 100,000 men began the slow and dreadful return. Winter came early. On October 29 the earth froze and the frost deepened and the Russian Cossack cavalry, used to the cold weather, harried the stragglers and outposts. In the crossing of one river the invaders lost 20,000 men. By this time most of their horses had perished. Napoleon, taking a sledge, hurried on ahead of the remnants of his army to reorganize the troops he had left in garrison in Germany. On December 14 the last hardy rabble of scarecrows and desperate men—*"grognards"*—struggled back over the Niemen. Marshal Ney, "the bravest of the brave," commanded the four men of the rearguard. He crossed last.

Napoleon raised new armies in France, but all Europe rose against him; and in a grim three-day battle around Leipzig the Russians, Austrians, and Prussians overbore him by sheer weight of numbers. Wellington, meanwhile, had won another battle at Vitoria in Spain, and had pursued the French through the passes of the Pyrenees into France. In the north, Napoleon, still fighting with amazing skill, was pressed back on Paris. In the south, Wellington's men reached Toulouse. Napoleon surrendered, and was sent in honorable exile to Elba.

His empire had fallen at last before the stubborn patriotism of the peasantries of Russia and Spain—a patriotism that he had never met in the multitudes of small German and Italian states. Britain's part in his overthrow was played by two "bands of brothers": Wellington's men of the Peninsula, and the seamen of those weather-beaten warships that kept the Mediterranean and Atlantic.

The statesmen of Europe gathered in Vienna to settle the affairs of all Europe, and they had not been long at this job before Napoleon escaped from Elba and landed in France, where he received an enthusiastic welcome, and where he raised new armies. He offered to keep peace, but the allies would not trust him. Their armies moved towards the French frontier, the Prussians under old General Blücher, the British, Dutch, and Hanoverians under the Duke of Wellington. Russian armies were gathering momentum far off. At Waterloo in Belgium on Sunday, June 18, 1815, Wellington's men stood firm all day against repeated French onslaughts ("They came on in the old way, and we beat them in the old way," said the Duke later). In the afternoon Blücher's Prussians appeared from the northeast and turned the defeat into a rout. The French broke before a general allied advance, and Napoleon gave himself up. He was this time sent to the lonely island of St. Helena in the South Atlantic. The Bourbon king, Louis XVIII, returned to Paris, and the statesmen in congress at Vienna went on with their task of trying to make Europe peaceful after twenty-five years of war.

So ended the long and wasteful wars of the French Revolution and Napoleon—the wars but not the results of them; for the ideas of the French Revolution spread everywhere. Men who were badly governed wanted freedom to share in their own government, and men who were ruled by foreign nations wanted freedom too. Two new forces were let loose—democracy, or the desire for personal freedom, and nationality, or the desire for national freedom from foreign domination.

7

MANY INVENTIONS AND NEW KNOWLEDGE: THE WORLD OF TODAY

Three Adventures

The tale of the last two hundred years can be told as three adventures: the adventure of politics; the adventure of invention; and the adventure of expansion over the earth.

Politics began as soon as one cave man made an agreement with another. Invention began as soon as men found out how to knap a flint or twist wool into long threads. Expansion began as soon as the first tribes wandered off to find new pastures.

All three adventures have moved at increasing speed during the past six generations. We are farther off in our ways of life and thought from the men of Napoleon's time than they were from ancient Rome. It actually took longer in Napoleon's time to journey from London to Rome than in the days of the Caesars. Now we fly the distance in a few hours. In Napoleon's time most men and women were unlettered peasants ruled by noblemen, just as their ancestors had been in Roman days. Now, everybody can read, and most men and women are townsfolk, and take some part in the government of their country. In Napoleon's time the outlines of the earth were known only in part. Now, most of the earth has been mapped, the ocean beds charted, and atlases are plentiful. New continents have been peopled, and radio unites the remotest places in a flash.

We expect new inventions all the time. We talk of journeys to the moon. This is the age of the scientist and the engineer. Men have gained, and are gaining, more and more knowledge of their surroundings, and more and more power to change their surroundings. This is sure. What is not so sure is whether they are learning wisdom to use their knowledge and power for the benefit of all mankind.

The Adventure of Politics: Kingdoms and Republics

History is full of kings. Long before the Jews asked Samuel for a king of their own, and he anointed Saul to reign over them, the river-valley civilizations were ruled by kings with names like Sargon and Hammurabi. There was a time when every city of the plain had its own king to do judgment and lead his men to war. In Egypt there were the princes of the Great House, Pharaohs like Amenhotep and Rameses and the rest—many dynasties of them. There were kings of the Hittites, those shadowy people whose ruined cities are being dug up today. There were kings of wealthy Tyre and Sidon. Persia had its kings; and Alexander the Great who overthrew Persia began as king of Macedon. His generals made themselves kings. And long before Alexander, the many Greek cities had had their own kings, the earliest known of whom appear in Homer's great poems—Agamemnon, Achilles, and all the mighty band of heroes who sailed their ships against Troy.

Rome, too, had its kings, Etruscan ones, until it expelled them and turned itself into a "republic" or commonwealth ruled by magistrates chosen each year from the leading citizens. Greek cities, of which Athens was the head and chief, had also been republics with assemblies of citizens who met to make laws. But throughout man's story kingdoms have been the usual sort of government. The word *king* is English. The Greeks called him *basileus*, the Romans *rex*, other races have used other titles—*sultan, shah, tsar, kaiser, maharajah, mikado*. It all came to the same thing: the rule of one man.

Rome and its amazing fortunes made a great difference. After becoming a republic, the city conquered the world; and then, having done this, became an empire under a *caesar* or *emperor*. Because Rome—which was in turn a republic and an empire—is the parent of all western Europe, there have been these two patterns of government ever since for men to copy. Every barbarian chieftain who led his armed band of English or Goths or Franks or Lombards into the lands of Rome looked on himself as a successor to the Caesars. He used Latin for his laws and in his "office" or "chancellery." Later on, when men wanted to live without kings they followed Rome's other pattern, and established republics.

The city of Venice, whose ships carried the spice cargoes of the eastern Mediterranean, was a republic of merchants. So was Genoa. Men often dreamed of a republic of Rome which should revive the glories of the ancient city. When the Dutch seamen and burghers won their freedom from Spain they formed themselves into a Dutch Republic. The English colonies in North America in 1783 turned themselves into a republic of United States. When the men of the French Revolution set up a French Republic many of them took ancient Roman names: even Napoleon was called, for a short while, "Consul."

The rulers in a republic might be actually more powerful than a king. The big difference is that in a republic it is easier to change one's rulers without war or revolution; there are rules for changing the rulers peaceably.

But there is another way of sorting out governments. It was suggested by that very wise Greek, Aristotle, Alexander's tutor. He observed that cities might be ruled by one man, by a few men, or by all the citizens. The first he called *monarchy*, the second *aristocracy*, the third *polity*—which we prefer to call *democracy*. Democracy is that form of government in which all men and women share in order to arrange things for the good of all. (This is, of course, much easier said than done.)

We must always keep in mind the two big differences between the politics of the ancient Greeks and Romans and our own. In ancient times each city governed itself. The state was a city-state, like Athens or Corinth or Rome. Today states are nation-states, like Spain or Denmark. In a city-state it is not hard for all men to help share in the actual government; they can all get into the big public meeting place. In our nation-states men can only share in governing by electing representatives to rule in their name.

The other difference is that in ancient times slaves did all the hard and dirty work. Today it is done by free men: and today one of the chief problems is who shall do the hard work and on what terms.

When Napoleon fell and his empire with him, some kingdoms of the west were much as they are now: Great Britain, France, Spain, Portugal, Holland, Norway, Sweden, and Denmark. There was also Russia, a strong monarchy centered in Moscow and St. Petersburg (Leningrad), with vast unexplored regions stretching far into Asia.

There were also two great empires which have vanished: the Austrian, made up of Austria, Hungary, Bohemia, and some Slav lands; and the Turkish, which included the Balkans (Serbia, Bulgaria, Rumania, and Greece), Asia Minor, Arabia, Syria, Palestine, and Egypt.

There was no united nation of Germany and no kingdom of Italy. Both Germany and Italy were merely names of regions.

The kings of Portugal ruled over Brazil, the kings of Spain ruled over the rest of South America. Great Britain held the seas. The United States of America was a young and free nation with a mighty continent behind it, waiting to be settled and made fruitful.

Most states were ruled by kings without constitutions, or sets of rules like those drawn up by clubs and societies which are binding on their members. Most rulers could therefore do more or less as they pleased. In Britain there was an unwritten constitution—one made by custom and habit; in the United States there was a written constitution or agreement made between the citizens as to the manner in which they should be governed.

Politics: Freedom

The emperors, kings, dukes, and counts of all the monarchies met in Vienna to arrange the affairs of Europe after twenty-five years of war and tumult. For two years, 1814–1815, this gay and glittering Congress of Vienna discussed the map. The imperial city was the center of banquets, entertainments, balls, receptions, and boar hunts; and the Viennese saw, day by day, the august and aristocrat peacemakers: their own slight, frail white-haired Emperor; the tall King of Prussia; the short King of Denmark; the jolly-looking Tsar of all the Russias; and the ministers—Wellington, soldierly, decisive; Lord Castlereagh, aloof, grave, burdened with care; Count Metternich, handsome and courtly; and Talleyrand the Frenchman, cleverest of them all, a man who had been a bishop before the Revolution, and who had survived all the chances and changes of French politics. It was due to his skill that the Congress accepted defeated France as a great power, and restored the French monarchy under Louis XVIII, brother of the ill-fated Louis XVI. Louis XVIII, corpulent and easygoing, had been in exile in England.

The rights of men to govern themselves or to be free from foreign rule were not considered. For all the Tsar Alexander and Count Metternich cared, the liberal ideas of 1789 might have been uttered in the moon. Yet in all lands men yearned for freedom from unjust laws and taxes and from despotism, from the fear of the dungeon and the gallows. They wanted constitutions to safeguard themselves. Liberty was in the air everywhere but in Vienna. There, the aristocrats redrew the map. They could not put Europe back as it had been in 1789, but they went as far as they could, and did all they could to make it safe for kings—that is, for the emperors of Austria and Russia, and the monarchs of Prussia and France. There were to be no more revolutions.

They murdered Poland. That gallant and unhappy kingdom which Napoleon had promised to revive, they buried again under Russia, Austria, and Prussia. "Every man but the Pole has a homeland; he has a grave"; these bitter words of a Polish exile and patriot are still true today.

To provide a bulwark against any further trouble from the French, the Congress gave the rich and historic region of the Rhineland to the King of Prussia, who, in consequence, bestrode the German states from east to west. The other German kingdoms and duchies, reduced to thirty-nine in number, were grouped into a *Bund,* or union, under the guidance of Austria. Austria lost her Netherlands (modern Belgium) to Holland, but was rewarded by the overlordship of North Italy.

Italy remained the name of a peninsula. In the south was the badly governed kingdom of Naples and Sicily; in the center were the dominions of the pope—the worst governed lands in the world; in the northwest was the small country of the foothills (Piedmont) ruled by the King of Sardinia and Savoy.

The work of the Congress was intended to endure. It was unlikely that it would; for the winds of freedom were moving in men's hearts, like the winds that stirred the woods where they met to plot rebellion, forming secret societies of patriots and sealing their vows with solemn ritual. The students of the German universities formed political groups. In Italy the patriots called themselves charcoal burners (*carbonari*). Citizens, workmen, noblemen, poets, and rough soldiers of fortune were among them. Yet even to join a secret society was a crime! Agricultural laborers in England were transported as convicts to Australia merely for meeting in secret to discuss how they might get higher wages.

Neither in Italy nor in Germany, however, were the first victories won in freedom's name, but in Turkey and the New World.

Among the Christian subjects of the sultan were the Serbians, who kept their fighting spirit in the Balkan hills. They had rebelled as early as 1804, and after a long, desultory war they won the right to become independent under a prince of their own race. Even Metternich could not pretend that the Turk was the heaven-sent ruler of the Serbians. Moreover, the Russians sympathized with them because they were fellow Slavs. The Russians were Turkey's neighbors and rivals on the Black Sea, and the tsar regarded himself as the protector of all Christians in Turkey. This was an echo of the old conflict of Cross and Crescent.

A more famous people, the Greeks, whose ancestors had first shown men how to combine freedom with civilized life, rebelled against the sultan in 1821. Like the western patriots, they, too, had formed secret societies, known as the "friends of Greece." The war was barbarous; for the modern Greek was just as ruthless as his ancient ancestors. In the Morea more than twenty thousand Turks were killed, and the Turks revenged themselves by massacring Greeks wherever they found them, and by a particularly hideous slaughter of the Greek population of Chios. The fame of ancient Greece held enchantment for westerners whose boyhood had been full of the stories of Leonidas and Pericles; and many volunteers from the west joined in the Greek War of Independence, among them Lord Byron, the poet:

> The mountains look on Marathon,
> And Marathon looks on the sea;
> And musing there an hour alone,
> I dreamed that Greece might still be free.

The Greeks had more powerful allies than the volunteers. When the Turkish pasha of Egypt sent his troops into the Morea to subdue the rebels, Anglo-French warships under Admiral Codrington blew the Egyptian navy to bits in Navarino Bay; and a Russian army invaded Turkey from the north. So the Turks were forced to give the Greeks their freedom, and Greece became an independent kingdom.

Thousands of miles away new nations were being born. When Napoleon captured Spain and Portugal, the Spanish and Portuguese colonies lost touch with their homelands. Brazil became an empire independent of Portugal, and remained independent, becoming later a republic. The Spanish colonies revolted in the eighteen-twenties and all gained their independence. Among their leaders the greatest was Simón Bolívar, and among the many English and French volunteers who helped them the most famous was Lord Dundonald, a seaman of the Nelson breed. South and Central America had been Spanish for over 300 years, and Spain had set her enduring mark on the whole continent in race, religion, and language. Now there came into being the republics of Paraguay, Bolivia, the Argentine, Peru, Chile, Ecuador, Colombia, Venezuela, Mexico, and Guatemala, dividing among them a continent of fabulous wealth and size. All the New World except Canada was freed from the old monarchies of Europe.

While Britain held the seas the New World was beyond the reach of Austrian and French bayonets. Italy and Spain were not. When revolts broke out in these lands an Austrian army marched into Naples, and a French army into Spain, and crushed them. The Austrians also put down revolts in Lombardy which had been inspired by the charcoal burners, many of whom were thrown into Austrian dungeons.

An insurrection in July, 1830, in Paris sent the French king in flight to England; and his cousin, Louis Philippe, who had more sympathy with democratic ideas, took his place. This revolt stirred men far and wide—uprisings occurred in Portugal, Poland, Germany, and Italy. They all failed. The Austrian troops in Italy used the utmost severity in putting down the rebels, especially in the dominions of the pope. Among the many patriots sent into exile was Giuseppe Mazzini, who had dedicated his life while still a student to the cause of Italian independence. He became the prophet of a national, free, and democratic Italy.

Only in the Netherlands was the revolt successful. There the people of the south rebelled against their Dutch rulers, and the European powers allowed them to set up their own kingdom of Belgium—the one we know now, named from the warlike people of the *Belgae* of Caesar's time.

Serbia, Greece, the South American republics, Belgium—these were the gains of Freedom. Under the old dynasties of Europe brave men still suffered the loss of their liberty. The monarchs were keeping their dominions in order and safe against revolution. Lord Byron had died in 1827, but his words will serve to mark these years after 1830:

> Yet Freedom! yet thy banner torn, but flying,
> Streams like a thunder-storm *against* the wind.

Politics: The Mother of Parliaments

The men who founded the United States of America formed their government on the pattern of the British parliamentary one, which they thought was the best the world had seen. But even then the British House of Commons needed reform, and needed it still more fifty years later. Many boroughs which returned members to the Commons were small and insignificant hamlets like Old Sarum and Gatton, each of which sent two members to represent their handful of people. Such places were elegantly known as "rotten boroughs." Other places with only a few voters, like Tavistock where but ten men were so privileged, were in the "pockets" of the great lords who paid the voters to send to the Commons men of their choice—sons or relatives or dependents. As a result most of the members of the Commons were entirely dependent on noble "patrons" in the House of Lords.

Nor was this all. A novelist in 1817 amused himself by writing of "the large populous city of No-vote which was situated at a short distance from the ancient and honorable borough of One-vote." There were plenty of cities of No-vote —Manchester, Halifax, Leeds, Sheffield, Birmingham, to name but a few; cities which were populous and growing fast owing to the increasing manufactures and trade of the late eighteenth century. Between 1781 and 1831 the island's population had doubled in number—and most of the increase was in these No-vote cities, which had therefore no say whatever in the government of the country. Yet, out of some 500 Members of Parliament, about 70 were elected by small places with hardly any voters at all. What kind of comic elections took place in the boroughs has been described by Dickens in his *Pickwick Papers* in his account of the goings-on at Eatanswill on polling day.

To be fair to our forefathers it must be said that many had been aware of this absurd state of things and had proposed to remedy it, before the outbreak of the French Revolution. The brutal frenzy of the French populace made the rulers of Britain afraid to give any power to anybody: and, of course, there were hotheads in this island who thought the French example ought to be followed. But the long wars caused distress and unemployment among farm laborers and working people, and there were serious riots and the burning of ricks and barns, and the looting of shops, and the military had to disperse rioters, and wild men talked of "committees of public safety." As trade recovered gradually, this agitation turned into a demand for a reform of parliament. By 1830 there was a group of M.P.s in favor of reform: and by 1830 the country was faced with threats of a possible revolution. In that year no fewer than 700 men were tried at Winchester for rioting. When parliament threw out Lord Grey's Bill for Reform in 1831, riots were renewed fiercely in the Midlands. In Bristol the mobs began to burn the city. Finally the Duke of Wellington and his party gave way and advised William IV to sign the Bill. Rotten and pocket boroughs to the number of 143 were abolished, and their seats redistributed among the new manufacturing towns. At the same time all townsmen who paid £10 a year in rent were given the vote. A reform was likewise made in the counties.

In this manner, when patriots in Europe were clamoring for

Many Inventions and New Knowledge

freedom from oppression, did the mother of parliaments reform herself—or rather, begin to reform herself; for the process continued. Further reform bills were passed in 1867 and in 1885, giving the vote to most adult townsmen and most adult countrymen. The enormous value of this is clear: an unpopular government can be changed when the time for the next election comes round.

The British parliament is an old institution, going back to the days of Edward I, the king who held that "what touches every man should be approved by every man." But we should notice a change in the *idea* of representation. In the Middle Ages a knight of the shire (i.e., a country member) represented all the other knights of the shire, or substantial farmers—men just like himself. Similarly, a burgess member (i.e., a city man) represented all the other burgesses of substance or guildsmen of his town—men like himself. Now, owing to the vast growth of population an M.P. is simply any good man whom the voters care to choose to represent them, not because he is like them, but to do his best to help in governing the land. A borough may elect a wealthy landowner; a county may elect a wealthy financier.

The nineteenth century was the great age of parliament. It is worth noting that the power of parliament was so strongly believed in, and its reputation so high, that one of the chief things desired by all working men was the vote: given that, they believed all other desirable things would follow. Indeed, this is an instance of the faith the islanders have always had in getting together and discussing their troubles—sensibly, not pushing their own claims too far, but ready to give and take.

The reform of the House of Commons was followed by a much needed reform of local government of towns and counties—the towns in 1835, the counties in 1888. Instead of having small groups of men chosen at random, or by themselves and their friends, to conduct business, both towns and counties were given regular and elected councils.

Invention: The Engineers

Since the beginning of things men have changed their surroundings by patient labor. They have terraced hillsides for vines, cleared forests, drained swamps, channeled rivers, made sea banks, erected vast monuments of brick and stone, built cities, and run roads across continents.

Never has the world scene undergone such sweeping changes as those which began about 1760—changes due to the engineers.

The engineer is a maker of clever or ingenious devices. He is ingenious on a large scale in building, bridging, trenching, tunneling, mining, and working in metals. His ancestors include all cunning artificers, especially the millwrights, the clockmakers, and the powerful army of smiths. His work depends on exact measurement, and therefore on mathematics; it depends also on the nature of materials, and therefore on physics and chemistry. Craftsmen, mathematicians, scientists —all these are his forerunners. He takes their knowledge and skill and puts it to practical use, subduing timber and rock and metal to his own design. He is the supreme architect of human industry.

His tools are themselves ingenious machines, like the sawmill, the power lathe, and the steam hammer, and they are moved by the power of falling water, expanding steam, explosive gases, or electric impulse. Such machines work a hundred times faster, more powerfully and more accurately than hand tools.

The engineer's work has brought to an end the old-fashioned societies of craftsmen and peasants, because his machines need the exact and orderly co-operation of many people. The ancient world used slaves. The engineer cannot do this in our civilization, which is founded on the freedom of all men. Yet, to get the willing co-operation of multitudes of free citizens is sometimes a perplexing task. Many machines need the use of men and women themselves as part of the machine, repeating a few simple muscular movements over and over again, day in, day out. The engineer himself may still take a craftsman's delight in his own work: but machine-minders spend days and days in doing jobs compared with which chopping wood and painting walls are wildly exciting.

Invention: Roads and Canals

After the last Roman gang had laid aside its spades, no useful work was done on Britain's roads for more than a thousand years. Droves of cattle trampled the tracks into quagmires. In summer pilgrims and peddlers trudged along the ruts, or rode ponies and horses; in winter folk just stayed at home. In some parts wooden posts were needed to mark where the highway went, for it was often indistinguishable from the surrounding field. York was a week's journey from London: Swift Nicks did it in a day or so in 1676, but he was a highwayman in a hurry. The *Gentleman's Magazine* in 1752 said that roads to the west were "as God left them after the Flood"—founderous, thick mud in winter and thick dust in summer.

Civilization depends on good transport. When, after 1700, London began to spread out, the roads were crowded with sheep and oxen and geese all on their way to feed the capital. Soon after 1700 turnpike trusts of private citizens began to repair stretches of highway, paying for the work by taking tolls of all travelers at tollgates erected across the road. By 1837 there were over eleven hundred of these trusts. Their work varied in quality, but they did employ some skilled road engineers. Thomas Telford is best remembered for his Holyhead Road and his suspension bridge across the Menai Strait. John McAdam gave his name to a type of road with a surface of small multangular stones pressed hard together into a solid mass. Because of these improvements, the old, cumbrous carriage slung on leather straps gave place to the lighter and speedier stagecoach mounted on steel springs. Between 1760 and 1840 the chief towns were linked by regular services of Tally-Hos, Nimrods, and Lightnings, all gaily painted, and drawn by teams of horses which were changed at each stage. Winter weather, of course, upset timetables, and sometimes coaches. Then, only the hardiest travelers could endure the outside seats, and there are grim stories of such passengers being found frozen to death at the end of the stage.

Moved by the slowness of the postboys (forty hours between Bath and London) a Mr. John Palmer suggested a service of mail coaches. The first in 1784 reached Bristol in fifteen hours. The Royal Mail became an event—a splendid vehicle clattering through tollgates, already opened at the sound of the posthorn, and passing along with all the village waving and cheering. "The absolute perfection of all the appointments about the carriages and the harness, their strength, their brilliant cleanliness, their beautiful simplicity—but, more than all, the royal magnificence of the horses—were what might first have fixed the attention." So wrote Thomas De Quincey of the nightly parade of mail coaches before they set out from Lombard Street for the chief cities of the kingdom. By 1835 over 700 mail coaches were in use, as well as thousands of stage coaches, employing multitudes of drivers, guards, grooms, and ostlers, and maintaining stables at hundreds of inns.

This era of the stage and mail coach was also the era of the canals—1760 to 1840.

Water carriage is easy and cheap. For a long time coasting ships—colliers—had been bringing coal ("sea coal") from the Tyne to the Thames; as, indeed, they still do. It was the Grand

Canal of Languedoc joining the Bay of Biscay with the Mediterranean that gave the Duke of Bridgwater his notion of a canal to carry coal from his pits at Worsley to Manchester. He employed James Brindley, a millwright of genius, to plan the work, and when the canal was finished in 1761 the price of his coal at Manchester fell by half. A veritable frenzy of canal building followed, linking river with river and town with town. Josiah Wedgwood could now make and sell his fine Staffordshire pottery without fear for its safe delivery. Northwich salt needed no longer to be transported on pack horses along the "saltways." Manchester cottons and Yorkshire woolens went in bulk in the barges. China clay, bricks, hardware, timber, coal, all became easily transportable, now that Severn and Thames were linked with the Midlands and with each other: and London, the largest market, was opened to the growing manufactures of the Midlands and north. Some canals carried passenger barges. The government moved troops on them. Houses and factories rose along their banks. There opened a prospect of a canal civilization— active, wealthy, busy, and quiet. By 1830 the frenzy of digging was over, the largest waterway, the Caledonian Canal, designed by Telford, being dug between 1804 and 1822. Unfortunately the canals varied much in depth and width, and the carriers who used them were often unpunctual and extortionate in their charges. The best canals have remained in use: the picturesque ruins of the others can be seen in long stretches of idle water, weed-grown, strewn with water lilies, the haunt of moorhens.

By the eighteen-thirties the engineers had another form of traction in active preparation: the steam railway, which depended on coal and iron and the advance of mechanical engineering.

Invention: Coal, Iron, and Steam Power

How the engineers began to change the scene of man's life is told best by a brief account of what we call the *industrial revolution*, which first took place in Britain, and which centered in the use of coal and iron.

Millions of years ago forests grew and decayed in stagnant swamps: and layers of rotting vegetation, crushed under the weight of later seas and sedimentary rocks, disappeared beneath the land surface. From these vast and incredibly slow events in geological time came the seams of coal upon which our civilization has depended.

Coal-getting is an ancient craft. For centuries it remained a local affair; for pits were shallow because of flooding, and coals were too heavy and bulky to be transported far. Tyneside coal was carried in coasting vessels to London, and was, in consequence, known as "sea coal"; and when canals came they were used by coal barges, and mineowners often built railways for their coal wagons to run easily from the pits to the canal wharf. But miners were restricted to shallow seams and outcrops until they could get a good pump to keep their workings free from water.

Steam power, known to the ancient Greeks, and a theme for curious speculation among the sort of men who liked "to make things go" (clockmakers, millwrights, and instrument-makers) was first used to drive a pump by the blacksmith Newcomen in 1705. It was cumbrous and needed a boy to release the spent steam after each stroke. But it worked, and was improved; and the pits went somewhat deeper. In 1784 James Watt, a scientific-instrument maker, added a separate condenser to release the surplus steam after it had done its job of pushing the rod or piston: and the pump became a steam engine, more or less as we know the thing. By simple mechanical contrivance the up-and-down or vertical motion could easily be turned into a rotatory one. In plain words, Watt's steam engine could turn a wheel. Hitherto, wheels had been turned by men, dogs, donkeys, horses, water, and wind.

More and more coal was needed. Those mighty comforting log fires of the old days, those fleets of wooden ships, those timbered halls, houses, barns, and mills, that clearing of the forests to make farms—all consumed the woodlands at a great pace. Timber grew scarce, fuel grew scarce—especially charcoal. By 1760 only a few dozen charcoal blast furnaces were at work; and the question was considered: Could mined coal be used in place of charcoal to smelt iron ore?

In such woodlands as the Sussex Weald and the Royal Forest of Dean the early iron masters worked near the source of their charcoal. From their furnaces, kept at intense heat for days on end by a primitive bellows-blast, they cast the molten iron into pigs which went to the forges. At these, the Masters of the Bloom melted and hammered them into shoes or tires or rails or hooks or hoes. About 1708 the Quaker ironmaster, Abraham Darby, discovered that by cooking or "coking" coal he could use it in place of charcoal in his blast furnace. It was a timely discovery. The iron-masters began to move to the coal fields of South Wales, the Midlands and the north, leaving behind in their age-old forests the slag heaps such as we see today in the Weald and Dean. In their new surroundings the descendants of the smiths who had started the Iron Age toiled at creating amid flame and fume our huge mechanical and iron civilization. The blacksmiths were the righthand men of the engineers. A series of inventions and improvements added knowledge to knowledge and skill to skill. In 1767 at Coalbrookdale they cast the first iron rails for colliery railroads. A bridge made of iron was erected across the upper Severn. One man devised a furnace in which the flames were "reverberated" or reflected down on the mass of ore and coke while the impurities were stirred out from it; and he also learned how to squeeze the softened blooms of iron through grooved rollers to make rails and bars. Another man heated iron with charcoal in small crucibles to make a specially toughened iron—or steel —suitable for springs and cutlery, and used by the Sheffield bladesmiths. The early ironmasters were men of fertile minds. Dr. John Roebuck of Carron in Scotland not only cast the famous naval guns, the carronades, but found out how to make sulphuric acid on a large scale.

Such was the beginning of heavy industry. Notice how coal and iron acted and reacted on each other: the furnaces needing coal, the mines needing iron for rails and pumps and engines. Between 1750 and 1830 the coal mined rose from 5 to 25 million tons, and the iron output rose from a few thousand to one million tons.

This transformation of daily life and labor took place in the Midlands and the north. So did the great change in the ancient crafts of spinning and weaving.

For centuries in farmhouses and cottages everywhere the womenfolk (spinsters) had drawn out and spun the threads to feed the murmuring looms and make "the countless list of woolen webs"—the worsteds, fustians, kerseys, broadcloths, and the rest. It was a household industry, although rich merchants gave out and collected the materials for the work. The island's wealth was founded on wool. With money from their fine cloth the pious merchants had built the lovely churches of East Anglia and Gloucestershire; with taxes on wool the kings had paid for their wars. The woolen merchants were the aristocrats of commerce. In 1700 the value of the wool sent out was one quarter of all exports. The main centers of the weaving trade were the Eastern Counties, Gloucestershire, and Yorkshire. But the machines that changed the textile industry were first applied to the newer trade of cotton, which was carried on chiefly in Lancashire, and supplied with raw cotton from the east. This new industry was not so settled in its ways as the older woolen one, and it was easier to introduce changes into it.

One weaver consumed the output of very many spinners. When John Kaye devised a flying shuttle to speed the looms,

MANY INVENTIONS AND NEW KNOWLEDGE

the spinners would have lagged behind sadly but for a whole series of inventions. In the seventeen-seventies and eighties, James Hargreaves, a Blackburn carpenter, made a spinning jenny which turned a great number of spindles at once; Richard Arkwright, a barber of Preston, invented a frame in which the threads were drawn between rollers before being twisted—and this strengthened them; Samuel Crompton, a Bolton weaver, made his famous "mule," a spinning machine which combined the good points of all the others. These machines, worked by water, or steam power, were quickly multiplied. It was now the turn of the weavers to catch up with the spinners, and this they were enabled to do by a power loom invented by Edward Cartwright, a clergyman. In and around Manchester the number of cotton mills increased from two in 1780 to over 50 in 1800.

So spinning and weaving left the cottages and moved into mills. Men and women moved into mills also; instead of working all hours at home they worked all hours in a mill. Weaving had so far been a man's job; now it was discovered that much of the simple work of tending the machines could be done by women and children. The woolen trade, which gathered mainly in the West Riding of Yorkshire where there were running streams to turn the wheels, was slower to adopt machinery. But by 1830 the trade was mechanized. Within the span of one lifetime whole townships were turned into woolen and cotton towns entirely dependent on the mills. The change-over did not pass peacefully. The inventions deprived cottage workers of their livelihood, and there were riots in which machines were smashed by wrathful weavers. Murder was not unknown. Rioters were killed, and hanged on the magistrates' orders. In truth the passing of the handloom weaver was a tragic event; and, in truth also, the new inventions in the coal and iron industries were often pushed forward with utter disregard for the human happiness and health of the workers.

James Watt's steam engines were manufactured by Matthew Boulton at his Soho works near Birmingham, and Boulton-and-Watt engines were soon at work turning wheels in breweries, flour mills, foundries, and rolling mills as well as the textile mills—in fact, in all places where rotatory movement was needed. One engine was used to drive a small boat on the Hudson River in 1807. The *Times* newspaper used a steam engine to turn its printing rollers in 1814. By 1830 there were some 300 engines working in and about Glasgow.

Such engines required extreme accuracy in their working parts. Blacksmiths who made them depended more and more on machine tools, operated not by hand but by machines.

All modern engineering depends on the machine-tool trade, which began in London with Joseph Bramah (1748–1844). Bramah's pupil, Henry Maudslay, invented an automatic screw-cutting lathe in 1800 which worked to one-thousandth part of an inch. Another invented a metal plane and a steam hammer. In 1834, Joseph Whitworth laid down standard sizes for screws and small machine parts. These expert mechanicians were all craftsmen of a nice ingenuity, and could design and erect any milling and cutting machinery. Imagine a modern engineering civilization in which every screw and nut and bolt had to be cut by hand!

Civil and mechanical engineers had a major invention in preparation: the steam railway. It was very badly needed to cope with the increased flow of goods.

It was a twofold invention: first, the railway, then the steam locomotive.

Railways along which a horse could haul loads of twelve tons were in use as early as 1700. These were wooden rails laid on ties with ballast between them to hold them in place. To save wear and tear, platelayers covered the wooden rails with iron plates. Then came cast-iron rails flanged on their outside edges. Then the flange was transferred to the wagon-wheels. Someone suggested covering the land with a network of such public railroads radiating from London. There were in 1824 more than 100 miles of such railroads in South Wales to serve the coal fields. Sometimes a stationary steam engine hauled wagons along them by means of a cable passing round a large drum.

If steam power could turn a wheel, it could, perhaps, turn the wagon wheels themselves—if an engine could be made accurately enough, and if the wheels did not skid.

The steam locomotive was sixty years in its development from 1769 when Nicholas Cugnot's steam carriage moved at two miles an hour along the streets of Paris until the day that George Stephenson's Rocket pulled a coachload of passengers along a railroad at Rainshill at 30 miles an hour in 1829. Many inventors had made steam locomotives and carriages with more or less success; Stephenson's was the best. When a new railway was opened in 1831 from Stockton to Darlington, his engine was employed; and he became the engineer of the first railway to be built for steam locomotives—from Manchester to Liverpool. On this his engine did 36 miles an hour—and hauled 250,000 people in the first six months. The steam railway had arrived, and not before it was wanted; for the canals could not cope with the masses of goods to be carried.

Thirty-six miles an hour was faster than ever man had

traveled. It was amazing, and to some people, very frightening. One man complained that it would destroy all quiet and beauty, that "the roaring of bullocks, the bleating of sheep, and the grunting of pigs" where trains passed, would "keep up one continual uproar through the night," and that all the countryside would be fouled with the smoke. But the Rev. Sydney Smith in 1842 wrote that "railroad traveling is a delightful improvement of human life. Man," he said, "is become a bird; he can fly longer and quicker than a solan goose." Owing to the prejudice against them the British railways cost fabulous sums to build: sometimes thousands and thousands of pounds were paid to lawyers even to prepare an act of parliament to allow a line to be made! And some landowners charged enormous sums for the strips of lands needed. In spite of this the benefits of railway transport were so obvious that men subscribed vast sums to build lines everywhere: and the invention was quickly adopted in all civilized countries.

Those hundreds of thousands of sheep, oxen, and geese that used to creep slowly to London were now packed quickly into trucks. The main roads coach traffic disappeared, and inns and stables were emptied. By 1842 the 2500 horses stabled at Hounslow, the first stage out of London, had gone; and one Norfolk inn was spared the cost and profit which it had made in sheltering 9,000 beasts on their way to the capital. Ostlers, stableboys, cattlemen, postillions, melted away in search of other employment. Here and there the mail or stagecoach still cheered the wayside hamlet: the *Quicksilver* coach posted from Falmouth to Plymouth as late as 1859. But for the most part a sabbath calm descended on the turnpikes, the inns decayed, and small market towns, not served by the railways, became sleepy backwaters. By 1850 the era of roads and canals had passed.

Invention: Gains and Losses

When Princess Victoria's uncle, William IV, died at Windsor in 1837, two horsemen, one of whom was the Archbishop of Canterbury, rode through the dawn to Kensington Palace to salute her as Queen. That was their speediest means of transport. Victoria, whose long reign, from 1837 to 1901, gave her name to an age, actually lived through a succession of ages if we reckon by the multitude of new inventions that changed daily life. When she died the railways were already a part of the island's landscape, and more than 2,000 of the noisy new motor cars were raising clouds of dust on the highways. At her accession her ships of war were still the "wooden walls of Old England"; before she died fleets of giant steamships had transported an army of half a million men to South Africa. An even more striking illustration of the change can be given from a West-of-England tombstone which records a father born in 1775 and his daughter who died in 1907. Their two lives spanned the years during which the rural and domestic life of their land was transformed into an urban and factory one depending on iron and coal and steam power. The fruits of the tree of knowledge fell so fast and thick among men that in the scramble to enjoy them there was too often very little regard for fair dealing. We are still trying to learn how to make sure that they are gains to humanity and not losses.

Among obvious gains have been the defeat of darkness and the lessening of disease. Until the nineteenth century all the world went by candlelight, or kept its oil lamps trimmed. Even the first wooden lighthouse on the Eddystone was candlelit. The means of irradiating the night came from coal. In 1816 gas lamps were used in the London streets; and thereafter the use of gas was spread by gas mains—a considerable engineering feat in itself; and a large new prosperous gas industry grew up whose monuments are the gasometers which now adorn our cities, and whose lamplighters at dusk were the joy of Victorian children. By 1880 gas had a rival illuminant in the electric lamp, which, after a slow start, gained favor so much that since 1900 it has all but ousted gas for lighting; and the lamplighter of today is the man at the switchboard in the power station. Whether or not we care to rise with the lark we are now no longer compelled to lie down with the lamb. The lengthening of our days by artificial light has increased enormously our output of work and our leisure.

The attack on disease was made by improved sanitation and drains, by a more plentiful supply of factory-made soap, by a more plentiful supply of cheaper cotton clothes. Medical knowledge was accumulated by hospital doctors, and hospitals gained greatly from the work of Florence Nightingale and other devoted women who insisted on higher and more skilled standards of nursing. The make-up and dosage of medicines and drugs were fixed by pharmacists, and knowledge gained in the use of drugs such as quinine. Doctors learned how to employ anaesthetics like ether and chloroform in operations, and published their records for others to read. The days were ended when wounded men were given rum and strapped down while the "sawbones" cut and sawed through a mangled limb! In 1865 Louis Pasteur taught doctors how to detect and combat the bacteria that cause illness; and in 1866 Joseph Lister taught them how to prevent gangrene in cuts and wounds. In 1895 Röntgen discovered the use of X rays to give photographs of the bones and internal organs of the body. So, throughout the century there was a steady improvement in health. Typhoid fever, diphtheria, and tuberculosis took their toll of lives, and there were outbreaks of cholera, but smallpox declined, and the plague was simply forgotten. Of old, smallpox was always well in evidence, and the pestilence which had all but ruined the civilization of the west in the sixth and again in the fourteenth century had frequently occurred in small outbreaks down to the eighteenth century.

The result of all this gain in health and medical skill was an increase in the number of people: fewer babies died and more adults lived longer. But for the loss of the emigrants taking ship to the New World, the increase would have been much greater. The population of Great Britain rose from 8 million in 1781 to 16 million in 1831, to 37 million in 1901, and to 45 million in 1931—far too many mouths to fill from the island's farms. Farming was profitable and its produce was increased—and the grain, root crops, and cattle and sheep were still among the very best in the world. But the crowded town populations came to depend on ships bringing grain and meat from abroad, in return for their coal, iron goods, woolens, cottons, pottery, and machinery. Great Britain depended for her life on exports. And the banks and insurance offices that supplied money for their factories and trade also lent money to foreign countries and for this received large sums in interest: London was the hub of the world's finance, and Britain's golden sovereigns were as famous as the gold bezants of Byzantium or the gold ducats of Venice had been in the Middle Ages.

But the onset of the Machine Age brought dire misery to thousands of unfortunates. People living in a few village hovels have the blessing of the open air all day; but people living in great clusters and rows of hovels in a new industrial town spent most of their days in steamy, noisy, and grimy factories. How towns grew may be illustrated by the record of Middlesborough and Birkenhead: neither of which existed in 1815. One is tempted to use Dr. Johnson's vivid phrase and say that they "rose like exhalations from the ground." Imagine a Greek (accustomed to laying out the plan of a new city with his measuring ropes) designing something like one of these! Of course, no one did design them—any more than the men of today arrange the killing of thousands on their unfenced roads. It just happens. In their haste to get money and power employers often forgot their duty to their fellow men and women. There was no forethought in the building of the hideous towns of the nineteenth century that grew up without dignity or charm. The profits made in them were spent in London or in pleasure cities at home or on the Continent. The workers—"hands"—knew nothing of the joy of living in a fine city; for them, architecture was a lost art, and civic pride an unknown virtue. So thousands led dreary lives on mere pittances for long hours of drudgery, toiling for an ironmaster, a cotton spinner, a coalowner, a chemical manufacturer. For many centuries plowmen and craftsmen had toiled long hours at work that was either healthy or skillful. Factory life was monotonous, wearying, unhealthy, and not usually skillful: wherever possible children and women were employed because they were cheap. In some mills workhouse children were "purchased" by the millowners, and whipped to their tasks. In some mines women and children, half-naked, dragged coal trucks on all fours along the underground galleries like beasts of burden. Many masters were ignorant men, many hard, many unheeding, some were downright scoundrels. A number were good Christian gentlemen who quickly joined with other citizens in persuading the government to stop such a dreadful misuse of human beings.

For a long time there had been a notion that men should be allowed to do as they pleased so long as they committed no crimes—did not poach on the squire's birds or game, did not thieve, or forge, or counterfeit, or maim, or kill, or slander. It was argued that no one would ever harm himself. No one would ever forget that there was a whirling machine unfenced behind him, so why fence it? Everyone would naturally avoid danger and poverty and hunger, and everyone was free to leave his work. This was not a helpful notion in the nineteenth century when so many enterprising men were acquiring wealth and power over the lives of their fellows. The flaw in it was that all men did not start equal, and many were compelled to accept degrading work for a few shillings a week in order to keep themselves and their families alive. The notion was broken down gradually by the persistence of good men like Lord Shaftesbury, who insisted that the parliaments should pass acts to regulate factory life. Investigations were made, workers and employers questioned, and factories were regulated—hours of work reduced, and safety precautions enforced. In 1901 a comprehensive Factory Act summed up all previous ones.

The British parliaments had much to do to overtake and keep up with the everlasting changes in social life and work.

MANY INVENTIONS AND NEW KNOWLEDGE

Their activity may be illustrated by a list of some of the things dealt with in their many Acts: highways, canals, railways, merchant ships, postal services, police, agriculture, tithes, banks, trading companies, insurance, trade unions, local government, schools, prisons, public health, poor laws, house building. In order to make sure that these Acts were carried out it was necessary to appoint more and more civil servants and more and more inspectors. In 1870 the old-fashioned way of appointing civil servants by favor gave place to open, competitive, written examinations—after the custom of the Chinese. If we add to these civil servants all those in the pay of the local councils from refuse collectors to town clerks, we shall find that the state is one of the biggest employers of labor.

It is important not to forget that the workers played their own part in redeeming themselves from drudgery and insecurity and injustice. In the early days of the century workmen began to join in groups to better their conditions of work, and at the same time help each other in distress and sickness. This was the beginning of trade unions. At first the government opposed them, but in 1824 an Act allowed men to form such unions; and later acts regulated them. In older days the villein-farmers had been protected, to some extent, against scoundrelly lords of the manor by the known custom of the manor; in the new factories there were no customs to safeguard the landless laborers; it was each for himself and the Devil take the hindmost. This is why trade unions were needed. Today they are among the important parts of our industrial organization. Some gain, therefore, came from all the misery of the industrial revolution, if only by its making men realize the old medieval principle of the Church lawyers: that no man should be allowed to profit by another's misfortune.

Meanwhile the workers themselves had also taken steps to improve their lives in other ways. A group known as the Rochdale Pioneers founded the first "co-operative society" in 1837. Others followed suit. In 1864 the Co-operative Wholesale Society was formed. Then, apart from this, dozens of Friendly Societies were run by workers, employers, churches, and philanthropists to encourage thrift and insure against want. In this also the insurance companies played their part.

So, out of a world fouled and ugly with slums and still afflicted by the cursed hunger for gold, the people began to prosper a little, to share a little in the benefits of the new knowledge and power. There were plenty of watchdogs on the lookout for injustice and oppression, and ready to prod a lazy government into action. Some men believed that only by government control of all great industries could the people's welfare be safeguarded, and they advocated socialism. Some of our industries are now socialized; and men are still quarrelling about them. Others, like Dr. Barnardo, took action on their own—and when they did so found a thousand willing hands to help them: Barnardo's Homes for Children are but one of hundreds of charitable ventures which have kept hospitals, almshouses, orphanages, for the outcast and rejected. One of the most hopeful things in the last hundred and fifty years is the great increase in voluntary help for the crippled, the fatherless, and the widow. In this the many Christian churches did front-line work: after the easygoing habits of the eighteenth century, a new spirit of duty and service—thanks largely to John Wesley—reanimated the churches and chapels. And a special mention must be made of the Quakers and of the Salvation Army, which, in their contrasting ways, followed the precepts of the New Testament, and tackled the age-old problems of misery and destitution.

There was one invention on which all the rest depended, that old invention of the German Gutenberg. Printing stored knowledge and spread knowledge, and more and more people read books. The old hope of William Tyndal's that all plowmen should read the Word of God still burned brightly, and religious publishing societies issued Bibles and Gospels and tracts for the people—not only in Britain but in every part of the habitable globe. There were men who thought it unwise to teach the poor to read—it might give them ideas above their station. But it was equally true that to leave them ignorant would be to bring them under the influence of bad men. As it happened there were large numbers of poor men who taught themselves to read.

There were, roughly speaking, two sorts of training at the beginning of the century: that given in the grammar schools and such like, and that given to apprentices. The aim of the schools was to train boys to be lawyers, clergymen, doctors, merchants, and clerks. The aim of the apprenticeship system was to train skilled craftsmen. Neither helped to train the farm laborer or the landless laborer who lived in the industrial towns.

Slowly and with opposition and difficulty the politicians arranged for all children to be taught simple reading, writing, and arithmetic. In 1833 only half of the children had any schooling. In 1870 each part of the country was permitted to compel children up to the age of thirteen to attend school. Since then the school-leaving age has been raised by easy

Many Inventions and New Knowledge

stages to fifteen. In 1876 all children up to the age of ten were compelled to attend school. The difficulties were great—expense of buildings, the task of training teachers, the loss to parents of the small sums of money which their little ones earned in the workshops. In the provision of parish schools the churches and chapels played a leading part, raising money and training teachers. They were being true to their ancient purpose of using books and the wisdom of the past to preserve Christian civilization. An enormous amount of good work was done by societies like that for Promoting Christian Knowledge in publishing good books.

The earliest grammar schools began at the church door in the Middle Ages; and the universities were founded by churchmen. When the Nonconformists in the seventeenth century were forbidden to use either the grammar schools or the universities, they founded excellent academies of their own. So true is it that religion and education always went together. They still do.

The ancient universities of England were thrown open to Jews, Catholics and Nonconformists during the nineteenth century; and other universities were founded. London had always had its famous schools of law and medicine; but a brand-new university was established there in 1828. Durham followed in 1832, Manchester in 1880, and the rest have received their charters during this century.

The printing of books and the spread of education to all people are completely new things in man's record. Learning of all sorts is so widespread today that one can guess that, if all the works of, say, Dante or Shakespeare were lost they might be rewritten from human memories. And the pyramids of scientific knowledge might be rebuilt from the minds of men. When we recall how much of literature and learning of the ancient world disappeared forever, we can be thankful for our condition now. We are most concerned to preserve the heritage of the past generations in our buildings, pictures, sculptures, literatures, and music.

It is still to be settled whether the spread of education results in more first-class works of imagination; for the conditions under which genius is produced are not known. Music is alone among the arts in being a thing of the last six centuries: at least, the preserved record of it. What music the sirens sang, as Sir Thomas Browne remarked, must remain a mystery. But, if we have lost such records of early music as were made, we do know its power was manifest to the Greeks, in whose fond tale the lute of Orpheus could influence even Pluto, the god of the underworld, and in whose speculations the whole system of stars moved in harmony. We are fortunate in our rich hoard of music composed in the last five centuries—and little of it could have been available to even a favored few without the printing press. The means we have today to keep our inheritance of beauty and share it with all men, to bring delight and to ennoble the mind, are without limit.

Politics: The Year of 1848 in Europe

When John Kemble dedicated his history of *The Saxons in England* to Queen Victoria, he remarked that she reigned over a land free from the tumult that filled all Europe in that year of 1848.

Revolutions and revolts, in fact, took place in France, Germany, Italy, Austria, Hungary, and Bohemia. Nearly sixty years had gone by since the French revolutionaries proclaimed the freedom of man, and over thirty since an English warship carried Napoleon to his last exile on St. Helena; yet the peoples of Europe still endured injustice and oppression under selfish rulers, sometimes foreign rulers. They still lacked constitutions, equal and just laws, fair taxation, and freedom of speech and print. By contrast, the ancient and decayed British parliament had been reformed in 1832, and was busy overhauling old laws and fashioning new ones to cope with the new sort of industrial society created by the use of machinery.

King Louis Philippe governed France with the help of groups of aristocrats and rich men. Not one citizen in a hundred had the vote, and it was still possible to forbid men to publish their opinions. Most Frenchmen, then as now, were peasants and not bothered overmuch with politics so long as they were left to profit from their farms; but the new factories had crowded the towns, especially Paris, with mechanics and unskilled laborers, many of whom were very poor or out of work. A new kind of town or urban society was coming into being—men without the solace or resources of the countryside. In February of 1848 a Paris mob clashed with the police. The riots grew—after the manner of Paris— and the rioters were joined by the National Guard. Louis Philippe left in a hurry, escaping by cab; and, later, sailed for England. The Parisians set up a second French Republic. To employ the workless the new government established "national workshops," and very soon there were some 100,000 men being paid for doing nothing in these places. No one could find work for them—one wag suggested that

Many Inventions and New Knowledge

they might spend their time bottling off the River Seine.

So far there had been excitement and confusion rather than any serious strife. When, however, a new elected Assembly (chosen, as it was bound to be, mainly by the peasants) closed the workshops, fierce street fighting began, and thousands lost their lives. It was worse than the beginning of the Revolution of 1789. After this appalling tragedy, the Second Republic settled down for a time with Louis Napoleon, nephew of the great emperor, as its president.

Louis Napoleon did not waste much time in imitating his uncle; for in 1852 he ended the everlasting quarrels among the political parties by proclaiming himself Emperor as Napoleon III. He had had many ups and downs of fortune. He had invaded France from Dover with a boatload of his friends, and had suffered imprisonment in Ham castle for six years. He had escaped from this place to England. He was audacious, and the magic of his name helped him. Indeed, he was full of good ideas and schemes for improving his country. He had intelligence and was something of a scholar. He was popular, and ruled for many years, during which—under a settled government, and with growing trade and industries—France prospered. But he did not solve the difficult problem of devising a truly free or democratic government for his people.

The February revolt of the Parisians stirred the Germans to clamor for free governments, and in ten states the rulers were forced to grant constitutions—which meant assemblies, and freedom of speech, of religion, and of the press.

The chief wonder of all was a revolt in Vienna, the capital of the Austrian Empire. This outbreak sent Prince Metternich in flight to England. (It is hard to imagine what the kings and rebels of Europe would have done without England as a refuge.) Then there followed nationalist uprisings in the Austrian Empire—of Bohemians in Prague, and of Hungarians in Budapest. After much fighting these were put down by the Austrian generals. In Hungary, where the armed conflict was bitter and prolonged, the rebels were only subdued with the help of a large Russian army sent in by the tsar to help his brother-emperor, and the Hungarians were cruelly punished for their rebellion.

In Austria and Germany the results of these 1848 rebellions were almost nil. The kings and dukes continued to rule as they pleased. But there had been a serious attempt to unite all the German states in a central parliament—a sort of shadowy "united states" of the Germans. The idea of a Germanic federation was in men's minds. It failed because of the rivalry of Austria and Prussia. In Prussia, where there had been street fighting in Berlin, the king did agree in 1850 to an orderly constitution controlled by his officials, landowners and army officers, with a code of law, and an assembly. This was not a parliamentary government of free men as in Britain or the United States of America, but it did provide a clear-cut and orderly system which lasted. And in Prussia the king in 1862 made Count Otto von Bismarck his chancellor. Bismarck was unscrupulous, but he had a vigorous and shrewd mind, without any petty envy or selfishness. He lived for Prussia.

The Italians had the double task of winning freedom from alien rule and also from despotism. Among the many makers of the Italian nation were Victor Emmanuel, the gallant king of Sardinia; Count Cavour, his wise and patient minister; Giuseppe Mazzini, the man who inspired the rebels by his impassioned and noble utterances; and Garibaldi, the beloved soldier.

Mazzini founded the Young Italy Association. Thousands of Patriots of all classes joined it, sworn to make Italy "one independent sovereign nation of free men and equals." Mazzini himself favored a republic, but was ready to support any kind of government which the people approved. Some others looked to the pope to unite the land, particularly to Pope Pius IX in 1846, who began to reform his own Papal States, reputed to be the worst governed lands in all Europe.

In 1848 there were revolts in Sicily and Naples, where the king granted a constitution. Sardinia and the Pope also granted constitutions. The men of Lombardy and Venice rose against their Austrian masters and were helped by the Sardinians: but all these were crushed by the Austrian whitecoats under the redoubtable Marshal Radetsky. It was after this that King Charles Albert of Sardinia abdicated and gave his throne to his son, Victor Emmanuel. The Venetians, led by the heroic Daniel Manin, endured a horrible siege before yielding to Radetsky's army.

The end of the sorry tale took place in Rome. There a republican government had been proclaimed by the people, and Mazzini was with them. The Pope fled. Upon this, Napoleon III, wishing to appear as the protector of the Catholic Church and champion of the Pope, sent an army to besiege Rome. Garibaldi led a legion of volunteers from North Italy to save the Roman Republic. His men fought magnificently to defend it, but the regular French troops stormed into the city and restored the Pope. The escape of Garibaldi and his men across the Apennines to the north was the heroic closing chapter of Italy's first bid for freedom.

Politics: Italy and Germany

The uprisings of men in the name of freedom seemed to have failed utterly: patriots and democrats had seen their ardent hopes destroyed by the Austrian generals and the Russians. Yet within twenty-five years of 1848, the Italians were a free and united nation under King Victor Emmanuel, and all the German kingdoms and duchies were joined in one powerful German Empire under William I of Prussia. In the making of Italy, France played a leading part—sometimes willing, sometimes unwilling. In the making of the Prussian Empire she played a part entirely unwilling. Great Britain took no active part: because neither the Rhine delta nor the ocean trade routes were in peril. Her wars were small ones, fought far away in Asia and Africa—except in 1854 when she joined Napoleon III in an attack on Russia in order to defend the Turks, and when warships and transports sailed into the Black Sea, to land a large Anglo-French army on the Crimea peninsula.

of patriots of all classes joined it, sworn to make Italy "one the men than the skill of their commanders; and none fought more bravely than the 25,000 Italians whom Cavour and Victor Emmanuel of Sardinia sent to fight by the side of the French and British regiments. Their valor raised the tiny kingdom of Sardinia to the level of a European "Power"— much to the disgust of Austria. But there was a much bigger shock in store for the Austrians; for in 1859 the French Emperor, Napoleon III, who had come to a secret understanding with Cavour, ordered a French army to invade Lombardy and drive the Austrians out. Two hard battles at Magenta and Solferino were sufficient to do this: and Lombardy was added to Victor Emmanuel's kingdom.

This sudden and startling action of Napoleon III as the champion of Italian liberty roused the patriots of Tuscany, Parma, Modena, and the Romagna, who drove out their Austrian masters, and placed themselves under the Sardinian king. To finish the good work, that heroic soldier of Italian freedom, Garibaldi, came into brisk and decisive action with his legion of red-shirted volunteers. With Mazzini's blessing and the practical help of Victor Emmanuel, he sailed from his own native city of Genoa amid great excitement. He and his men were outward bound for the conquest of Sicily from the King of Naples. North Italy and Central Italy were already the realm of Victor Emmanuel: he would add South Italy.

He did. His impetuous red-shirts swept across Sicily and then crossed to the mainland where they routed the Neapol-

THE UNIFICATION OF ITALY UNDER THE HOUSE OF SAVOY—
KINGS OF SARDINIA AND PIEDMONT

itans. Meanwhile, King Victor Emmanuel came riding south, and he and Garibaldi entered Naples in triumph in 1861.

Within three years in this manner all Italy was united, while the foreign ministers of the great powers followed events with approval, or anxiety or alarm, according to their own hopes or fears. The thing was done, and a new nation born. Only the old republic of Venice and the city of Rome lay outside the king's power—the one still occupied by the Austrian whitecoats, the other ruled by the pope and protected by a French army.

The fate of these two cities was decided by events north of the Alps, in which the chief actor was the Iron Chancellor of Prussia, Count Otto von Bismarck.

Ever since its beginning as a borderland against the heathen Slavs, Prussia had been a military state. Alone among European kingdoms she had produced in Frederick the Great a king who was also a soldier of genius. The Prussians had taken a leading part in the war of liberation against Napoleon: it was their army under the aged Marshal Blücher whose arrival on the battlefield of Waterloo sealed the allied victory in 1815.

Bismarck, a burly and grim Prussian landowner who became chancellor to King William I in 1862, was a hard man, clear-sighted and single-minded in politics, wholly devoted to his purpose of making his king the master of all the Germans. He had no use for parliaments or speeches. He admired force. The best of arguments was, to use his own elegant phrase, "blood and iron": that is, war. And for war Prussia was superbly prepared. Under von Moltke, a great soldier, her army was made a perfect instrument for attack—well-drilled, well-equipped, and marshaled by a skilled and intelligent general staff. Just as Napoleon had studied the wars of Frederick the Great, so von Moltke and his officers studied the campaigns of the great Corsican. Bismarck had the guns and the bayonets to carry out his policy. But he had to take into account the friendship or hostility of the three European powers—Russia, Austria, and France.

In 1863 the Poles rose in rebellion against Russia. Bismarck earned Russian gratitude by allowing the Russian army to move across Prussian territory to crush the Poles, who were duly and cruelly brought back to submission.

Three years later Bismarck struck suddenly and in great strength, first occupying the North German states, and then attacking Austria. The Prussians routed the Austrians at Königgrätz, 1866, and this one defeat was enough. The war lasted only seven weeks. It left the Prussians the acknowledged masters of Hanover and all North Germany, with the southern kingdoms of Bavaria and Württemberg as allies. In a lightning campaign (a *blitzkrieg*) the Hohenzollern King of Prussia had wrested the leadership of the German race from the Hapsburg Emperor of Austria, whose ancestors had held it since the Middle Ages. Sardinia profited; for, in return for some not very successful Italian attacks on the Austrian troops in Italy, Bismarck arranged at the peace that Austria should surrender Venice and its territories to King Victor Emmanuel.

Bismarck's full intention was uncovered in 1870 when three Prussian armies invaded France. It was Napoleon III who actually declared war, but Bismarck had planned and provoked it, and von Moltke and his able generals had it all under control. The French fought with their traditional bravery but lacked firm leadership. This Franco-Prussian War revealed the power of the Prussian army, which moved under one will to victory, to swift victory. One French army surrendered at Sedan, another at Metz. Napoleon III was among the prisoners of war, and the Prussians laid siege to Paris and took it.

In the palace of Versailles in 1871 King William I of Prussia was acclaimed the first Emperor (Kaiser) of the German Empire. There were old men in France who had marched under Napoleon I into Prussia, and old men in Germany who had fought against Napoleon I in the War of Liberation.

France was compelled to surrender Alsace and Lorraine to the new German Empire. And the war led directly to the completion of the new Italian kingdom; for Napoleon III had been forced to bring home his troops from Rome, which was thereupon occupied by Victor Emmanuel. Rome, for eighteen hundred years the religious capital of Christendom, became the national capital of Italy. Since it was unthinkable that the pope should be the subject of any earthly king, Pius IX withdrew to that part of Rome known as the Vatican City, which remained under his rule, and quite outside the government of the king.

The distress and anger of the French at the defeat led to a rebellion of patriots and socialists in Paris. They took charge of the city and appointed their own government. The disciplined German army watched the French army lay siege to the capital and fight its way in. In six weeks of bitter struggle thousands lost their lives and many buildings were sacked and burned. After order had been restored, a new parliamentary constitution was agreed on by the politicians, who modeled it as far as they could on the British one. For some time they intended to restore the old monarchy, but in the end the French settled down under a president. It was the Third French Republic.

Such were the grim and tragic events that heralded the entry of the Prussian Empire into European and world history.

For the next forty years, 1871 to 1914, the political pattern of western Europe stayed without change. There were the three great land empires of Russia, Prussia, and Austria, a new kingdom of Italy, and a new republic of France. They all grew continually in population and wealth, in industry and commerce. They all kept large conscript armies. They lived in peace and prepared for war. In the southwest were the kingdoms of Spain and Portugal, untouched by these happenings. In the southeast lay the dominions of the Turk, backward, wasted by neglect, despotic, lazy, and inefficient. Great Britain, the supreme naval and mercantile power, occupied herself in manufacture and overseas trade and colonies.

Europe bristled with armaments, but fired no shots in anger; in the three land empires the landowning aristocracy governed the peasants of the countryside, and the townsfolk were beginning to discuss socialism and to question the rights of men to govern others just because they were nobly born or rich. But those forty years were a time of increasing prosperity and increasing co-operation between nations. It seemed possible that, with wisdom and patience, the nations of Europe might be brought to diminish the barriers of frontiers and misunderstanding until they could live in peace as Europeans—just as the earlier citizens of their lands had done under the best of the Roman emperors.

Politics: Russia and Revolution

Unlike the lands of the west, Russia had never been nursed by an ancient civilization; and her church—the Greek Orthodox one—had never been a learned and civilizing church like the great Latin Church of the west.

Russia was vast and her people backward. Most of them were serfs living in village communities, paying dues to landowning noblemen. There were few merchants, businessmen or manufacturers. Above all the government of Russia was despotic. Her tsar was more powerful than the Roman Caesars whose title he bore: he was the Protector of Holy Church, the Father of his people, the Autocrat of all the Russias. His will was law.

The successors of Peter the Great continued, in a slow way, to "westernize" their country—especially the German-born tsarina, Catherine the Great. The main influence was French because France led Europe in the arts during the eighteenth century, and educated Russian noblemen spoke French. That Russia belonged to the European group or "concert" of Powers was made plain in Napoleon's time by the presence of the tsar's armies operating in Germany and Italy. It was made very plain when the Tsar Alexander I attended the peace conference at Vienna in 1815, and afterwards helped the Austrian emperor to put down rebellions. And Russia was open to western ideas.

The liberal ideas of the men who made the American and French revolutions gained ground throughout Europe during the nineteenth century. All men should be free to enjoy life and leisure under just and equal laws, without fear, expressing their opinions in a free press, and taking some part in their government. Such ideas stirred in the hearts of some Russian noblemen and students: and such ideas made greater the contrast between the pleasant leisured lives of the Russian gentry and the wretched lives of the Russian serfs, who lacked education, who were tied to their fields, who could be flogged by their masters. In Russia it was as if the nineteenth and ninth centuries had met! There was no middle class, such as grew up in the Middle Ages in France and England, to bridge the gap between the extremes of society.

There had been many serious peasant revolts before 1800. In the last of these, led by a Cossack adventurer named Pugachev in 1773–75, no fewer than fifteen hundred landowners were killed. At the accession of Nicholas I in 1825 a group of army officers of liberal opinions revolted. They were put down; and Nicholas revealed himself to be a stern, unyielding autocrat who wished to run his country as a commander-in-chief runs an army. Peasant revolts continued. Between 1845 and 1860 there were, in different places, some eight hundred uprisings, in which more than three hundred landowners perished. It was against this background of unrest and violence that the Russian governments organized their secret police and network of spies, and used their Siberian wastes as places of exile for agitators and for men unlucky enough to be denounced by the tsar's agents. Then, what should have proved a blessing merely brought more confusion and unrest. For when in 1861 the liberal-minded Tsar Alexander II set free the serfs—"emancipated" them— fifty million of them did become free men, but often only to find they could not live on the two acres allotted to them. They were free, indeed, to wander to the towns, where they became laborers or landless unemployed. By this act of

Many Inventions and New Knowledge

1861 the whole roots of Russian society were disturbed. Alexander II also overhauled the courts of justice, and established local councils *(zemstvos)* to conduct local affairs. The reformers, who wanted much more done, were disappointed with these changes, and old-fashioned people were, of course, angry at any change. The cause of the liberal-minded reformers was not helped by the assassination of Alexander II in 1884. Unrest continued all through the later years of the century, and revolutionary parties increased in number and membership. Of these there were the ordinary reformers—men like the radicals in Britain who wanted a thorough reform along liberal lines; and there were also two types of extremists, anarchists and communists.

Anarchists were men who so despaired of reforming or improving the government that they wanted to destroy all governments and all rulers. For them, any bomb thrown at any governor or man in authority was a good thing. No doubt, if all men were perfectly good there would not be need for very much government.

Communism means holding all things in common, sharing alike. It is an extreme form of socialism which means the possession and control of land and industries by the people in order to make sure of a fair share of goods for all. Socialism had been preached in England and France quite early; common ownership and sharing were familiar things. The monks had shared their goods, and many things had been owned in common ("corporately") by the guilds. A good example of sharing and common ownership is provided by the co-operative societies who own and manage large shops, distributing the profits to their members. But Karl Marx, a German Jew who came to live in England, worked out an extreme form of communism. He preached—with the fervor of a Hebrew prophet—that all human history was a relentless struggle between the *have's* and the *have-not's;* and that it was the duty of all poor men to create turmoil and confusion in order to hasten the break-up of society so that a new classless one could be established. In any case the coming of the classless society was bound to happen, because the sort of society where men can become millionaires is, he said, bound to break up. There was a lot of hatred in Marx's creed, and some muddled thinking. But it made two strong appeals: first, and naturally, to the downtrodden and unfortunate; and secondly, to ardent spirits who felt they would be carrying out the purpose of all the ages—they would become apostles of destiny, full of a sacred devotion to right human wrongs. Unfortunately, they also believed that it did not matter if they practiced lies and cruelty to bring about their perfect state. The end would justify the means. Marxian communists did not bother about goodness. The important thing to note, here, is that Marx was moved to his indignation, as were countless other men, by the evils of the industrial revolution in England, and he based all his hopes on the skill-less, unemployed, town laborers. These unfortunate men are one of the results of modern civilization. There were men, like William Morris, who hoped to build a new civilization based on the happy lives of countrymen. Not so Marx. He did not think of peasants as citizens of his utopia. He saw his communism beginning in the west in the great towns and industrial societies.

Meanwhile, the land which grew more and more ripe for revolution was Russia. Revolts and strikes of workmen went on. All the while her industries were increasing slowly, sometimes by direct help, as from men like John Hughes who founded the Krivoi ironworks, sometimes by loans, especially from the French, which enabled the Russians to build their railways and other public works. These loans were one result of the gradual alliance of France with Russia after the Franco-Prussian War of 1870, when both lands began to dread the enormous military power of the new German Empire.

Russia, today, means all the territories, ruled from Moscow, that stretch from the German borders to the frontiers of China, to the shores of the Arctic, to the highlands of Persia and the Caucasus. It spans two continents. Yet it was not until the eighteenth and nineteenth centuries that the Russians of the regions about Kiev and Moscow began to extend their power over this massive hinterland of Europe and Asia. As surely as the Americans colonized their continent, moving westward from the coast, following a troubled frontier toward the sunset across forests and prairies and deserts, so the Russians colonized their continent—but beginning from the inside and moving outwards, north and east and south; first, the forest people, hunters, fur trappers, and fishers; then the herdsmen and plowmen who cleared the lands along the waterways to raise stock and crops of rye; then the miners seeking veins of iron and lead; then the officers of the tsar to bring his authority over the new lands. There were wars. Like America, Russia bred its own races of frontiersmen, hardy, independent groups of horsemen who foraged far and wide, grazed their cattle, and were hard to bring into settled ways of life. They are well known in history as the Cossacks of the Don and the Volga.

Not until 1775 did the tsars subdue the warlike Tartars of

the middle Volga region this side of the Ural Mountains; not until 1783 did they conquer the Crimea from the Turks —those ancient enemies against whom they fought eleven wars, and not until the eighteen-sixties did they overcome the resistance of the men of Georgia and the Caucasus. They founded the port of Vladivostok on the Pacific Coast in 1860. The long Trans-Siberian railway was not finished until 1896—and even then it ran for part of its way across Chinese land: the all-Russian route was not completed until 1916.

This expansion of Russia into Asia alarmed British soldiers, who dreamed of Russian armies pouring steadily through Afghanistan down to the plains of India. The British Lion and the Russian Bear were, in fact, rivals for the Afghan alliance. Russian expansion in the Far East brought about the Russo-Japanese War of 1905; for Japan also was an imperialist power seeking to extend her influence on the mainland of Asia. The Russian army and navy suffered heavy disasters at Japanese hands. The Russian Baltic fleet sailed all the way to the Far East only to be sunk by the Japanese navy.

This humiliating defeat encouraged revolts by all malcontents, for it proved, as had the Crimean War, that the tsar's government was inefficient as well as corrupt and oppressive. Hundreds of rioters were shot down in St. Petersburg and there was an armed rising in Moscow. Later three million workers came out on strike. Such disturbances forced the tsar to grant a constitution with a parliament, or *duma*. In spite of this the peasants, now numbering seventy-five million, rose in widespread revolts in 1906. Strikes and shootings went on year after year till 1914. Russia was the land of assassination, of plots, of secret police and secret arrests.

Russia was still in a state of chronic unrest, still on the verge of revolution, when the tsar entered the First World War against Germany, as the ally of the French. The war rallied the patriotism of all classes—nobles, workers and peasants: and it seemed that with powerful allies to help her Russia might, through victory, achieve better and happier times.

Expansion

It is a melancholy fact that all the globe from China to Peru has taken to wearing the somber clothes invented by Europeans after the French Revolution. We export our habits more easily than our civic virtues or our religion. It is easier to turn a Malay or a Zulu into a mechanic in dingy overalls than to teach him to live in Christian charity with his fellows. Too often we think that a man with a gun, or dressed in a suit of coat and trousers, is more civilized than one with a knife and adorned merely with a loincloth. It is, of course, our great power that has most impressed non-Europeans ever since Columbus scared the Caribs with his gunfire. That gunfire—and our luxury and machinery—appears to be the white man's magic; and this can even deceive ourselves. The true white man's magic lies deeper: it springs from the wisdom of Greece, the religion of the Jews, and the laws of Rome.

For four centuries Europeans have sailed to all parts of the world, trading, seeking markets, taking hold of half-empty continents and tropic islands, and living on the natural wealth of the tropics—sugar, cotton, rice, spices, tea, coffee, rubber. The story is as varied, as heroic, as terrible, as cruel, as human life itself. It is a story of separate nations, separate adventurers, separate trading companies, separate—and sometimes hostile—churches, all striving against each other. This manifold adventure of the white races with the brown, black, and yellow races, has been made from every sort of motive from the "cursed hunger for gold" to the pure zeal of the cause of Christ. We have exported our wars and our hatreds. When the Romans acquired a great land empire they often sent their best men abroad to govern provinces, and even their emperors settled provincial affairs. The European nations have seldom sent their leading statesmen to rule abroad, or their chief bishops to preach the gospel. Their overseas adventures have been, to a very large extent, haphazard ones.

Expansion: The Tale of Empire and The Pax Britannica

The five nations that acquired overseas empires were Portugal, Spain, Holland, France, and Britain. By 1830 the position was as follows:

Britain had lost her American colonies, Portugal had lost Brazil, and Spain had lost her dominions in South and Central America. The new nations set free from European domination carry the stamp of their origin: the language and law of the United States are British; those of Brazil, Portuguese; those of the other South American republics, Spanish.

The Portuguese Empire at its height comprised, besides Brazil, some dozens of fortified trading posts along Africa and throughout the Indian Ocean. Most of these were cap-

MANY INVENTIONS AND NEW KNOWLEDGE   247

tured by the Dutch, leaving to Portugal only a few stations, like Diu and Goa in India. The present Portuguese possessions in East and West Africa remain from the days when the kings of Portugal were lords of the eastern seas and masters of the sea route to India.

The Spaniards had possessed many rich islands. Jamaica was taken from them by Britain in 1655, and Trinidad by Britain in 1797. Cuba in the West Indies, and the Philippines in the Pacific, were both captured by Britain in 1762, and both handed back again. Much earlier—in 1702—the British had captured the southern tip of Spain itself—Gibraltar—which they still hold as a fortress.

The Dutch had once upon a time built a town called New Amsterdam, which the British captured and renamed New York—a fine port which went along with the rest of the American colonies when they rebelled in 1776. The remarkable Dutch East India Company, which drove the Portuguese from the east, was a "power" in itself, making war and peace, issuing its own coinage, sending out famous navigators to search the southern seas and discover the coasts of Australia, Tasmania, and New Zealand. The Dutch fleets even had their own ghostly legend—the tale of the *Flying Dutchman*, a fully rigged ship seen driving before the storm, with all its crew dead from scurvy, a fearful sight for superstitious mariners. The heart of the Dutch Empire was Java and the tropical East Indies, teeming with natural wealth. These were all taken by Britain in 1811, and all restored to Holland. The Dutch possessions taken and kept by Britain were Malacca in 1795; Ceylon in 1797; and the Cape of Good Hope in 1809.

The British East India Company had driven the French Company from the mainland of India in the Seven Years' War. The French retained small coastal settlements, such as Pondicherry and Chandernagor. Britain captured and kept the isle of Mauritius. She captured and kept the important French colonies of Nova Scotia and Canada. She captured but gave back to France the two wealthy West Indian sugar islands of Martinique and Guadeloupe no less than four times.

When Robert Clive was accused of taking money from the Indians he retorted that, on thinking it over, he was astounded at his own moderation. So might Britain herself have said; for the possessions she had restored to other nations were worth untold riches. Even so, her Empire in 1830 surpassed all dreams of empire. To the possessions already named we must add Malta, Bermuda, the Bahamas, and Guiana; Newfoundland and the Hudson Bay Territory stretching illimitably across the prairies and frozen north of Canada; Australia, Tasmania, and New Zealand and many islands in the Pacific. Besides these she held forts on the west coast of Africa—old slaving stations now happily freed from their ghastly traffic by the law of 1806 which forbade the slave trade. Moreover, her East India merchants were masters of Bengal and much else of the Indian peninsula.

Britain's own overseas colonists were not very numerous—some thousands of loyal Americans in what is now Ontario; a few thousand ex-soldiers in New Brunswick and at the Cape of Good Hope; a few planters in the West Indies; a convict settlement in New South Wales together with a few sheep farmers. Most of her white subjects overseas were foreigners—Cape Dutchmen ("Boers") in South Africa, and Catholic French Canadians about Montreal and Quebec.

Like that of Venice, Britain's Empire had been created by trade. It was the work of her seamen and merchants. It was a London merchant who wrote a book called *England's Treasure by Foreign Trade*, a title that explains itself; and it was an English nobleman who warned his countrymen: "Look to your Moat; the first article in an Englishman's political creed must be, That he believeth in the Sea." The books that her boys read were Lord Anson's *Voyage Round the World*, and those exciting tales of distant islands, *Robinson Crusoe* and *Gulliver's Travels*.

From 1815 to 1914 the peace of Britain was on all the seas. Her navy rode unchallenged, and her merchantmen, and those of all other lands, came and went unhindered on their lawful occasions. There were no rivals. The Dutch had their energies absorbed in their own rich and sufficient empire of the Spice Islands: France was still seeking to learn how to govern herself: Germany did not exist, nor Italy, until 1870. Britain possessed a steady government, one able and willing to improve itself. She had enjoyed real internal peace for centuries—for the civil wars had not wasted her. She had a long tradition of trade. Her citizens had accumulated riches, and in the eighteenth century they showed an astonishing activity of invention and manufacture that made her the workshop of the world. No wonder then that her empire grew over backward and empty lands—

> Kingdom in kingdom, sway in oversway,
> Dominion fold in fold.

How her dominions became self-governing nations, how she organized and governed India, and how she acquired vast new lands in the last continent to be revealed—Africa—is one of the major themes of nineteenth-century history.

Expansion: The British Dominions

Around Quebec and Montreal were the French settlements planted in the seventeenth century, a New France, peopled with sturdy peasants and townsfolk from Normandy, living a simple and heroic life in that remote, wooded and well-watered land, a thousand miles from the open sea. There they defended their villages against the Indians; there they farmed as their ancestors had farmed in Old France; there they sang the gay songs of their homeland; there they went to Mass and kept the festivals of the Church; and there they welcomed home the *voyageurs* on their return from the wilderness of lakes and streams of the west and north.

In the Niagara peninsula, about a township loyally christened Kingston, the refugee Americans came to settle during the rebellion of the American colonies against George III. These newcomers endured great hardships, beginning life again, living in huts, growing hardly won crops, and grinding their grain by hand—until help in provisions and clothes and implements was sent from Britain.

These two settlements of Upper and Lower Canada were utterly different in language, laws, religion, and customs; and while one was a conquered land, the other was fanatically loyal—so much so that any new British settlers were almost as unwelcome to them as to the French *habitants* of Quebec.

When discontents in both settlements came to the point of rebellion in 1837, Lord Durham, who was sent out to investigate matters, reported that he found "two nations warring in the bosom of a single state." His remedy was that they should be united under their own chosen government so that they might grow to be proud of their own nationhood. This was done; and despite many difficulties, it worked, thanks largely to a wise governor.

Times were changing rapidly. The new steamships of the Allan Line were bringing in new settlers in the fifties and sixties, and population quickly doubled. Railways were constructed to link Kingston and Quebec to the Atlantic. Far-seeing men held that the "two nations" of the Canadas, together with the provinces of Nova Scotia and New Brunswick, and the vast empty lands of the Hudson Bay Company in the west and north, should all be joined in one political federation and linked by a transcontinental railway. The Civil War in America caused alarm, because no Canadian wanted a highly armed state on its long and lonely frontier. In 1870 the cavalry which had put down a rising of half-breeds in the Red River district carried out a famous exploratory ride across the prairie to the foothills of the Rockies. These troopers were the first members of the Canadian Mounted Police.

In 1881, all the way from the Great Lakes to the Pacific coast, some 9,000 laborers began working on the Canadian Pacific Railway. There were grading gangs, tunneling gangs, track-laying gangs, dynamite gangs, and bridge-building gangs, living in camps and feeding on the herds of cattle which moved slowly up from the American plains to the scene of action. Thanks to the Canadian Mounted Police there were no disorders, no Indian attacks. Year by year the work went forward along the plains and in the high solitudes of the Rockies, where thousands of Chinese coolies helped to hew out the track, and engineers threw trestle bridges across the ravines. At last, in 1885, the lines from east and west met in the Eagle Pass, and the steel artery of the new Canadian Dominion was complete.

Slowly at first, then more and more quickly, the prairie wheatlands were occupied and the dairy and fruit fields of the Pacific Coast were taken up. It was no longer necessary to travel around Cape Horn to reach Vancouver. The Dominion of Canada had been formed in 1867. Manitoba joined in 1870, and British Columbia in 1871—on condition that the railroad was built. The political pattern was finished in 1905 when Alberta and Saskatchewan became provinces. The new federal state extended from ocean to ocean, and northwards across the frozen wastes to the Arctic Circle.

Meanwhile, beneath the stars of the southern hemisphere, another continent was also being peopled and farmed: the faraway Southern Land of strange plants and animals, a place of dark mountain forests and landscapes of softened grays and olives and purples, a land whose heart is not a prairie but a desolation and a desert. What began there as a convict station, six-months' voyage from Europe, grew slowly into the shepherd's paradise of New South Wales, Queensland, and Victoria, where the merino sheep wandered on vast grasslands and downs. The few free farmers and explorers opened up the fertile territories, and the navy surveyed the coasts. A new interest in colonization at home in Britain led to the founding of settlements around Perth in Western Australia and around Adelaide in South Australia. But population lagged until 1851. In that year a man who had been in the California gold rush of 1849 found gold in New South Wales. Others picked up gold nuggets at Bendigo and Ballarat in Victoria. A rough multitude of prospectors and diggers swarmed in; the ports were emptied and whole ships' crews deserted in the hopes of making easy fortunes. Few did this, but the gold rush raised the population to over a million by 1858. By this time steamships were bringing in settlers after a voyage of only six weeks, and the disappointed diggers stayed to take up other work. The ports grew and the gold was used to import the luxuries of civilization; and as population increased so did farming and business. Guided by its experience with Canada, the British Parliament gave self-government to the Australian states. A later gold rush took place in 1892 to Western Australia, where mines were opened at Kalgoorlie and Coolgardie. In 1900 the separate states joined together in a self-governing Commonwealth of Australia.

Twelve hundred miles from New South Wales are the islands of New Zealand, found and named by the Dutch, surveyed by Captain Cook, visited by whalers, sealers, and missionaries. To the last we owe the skillful writing down of the Maori language of the natives. The Maoris were attractive cannibals, of splendid physique, intelligent, and sporting, who rejoiced in tribal warfare. For many years after Captain Phillip's convicts had landed in Australia the New Zealand coasts were a sort of no man's land where the scum of the South Seas mingled with Maoris and traded muskets and blankets for pigs and pickled human heads—tattooed ones.

It was the new interest in colonization that made New Zealand the place we know. After a treaty in 1840 with the Maori chiefs, a New Zealand Colonization Society sent out groups of settlers chosen by the churches: the Scots Presbyterians, for instance, went to Otago, the Anglican Churchmen to Canterbury. Sheep, dairy, and fruit farming occupied them in islands of a mild climate and luxuriant vegetation. In 1854 the settlers were granted self-government. Since then the story of the islands, except for a sharp Maori War in 1860, has been peaceful and prosperous, with a steady inflow of immigrants, mainly from Britain. In 1907 New Zealand was proclaimed a Dominion under the British Crown.

Expansion: The United States of America

In 1827 the sailing ship *James* foundered off Newfoundland with 160 Irish emigrants on board. Indeed, in that year, seventeen crowded emigrant ships bound for America went down with the loss of hundreds of poor souls who had already suffered the misery of the Atlantic crossing. Seldom a year passed without some such disaster, and not always at the end of the voyage. In 1849 the *Floridan* with German emigrants from Antwerp was wrecked off Harwich. In 1850 a hundred

Irish perished when the *Edmund* struck on the rocks of County Clare. These were incidents in the great migration from the Old World to the New, which, beginning in the 1780s, continued throughout the nineteenth century. Until the 1850s it was carried in sailing vessels subject to every chance of wind and weather.

Most of the emigrants were poor, many were destitute and desperate. They included highland crofters turned off their holdings; English artisans, hand weavers and mechanics, out of work in the depression of trade that followed the Napoleonic War; peasants whose land had been taken by their landlords; above all, Irish peasants ruined by the failure of their potato crops, and evicted from their hovels because they could not pay rent. From Europe, especially from the German states, came thousands of refugee farmers and craftsmen, eager to start life afresh, away from the tyrannies of Europe. So true is it that the misery and despair of the Old World peopled the New World. The victims of famine in Ireland, unemployment in England, revolution and tyranny in Europe, swarmed overseas. In the ten years from 1815 to 1825 about 70,000 left Britain; in 1850 no fewer than 250,000 sailed, mostly Irish. Many landed at Quebec and traveled thence into the United States. Great numbers landed at New York every year—in 1847, for instance, 100,000 men and women, half of them German, half Irish. The discomfort and length of the voyages were lessened with the coming of the Cunard liners to New York in the forties and the Allan steamships to Quebec in the fifties. Altogether, in the century ending in 1890 no fewer than eleven million people crossed the ocean, nine million to the United States. Nor did the flood of emigration stop then.

The newcomers found a nation already on the move towards the good lands of Tennessee, Kentucky, Ohio, and the farther-off territories of Illinois, Missouri, Indiana, Alabama, and Mississippi—which all became states of the Union before 1821. Horsemen and wagoners journeyed along the new national turnpikes out of New York State or along Braddock's old marching road out of Pennsylvania westward. They were not the pioneers. Those were the fur traders and the half-wild hunters, men who always moved away from the settled communities. But all who ventured west were thrown back on their own resources for everything. The Indians were driven from their hunting grounds with many a murderous combat, many a foray by the United States militia, and ambushes, scalpings, and massacres. Farther west the settlers followed well-marked trails blazed by the frontiersmen, leading to Santa Fe in Mexico (now New Mexico) and to

MANY INVENTIONS AND NEW KNOWLEDGE 253

California and Oregon. Riflemen guarded caravans of prairie schooners, as the heavy covered wagons were called, living mostly on buffalo meat in plains where the horizons were sometimes black with the vast humpbacked herds. The buffalo all but vanished under the ruthless slaughter from the guns. At night the wagons were laagered to fend off surprise Indian attacks. In this eager, hopeful, and hardy winning of a continent of prairie and sagebrush and giant forest, the mighty rivers played a useful part. It was a simple thing to run the wagon onto a raft to float down the Ohio. The Mississippi in the eighteen-thirties was already a water highway for broad steam-paddle boats with tall funnels.

So the best land was taken up. So the desert and the cactus wilderness were traversed, and the high snowy passes of the Rockies conquered by a new nation of adventurers. The coming of the railroads speeded everything. In 1869 a transcontinental line was completed; the last spike of it being driven in at Ogden (Utah) when the eastern and western sections met.

Joseph Priestley, the English scientist, a staunch believer in the power of reason, was full of enthusiasm for the newborn American Republic. In 1791 he wrote that it was most unlikely that there would ever be a civil war in the United States—only the "unreasonable" monarchies endured such evils. But less than a hundred years afterwards there *was* a civil war in America, a fierce and bloody civil war between the Northern states and the Southern ones, 1861 to 1865. Virginia, the Carolinas, Georgia, Tennessee, Arkansas, Louisiana, Alabama, and Mississippi broke away from the Union and elected their own president. The Northern states made war on them to compel them to stay in the Union. This may sound rather odd seeing that we usually agree that men should be free to choose their own government! But in fact, there had long been a difference between South and North, the South being a land of slave plantations, the North being commercial and industrial; the South was full of aristocratic plantation houses of landowners living on the profits from cotton and tobacco, while the North was a land of merchants, manufacturers, and free farmers. The background of the strife was Negro slavery. Many Northerners wished to set the slaves free, and, during the war, President Abraham Lincoln announced the abolition of slavery.

Lincoln had been brought up in log shanties in his native Kentucky and in Indiana, and, largely self-educated, became a lawyer. By his undaunted and patient leadership he carried the North to victory over the South, despite the fact that the South was led by the most talented soldier—Robert E.

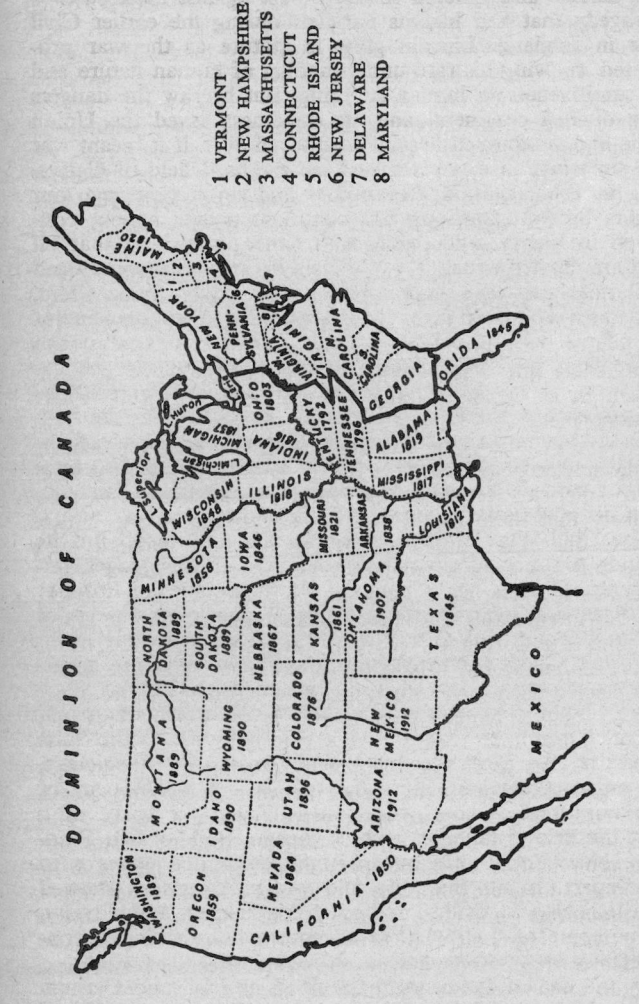

1 VERMONT
2 NEW HAMPSHIRE
3 MASSACHUSETTS
4 CONNECTICUT
5 RHODE ISLAND
6 NEW JERSEY
7 DELAWARE
8 MARYLAND

WESTWARD EXPANSION OF THE UNITED STATES

MANY INVENTIONS AND NEW KNOWLEDGE

Lee. It was, indeed, a tragedy of the war that two such men as Lee and Lincoln should be set against each other—a tragedy that had had its parallels during the earlier Civil War in England. Lincoln grew in stature as the war progressed, showing his rare understanding of human nature and his sensitiveness to human suffering. But he saw the dangers of a divided continent, and his steadiness saved the Union as he had determined it should be saved even if it meant war and suffering. In a noble speech on the battlefield of Gettysburg in 1863, he said: "Fourscore and seven years ago our fathers brought forth on this continent a new nation, conceived in liberty, and dedicated to the proposition that all men are created equal. . . . We highly resolve that these dead shall not have died in vain; that this nation, under God, shall have a new birth of freedom; and that government of the people, by the people, for the people, shall not perish from the earth." To us who have seen freedom in the utmost peril all over the world during our own century, Lincoln's words sound still like a clarion. This was the man from the poor wooden cabin whose parents had no advantage save the freedom of those who ventured west, and who himself had come to the greatest place of honor through freedom. Even his adversaries respected "Father Abraham."

The Civil War left bad memories and bitterness. But its wounds did not affect those thousands of new eager immigrants still pouring in from the old monarchies of Europe: and American expansion went on with increasing energy. It cannot be said that America settled down—she has never done that! The newcomers worked around the clock, toiled for profit, invented, traded, manufactured, farmed with vigor —and all the time strove to establish a uniform system of education complete from the village schoolhouse to the State university. America became a land of farmers, engineers, and millionaires: and, as in the Old World, a new sort of man was created—the businessman. Within the space of a short lifetime, great cities arose, Chicago, Buffalo, San Francisco. New York, built on an island, expanded upwards in skyscrapers. In all their life and works Americans showed an astonishing ingenuity, a thirst for quickness and novelty, the outcome of their restless adventure in subduing a continent.

By the end of the century the flood of Irish and German settlers had overlaid the older and traditional societies of New England and Virginia and Dutch New York. The days of Rip Van Winkle of Sleepy Hollow and of the village folk of Massachusetts had passed. Yet this extraordinary nation, continually enlarged by the exiles of other lands, kept true to the principles of its founders who had built on their heritage of England's medieval law and custom; and the leaders of the United States had the task of winning and molding to their tradition the most diverse peoples—Germans, Irish, Slavs, Greeks, Jews, Italians, and even Chinese and Japanese on the Pacific Coast, where also were Spaniards, descended from the time when Spain ruled California. One writer aptly called America the "melting pot" of the world, where all sorts of races were commingled.

For a hundred and fifty years after its foundation the United States pursued its way unentangled in the affairs of its many motherlands in Europe. It kept its law and constitution and absorbed those many millions who desired freedom and work. We need not be surprised that its citizens had small interest in the doings of the outside world: they had a big enough world of their own, and there was more than enough to do there. In any case, the immigrants had left the Old World deliberately turning their back on it in order to make their own New World. Why should they worry about Europe?

Expansion: India

By the mid-nineteenth century the merchants of the East India Company controlled all India up to the hills of the North. This had come about by treaty and conquest in a land where there was no unity and no idea of unity; where Hindus and Mohammedans were intermingled and hostile; where there was no one law, but a thousand superstitions and barbarous customs, and a thousand governments. The Company's agents and soldiers, supported by the officers and soldiers of the Queen, brought one law and one authority. More than one Anglo-Indian army had marched into the wild mountains of Afghanistan beyond the northwest frontier —a military zone just as much as Hadrian's Wall had been in ancient Britain, or the Roman *limes* in the Rhineland.

The possession of India led to the conquest of Burma, a land of jungles, and to the control by treaties of the Malay States of the Malay peninsula—a land which was to become very rich from its tin ores and its rubber trees. Singapore, founded in 1819, became a center of eastern seaborne trade, the meeting place of Chinese, Indian, Arab, Malay, and East Indian merchants. One adventurous Englishman, Brooke, became the rajah (or ruler) of Sarawak—a large part of the great island of Borneo; and by the end of the century half that island was a British possession. From the Cape of Good Hope to Singapore the Indian Ocean was a British sea.

Many Inventions and New Knowledge

By the end of the seventeenth century the English East India Company had factories in Calcutta, Bombay, and Madras, and traded with China. Its merchants built their own dock at Blackwall on the Thames, built their own massive ships, made their own ropes and sails, even their own casks. Their ships were so heavily gunned that they were more like royal ships than merchantmen. They could, and did, engage and sink foreign warships. The Company's factories abroad, where goods were stored for loading, were like colleges, with a governor, a chaplain, a chapel, and a common dining room. They raised regiments of Englishmen and regiments of Indians (sepoys). In fact, they acted in every way as a sovereign power. During their struggle with the French Company in the eighteenth century the king's regiments were sent out to help them, and at the end of that century a royal governor was sent out to govern the land empire which the traders had acquired.

The like of this had not been seen before, and is not likely to be seen again: and the marvel is not that these traders made so much profit from their empire, as that so many of their servants did their utmost to bring peace and justice to a land in confusion and decay, where the population ranged from high-principled Brahmans, saintly Buddhists, and chivalrous Rajputs to idol-worshiping tribes living in filth and ignorance.

After a mutiny in the Bengal sepoy army in 1857, the Company came to an end. Henceforward India was ruled by a viceroy and his council under the Queen. One third of the country was made up of 600 native states under their own princes, who varied in power and dignity from the Nizam of Hyderabad, ruler of a land as big as England, to the chieftain of a single village. The other two thirds were governed in the Queen's name by about a thousand civil servants, a picked and devoted band of men, each of whom administered his district like a benevolent despot, sometimes being the only white man amidst a quarter of a million natives. This remarkable civilian government was matched by a no less remarkable army of 250,000 men, of whom 75,000 were British—one British regiment brigaded with three Indian ones—and all commanded by British officers. The Indian infantry and troopers were recruited from the warlike races—Punjabis, Sikhs, Marathas, Dogras, and Rajputs, with Pathans and Gurkhas from across the borders. It was an army the like of which the world had never seen, for pride, valor, and devotion to duty. Nor was it maintained to keep India in subjection. Its chief duty was to safeguard the frontier. A third, and still more remarkable thing about this strange Indian Empire was that the ordinary man and woman in Britain knew so little about it and cared less.

Under British rule India enjoyed internal and external peace. Moslems and Hindus wrangled and rioted but never fell into outright war. And India began to share the benefits of western engineering: roads, railways, telegraphs, canals, lighthouses, bridges, reservoirs—all these were built. More efficient forms of farming were introduced and some of the jungle cleared. Floods, famines, and pestilences were brought partially under control, and their dire effects lessened. Coal and iron were mined, cotton, sugar, and jute grown. Mills and factories were erected. Forests were preserved for timber. These things do not take so long to do; they are the less valuable part of the white man's magic. More difficult it is to make a good system of education or a public health service: but with the very extensive help of Christian missionaries these things also were begun. By the close of the century India had its own universities and medical schools. And by the close of the century, in spite of the enormous one third of all that of the whole British Empire.

In fact, India was the most orderly and best governed growth of its population, its seaborne trade amounted to part of Asia.

Expansion: The Far East

The story of Europe is much less than half the tale of humanity. Away beyond the forests and plains of Central Europe and the highlands of Persia there was a vast region of grazing lands from which uncouth tribes of Huns and Tartars descended on the eastern frontiers of Europe, where they were regarded as scourges sent to punish wicked men, or as beings uprisen from the infernal world. These wild horsemen also raided the western frontiers of a very ancient civilization in the Far East—the Celestial Empire of the Chinese, whose early rulers built a Great Wall, eighteen hundred miles long, to keep the raiders off.

Chinese civilization goes back to a dim antiquity three thousand years before Christ. It has its own long history of empires and dynasties, wars and conquests. It developed its own system of writing on paper, and its own methods of building, agriculture, and commerce. It had its own literature and fine art, its own games (including one of football with seventy ways of kicking a ball!) and its own drama. It existed unbeknown to westerners, never in any sort of direct contact —except, perhaps, fleetingly, when Alexander's spearmen

MANY INVENTIONS AND NEW KNOWLEDGE 259

marched into India, and gave the races north of that peninsula some knowledge of Greek ways. Solitary travelers reached China from the west, and a thin trickle of trade in silks was carried on through a long chain of merchants; but Europe's first full acquaintance with China began when a Portuguese ship anchored in Canton in 1514. There were many Chinese to be found in Malacca, where Chinese junks were a familiar sight. After the Dutch and English had supplanted the Portuguese in eastern waters, their ships traded in Chinese ports. The English East India Company set up an agency at Canton in 1715 where its agents traded with due ceremony with the hong merchants, giving bales of woolen cloth for chests of tea.

Tea, now a delightful commonplace of our homes, is the supreme gift of China, the Indian variety being cultivated later to supply our enormous demand. Another famous export of the Far East was its fine porcelain—particularly that of the Ming Dynasty; for the Chinese were skilled potters and their vases and figurines and cups and saucers are much sought after by collectors. Their skill has, indeed, its just commemoration in the word we use for our tableware—china. Another tremendous gift to the West is the great and lovely multitude of shrubs and flowers brought by our botanists during the past two centuries from all the Chinese provinces.

Chinese ideas of law and trade and manners were strangely unlike European ones, but their sense of virtue and duty was the same. They were cheerful, noisy, loyal, hard-working, patient, courteous. They kept no hard and fast class distinctions like the Western ones between aristocrats and populace. Of the four main occupations they held that of the scholar in highest honor; then that of the farmer. The craftsman came next, the trader last. (This is practically the entire reverse of the Western order.) From the scholars, versed in the ancient Chinese classics, they chose their governors and officials.

To study the best things in Chinese civilization is to see our own lives and habits in a new light. The wisdom of their philosophers such as Confucius and Mencius is no less a treasured heritage of all mankind than that of our own sages. The Chinese Empire was larger than Europe, and had endured centuries longer than any other in the history of the world. The most striking quality of Chinese life was its sameness throughout the whole of the Christian centuries of the West—till the West forced itself on China, and brought its own restlessness to the Far East.

The story of Western commerce with the Chinese is one of

which we cannot be proud. In 1834 the British made war on the Chinese to compel them to let Indian opium be imported. In a later war conducted by British and French troops the beautiful summer palace of the Manchu emperors was wantonly burned down. To secure their trade and the profits it earned them, the European Powers forced the Chinese to give them certain ports—Canton, Amoy, Foochow, Ningpo, and Shanghai—in which their merchants could live and through which they could pass their goods. The British possessed themselves of Hong Kong. That many Chinese did not want the "foreign devils" in their homeland need not astonish us. Imagine our indignation if the Manchu emperors had despatched merchants to force their way into Antwerp or London. The Christian missionaries took pains to understand the Chinese and did much splendid work among them. But too many Western traders saw themselves as the superior "civilized" people and the Chinese as "natives." It was a great mischance for China that the Manchu rulers were weaklings during the latter part of the nineteenth century; for through this China was disturbed by civil wars and strife for many years—in fact, almost continuously. It was, perhaps, in something like the condition of Europe during the later years of the Roman Empire. It was also most unfortunate for the Chinese that the Japanese turned themselves into a strong power equipped and armed with the white man's machines and weapons—the wrong magic.

Japan was awakened by the white man's lust for trade at all costs. The Americans compelled the Japanese to receive merchants in 1854. Thereafter the diminutive islanders proved very apt pupils at learning Western technical skills and science, and soon made themselves an industrial nation with a powerful navy and army led by a strong aristocracy. In 1894 Japan seized Korea from China. This made the jealous Western nations, Britain, France, Germany, and Russia, seize Chinese ports.

The civilized territories of China were now, like those of uncivilized Africa, at the mercy of all the ambitions, greeds, and rivalries of the Great Powers. When Chinese patriots, known as "Boxers," gathered together and killed European engineers and missionaries, the Great Powers joined forces to sack and loot Peking and other places, and many of their troops behaved barbarously (1899–1901).

A few years later, in 1904, Russia and Japan came into conflict over which of them should control Manchuria. They fought their war in Chinese territory and Chinese waters. The Japanese defeated the Russians and sank their fleet.

In 1911 China became, in name, a republic. In fact the

empire of the Manchus was divided. No single authority was recognized, but rival governors and soldiers marched and fought against one another. Law and order were maintained in the Treaty Ports by the Western Powers, but within four years these were themselves engaged in a war which involved most of the world.

Expansion: Africa

Thanks to their Mounted Police the Canadians had little trouble with the redskins; the Australians met no opposition from the primitive blackfellows; and though the Americans and New Zealanders fought against the Red Indians and Maoris respectively, they never enslaved them.

In Africa the tale was tragically different. That massive continent, whose northern shore had once been the home of ancient Christian civilization, kept its secrets longer than the others. The curse of slavery lay on it, and unnumbered multitudes of its Negroes were traded, even by their fellow Negroes, like chattels to the Arab merchants of the east or to the European ship's captains of the west. Most of its history can be summed up in a few terrible words: ignorance, poverty, famine, disease, war, fear, superstition, and slavery. Long before any white men knew where Africa's rivers ran, or where her mountains rose to the clouds above lakes as large as inland seas, they had forcibly transported whole populations of blacks to toil on the sugar, tobacco, cotton, and indigo plantations of the New World; no fewer than six million terrified souls were so taken into slavery during the eighteenth century from some forty slave stations along the tropical west coast. At the end of that century Africa meant to the Europeans just this commerce in "black ivory," with a lesser traffic in elephants' tusks, gold dust, and mahogany. Along the Barbary Coast of Algeria there were corsairs, or piratical Moslems. Egypt lay idle and decaying under Turkish rule. Six thousand miles away at the Cape was an insignificant colony of Dutchmen, or Boers. Of the tropical and subtropical interior nothing was certainly known. Africa was in every sense a "dark continent."

After Britain annexed South Africa in 1807 the Boers and their new rulers disagreed over the natives. To the Boers all natives were a lesser breed of humanity to be used as slaves, treated maybe kindly, even trusted to be nurses to their children, but always kept sternly in their place. In Great Britain at that time the missionary zeal was beginning that sent dozens of young men to convert the heathen in the Pacific

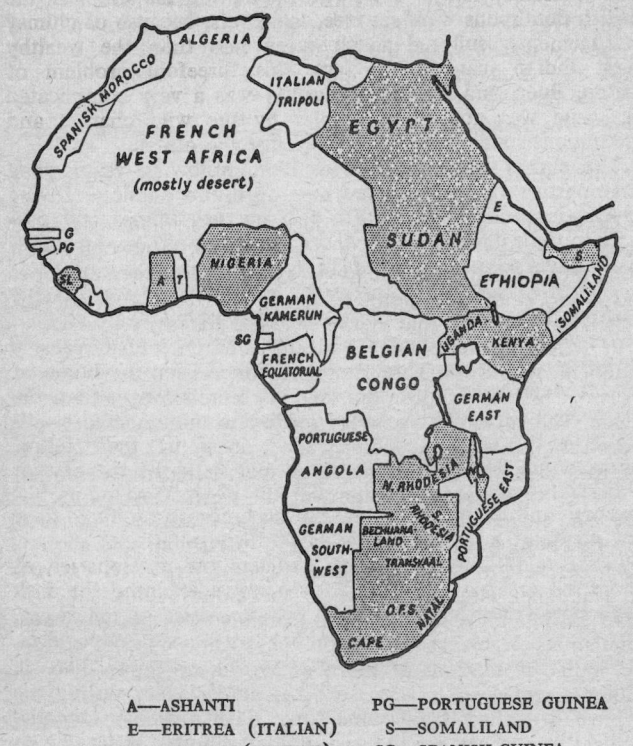

A—ASHANTI
E—ERITREA (ITALIAN)
G—GAMBIA (BRITISH)
L—LIBERIA
N—NYASALAND
OFS—ORANGE FREE STATE
PG—PORTUGUESE GUINEA
S—SOMALILAND
SG—SPANISH GUINEA
SL—SIERRA LEONE
T—TOGOLAND

EUROPEAN OCCUPATION OF AFRICA: THE POSITION IN 1914

British possessions are shaded. Only two small states were left under native rule—Ethiopia and Liberia

After the 1914-1918 war Britain took German East and German Southwest Africa; France took the German Kamerun and Togoland

Islands and in Africa. The missionaries and Boers did not take the same view of the Negro. When all the slaves in the British dominions were set free, the Boers, because of clumsy arrangements, suffered much more loss than the wealthy West Indian planters. In fact, this threefold problem of Briton, Boer, and Bantu (or native) was a very complicated one, and was not made simpler by the wild charges and accusations made by each side against the other.

The climax came in 1836 and the following years when large parties of Boers packed their furniture on slow moving ox wagons and set out north seeking new homes and pastures in the wilderness, then the hunting grounds and pastures of Zulu warriors. This Great Trek was for them a journey of an oppressed people to a promised land; for they were deeply religious in a dour Old Testament way, and regarded their Bibles with as much affection as their guns. It was heroic and tragic. Many of them were massacred by the bloodthirsty tribesmen. Those who fought their way through established two new states, one on the Orange River and one in the Transvaal.

Meanwhile the French were in action in the extreme north. They conquered Algeria, ridding the Mediterranean of the corsairs, and then began making schemes for joining their new conquest to their stations on the Senegal River.

In the middle of the century travelers and missionaries, of whom the greatest was David Livingstone, explored the dark interior of Central Africa, tracing the courses of the Niger, Nile, Zambesi, and Congo, and discovering the great lakes. They revealed the appalling savagery and revolting horrors of tribal life and warfare. They revealed also the enormous natural riches of the continent. This was a twofold challenge to the European nations: first, to bring the light and love of the Gospel to the black heathen; and secondly to seize as much land as possible for the sake of the profit. The result was a scramble among the Great Powers to acquire African lands in the eighties and nineties.

Through the efforts of their King Leopold the Belgians annexed the large Congo basin, where they began planting rubber and were later to discover valuable minerals. Britain extended her power over the Niger lands, creating "Nigeria," besides taking Nyasaland and Uganda. The Portuguese were already in possession of Angola and of Portuguese East Africa—relics of their earlier epic days of discovery in the fifteenth century. The Germans, latecomers to colonial enterprises, secured the Cameroons and large territories in East and West Africa. The French succeeded in their prolonged effort to stretch their power in a compact block of land from the Mediterranean to the coast of Guinea, including the Sahara Desert. In a very few years all Africa, outside the old native Christian country of Abyssinia (Ethiopia), and that of Liberia on the West Coast (settled by freed slaves), was shared out among the Great Powers.

Even Egypt was occupied. There, in 1859–1869, a French engineer, de Lesseps, constructed the Suez Canal to shorten the sea route to the East, and at once Egypt became important. Bad and bankrupt government led Britain to occupy and govern it as a "protectorate," that is, for its own benefit, in 1882; and Britain had to keep order in the Sudan as a result. The Suez Canal was a vital link in British imperial communications, and Egypt lay at the center of British trade and strategy.

Missionary zeal was soon proved by the devoted work of men in every part of the continent, by the preaching of the Gospel, and the slow and arduous beginning of medical and educational services by the churches. The missionaries recorded in writing the many native languages. With government help the work still goes on. But in the far south events moved towards a major catastrophe.

In 1877 Britain annexed the Boer republics. In 1879 a British force was wiped out by Zulus. In 1880 another British force was wiped out by Transvaal Dutch at Majuba. The Zulus were later subdued and their land annexed. The Transvaalers were left alone by the British government—but not by the adventurers. Diamonds had already been found at Kimberley, and now rich deposits of gold ores were discovered on the Witwatersrand (the *Rand*) in the Transvaal, 1886. At once a great mob of gold-seekers rushed in to stake their claims, and in a few years the tiny Dutch dorp of Johannesburg was turned into a wealthy town, the center of the richest mining industry in the world. These foreigners, or "outlanders," were not exactly the cream of civilization: and their contrast to the strict and old-fashioned Boer farmers with their outlook of Old Testament patriarchs could hardly be exaggerated. The president of the Transvaal was old Paul Kruger, a typical Boer farmer, who had taken part as a small boy in the Great Trek to help gain this country as a homeland.

One of the men who made millions of money out of the diamonds and gold was Cecil Rhodes, the son of an English clergyman. In 1890 he was prime minister of the Cape. He used his wealth to form a company to seize all the native lands north of the Transvaal, and the company's well-equipped expedition did this. The newly acquired land was named Rhodesia. The Boers were now entirely surrounded by British territories.

Rhodes organized an armed raid into the Transvaal to help the outlanders of the Rand, who were, in fact, being rather badly treated by the Boers. The raid failed miserably. In 1899 ill-feeling between Boers and Britons reached such a tension that the Transvaal and Orange Free State horsemen mustered in their commandos and rode in to the British colony of Natal. They brought artillery, purchased in Europe, and they were expert riflemen. They were mobile. In this they remind us strongly of those mounted archers that Britain herself produced in the Middle Ages. The war that followed began with a series of British defeats, and Britain only achieved final victory in 1901 by bringing into the field over a quarter of a million troops, including many mounted ones from her dominions. She lost six thousand killed and twenty thousand more who died of fever and dysentery. The other European nations were neither convinced of the righteousness of Britain's cause nor impressed by the intelligence of her generals. Wisdom prevailed at Westminster in that peace of 1906 which gave the Boers complete self-government within a Union of all the South African colonies.

The heirs of da Gama, of Columbus, of Cabot, of Cartier, of Tasman and Cook, had by 1900 laid claim to all lands in all the continents. The imperial eagle of Russia was supreme over an empire that reached to Mongolia, and the republican eagle of the United States spanned America. The world was owned by Europeans save for a China in great disorder; a Japan in good order, disciplined, armed and overpopulated, seeking new lands; and the cluster of broken lands in the Near East where the Turk took his ease at the expense of his miserable subjects.

The world had "spread upon" Europe as it had once spread upon ancient Rome. But Rome had one senate and one army. Europe had many. Rome governed mostly white peoples akin to her own sons. Europe had millions of backward and colored races in her care. The best of Romans could bring a Roman peace to her empire. There was no such thing as a European peace. Instead, the rivalries of the European states engulfed the world in their own bitter strife.

The Nations in Their Harness, 1914—1918

The new Germany quickly became a rich industrial and mercantile empire. She wanted colonies, and in the scramble for unoccupied parts of Africa she acquired in 1884 large

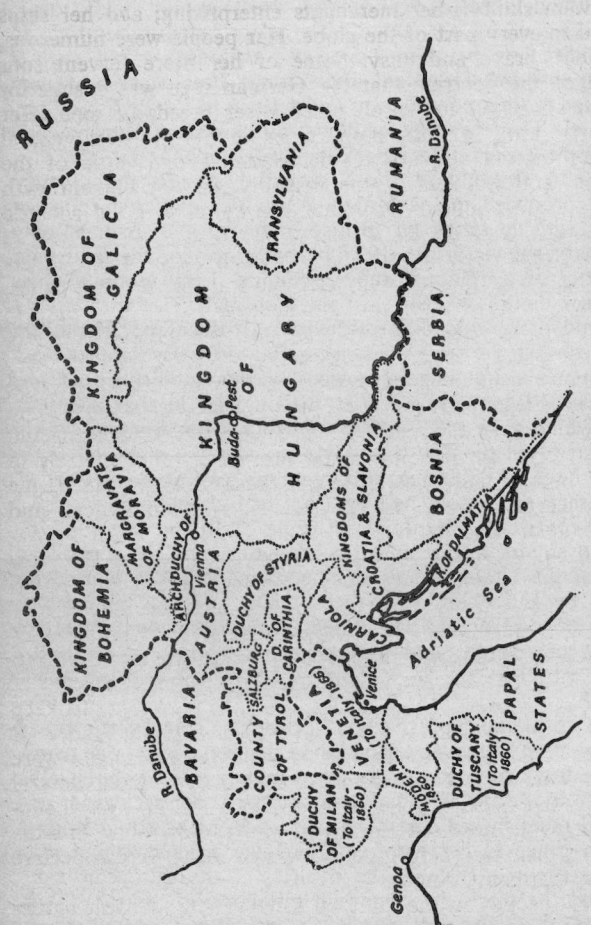

THE KINGDOMS AND DUCHIES OF THE HAPSBURG EMPIRE OF AUSTRIA-HUNGARY, 1914:
A feudal and monarchical bulwark of Western Christendom

territories in the southwest and the east of that continent, as well as Togoland and the Cameroons. She also occupied northern New Guinea. Her engineers, craftsmen, and scientists were skillful, her merchants enterprising; and her ships traded to every part of the globe. Her people were numerous, obedient, brave and busy. Some of her more fervent sons preached the doctrine that the German race was a superior one, destined to master all other lesser breeds of men. Her conscript army was the best trained in Europe. Her general staff of officers despised the Russians, thought little of the French, and still less of the British. And not content with having a great military machine, she began to build a battle fleet to challenge the British navy.

This threat drew France and Britain together in an understanding, or *entente*, in 1904. Russia and France were allies. Germany and the Austrian Empire were allies. To complete the circle of alliances and rivalries, Russia and Austria were jealous of each other's influence in the Balkans. So there were two groups of Great Powers, jealous and afraid of each other. But Europe had enjoyed forty-odd years of peace and prosperity, and there seemed no reason why, apart from human folly, the nations should not settle their quarrels in peace. In fact, there was an International Court at the Hague where learned jurists judged disputes between nations and settled them peacefully.

In June, 1914, the Archduke Ferdinand, heir to the Austrian throne, was assassinated in Sarajevo in Bosnia. Asserting that the deed was planned by Serbians, Austria demanded full satisfaction from the Serbian government. But she allowed no time for calm negotiation. Instead she declared war. Russia championed her fellow Slavs of Serbia. In spite of most desperate efforts by ministers and ambassadors to keep peace, Germany declared war on Russia and on France. It is clear that the Austrian and German general staffs were set on war. By their invasion of Belgium, a small neutral country, the German generals hoped to wheel an overwhelming army into northern France by the easiest route; but the result of their treacherous action was to make Britain declare war on Germany, August 4, 1914.

A few people on the cliffs of Kent saw the British battleships moving in long lines through the straits northward. The navy was on its way to battle stations in Scottish waters. Other holiday-makers found themselves delayed in sidings while long troop trains passed. The first seven divisions of the regular army were gathering at Southampton for their voyage to France. Men left their farms, their factories and offices to fall in behind marching companies of soldiers. They crowded the army depots. For the first time in her history Britain became a nation in arms. And from all parts of the world her sons hurried home to join up. India and the Dominions offered their armies and their wealth. The feeling against Germany was amazingly strong. Even then, at the outset there was the resolve: Germany has appealed to force; she shall have force, and to the uttermost. The war was a crusade:

> What of the faith and fire within us,
> Men who march away,
> Or ere the barn-cocks say
> The night is growing gray—
> What of the faith and fire within us?

For the French conscript who went stolidly to his depot, for the French reservists who helped to stoke their homeward-bound liner from South America, for the British volunteer who sprang to arms, this was to be the uprising of all decent men against the intolerable threat of aggression. It was a war to end war.

Such a response made nonsense of the German intention to fight a *blitzkreig*, a lightning-war, first overthrowing the French, and then turning eastward to defeat the Russians.

True, it was a near thing in France. But by good fortune and valor the French armies rallied against the invaders and drove them back to the Marne. The gallant Belgians had done what they could, and the British army played its small and effective part. The blitzkrieg became a stalemate; both combatants dug in, all along the line from the Vosges Mountains to the Belgian coast. For four years this western front was a battlefield of trenches and shell craters where millions of men fought a sort of siege warfare. Human folly and human heroism were given full scope in a war that involved most of Europe; for the Turks joined Germany in 1914, and the Italians declared war on their old enemy, Austria, in 1915.

Germany, Austria, and Turkey became a gigantic fortress or fortified mass of land, besieged at all possible points. Russian armies attacked it from the Baltic to the Balkans; Russians also invaded Turkey from the Caucasus Mountains; an Anglo-Indian force landed in the delta of the Tigris in Mesopotamia; another British army defended the Suez Canal; the Italians clambered and fought along the Austrian Alps; while from Switzerland to the Belgian coast French, British, and Belgian armies defended Paris and the Channel Ports.

In 1915 a gallant attempt was made by British, Australian, New Zealand, and French troops, supported by battleships,

Many Inventions and New Knowledge

to capture the Gallipoli Peninsula, and so open a sea route to Constantinople and to the Russian ports of the Black Sea. Its success would have taken Turkey out of the war and brought much-needed succor to the Russians. But the attempt failed after furious fighting. The Turks were saved by the skill of an officer named Mustapha Kemal: and the Russians remained isolated from their allies.

In France and Flanders men lived like ants in the ground, emerging at times to attack in face of machine-gun and rifle fire and bursting shells, and dying to gain a few muddy yards —or none at all. Attack and counterattack; raid and counterraid; trench against trench, sap against sap; mine and countermine—this was the daily round of thousands of men. Every device of destruction was used: grenades, bombs, mortars, shrapnel, high explosive, and clouds of choking poison gas, first let loose by the Germans. The havoc of the guns turned whole landscapes into muddy and barren desolation. Ambitious attacks were elaborately mounted; they failed, leaving heaps of dead and wounded and crippled—leaving also the somber names of the places where they happened— Loos, Ypres, Neuve-Chapelle, Chemin des Dames, Messines, Verdun—as records of folly and heroism beyond credence. The eager volunteers who rushed to the colors in 1914 went into a grand attack in 1916 along the Somme, and lost 60,000 men killed and wounded on the first day. No man living had wisdom enough or skill to use their valor profitably. Airplanes flying and fighting overhead added to the general confusion and destruction. No leader on either side had the slightest idea how to end the dreadful conflict except by a grim sort of arithmetic of death—flinging more and more men against the fortified lines. British tanks were first used on the Somme and might have broken through, but they were too few.

Without their navies the Allies could not have carried on the war at all. It was the cruisers and armed escort ships that blockaded Europe and kept supplies from reaching Germany; that protected the fleets of merchantmen that bore the minerals, food and munitions of the New World to the Allied arsenals and docks; and that safeguarded the great liners crammed with troops. One British blockading squadron spent most of its time patrolling between Iceland and Norway. When in 1916 the battleships of the German High Command streamed out from their bases into the North Sea, a sharp encounter with the advance flotillas of the British Grand Fleet off Jutland sent them hurrying back to harbor— where they stayed.

In 1917 the Allies met their worst fortunes. So far the

large Russian armies had held in action equally large German forces along a vast battlefront from the Baltic to the Balkans, where whole armies moved backwards and forwards across East Prussia, Poland, and Galicia. The Russian losses were enormous, and their supplies of guns and ammunition quite inadequate. Their bravery was astonishing. But in March, 1917, a popular revolution began in Russia. The tsar was deposed—and later murdered with his family. Like the French Revolution the Russian one was started by men of fair minds and good intent, but quickly fell into the hands of ruthless and bloodthirsty fanatics—in this case, the communists under Lenin, who speedily made a peace with the Germans. So the German armies of the east were releasd to help those in the west.

Then the French armies mutinied, and while they were recovering their discipline, the British fought a long, dreary, and costly battle in the mud of Passchendaele. Then a German army appeared on the Italian front and swept the Italians back into the plains, where their retreat was only stopped by the arrival of French and British divisions sent from France.

These setbacks were balanced by the entry into the war of the United States, whose people were angered by the ruthless sinking of merchant ships, including passenger liners, by German submarines. The supplies needed by the Allies were all seaborne, and by 1917 the German submarines were sinking cargoes at a devastating rate. In spite of the convoy system, reluctantly adopted by the admirals, the outlook was very grim. With the entry of America the prospect improved. American naval units went into service at once. American shipyards turned their immense energies into building ships. And no less welcome were the large contingents of American troops landed in France, and ever increasing until they were coming at the astonishing rate of a quarter of a million each month. They were not the first troops from across the Atlantic; for from the first months of the war the Canadians had despatched armies to take their place with the British.

In March, 1918, the Germans made a last determined attack. They overran the British Fifth Army and drove back the French. After a perilous time the gaps were sealed. The arrival of the Americans gave the Allies ample reserves, and by now their continual setbacks had compelled them to accept the orders of a commander-in-chief—a Frenchman of courage and character, Marshal Foch. He took charge. In July he began a series of sudden and fierce attacks, first here, then there, up and down the whole line, allowing the enemy no respite whatever. He had enormous supplies. Guns stood wheel to wheel along the battle lines. Army after army, French, British, American, moved into action supported by storms of artillery fire; and the tempo increased until the whole front was mobile. Under these continual assaults the German defenses crumbled, and soon the Allied gunners were unlimbering in open country and firing from field positions; and the infantry were outrunning their supplies. By November the Germans were in a general retreat.

News of success flowed in from other theaters of war. The Serbians, reformed and rearmed at Salonika, swept back to their homes, a nation of fighting men. General Allenby's army from Egypt fought the Turk through the hills of Judea, while his yeomanry and colonial horsemen rode the length of Palestine to trap the fleeing enemy. Damascus fell. In Mesopotamia General Maude's men advanced up the rivers to join hands with Allenby's. The Italians were in pursuit of the Austrians across the mountains.

So the Great War ended in an armistice, or cease-fire, on November 11, 1918. Germany and Austria were in revolution. Constantinople was in Allied hands. British, French, and American bugles sounded on the Rhine. The awful suffering and loss, the disastrous follies and superb heroisms, were over. It remained for the Allied statesmen to make a lasting peace.

Fallen Empires

The 1914–1918 War brought to an end the empire of the Russian tsars, the empire of the Ottoman Turks, and the empire of the Austrian Hapsburgs. All the eastern approaches of Europe were left in confusion.

The Russian Revolution of 1917, during which multitudes of people lost their lives, left the central government in the hands of the Marxian Communist Party under Lenin, a man of great political skill. The revolutionaries set up *soviets,* or councils, everywhere, transforming the tsardom into a Union of Soviet Socialist Republics (the U.S.S.R.) under a red flag bearing a hammer and a sickle—for neither of which they had any use. Their aim was to make Russia a land of factories, machines, and tractors, with its people turned into a proletariat, or mass of landless laborers. In place of the old aristocrats would be the members of the Communist Party.

These were ruthless in crushing opposition. But Russian rulers had always been tyrants. The chief difference was that these new masters were more efficient in their tyranny. As members of an international party of communists whose purpose it was to overthrow all existing governments, they could hardly expect existing governments to be friendly. In consequence, the Russians remained apart from the civilized world. Here again there was really little change, since Russia, by her geographical position, had always been somewhat isolated from the mainstream of Western life. The links that existed—old artistic and mercantile friendships—were severed by the determination of the Soviets to foster hatred, malice, and discord in other lands.

To restore order and work in a people disheartened, backward, ignorant, leaderless and defeated, would have been hard enough in any case, but the Soviets wanted to force all their subjects into one political mold. They sought to dominate the lives and the minds of men, just as the tribes of Africa dominate the lives and minds of their members, so that everyone thinks and acts in the same way at the same time. It is easier to rule people this way. They wanted the state to own everything and manage everybody—to make a society like the old Inca nation of Peru, but an industrial one, not an agricultural one. Curiously enough, the peasants had little use for Soviet communism. The Marxian revolutionaries of Russia, like the French revolutionaries of 1789, found their most stubborn opponents in their peasantry. A new word was coined to describe this sort of society—"totalitarian."

The achievements of the Soviet leaders, first under Lenin, and after his death under Stalin, were remarkable enough. They built roads, drained swamps, dug mines, made new industrial towns, and erected power stations. They devised a system of universal education and turned an illiterate people into a literate one. They explored the recesses of their vast land, opening up industries in the far frozen north and in the subtropical south. They had at their disposal one-sixth of the habitable world, full of untold natural wealth in vegetation and minerals. They made an epic of toil and suffering: they wiped out the middle class—or, as they called it the "bourgeois" class; they made war on the peasants; they transported entire populations from their homes to strange places; they sent thousands to slave and die in labor camps; they kept the secret police—who are always needed in a tyranny. Then they accused each other, arrested their comrades and had them shot—just as the French Revolutionaries had guillotined their comrades; but whereas the French leaders went to their deaths shouting defiance, the communists acknowledged their faults and begged forgiveness.

It was all very odd and sad, utterly unlike the politics of the West even in the Dark Ages. One English historian (in

--- The frontiers of the old empires of
Germany, Austria, Russia, and Turkey

THE FRAGMENTATION OF EASTERN EUROPE:

All these states except Austria, Greece, and Turkey are now dominated by Soviet Russia—which also controls Eastern Germany

1912) had called the Slavs the "vilest and least civilizable" branch of the white race. He referred to those of the Dark Ages, but indeed his words might fairly describe the behavior of many of the Russian revolutionaries. Shorn of all the high-sounding talk of a communist paradise on earth—which might mean men living in amity and equality and mercy with each other—the Russian brand of Marxism was plain brutality and utter disregard for civilized values. Lenin had genius of a political sort. Stalin, his successor, was a bloodthirsty tyrant. The U.S.S.R. was something new and very ugly—a mighty people in a mighty land controlled by a group of men who scorned all the values and laws that the West had inherited from Greece, Judea and Rome.

Somewhere, under the dreadful mask of political savagery, the old character of the Russian people waits, maybe, to show itself once more—patient, tolerant, humorous, loyal, and devout. Somewhere the old Russia of the great Russian novelists, poets, and musicians, still exists.

The break-up of the Turkish Empire, a ramshackle affair, left the Turks with only the fine city of Constantinople and Asia Minor; and, but for the fiery patriotism and energy of Kemal Attaturk, their possessions would have been even smaller. It was Attaturk who rallied his people and drove a Greek army in headlong flight from Asia Minor in 1920. Attaturk created the new modern Turkey, making his people adopt Western dress, habits, ideas, alphabet, and education. He completely transformed old Turkey into a busy agricultural and mercantile state. There are still old peasant women wearing veils even while they toil in the fields; but the younger women are attired like their sisters of France and Britain. Today, Turkish scholars excavate and study the ruins of lost empires in Asia Minor—and they include university women in their ranks. Turkey was an old enemy of the Russians in tsarist days. And still today the hardy and intelligent Anatolian soldiers of the army keep armed watch along the Soviet Russian border in Armenia. In a strange reversal of fortunes the modern Turk guards the flank of the civilized West just as the Venetians used to guard it against the Turks of old!

The rest of the Turkish Empire lies in fragments—Arab kingdoms and republics: Iraq (Mesopotamia); Syria; the Lebanon; Trans-Jordan; Arabia. In their lands are the rich oil fields leased to the oil companies of the U.S.A. and Britain. Into the ruined and long-wasted East, ruled by men without experience, and inhabited by the poorest of herdsmen and wanderers, flows the gold of America and the West to pay for the oil which alone keeps civilization going. All this

MANY INVENTIONS AND NEW KNOWLEDGE 275

Near Eastern block of small and weak states is in a condition of unrest and change. Like the small Balkan states of the nineteenth century, they are a source of danger to world peace because of the rivalry between Russia and the West.

For a long time leading Jews had nursed a hope that one day their people would return to Jerusalem. A "Zionist" movement was started to bring this about. The Allies of the 1914–1918 War promised to set up a "national home" for Jews in Palestine. In 1920, under the protection of the British army, this was done. The state of Israel was founded, and thousands of vigorous and intelligent Jews from all over the world took advantage of this opportunity to live under their own Zionist government. These pioneers and their successors have built up a modern state, with fruit farms, and mineral works along the shores of the Dead Sea. They have made a Hebrew University at Jerusalem staffed by brilliant men. But their arrival and their energy has not been welcomed by the Arabs, many of whom have been driven out of their old homes and are now hapless refugees. The hostility between Jews and Arabs is extremely bitter.

The most striking outcome of the war was the break-up of the Hapsburg Empire of Austria. Some strips of borderland went to Italy and to Serbia (renamed Yugoslavia). The main part broke up into three republics—Austria, Hungary, and Bohemia (renamed Czechoslovakia). Austria, the land about Vienna, was far too small to support itself; Hungary was a rich agricultural plain inhabited by peasants under their landowning lords; and Czechoslovakia was a country with a goodly number of industries and skilled craftsmen and artisans. They had all previously depended on one another: and now they were separate states.

Other new states appeared in the lands once held by Germany and Russia; along the Baltic coast were the small republics of Esthonia, Latvia, and Lithuania; and in the midst of the great plains the ancient Catholic kingdom of Poland reappeared as the Polish Republic.

If we add to these the small countries of the Balkans—namely, Rumania, Albania, Bulgaria, and Greece, there were no fewer than eleven small states, all with grievances and grudges about their frontiers, spread across the whole of eastern Europe from the Baltic to the Mediterranean. They formed a belt of "buffer states" between the two powerful nations of the Germans and the Russians.

Since 1918 the history of Europe, and of the world, has turned on this fact. All the eleven states were easily conquered by the Germans in 1939–1945; and, today, all of them except Austria, Yugoslavia, and Greece, are dominated by the army of communist Russia. Lord Acton, the great English historian, foresaw in 1900 the grave danger from the German and Russian armies; but the politicians and people who made the peace treaties of 1918 could not foresee the tragic suffering and fate of these many small states; on the contrary, they hailed their appearance as signs of a new world in which every nation should choose its own government, and then live in concord with its neighbors.

Twenty-one Years Between Wars, 1918—1939

The task of the peacemakers at Versailles was all but impossible; they were required to settle a weary, shattered, and ignorant world, and they were not very clever men. One hope did burn brightly. The "war to end war" must be followed by a solemn covenant between nations forswearing forever the use of force. Some such scheme had been the dream of many statesmen and philosophers in the past, and there was already in existence a body of international law and an International Court of Justice at The Hague, which had ended many disputes peaceably. Now, under the guidance of many leading men, including President Wilson of the U.S.A. and Field-Marshal Smuts of South Africa, a League of Nations was established with its headquarters at Geneva. This League was a large and persistent attempt to keep peace through debates and conferences, and its various committees did very useful work in getting the nations to co-operate in welfare work and communications. But the League failed to prevent war between the great powers, and men will go on arguing for a long time yet why it failed. Perhaps it never really had a fair start: the U.S.A. was not a member, nor were Russia and Germany for some years, and at no one time did all the great nations belong to it. Nations quarreled in public in its assemblies—and for some odd reason nations are not held in honor if they apologize or forgive in the way that individuals do.

The French had one overmastering desire. They wanted to be made perfectly safe against German attack, for they feared the Germans. The Germans, still the most numerous, industrious, and skillful people in the midst of Europe, tried to make their new republic work—and a defeated nation always finds it hard to accept a new form of government. The victors at Versailles insisted that Germany should publicly acknowledge her guiltiness in beginning the war, that she should be disarmed and kept poor, and that she should go on paying for years a crippling indemnity in money and goods for all the losses and damage of the war. Far from feeling that they had been defeated in fair fight, the German soldiers who had withstood the world's armies for four years, and who had marched back in good order to their Fatherland, still felt themselves to be better men than either the French or the Russians.

The declared purpose of the Russian communists to spread communism abroad merely increased the long-standing rivalry between Russia and Germany for the mastery of Eastern Europe. The fear of Russian power and aversion from its communist doctrine that the end justifies the means, is part of the melancholy background of all modern politics.

Communism spread in France, Spain, and Italy. It weakened French political power—already weak enough through the inability of the French to agree about government—and it upset Italy, a poor country that had suffered much but gained little glory or profit from the war. Gang warfare and political banditry between Italian communists and their opponents led to grave disorders. In 1922 a journalist named Benito Mussolini led his "Blackshirts" in a march on Rome to restore law and order. Mussolini became a dictator—*Il Duce* (or the Leader) and did as he pleased, setting up a tyranny as strong as that desired by the communists, whom he hated. He adopted as his sign the *fasces* carried of old by the Roman *aediles*—the men who kept order in Caesar's day. His party were known as *Fascists*. He and his party set about making Italy a strong military power and a colonial power, reviving the might of Rome. He made men work, forbade strikes, and conscripted all men and boys into the armed forces. A great deal was accomplished: swamps drained, roads built, banditry abolished. Such things can always be achieved by the use of force. Mussolini's rise was due to Italy's lack of experience in parliamentary government, to the ignorance of the people, to the plots of the communists, and the poverty and unemployment that abounded. Italy has a large population and few natural resources. To Mussolini his countrymen were the natural successors of the Romans: to many of his countrymen Mussolini was a savior. He was, in fact, a mixture of bandit, patriot, and tyrant.

Much of the trouble between nations and parties everywhere is economic: it concerns manufacture and trade, and who shall do what work and on what terms. After 1918 there was a boom of prosperity. But in 1931 there began a slump or a falling-off in world trade—plenty of work to be done (there always is) but a complete lack of confidence, so that trade came almost to a standstill. Money exchanges between nations broke down, no one could afford to buy the goods with which the warehouses were stored, fleets of fine merchantmen lay rusting in harbors and slack waters because no one could afford to hire them, the wheels in the factories stopped. Brazilian coffee was dumped into the ocean, American wheat burned, and milk poured down the drain. Millions of men were without work, even in the U.S.A., which had enough food for all and more than enough work to last everyone in the world for ages. The world seemed to be bewitched. It was a grim and fantastic situation, and only very slowly did trade revive and unemployment dwindle.

The attempt of the victors to keep Germany poor and make her pay for the war caused trouble there: trouble which was enormously worsened by the slump. Germany went bankrupt and most of her middle classes were ruined. There was a vast unemployed population. Again there were political gangs and lawless strife, out of which one ruthless party emerged and seized power—the National Socialists, or "Nazis"—led by Adolf Hitler, an ex-corporal of humble origin. In 1933 Hitler became *Der Führer* (the Leader)—a dictator. He organized his followers as troops. He put down all opposition with cold-blooded ferocity. His aims were simple and terrible: to make men work and obey; to kill all communists and Jews; to bring all Germans in whatever part of the world under his authority; and to make the German people, who were in his eyes a ruling race destined to master all others, supreme in the world. He aimed at conquering the fruitful plains of western Russia and the oil fields of the Caucasus. At the same time he would compel the peacemakers of Versailles to reverse their decisions. He made no secret of all this: and the rest of Europe watched him while he carried it out.

His power was due to the breakdown of democratic government in Germany, where it had never been practiced before the war; to the despair of the people; to the vulgar hatred of rich Jews and the vulgar belief that all economic troubles were due to them; and to the desire for revenge. His power was also due to two special causes: the habit of Germans of obeying any orders, and to the fact that many German officers supported him. They hoped that after he had united Germany and made it strong they could get rid of him. They were mistaken.

Naturally Hitler made an alliance with Mussolini. Both were utterly unscrupulous, both believed in the old Satanic

MANY INVENTIONS AND NEW KNOWLEDGE

principle—dear also to the communists whose plots had helped to cause confusion in Germany and Italy—that the end justifies the means: Hitler, indeed, openly proclaimed that if a lie is big enough and repeated often enough men will believe it. Both demanded instant and abject obedience. Both posed as patriots.

While the democracies of France, Britain, and the U.S.A. were living on hopes, quarreling among themselves, and letting their armies and navies melt away, three groups of ruthless men knew exactly what they wanted—and were prepared to take it by force: Adolf Hitler and his Nazis, Benito Mussolini and his Fascists, and Stalin and his fellow Communists. Naturally there were hundreds of private citizens in the democracies who knew these facts. No one, for instance, who watched the very school children drilling in military formation in Germany could fail to foresee the tragedy that might come.

In 1934 Mussolini attacked Ethiopia, and by 1936 had conquered it, in spite of tremendous indignation voiced throughout the democracies. In 1936 a violent civil war broke out in Spain, a country which had missed the war of 1914–1918. With the customary ferocity of Spaniards, communists and liberal or democratic forces fought against the army officers and "conservatives." Churches were sacked and burned, cities bombed, prisoners executed. Volunteers from other countries flocked in to help the Spaniards ruin their land in the sacred name of some political party. Hitler sent troops disguised as "travelers," Mussolini sent regiments to help the Spanish generals against the communists. In the end the Spanish army General Franco won and became a dictator in 1939. This war illustrated the confusion of mind in the democracies. Such was the shocking state of politics in Europe that no democrat could support a popular cause without allying himself with the communists; yet if he opposed a popular cause he allied himself with the equally repugnant Nazis and Fascists.

To make matters worse, there was open and undisguised aggression in the Far East, where the Japanese, under their military aristocrats, were invading Chinese provinces and creating havoc there. The League of Nations solemnly condemned this, but the League had lost all moral authority. Many nations had withdrawn from it. In December, 1939, it expelled Russia because the Russians had made war on Finland. This was the last thing the League did; for all Europe was again at war, a war which seemed, to those involved in it, a resumption of that of 1914–1918, after a muddled and disastrous truce.

The Nations in Their Harness, 1939—1945

In 1936, in defiance of the peace treaties, Hitler marched his troops into the Rhineland. In 1938 he seized Austria. In 1939 he seized Czechoslovakia, gaining thereby the Skoda armament works. France and Britain made no attempt to prevent or reverse these monstrous iniquities, but the British began rearming and adopted conscription; and they let Hitler know that if he attacked Poland (as he threatened to do) they would go to war. Hitler attacked Poland and occupied as much of it as he could; for Stalin craftily moved his Russian divisions into most of it as a safeguard against the growing might of Germany. So, after a brief freedom of twenty-one years, unhappy Poland was again partitioned.

The nature of the Second World War which began in September 1939 was determined by three inventions perfected since 1918: the fast and heavy bomber; the armored fighting tank; and wireless telegraphy and broadcasting.

Powerless to save Poland, the Allies were powerless to do anything else. For eight months, in darkness, depression, fear, and alarming secrecy, the conflict halted, except at sea where German mines and submarines sank ships. The Allies waited for Hitler to act. In May, 1940, he acted swiftly, treacherously, and with complete success. His armies and air force seized Denmark, Norway, Holland, and Belgium. His armored divisions drove through the Anglo-French armies as they swung up to defend Belgium. Paris fell, France surrendered, and a million Frenchmen marched into captivity. The British expeditionary force was rescued from the beaches of Dunkirk by a swarm of small craft—naval units, fishing vessels, yachts, pleasure steamers. All this the Germans accomplished in two months of *blitzkrieg,* and their own losses were comparatively trivial.

Britain had no guns, tanks, or even rifles worth mentioning. But Spitfire and Hurricane fighters of the Royal Air Force, guided by a new radar device, destroyed the German bombers that attacked harbors and airfields, and so prevented a German attempt at invasion. The few hundred fighter pilots saved civilization: another thousand such—had they been ready—might have saved France. After this "Battle of Britain" London suffered aerial bombardment night after dreary night for months on end, with grievous loss of life and damage.

It was a sorry reversal of fortune for Britain. Her countrymen stood to arms with pikes and sporting guns while the rescued battalions were being re-equipped. What ardors and endurances her heroic navy and merchant service underwent could only be described in a detailed history. She stood alone:

and in the eyes of most of the world she was doomed. The gathering might of her Dominions would come to her aid, provided that she could keep the seas, but she could not hope to make a victorious war without a strong ally in Europe. Gradually her factories and arsenals began to mend matters, and munitions of war began to flow in from the U.S.A., where Franklin Roosevelt was president. Most important of all for Britain was her own change of government: under the shock and shame of the disasters, Winston Churchill was acclaimed prime minister. He was a warm friend of Roosevelt. He was a soldier and a man of vision who soon dominated the war by his fortitude, his fertility of mind, and his grand and inspiring eloquence.

Britain's cities were bombed. Her ships were sunk. Her people were conscripted and rationed. One triumph lightened the gloom. In December, 1940, General Wavell, advancing with two divisions from Egypt, destroyed an Italian army of 150,000 men in Libya, and before May, 1941, other British troops had driven the Italians from Ethiopia. But another *blitzkrieg* by the Germans put all the Near East in peril. Hitler's armies occupied Hungary, Rumania, Bulgaria, and Yugoslavia, and then attacked Greece. The Greeks fought back, helped by a British force landed from Egypt, but the German tanks and planes carried all before them. In a few days the Germans reached Salonika and Athens, and then took Crete by a massed parachute attack. Again the Royal Navy rescued large British forces from Greece and Crete. By May, 1941, all Europe west of Russia was in vassalage to Hitler. Moreover, a German Afrika Korps under Rommel landed in Libya and threw the British back to the Egyptian border. Britain still stood alone.

Then Hitler gave Britain a continental ally. On June 22, 1941, the anniversary of Napoleon's invasion of Russia, seven German armies drove into eastern Poland and Russia without the slightest warning. Within a month they were at Smolensk, and before the winter they were before Leningrad and Moscow, and had occupied the industrial Donetz basin and the oil fields of the Caucasus. Like the French in 1812, the Nazi armies in the winter of 1941–42 were broken by the devastating frosts which wrecked their armored vehicles. The Russians were tough fighters, and behind the Germans were thousands of "partisans"—civilians by day and guerrillas by night. The war was frightfully savage, and Hitler set out to enslave the whole population of the conquered lands! The Russians transported their war factories with incredible toil back to the Urals where they were safe; and in gigantic tank battles before Moscow they held the invaders while they raised and massed new armies in Siberia. No country suffered in the war more than Russia.

The winter of 1941 saw another sudden transformation. In December, Japanese bombers, without any declaration of war, wrecked the American naval base at Pearl Harbor in the Pacific, and invaded the Philippines. Within three months the Japanese occupied Hong Kong, Indochina, Malaya, and Burma. They took the whole of the Dutch East Indies. They took the British naval fortress of Singapore and captured 70,000 British troops.

The United States was now in the war on the side of Great Britain against Germany and Japan. But the outlook for the democracies of the world could hardly have looked bleaker: the Germans and the Japanese held the initiative and controlled all Europe and Southeast Asia, and a German army threatened Egypt. This was in the spring of 1942.

Before the end of the year the Allies had gone over to the offensive in all three theaters of war.

In May and June American carrier-borne planes sank Japanese warships in the Coral Sea and off Midway Island. Thereafter, for the next two years American naval forces, aircraft, marines, and troops assaulted island after island, slowly recovering the mastery of the Pacific and setting up air bases. It was, inevitably, a long job. There were the most furious naval and air battles in the seas about the Solomon Islands, Papua, and New Guinea, while American and Australian troops cleared the island jungles of their fanatical Oriental defenders, who fought to the death. Meanwhile, in Arakan, an army of British, African, Indian, and Chinese divisions, also operating in dense jungle, slowly pushed their way south to Upper Burma and to Mandalay.

In October, 1942, General Montgomery smashed Rommel's Afrika Korps at El Alamein in Egypt, and chased it across the Libyan Desert to Tunisia. At the same time a large Anglo-American army was landed in Algeria. Rommel's army, caught between the two forces, surrendered at Tunis in May, 1943. North Africa was now free, the appalling naval hazards of the Mediterranean were diminished, and the heroic island of Malta succored after its prolonged attacks from the air. In July the Allies seized Sicily. In September they invaded the south of Italy, and under the command of the British General Alexander, they began a slow and costly advance up the peninsula. The Italian government surrendered, but the Germans held on skillfully, and by May, 1944, the Allies were still south of Rome.

In November, 1942, Russian armies closed in on a quarter of a million Germans commanded by von Paulus at Stalingrad on the Volga, and took or destroyed them by January, 1943. Then, attacking repeatedly with army after army all through the summer, autumn, and winter of that year and the spring of 1944, they drove the Nazis back to the frontiers of Poland and Rumania.

Hitler's fortress of Europe was under siege. Since 1942 fleets of Allied bombers had been blasting his towns with increasing power, hundreds of planes—sometimes over a thousand—operating at once. At sea the Allied navies and aircraft were steadily overcoming the packs of German submarines which had played havoc with the convoyed merchantmen. Under the Nazi yoke daily life for millions had become a nightmare of tyranny, suspicion, dread, and suffering. Hitler and his gang of infamous associates had turned Europe into a slave state of subject peoples ruled by the "lordly" Germans. Every land had its ruthless Nazi governor and its secret police. Thousands of wretched people were forced into war factories and camps, shifted about like cattle, torn from their homes and families, overworked, underfed; and thousands were thrown into ghastly concentration camps like Buchenwald, to live half naked in filth, to die of disease, to be flogged, tortured, shot, or gassed in gas chambers, and burned in incinerators. All Jews were wiped out. "Man's inhumanity to man" could not go farther. As the Allied army pushed up Italy and the Russians drew nearer, so the barbarities increased. Into this sealed and tragic Europe were dropped parachutists from Britain to direct saboteurs and encourage patriots. Into this continent of mourning and despair broadcast messages of hope came daily from Allied stations.

In June, 1944, under General Eisenhower's direction, the greatest fleet ever organized moved from the many harbors of Britain to the Norman coast, taking its own concrete artificial harbors with it! Allied aircraft gave it perfect cover. As the American, British, and Dominion divisions landed, they spread out, fought grim battles, and advanced. Another American army was landed near Marseilles and came up from the south. German resistance was so strong that it took a year to overcome it. The Allies reached the Rhine and crossed it in the south. The Russians thrust forward all their armies, and made a wide sweep southward to free the Balkans. The Nazis bombed England with pilotless aircraft and rockets. They flooded Holland. They fought like demons all the way back to their devastated cities, which were still under nightly bombardment.

In the end, with the Russian tanks and guns in Berlin, and the western Allies moving fast in Germany itself, Hitler shot himself in his air-raid bunker in Berlin. In May, 1945, some German officers arranged the unconditional surrender of their people and army. The war in the west was over. The victors could see what it was they had conquered—a continent of millions of refugees and shattered cities.

By this time the German army in Italy, driven up to the Alps, had surrendered, and Italian patriots had murdered Mussolini. In the East, Rangoon was freed, and large British and American armies were being prepared for the assault upon Japan.

The Japanese war lords were called on to surrender. They refused. On August 6, 1945, an atomic bomb was exploded over Hiroshima, and the flames and radiation killed 80,000 people at once. Another bomb over Nagasaki two days later killed 40,000. The Japanese had already suffered terrible bombing from ordinary high explosives. The dreadful carnage at Hiroshima and Nagasaki ended their war. They yielded everything, placing themselves at the disposal of the victors.

Inventions Without End and People As the Sands of the Sea

The adventure of invention goes on at a bewildering pace. Our engineers make the most complicated machines, which need power to drive them, and our scientists are making discoveries all the time. Sometimes it seems as if they will not stop until they have taken the universe to bits and put it together again.

Men contrive mechanisms to pull and thrust, to turn and twist and roll—all governed and timed exactly by the wheel which itself moves at once in all directions yet follows none. Such machines will take in planks of aspen wood at one end and throw out matchboxes at the other; or take in molten lead and eject it in the shape of solid bullets; or weigh, wrap, and label packets of tea—and so on. Machines work for us. They need power—measurable and controllable power of the kind that will drop a steam hammer to within a thousandth part of an inch above a watch glass.

Since Faraday discovered the interaction of magnets and electric currents (1832), men have perfected dynamos to generate electricity, and housed them in power stations, some of which use the energy of burning coal, some the energy of falling water. The hydroelectric power stations at Niagara Falls send out electric currents to places more than 300 miles away; the Russians are completing giant hydroelectric plants on the Volga; and in Scotland the engineers are busy damming the rivers and harnessing the water fall of the highlands. So far, however, only a tiny fraction of the world's available water power is in use.

A new fuel and source of power was discovered about 1860 in the subterranean oil of Pennsylvania, an oil which is refined into gasoline, and from which chemists extract paraffin, benzine, and hundreds of other substances, including vaseline. By exploding gasoline vapor in cylinders Gottfried Daimler, in 1886, made a gasoline engine. So the automobile appeared on the roads—the forerunner of all mechanical transport from motorcycles to bulldozers. By 1933 the engine, improved by a thousand designers, had been transformed into the Rolls-Royce "Merlin" which drove the British Spitfire through the skies.

In fact, the comparatively lightweight gasoline engine made flight possible. The first men to skim along above the ground were the Wright brothers in America in 1900. In 1909 Blériot flew across the Channel: in 1919 Alcock and Brown flew across the Atlantic. The rest of the tale is summed up in the furious air warfare of 1939-45 and the giant Viscounts and Britannias of today's airlines. An important part was played in aviation by those metallurgists who speeded the extraction of aluminum from its ores (300 *pounds* produced in 1884, well over a million *tons* in 1951), and who invented all kinds of tough, light aluminum alloys of which planes are made. Since 1941 the jet engine has come into use both for planes and rockets.

Since the 1880s there has been great development of "light" engineering such as produces bicycles, sewing machines, typewriters, and adding machines. These, like cars and planes, are made possible only by the giant powered machine tools that mold and cut and stamp and forge their parts.

Photography began in 1824. A camera taking a celluloid film was invented between 1880 and 1890, and by the end of the century motion pictures were projected onto a screen. Motion pictures were popular before 1914, the "talkie" came in 1928, and the effect of these triumphs of the photographer's art is plain to see in our cities. Other triumphs include cameras to augment our vision—to reveal things too small or too fast for our eyes—the motion of a bird's wing, or the structure of substances like steel—and aerial photography, which has enlarged our knowledge of the earth, and of the past.

The sending of coded messages along electric wires was

done as early as the 1840s. The telephone came in 1876. The use of waves in space, i.e., "wireless," was demonstrated by Marconi in 1896, and by 1901 messages had been sent across the Atlantic. In 1921 the radio engineers had ready a new miracle: broadcasting. Crystal receivers soon gave place to thermionic valves. In the cinema the picture came before the sound; in radio the sound preceded the picture: that was analyzed, and transmitted by waves through space, and reintegrated on a screen in 1936. We call it television. Here again these things are but toys compared with the control of waves by radar for guiding planes, ships, and missiles and for searching the remote places of the universe.

All matter, animal, vegetable and mineral, is grist for the magic mill of the chemists and physicists. In a sort of wizard's parlor game they change and transmute everything into something else. Out of coal they extract dyes and scents, creating colors never seen on land or sea, and perfumes excelling those of Arabia. They turn cellulose into artificial silk, benzine into nylon thread. They squeeze or compress the gas ethylene until it turns into polythene. The list of new substances from detergent powders to cosmetics for adornment, stretches to a tedious length: and old familiar materials are cut and joined and fused and varied endlessly to make all types of alloys and steels, concrete, glass, cardboard, plywoods. It is clear that the ingenuity we inherit from our brave ancestors of the Stone Age who invented fishhooks and baskets and cloth, has not failed us.

Science probes ever deeper into the nature of matter itself. Since Madame Curie investigated radium in 1898, the study of radioactive elements has never ceased. Since Rutherford in 1919 used radioactivity to chip a particle or so from the atom, the hunt has been persistent; and the quarry has been the control of atomic energy. The nature of matter, the nature of electricity, the nature of the invisible particles of which all the universe is made—all this is under the keenest scrutiny. So far the research has led to the atom bomb and the hydrogen bomb; and more recently and hopefully to the atomic power station like Calder Hall. Perhaps the earth will at length be enriched by our controlling the sources of all energy until we have power without stint.

The earth is at the moment increasing its difficulties by adding fast to its population, adding in fact 4,000 new human beings every hour, which makes 35,000,000 a year. Most of these are born to be undernourished, most of them add to the backward races. If all are to be well-fed, and supplied with the good things of life, there will be need of far greater wisdom than can be discerned in the past. There will be need for tolerance and understanding between races and nations. There will be need of a great deal of the white man's nobler magic. And of course there will certainly be need of power controlled and expended for the general good.

The Present Passing into the Future

Cables, wireless, and air transport link up the whole world closely and immediately, and the expansion of Western habits, ideas and peoples goes on at a great pace. Emigrants continue to flow from Europe to the new continents, some still, unhappily, as refugees, like the Hungarians fleeing from communist tyranny. From the new continents and from Africa come reports of mineral wealth in metals and oil discovered by expert geological survey, and so new mine fields and new industries are opened up. Inside their own mighty land the Russians continue to expand and develop their own mines and forests right up to the Arctic Circle. Indeed, both polar regions are under siege. In the geophysical year of 1958 an American expedition encamped at the South Pole, while English scientists explored Antarctica. And men have begun to explore the depths of the sea, and to send their rocket-propelled instruments—Russian *sputniks*—hurtling in space above the earth.

Canada, Australia, New Zealand, and America prefer white settlers. But the lands most teeming with people, overcrowded and poor, are the Asian ones of China, Japan, and India whose surplus populations have nowhere to go. Many Europeans are settling on the healthy fertile and temperate uplands of Central Africa, in Kenya, Tanganyika, and Rhodesia; but in Africa the increasing national feeling of the Negro races gives rise to ill-feeling and distrust—which are not eased by the stubborn determination of the South African Dutch to keep *their* Negro peoples separate and servile ("apartheid"). In addition to this difficulty, the ancient rivalry of Christian and Moslem has been reawakened by the new spirit of nationality—and many Negroes are Moslems.

Religious animosity and national feeling has led to a long and bitter war in Algeria between the French and some of the natives. It is a war that is draining France of her wealth. National feeling in the Moslem states of the Near East is creating very hard problems there. The Egyptians, from whose land Britain withdrew her garrisons, seized the Suez Canal in 1957 from the Anglo-French Company which owned it. But the most striking change and source of unrest in the Near East is the growth of the Jewish state of Israel. Jews still settle there from other lands, and collect money from their fellow Jews who remain in other lands. Israel grows and flourishes, after seizing as much territory as possible, and setting in flight the Arab inhabitants—thousands of whom are still homeless and destitute refugees. The Jews work on the time-wasted lands, making them blossom as the rose, planting trees in the southern wilderness and turning the flintstone into a springing well in approved Old Testament style. They are doing this with the skill and zeal of a race that has endured two thousand years of persecution, and yet has kept its own traditions. Israel may become a mighty power. At present she is well-hated by all the Arab states.

The expansion of Western science and technical skill also goes on among Asians and Africans, who acquire that sort of white man's magic with great ease. Chinese, Japanese, Indian, and African scientists are now in the vanguard of the assault along the frontiers of knowledge on the unknown powers and things of the natural order. But most Asians and Africans are poor, ignorant, and undernourished. Some still live on the edge of the Stone Age! There are startling contrasts: the Negro Doctor of Philosophy trained in an African college comes from a thatched kraal in which his parents lived in dread fear of the witch doctor; and the sheik in southern Arabia drives his luxurious limousine among the tribesmen whose way of life differs little from that of the age of the crusades.

The adventure of politics goes on in this world of incongruities where the Stone Age and Atomic Age jostle each other. The Western ideal of democracy is based on the medieval invention of parliament, and worked by a system of voting. It means that, as far as possible, men shall govern themselves by reaching agreement through discussion; that they shall have the power to change their governors when they think fit; that none shall oppress his fellows; that everyone shall be free to speak his mind without suffering for his opinions. All this depends on a habit and tradition established in Christian Europe for centuries.

When the Second World War ended, three men dominated the scene—Winston Churchill, Roosevelt, and Stalin. With their advisers they set up a United Nations organization to replace the League of Nations. Its members were pledged to settle their disputes by discussion, and to work together for the welfare of all peoples. An enormous amount of good practical work was done and is still being done to rescue and resettle the millions of war refugees, and to help people in poor countries with money and goods. In this the nations

MANY INVENTIONS AND NEW KNOWLEDGE

are working together splendidly. But the world is still in arms.

Since 1945 two somber facts have darkened the counsels of the United Nations. The communists of Russia and the democracies led by America, France, and Britain are deeply mistrustful of each other. Fear and envy and suspicion govern their actions. And these unkind feelings are deepened by the devastating power of the atomic bomb and the more devastating power of the hydrogen bomb, which both sides have.

The earth has become a "cold" battleground upon which the two mightiest nations, the U.S.S.R. and the U.S.A., face each other. At the end of the War in 1945 Germany was split between the Russians and the other victors: it is still divided, the Russian armies occupying the East and the American, British, and French armies the West. Similarly in the Far East, after the defeat of Japan, the lovely land of Korea was divided, with the communists in the North and the Americans in the South. In 1950, when the Americans withdrew their forces, the North Koreans, inspired by the communists of Russia, invaded the South "to restore order"! Without any hesitation the Americans re-entered South Korea and called on the other United Nations to lend a hand to repel aggression. British, Dominion, Norwegian, Turkish, and other contingents were sent to help. After a hard struggle they won back the South and crossed into the North. Then a large Chinese communist army poured in. By skillful warfare and bold resolution the South was saved. Needless to say, Korea suffered through this wanton war from all the familiar horrors of starvation, famine, and refugees.

The gulf separating the communists from the democracies is a deep one: each rejects the other's way of life and the other's good faith. Each remains in arms striving to bring to perfection the most deadly weapons.

Russia dominates all Eastern Europe except Turkey and Greece. The U.S.A. keeps its artillery, planes, and tanks in Germany, and has military bases in western Europe. The old European overseas empires have crumbled. The Dutch have lost their rich East Indies; the French have lost Indochina, and are even now trying desperately to keep Algeria. After its long nightmare of anarchy China has turned communist and has thrust out the Western merchants and missionaries.

The British Empire has suffered startling change, but not startling loss, by yielding self-government to its Asian and African members. First, to the subcontinent of India, which chose to split into two dominions, India and Pakistan (1947), though not without much bloodshed and bitterness; then to Ceylon and Burma (1948); and lastly to the Gold Coast, romantically renamed Ghana (1957). Further such changes are in prospect. All these are now at liberty to do exactly as they please, even to leave the Empire; for only complete liberty can safeguard liberty. They all have laws and constitutions of their own, after being associated with the island of Britain whose constitution was considered perfect by the fathers of the American Republic. But, as it has been nobly said by a citizen of that republic: "Liberty lies in the hearts of men and women; when it dies there, no constitution, no law, no court, can save it. While it lies there it needs no constitution, no law, no court to save it."

EPILOGUE

News of this World

The restless curiosity to search out and discover what is happening in all the world about us—in the heavens, in the earth beneath, and in the waters under the earth—brings, every year, fresh news of our home. By means of microscopes and telescopes and electronic devices we learn of things undreamed of by our ancestors. We learn about the atoms of which all matter is made; and we build atomic power houses to use the energy locked up inside these invisible particles. We learn of galaxies of stars so remote from the earth that the light they send out takes millions of our years to reach us. We trace the histories of all living creatures, uncover the monsters of the deep, and reconstruct pictures of weird animals that died out long before men arrived on the earth.

We are creatures that can live only within a few degrees of heat and cold, yet we measure the forces that keep the stars in their ancient places. The Psalmist cried out, "O Lord, how manifold are Thy works!" We know this with a far greater field for wonder than he had. We know this even if we study only one smallest part of all creation—such as mosses or shellfish.

Our men of science tread in the steps of the Greeks, of Copernicus and Galileo, of Vesalius and Kepler, of Harvey and Newton, of Lavoisier and Dalton, of Darwin and Clerk-Maxwell, of Einstein and Rutherford, and all the others who gave their time and their skill

> To follow knowledge like a sinking star,
> Beyond the utmost bound of human thought.

They bring us the news of their discoveries. Where they lead, the engineer, the inventor, and the technician follow, using what they have discovered to make our lives more comfortable, to give us more power over our surroundings, to give us new machines, new materials, new drugs for healing, new metals and fabrics for delight and use.

Knowledge and power are desirable. As men have always known, they can be used for evil purposes as well as for good ones.

News from Nowhere

The poet William Morris called his story of a perfect people in a perfect land, *News from Nowhere*, and it is an apt title. Men have always welcomed tales of the Fortunate Isles, legends of a golden age, or the promise of an earthly paradise. Throughout the centuries of sorrow and toil, something dearer to them than knowledge has been the hope of men: they have desired the triumph of good over evil, of justice over injustice, of love over hate.

Behold, a king shall reign in righteousness, and princes shall rule in judgment . . . Then shall the lame man leap as an hart, and the tongue of the dumb sing; for in the wilderness shall waters break out, and streams in the desert. . . . And the ransomed of the Lord shall return, and come to Zion with songs and everlasting joy upon their heads: they shall obtain joy and gladness, and sorrow and sighing shall flee away.

These were the words of Isaiah spoken to ancient Jewry in the eighth century B.C. The dream of St. John in the first century A.D. was of a Christian paradise:

And I saw a new heaven and a new earth: for the first heaven and the first earth were passed away; and there was no more sea. And I, John, saw the holy city, new Jerusalem, coming down from God out of heaven.

Such a vision was the comfort of multitudes of bondsmen and bondswomen of the Roman Empire, those slaves in a slave-ridden world, without hope of joy or prosperity.

Meanwhile, the Greeks also had speculated on a perfect city. Plato described one in his dialogue about the *Republic;* but like the wise Greek that he was, he said: "Until philosophers are kings, or the kings of this world have the spirit of philosophy, cities will never have rest from their evils." This truth was borne out by the fate of the Greek cities —Athens, Corinth, Syracuse, and the rest—which were broken and ruined in the evils of civil war.

EPILOGUE

Centuries later the fall of Rome and the passing of her palaces and temples, her peace and law, seemed to bring all hope to an end. Pagans looked back to a golden age that had vanished. Earth offered no solace. The best of men entered the Church of Christ where they cherished the hope of St. John's dream of the "Blessed City, Heavenly Salem."

> For thee, O dear, dear country
> Mine eyes their vigil keep;
> For very love, beholding
> Thy happy name, they weep.

The revival of Greek learning turned men's minds again to the earth. There were new visions of a perfect state where men lived under the guidance of guardian-philosophers. Sir Thomas More called his book *Utopia*—which means "Nowhere"—but, like Plato, he had his doubts: "It is not possible for all things to be well unless all men be good; which I think will not be for a good many years yet," he said. Francis Bacon described a sort of scientific island-state in his book entitled *The New Atlantis*.

As time went on, men began to hope for universal peace among nations, and with it, justice for all men, rich and poor. Spanish churchmen, Dutch lawyers, English Quakers, all devised schemes for this. There came into being, gradually, a code of international law, and ambassadors were sent abroad to help international understanding. The makers of the American Republic proclaimed that "all men are created equal." The men of the French Revolution marched forward with "Liberty, Equality, Fraternity" as their watchwords. The idea grew that men can, and must, remake their own world into a place of joy and peace for everyone. Some thinkers in the eighteenth century believed that good sense and reason would persuade men to do this: as reason increased its sway over their minds so they would abolish war and crime and cruelty and poverty. "The reign of Reason will ever be the Reign of Peace."

Envy, malice, and uncharitableness are deep-rooted things. We are still hard at work trying to bring the afflicted nations into concord. The League of Nations after the First World War, and the United Nations after the Second, are both attempts to turn the visions of "nowhere" into reality. This is the hope of all good men, the dream of all true statesmen; and, although fear may be a bad motive, the fear of the devastation of future wars also plays its part in urging men to seek peace and co-operation.

The Living Past

We are what we are because of the past. The years that have gone live in us, and not only recent years but far-off ones, because nowhere in the record of mankind—our own ancestors, our own families—is there a complete break and a rebeginning.

We are part of a long story, part of a great and ever-growing web of countless lives, and the present is what it is because of all that has gone before—because forgotten empires rose and fell in antiquity; because unknown men marveled at the splendor of the heavens in ancient Babylon; because unknown Greeks obeyed the Greek captains who defeated the Persians; because the Romans destroyed Carthage; because Mark Antony fell in love with Cleopatra; because the western Christians grew tired of trying to drive the Arabs from Egypt; because the merchants of the West traded with India and China for profit; because Columbus discovered America, and Luther preached against the pope, and Napoleon overran Europe. The list could go on forever.

All this is true whether we know the story or not. But in our printed records we keep the works of great and famous men such as Plato and Homer and the Jewish prophets; Dante and Shakespeare; Bach and Mozart; and hosts of others. They are dead, but their works speak still to us.

Any record of history is bound to be mostly the story of great men, leaders and thinkers and artists. "The greater part must be content to be as though they had not been, to be found in the register of God, not in the record of man": so wrote Sir Thomas Browne, the Norfolk physician, in 1650. Yet the work of this unrecorded "greater part" endures today. For our civilization is an inheritance made and kept by millions of unknown craftsmen who brought their labors to an excellent work, and also by the good faith and loyalty of millions of unknown hearts.

The Jews, almost alone among nations, have realized the value of history, and they have taken the utmost pains to keep their own records. We can best sum up in the words of the writer of their book called Ecclesiasticus:

Let us now praise famous men, and our fathers that begat us ... Such as did bear rule in their kingdoms, men renowned for their power, giving counsel by their understanding ... Leaders of the people by their counsels, and by their knowledge of learning meet for the people, wise and eloquent in their instructions ...

Epilogue

All these were honoured in their generations, and were the glory of their times. There be of them that have left a name behind them, that their praise might be reported.

And some there be, which have no memorial; who are perished as though they had never been . . . but these were merciful men, whose righteousness hath not been forgotten. Their seed shall remain for ever, and their glory shall not be blotted out. Their bodies are buried in peace, but their name liveth for evermore.

INDEX

Achaeans, 28, 33
Aeschylus, 35, 37
Afghanistan, 245
Africa, 261-65
Aircraft, 285
Alans, 65
Albania, 275
Alchemists, 183
Alcock, 285
Alexander, 38-40
Alexander I (Russia), 214, 275
Alexander II (Russia), 242-43
Alexandria, 62, 78
Alfred, 84-86
Algeria, 287
Alsace, 240
Ampère, 186
Anglo-Saxons, 67-70
Anne, Queen, 175, 176
Antarctica, 287
Antioch, 62, 78
Arabic Spain, 87-89
Arabs, 77-79
Archaeology, 16-18
Argentina, 216
Aristotle, 37, 108, 133, 185, 186, 213
Arkwright, 225
Armada, Spanish, 156-58
Armor, 96
Asia Minor, 58, 117
Assyria, 27-29
Athelstan, 86
Athens, 35-39
Atom Bomb, 284
Augustus, 12, 50
Australia, 129, 161, 191, 250-51
Austria, 89, 141, 176-77, 213, 235, 275

Avignon, 102

Babylonia, 26
Baden, 207
Balkans, 117
Barbarians, 65-72
Barnardo, Dr., 232
Bastille, 200
Bavaria, 207, 240
Becket, Thomas, 102-03
Bede, 77
Belgium, 217, 280
Bible, A.V., 149-50
Birmingham, 193
Bishops, 70-71, 99, 163
Bismarck, 236, 239-40
Black Death, 102
Blenheim, 176
Blücher, 210
Boers, 261-63
Boer War, 265
Bohemians, 142, 235
Boleyn, Anne, 147
Bolivia, 216
Borneo, 125, 256
Boxers (China), 260
Boyle, Robert, 186
Braddock, 179
Brahe, Tycho, 185
Brazil, 125, 171, 216
Bristol, 193
Bronze Age, 14-16
Brooke, 256
Brown, 285
Bulgaria, 275
Burgundians, 65, 131
Burke, 188
Burma, 282, 289
Byrd, 160

INDEX

Byron, 216

Cabot, 128
Calvin, 143, 145-46
Canada, 167, 169, 181, 182, 191, 249-51
Canals, 221-22
Canterbury Pilgrims, 103-04
Canute, 87
Cape of Good Hope, 122, 161, 203
Caribs, 125, 246
Carnot, 202
Carolina, 170, 171
Carthaginians, 30, 41, 44-45
Castles, 97-98
Catacombs, 59
Cathedrals, 112-13
Catherine of Aragon, 147
Catholics, 71
Cavendish, 186
Cavour, 236
Caxton, 138-39
Ceylon, 203, 247, 289
Chaldeans, 29
Champlain, 170
Champollion, 17
Chancellor, 142
Charlemagne, 80-81
Charles Martel, 79
Charles I, 162-64
Charles II, 165
Charles V, Emperor, 143-44
Chaucer, 103, 104, 114
Chénier, 202
Chicago, 255
Chile, 216
China, 258-61, 289
Chivalry, 105
Church, The, 112-13
Churches, medieval, 98-99
Churches, 18th-century, 197
Churchill, 281, 288
Christians, Early, 57-59, 60-64
Cicero, 134-35
Cincinnatus, 44
Cinque Ports, 114
Civil Service, 231
Clerk-Maxwell, 186

Clive, 179, 182, 247
Coal mining, 222-24
Coffeehouses, 195
Coke, 162
Colbert, 167
Colombia, 216
Columbus, 124-25
Communism, 243, 277
Concentration Camps, 283
Confucius, 259
Congo, 263
Constantine, 62-63
Constantine Palaeologus, 119
Constantinople, 63, 72, 79, 83, 117-19, 134, 135, 269, 271
Co-operatives, 231
Copernicus, 139-40, 184
Cordova, 88, 120
Cortés, 127
Cossacks, 244
Cotton Industry, 224-25
Craftguilds, 105-06
Craftsmen, 183-84
Cranmer, 149
Crassus, 49
Crete, 17, 27-28, 32
Crimea, 237, 245
Cromwell, 164-65
Crusades, 91-94
Culloden Moor, 177
Cuneiform, 21, 25
Curie, Mme., 286
Cynics, 55
Cyrus, 30
Czechoslovakia, 275, 280

Daimler, 285
D'Albuquerque, 124
Dalton, 186
Damascus, 26-27, 78
Dante, 109, 139
Danton, 202
Darius, I, 31
Darnley, 151-52
Darwin, 186
Da Vinci, 137, 139
Denmark, 89, 280
Descartes, 185
Diaz, B., 122

INDEX

Diet of Worms, 145
Donatello, 136
Dorians, 28, 33
Drake, 155-56
Dupleix, 178
Dutch Colonial Empire, 247, 282

East India Company, 188, 257, 259
Ecuador, 216
Edinburgh, 193
Education, 232-33
Edward VI, 148
Egypt, 17, 18, 20-23, 204, 264
Eisenhower, 283
Electricity, 186, 228
Elizabeth I, 149, 151, 152, 156, 158, 160, 173
Emigration, 251-52
Enclosures, 196
Engineers, 219-20
Epicureans, 55
Erasmus, 136
Erech, 18
Esarhaddon, 29
Esthonia, 275
Ethiopia, 279
Etruscans, 41-42
Euripides, 33, 37
Evans, 17
Exeter, 193

Fairs, 106
Faraday, 186, 284
Feudal Army, 96
Fleury, Cardinal, 176
Florence, 136
Foch, 270
France, 141-42, 174, 199-210, 213
Franklin, 186
Franks, 66, 70, 71, 79
Frederick II (of Sicily), 93
Frederick the Great, 177, 179, 182-83, 239
Frederick William I, 174
French Empire, 247
Friars, 99-100, 115

Galileo, 185
Gallipoli, 269
Galvani, 186
Garibaldi, 236, 237
Gaslight, 228
Gasoline Engines, 285
Gaul, 48-49
Gauls, 42, 48
Genoa, 212
George I, 176
George II, 176, 182
George III, 174, 182, 200
Georgia (Russia), 245
Germany, 162, 213, 235, 239-40, 266-68
Ghana, 121, 290
Gibraltar, 176
Gilbert, Sir H., 155
Gilbert, William, 186
Glauber, 186
Godfrey of Bouillon, 91
Gods, Pagan, 55
Gothic Architecture, 113
Goths, 66, 70-72
Granada, 120
Great Britain, 162-74; population, 229; trade, 229; colonial empire, 246-48
Greece, Ancient, 28-41; art, 34-35; civilization, 39; drama, 34; games, 34; language, 135
Greece, Modern, 216, 275, 276
Grenville, Sir R., 155
Guatemala, 216
Gutenberg, 137-38, 232

Hammurabi, 26
Hannibal, 45-46
Hanover, 205, 239
Hansa, 116
Harappa, 18
Harold Godwinson, 90
Harvey, William, 186
Henry, the Navigator, 121
Henry VII, 146
Henry VIII, 146-48
Hermits, 62
Hieroglyphics, 17, 21

INDEX

Hiram, 15
Hitler, 278-79, 283
Hittites, 23-24, 27
Holland, 141, 153-54, 161, 203, 207, 212-13, 215, 280
Holy Roman Empire, 80-81, 89, 141, 207
Homer, 16, 17, 28, 32
Hottentot, 123
Hudson Bay Company, 249
Huguenots, 146, 154, 160, 171
Hundred Years' War, 95
Hungarians, 89, 117, 119, 235, 275
Huns, 66, 71
Hyksos, 23

Ikhnaton, 23
Incas, 14, 127
India, 123, 178-79, 182, 256-58, 289; army, 256; civil service, 257
Indochina, 289
Indo-Europeans, 24
Indus Valley, 18
Inquisition, 152-53
Ionians, 33
Ireland, 83, 165
Ironworking, 223-24
Israel, 275, 287-88
Italy, 134, 142, 207, 213, 214, 215, 237-39, 282; Gothic War, 73; craftsmen, 134
Ivan the Terrible, 173

Jacobites, 175, 177-78
Jamaica, 165
James I, 152, 160, 162
James II, 166
Japan, 245, 260, 282, 284
Jefferson, 189, 190
Jerusalem, 16, 60, 62, 78, 91
Jesuits, 152-53, 171
Jews, 27-30, 56, 59-60
Joan of Arc, 95
John, King, 101
Johannesburg, 264
Johnson, Dr., 229
Julian, 65

Julius Caesar, 49-50
Justices, 107
Justinian, 72-73

Karnath, 23
Kelvin, Lord, 285
Kemal Attaturk, 269, 274
Kepler, 185
Khafre, 22
Kingship, 211
Knighthood, 105
Knights Templar, 91
Knights of St. John, 91-94, 119, 153
Korea, 260, 289

Latvia, 275
Laud, 163
La Vendée, 202
Lavoisier, 186, 202
Layard, 17
League of Nations, 276, 279
Lenin, 271
Leo X, 136
Leonidas, 36
Lepanto, 153
Lincoln, Abraham, 253-54
Lister, 229
Lithuania, 275
Livingstone, 263
Lloyd's, 195
Locke, 186
Lombardy, 203, 217
London, 106, 159, 193-95, 200
Lorraine, 240
Louis XIII, 166
Louis XIV, 167, 168, 174, 176
Louis XV, 167, 168, 176
Louis XVI, 174, 199, 200
Louis XVIII, 210, 214
Louis Napoleon, 235-36
Louis Philippe, 217, 234
Louisiana, 171
Luther, 144-45

Machines, 226, 229-30
Magellan, 125
Mail Coaches, 221
Malta, 153, 282

INDEX

Manors, 110-11
Marathon, 35
Marconi, 286
Marco Polo, 115-16
Maria Theresa, 176, 179
Marie Antoinette, 202
Marius, 48
Maoris, 13, 251
Mark Antony, 50
Marlborough, 175-76
Mary Queen of Scots, 151-52, 156
Mary Tudor, 148-49
Maryland, 169
Marx, 243-44
Massachusetts, 188, 190
Mathematics, 184-85
Mazarin, 167
Mazzini, 217, 236, 237
Medici, Lorenzo de', 136
Medicine, 228-29
Mencius, 259
Mesopotamia, 18-20, 268, 271
Metternich, 214, 235
Mexico, 127
Michelangelo, 136-37
Miracle Plays, 107
Mitanni, 24
Mohammed, 77-78
Mohammed II, 119
Mohenjodaro, 18
Monks, 63, 99-100
More, Sir. T., 147
Morris, 244
Moscow, 209
Music, 113-14, 160, 233-34
Mussolini, 277
Mycenae, 17

Naples, 217
Napoleon, 203-10
Navarino, 216
Nebuchadnezzar, 29
Nelson, 204, 205
Netherlands (Belgium), 151, 176, 201
New Brunswick, 190
New England, 169, 171
Newfoundland, 128
New France, 169
New Netherlands, 169
Newspapers, 194
Newton, 185
New York, 161, 169, 171, 190, 255
New Zealand, 251
Ney, 209
Nicholas I, 242
Nigeria, 263
Nineveh, 17, 29
Normans, 84, 90
North, Lord, 188
Norway, 280
Norwich, 193
Nova Scotia, 190
Nursing, 228

Ohm, 285
Otto the Great, 89
Oxen, 110

Pakistan, 289
Palestine, 271
Paper, 138
Paraguay, 216
Paris, 193, 200
Parliament, 100-01, 217-19, 230-31
Pascal, 185
Pasteur, 228-29
Pearl Harbor, 282
Peloponnesian War, 37
Peninsular War, 208-09
Pennsylvania, 170-71
Pericles, 37
Persians, 29-32, 36, 79
Peru, 216
Peter the Great, 173
Petrarch, 134-35
Pheidias, 37
Philadelphia, 171, 188-89, 190
Philip II of Spain, 149, 151, 156, 158, 161
Philip III of Spain, 161
Philistines, 28
Phoenicians, 15, 27
Photography, 285
Phrygians, 27

INDEX

Pilgrimages, 112
Pitt, William, 181, 182
Pius IX, 236, 240
Pizarro, 127
Plato, 37, 136
Pompey, 49
Poles, 117, 119, 172, 215, 280
Polybius, 45-46
Popes, 101-102
Portuguese, 120-24, 141, 161, 214, 216, 246-47
Prayer Book, 149
Priestley, 186, 198, 253
Printing, 137-39, 232
Prussia, 89, 142, 174, 182-83, 236, 239-40
Pyrrhus, 44

Quakers, 170, 171
Quebec, 182, 252

Radio, Radar, 286
Railways, 226, 249
Raleigh, 156, 159
Rameses, 28
Rawlinson, 17
Redskins, 170
Renaissance, 136-37
Rhineland, 70, 215
Rhodes, Cecil, 264-65
Richard Lionheart, 117
Richelieu, 166-67
Roads, 220-21
Robespierre, 202
Rome, 40, 42-43, 66-67, 136, 212, 239, 240
Roman Empire, 11-12, 48-54, 68, 70
Roman Law, 51, 73
Röntgen, 229
Roosevelt, 281, 288
Rumania, 275
Russia, 83, 142, 173-74, 209, 241-45, 270, 271-74, 281

Saladin, 91-93
Salamis, 36
Samnites, 43
Saratoga, 189
Sardinia, 44, 215, 236

Sargon, 25-26
Saxe, 175
Schliemann, 17
Science, 183-87
Scipio Africanus, 46
Seamen, 114, 129-30, 158-59
Sedan, 240
Semitic Peoples, 24
Serbians, 117, 119, 215
Shaftesbury, Lord, 230
Shakespeare, 159
Sheffield, 193
Sicily, 44, 90, 93, 236, 237, 282
Sierra Leone, 123
Silesia, 176
Singapore, 256
Slavery, 46, 127, 253, 261-63
Smith, John, 168
Smiths, 15-16
Smuts, 276
Sobieski, 173
Solomon, 15-16
Sophocles, 35, 37
South America, 216
Spain, 79-80, 87-89, 120, 141, 150-51, 208, 214, 216, 217, 246-47, 279
Sparta, 35-36
Spenser, 159
St. Aidan, 76
St. Bartholomew, Massacre of, 154
St. Augustine of Hippo, 67
St. Augustine, 75-76
St. Basil, 63, 70
St. Benedict, 63, 65, 75
St. Boniface, 77
St. Columbanus, 77
St. Francis of Assisi, 99-100, 110
St. Gall, 77
St. Gregory, 64, 75-76
St. Jerome, 108
St. John Chrysostom, 70
St. Louis, 94
St. Luke, 12
St. Patrick, 74, 76
St. Paul, 52, 58
St. Thomas Aquinas, 108

INDEX

Stagecoaches, 221, 227
Stalin, 274, 288
Stalingrad, 282-83
Steam Engines, 223, 225, 226
Stephenson, 226
Stilicho, 66
Stoics, 55
Stone Ages, 13
Suez Canal, 264, 287
Sulla, 48
Sumerians, 25

Tarquins, 42-43
Tartars, 115, 173
Tertullian, 61
Theodore of Tarsus, 76
Theodoric, 72
Thermopylae, 36
Thirty Years' War, 162
Ticonderoga, 181-82
Tiglath Pileser, 29
Town Planning, 192-93
Trade Unions, 231
Trafalgar, 205
Transvaal, 264
Trent, Council of, 152
Trinidad, 203
Troy, 16, 17, 28
Turkey, 141, 172-73, 274-75
Tutankhamen, 23
Tyndal, 150
Tyre, 15-16, 27

Umbrians, 43
United Nations, 288-89
United States, 190-91, 213, 214, 251-56
Universities, 108, 233
Ur, 18, 25

Vandals, 66, 70
Vauban, 167-68
Valley Forge, 189

Venezuela, 216
Venice, 93, 114-15, 124, 162, 203, 212, 236, 239
Ventris, 18
Versailles, 167-68, 200, 276
Vesalius, 186
Victor Emmanuel, 236, 237
Vienna, Congress of, 210, 214
Vikings, 81-83
Virginia, 168, 171
Volta, 186
Von Moltke, 239, 240
Vulgate Bible, 108

Walpole, 176
War, First World, 267-71
War, Second World, 280-84
Washington, George, 179, 188-90
Waterloo, 210
Watt, 225
Wellington, 208-10
Welsh, 68
Wesley, 197
Wessex, 84-85
West Indies, 125, 171
William of Normandy, 90
William of Orange, 166
William III, 174-75
Willoughby, 142
Wolfe, 182
Wolsey, 146-47
Woolen Industry, 224-25
Woolley, 18
Wren, Sir. C., 187, 193-94
Wurtemberg, 207, 240

Xenophon, 37
Xerxes, 35-36

York, 193
Yorktown, 190
Yugoslavia, 275

The Mentor Philosophers

The entire range of Western speculative thinking from the Middle Ages to modern times is presented in this series of six volumes. Each book contains the basic writings of the leading philosophers of each age, with introductions and interpretive commentary by noted authorities.

"A very important and interesting series."
—*Gilbert Highet*

50 cents each

THE AGE OF BELIEF: The Medieval Philosophers edited by Anne Fremantle. (#MD126)
"Highly commendable . . . provides an excellent beginning volume." —*The Classical Bulletin*

THE AGE OF ADVENTURE: The Renaissance Philosophers edited by Giorgio de Santillana. (#MD184)
"The most exciting and varied in the series." —*New York Times*

THE AGE OF REASON: The 17th Century Philosophers edited by Stuart Hampshire (#MD158)
"His (Hampshire's) book is the most satisfactory addition to an excellent series." —*Saturday Review*

THE AGE OF ENLIGHTENMENT: The 18th Century Philosophers edited by Sir Isaiah Berlin. (#MD172)
"(Sir Isaiah) has one of the liveliest and most stimulating minds among contemporary philosophers." —*N. Y. Herald Tribune*

THE AGE OF IDEOLOGY: The 19th Century Philosophers edited by Henry D. Aiken. (#MD185)
". . . perhaps the most distinct intellectual contribution made in the series." —*New York Times*

THE AGE OF ANALYSIS: 20th Century Philosophers edited by Morton White. (#MD142)
"No other book remotely rivals this as the best available introduction to 20th century philosophy." —*N. Y. Herald Tribune*

Other MENTOR Books You Will Enjoy

THE PUBLIC PHILOSOPHY   **by Walter Lippmann**

    A penetrating and challenging analysis of the changing state of Western democracies, by one of America's most influential political commentators. (#MD174—50¢)

BOOKS THAT CHANGED THE WORLD
                          by Robert B. Downs

    Histories of sixteen epoch-making books, from Machiavelli's *The Prince* to Einstein's *Theories of Relativity*.
(#MD229—50¢)

THE NATURE OF THE NON-WESTERN WORLD
                          by Vera Micheles Dean

    A noted expert on foreign affairs throws new light on the conflict between East and West. (#MD190—50¢)

RUSSIA AND AMERICA: Dangers and Prospects
                          by Henry L. Roberts

    A penetrating discussion of the global tension created by atomic discoveries, our relations with Russia, and the policies needed to meet the Communist challenge.
(#MD182—50¢)

THE SHAPING OF THE MODERN MIND
                          by Crane Brinton

    The concluding half of *Ideas and Men*—a self-contained history of Western thought since the Renaissance.
(#MD173—50¢)

THE TRUE BELIEVER   **by Eric Hoffer**

    A provocative analysis of the nature of mass movements and the fanatics who give them power. (#MD228—50¢)

THE WORLD OF HISTORY, Crane Brinton, Alfred Kazin and John D. Hicks, advisory editors

    A stimulating selection of the best in contemporary historical writing. (#MD109—50¢)

To Our Readers: We welcome your request for our free catalog of Signet, Signet Key, and Mentor Books. If your dealer does not have the books you want, you may order them by mail, enclosing the list price plus 5¢ a copy to cover mailing. The New American Library of World Literature, Inc., 501 Madison Avenue, New York 22, New York.